W9-BAP-953

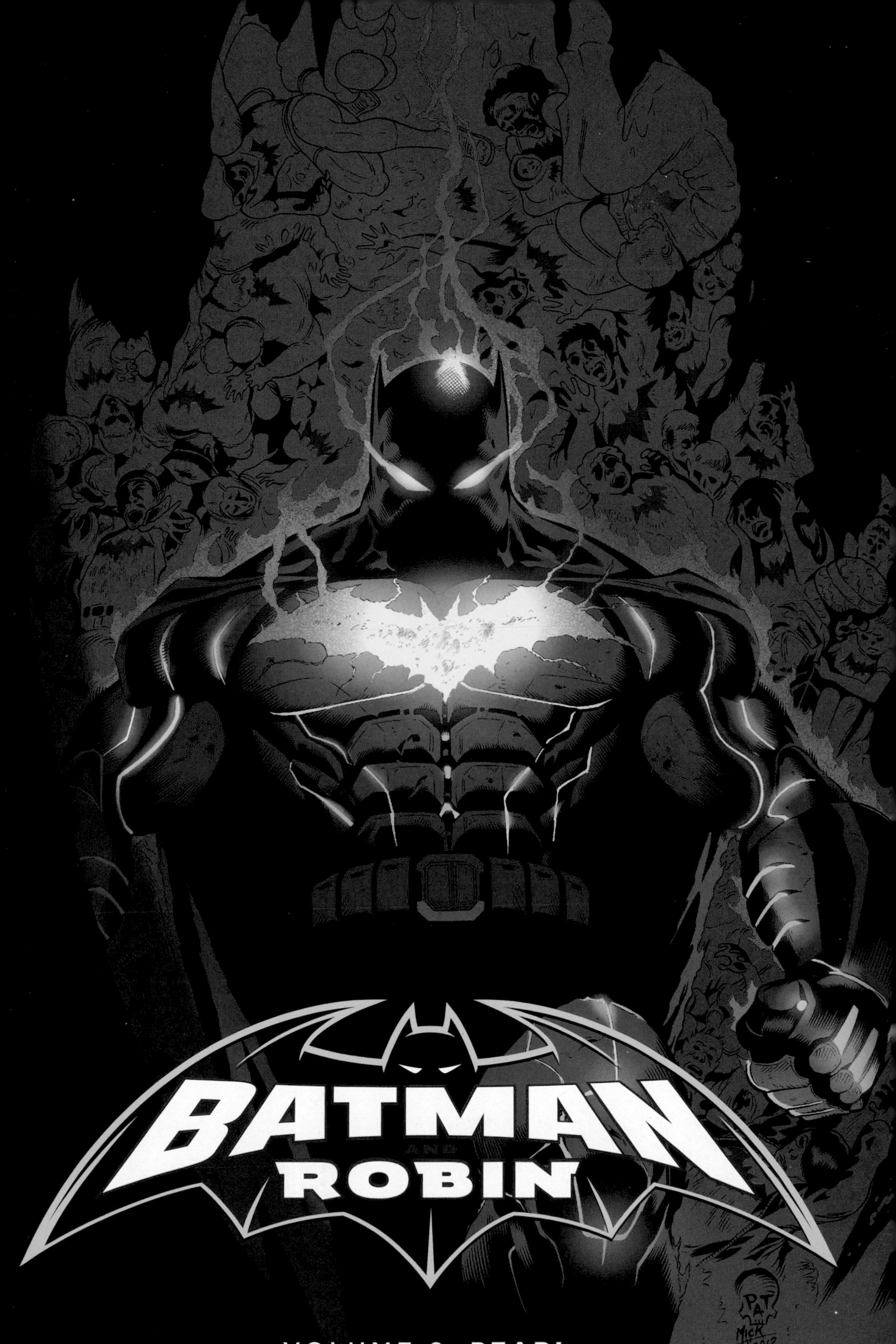
BATMAN
AND
ROBIN
PAT
MICK 2012

VOLUME 2 **PEARL**

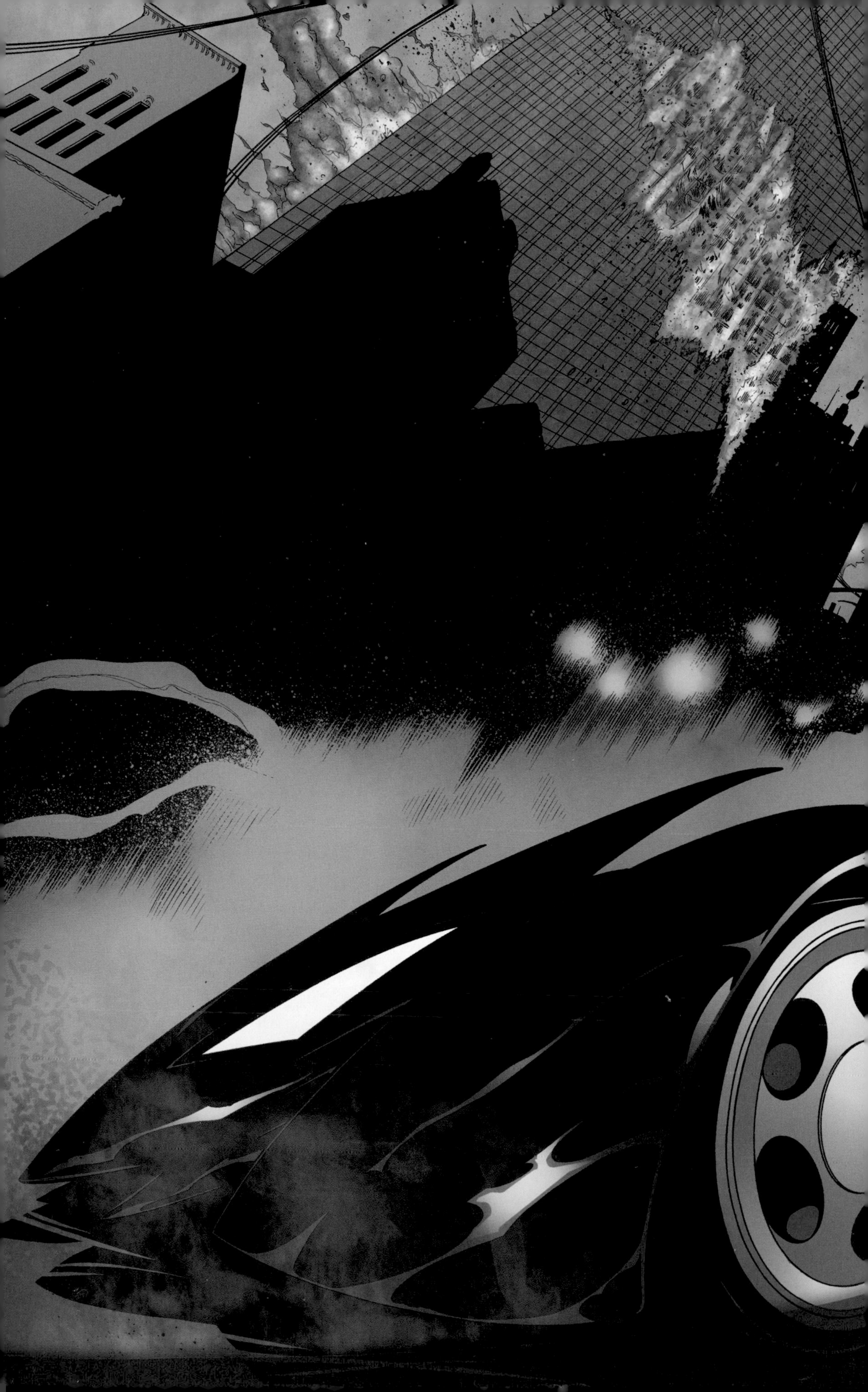

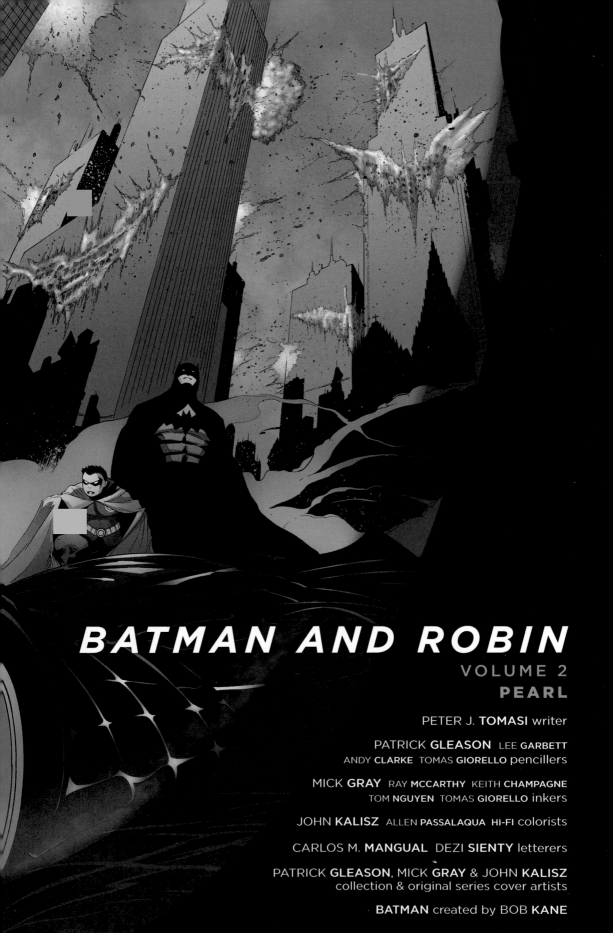

BATMAN AND ROBIN

VOLUME 2
PEARL

PETER J. **TOMASI** writer

PATRICK **GLEASON** LEE **GARBETT**
ANDY **CLARKE** TOMAS **GIORELLO** pencillers

MICK **GRAY** RAY **MCCARTHY** KEITH **CHAMPAGNE**
TOM **NGUYEN** TOMAS **GIORELLO** inkers

JOHN **KALISZ** ALLEN **PASSALAQUA** HI-FI colorists

CARLOS M. **MANGUAL** DEZI **SIENTY** letterers

PATRICK **GLEASON**, MICK **GRAY** & JOHN **KALISZ**
collection & original series cover artists

BATMAN created by BOB **KANE**

RACHEL GLUCKSTERN MIKE MARTS Editors – Original Series HARVEY RICHARDS Associate Editor – Original Series
RICKEY PURDIN KATIE KUBERT Assistant Editors – Original Series RACHEL PINNELAS Editor
ROBBIN BROSTERMAN Design Director – Books ROBBIE BIEDERMAN Publication Design

BOB HARRAS SENIOR VP – Editor-in-Chief, DC Comics

DIANE NELSON President DAN DIDIO and JIM LEE Co-Publishers
GEOFF JOHNS Chief Creative Officer
JOHN ROOD Executive VP – Sales, Marketing and Business Development
AMY GENKINS Senior VP – Business and Legal Affairs NAIRI GARDINER Senior VP – Finance
JEFF BOISON VP – Publishing Operations MARK CHIARELLO VP – Art Direction and Design
JOHN CUNNINGHAM VP – Marketing TERRI CUNNINGHAM VP – Talent Relations and Services
ALISON GILL Senior VP – Manufacturing and Operations
HANK KANALZ SENIOR VP – Vertigo & Integrated Publishing JAY KOGAN VP – Business and Legal Affairs, Publishing
JACK MAHAN VP – Business Affairs, Talent NICK NAPOLITANO VP – Manufacturing Administration
SUE POHJA VP – Book Sales COURTNEY SIMMONS Senior VP – Publicity
BOB WAYNE Senior VP – Sales

BATMAN AND ROBIN VOLUME 2: PEARL

Published by DC Comics. Cover and compilation Copyright © 2013 DC Comics. All Rights Reserved.

Originally published in single magazine form in BATMAN AND ROBIN #0, 9-14. Copyright © 2012, 2013 DC Comics. All Rights Reserved.
All characters, their distinctive likenesses and related elements featured in this publication are trademarks of DC Comics.
The stories, characters and incidents featured in this publication are entirely fictional.
DC Comics does not read or accept unsolicited ideas, stories or artwork.

DC Comics, 1700 Broadway, New York, NY 10019
A Warner Bros. Entertainment Company.
Printed by RR Donnelley, Salem, VA, USA. 5/3/13. First Printing.

HC ISBN: 978-1-4012-4089-9
SC ISBN: 978-1-4012-4267-1

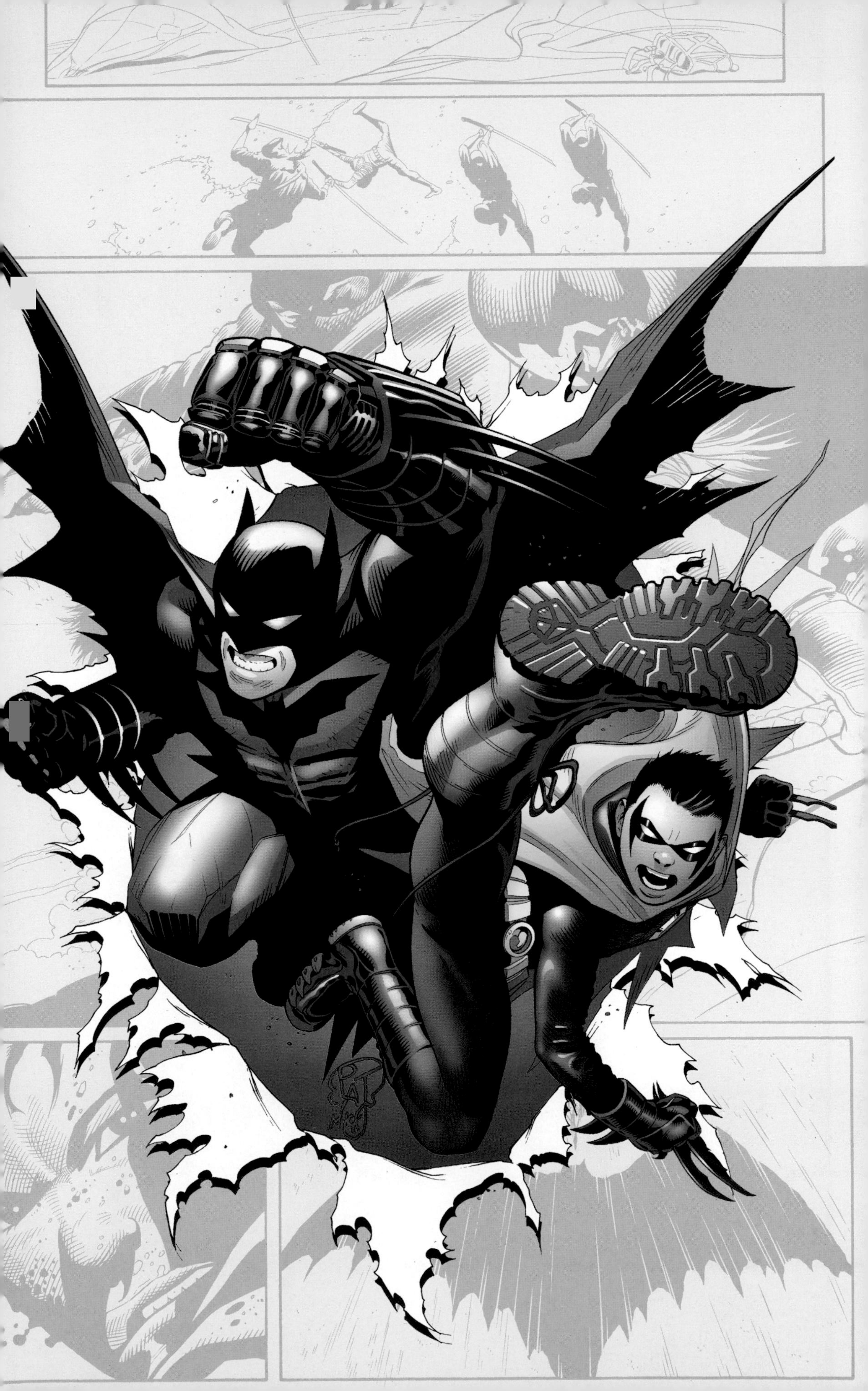

SOMEDAY NEVER COMES

PETER J. TOMASI writer PATRICK GLEASON penciller MICK GRAY inker
cover by GLEASON, GRAY & KALISZ

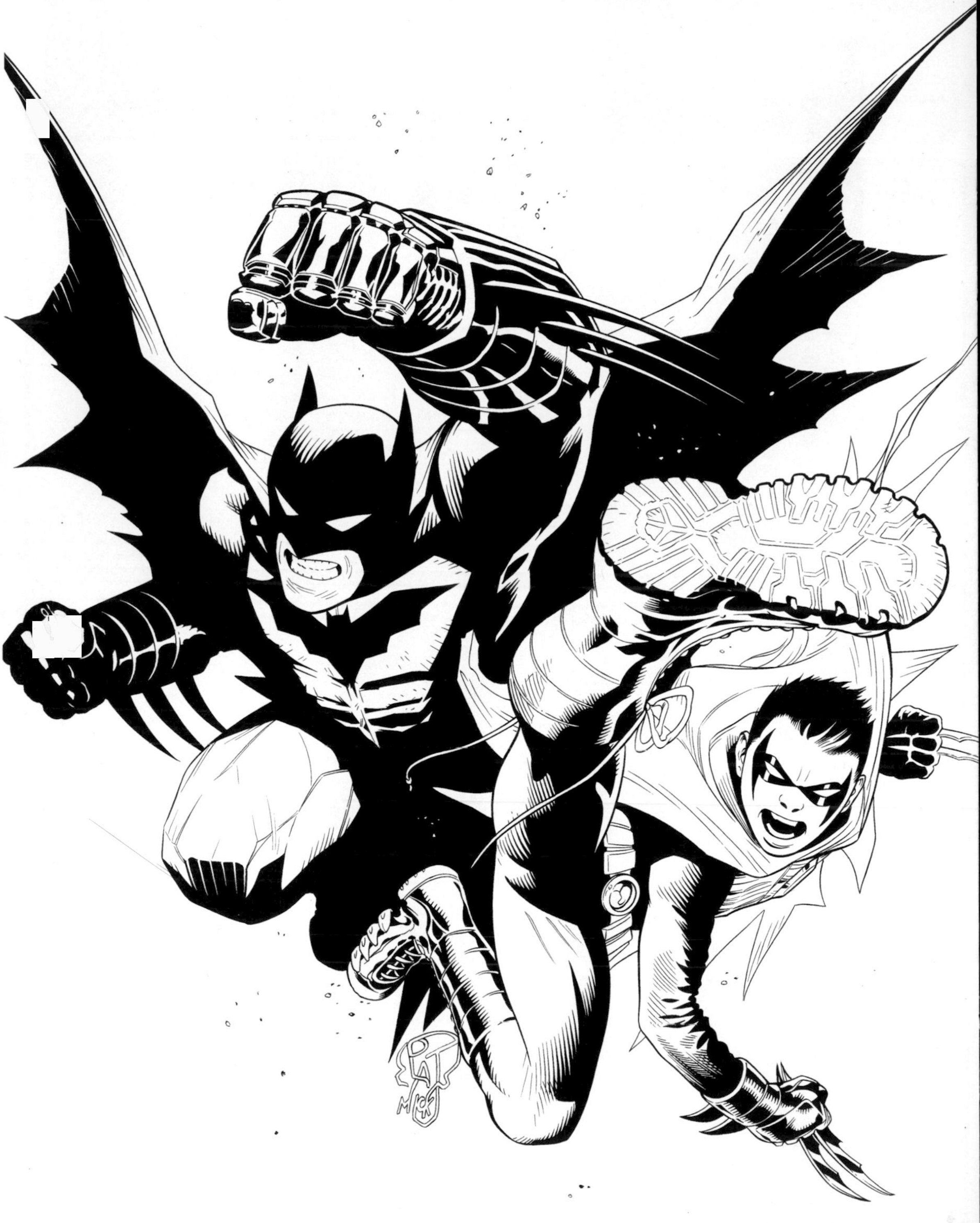

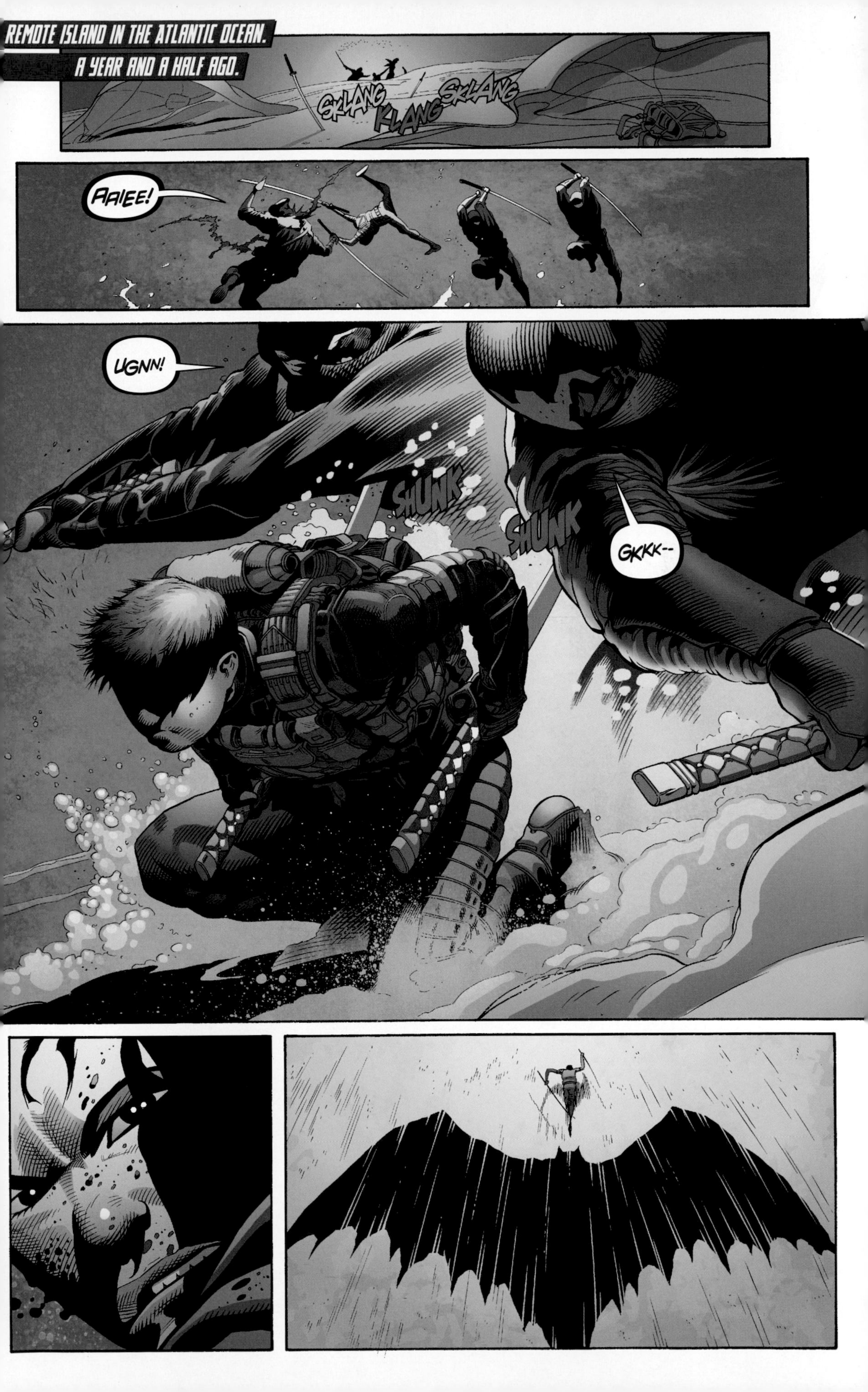
REMOTE ISLAND IN THE ATLANTIC OCEAN.
A YEAR AND A HALF AGO.
SKLANG
KLANG
SKLANG
AAIEE!
UGNN!
SHUNK
SHUNK
GKKK--

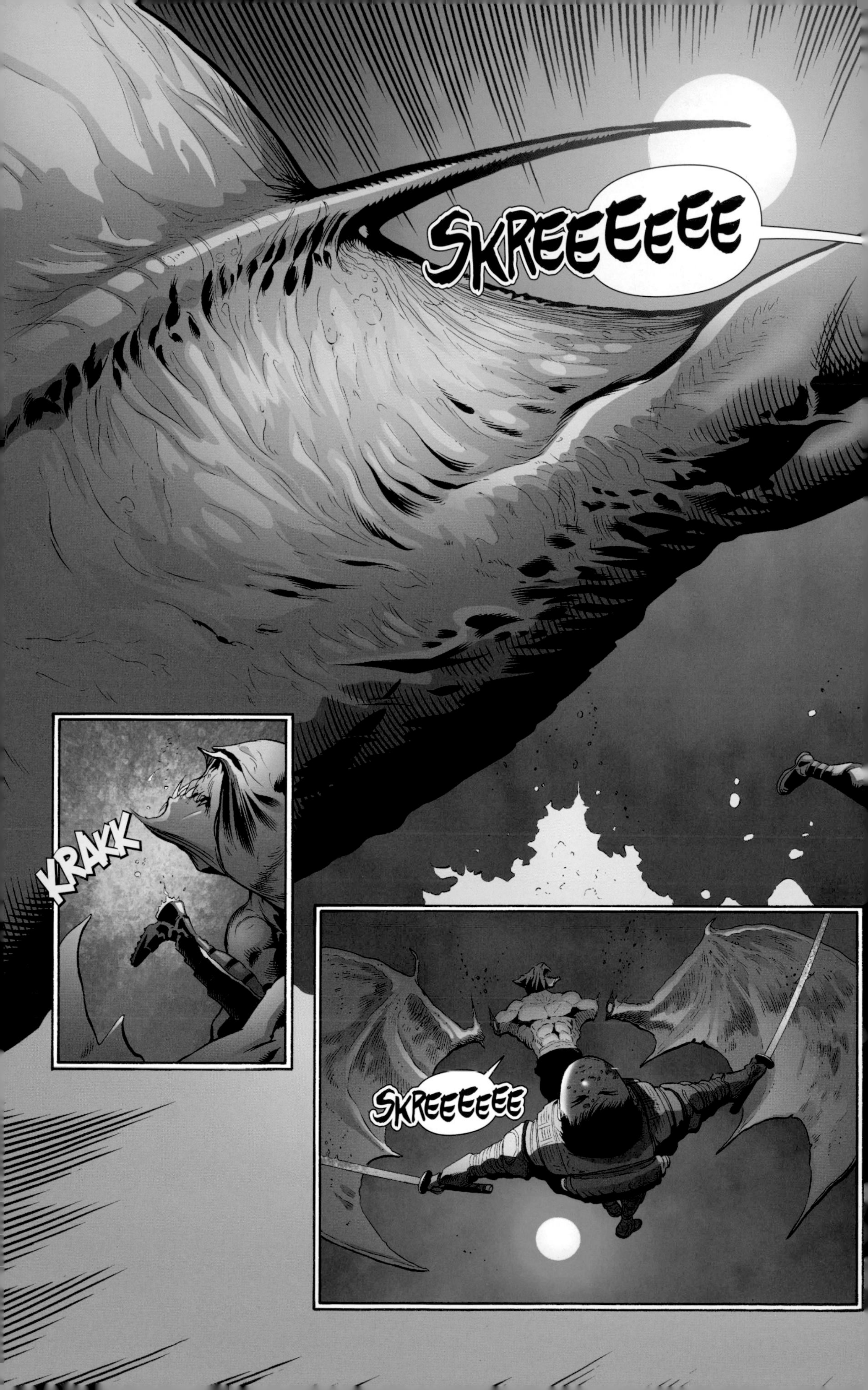
SKREEEEEEE
KRAKK
SKREEEEEE

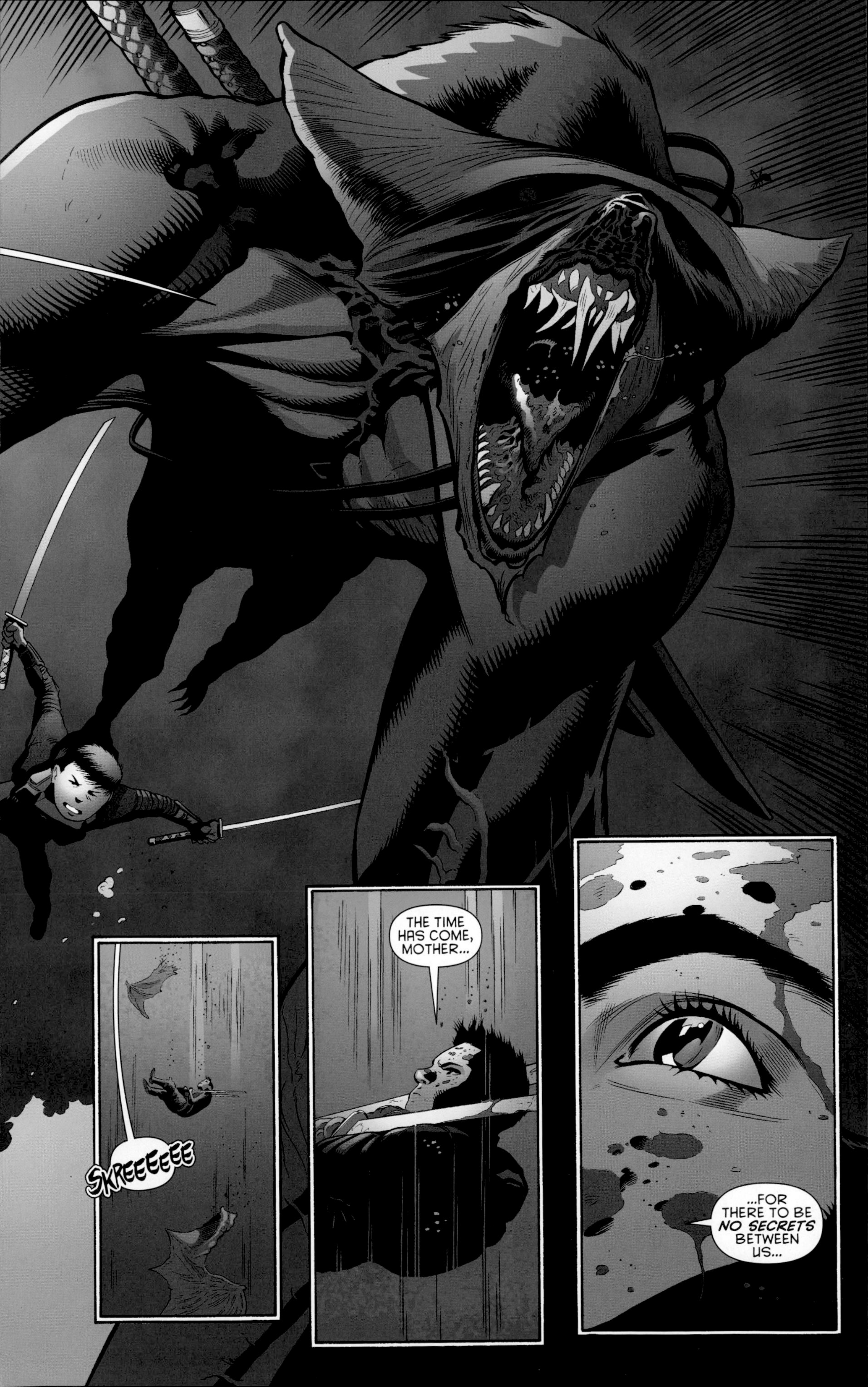
SKREEEEEE
THE TIME HAS COME, MOTHER...
...FOR THERE TO BE NO SECRETS BETWEEN US...

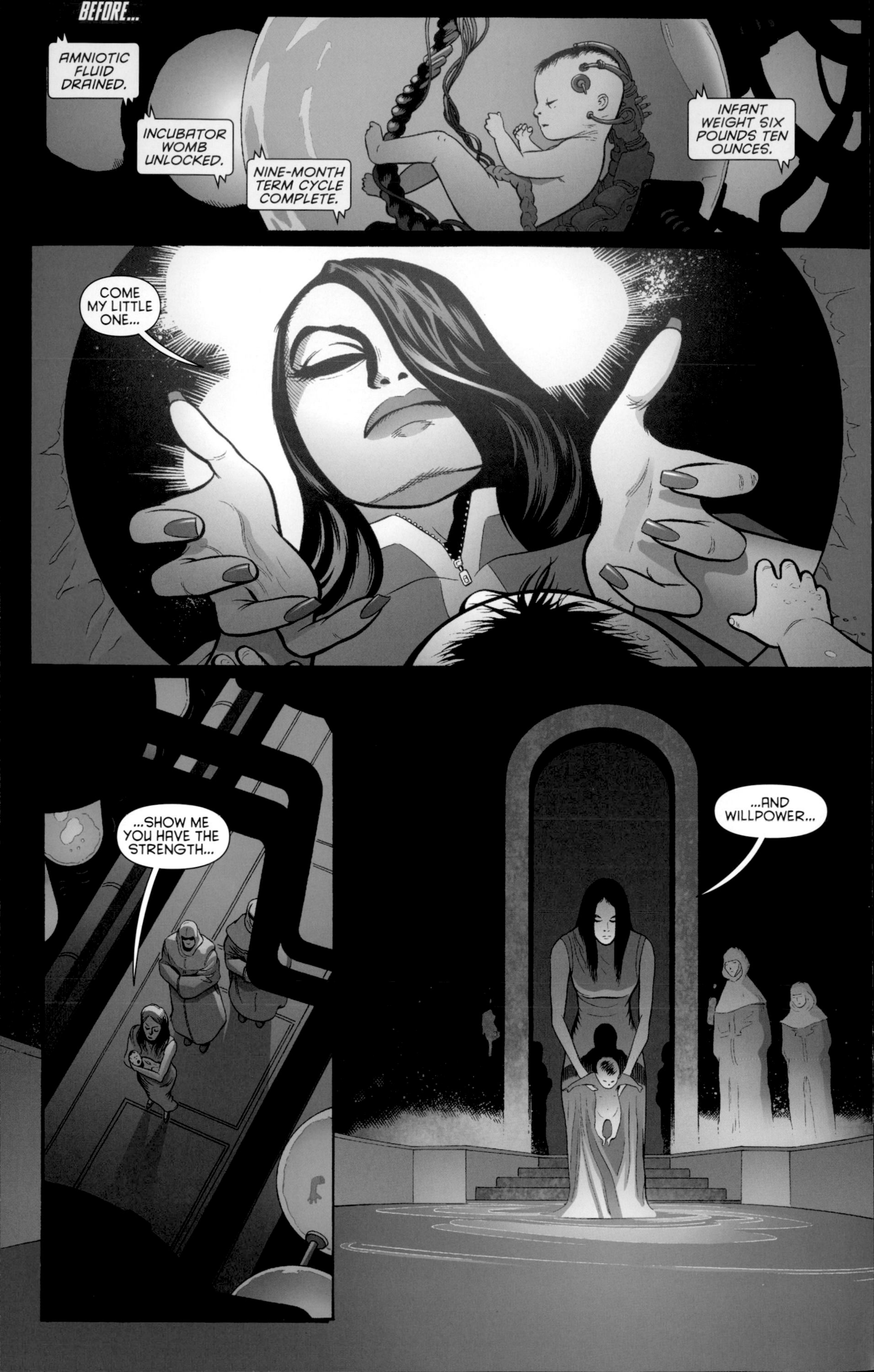
BEFORE...
AMNIOTIC FLUID DRAINED.
INCUBATOR WOMB UNLOCKED.
NINE-MONTH TERM CYCLE COMPLETE.
INFANT WEIGHT SIX POUNDS TEN OUNCES.
COME MY LITTLE ONE...
...SHOW ME YOU HAVE THE STRENGTH...
...AND WILLPOWER...

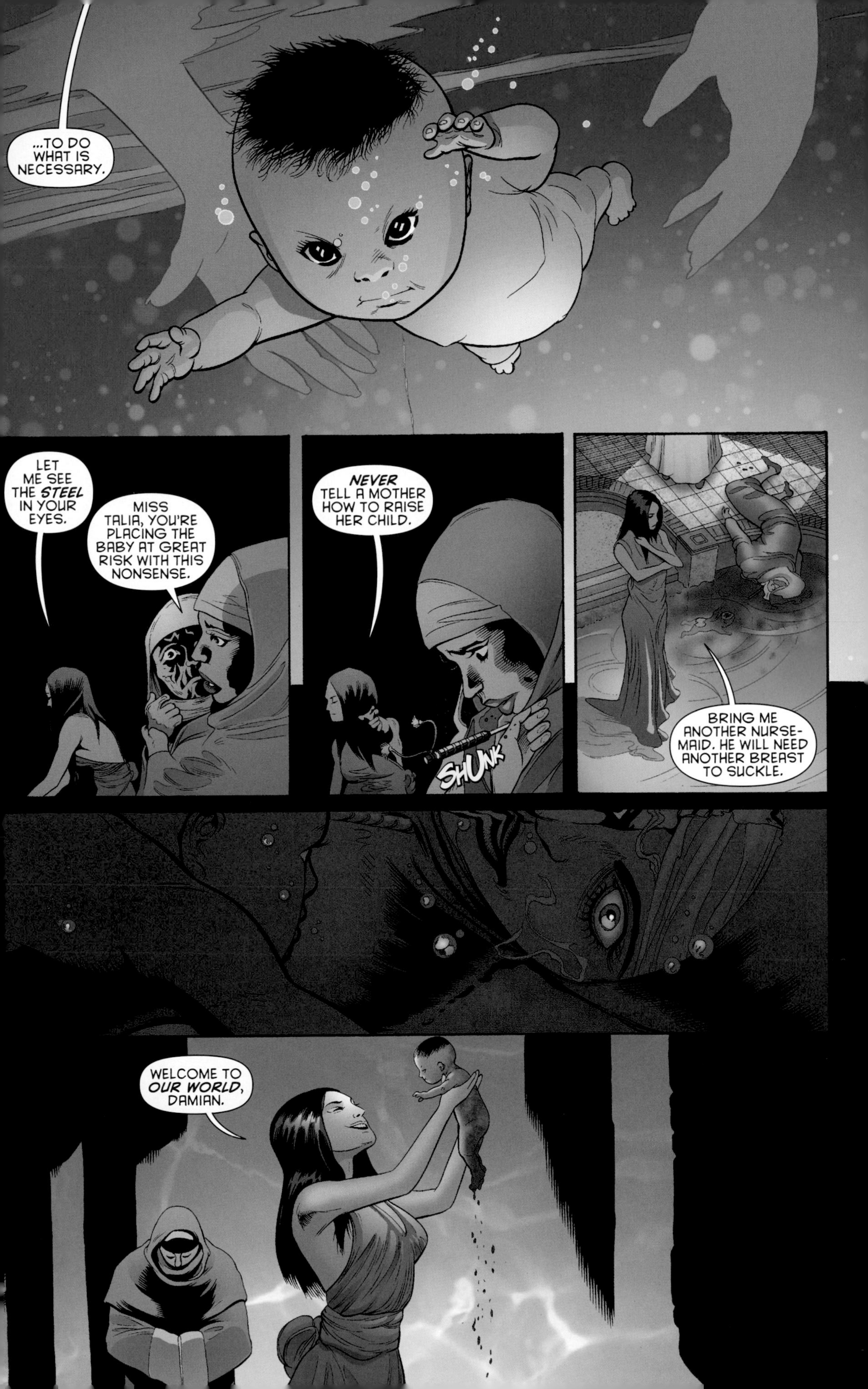
...TO DO WHAT IS NECESSARY.
LET ME SEE THE STEEL IN YOUR EYES.
MISS TALIA, YOU'RE PLACING THE BABY AT GREAT RISK WITH THIS NONSENSE.
NEVER TELL A MOTHER HOW TO RAISE HER CHILD.
SHUNK
BRING ME ANOTHER NURSE-MAID. HE WILL NEED ANOTHER BREAST TO SUCKLE.
WELCOME TO OUR WORLD, DAMIAN.

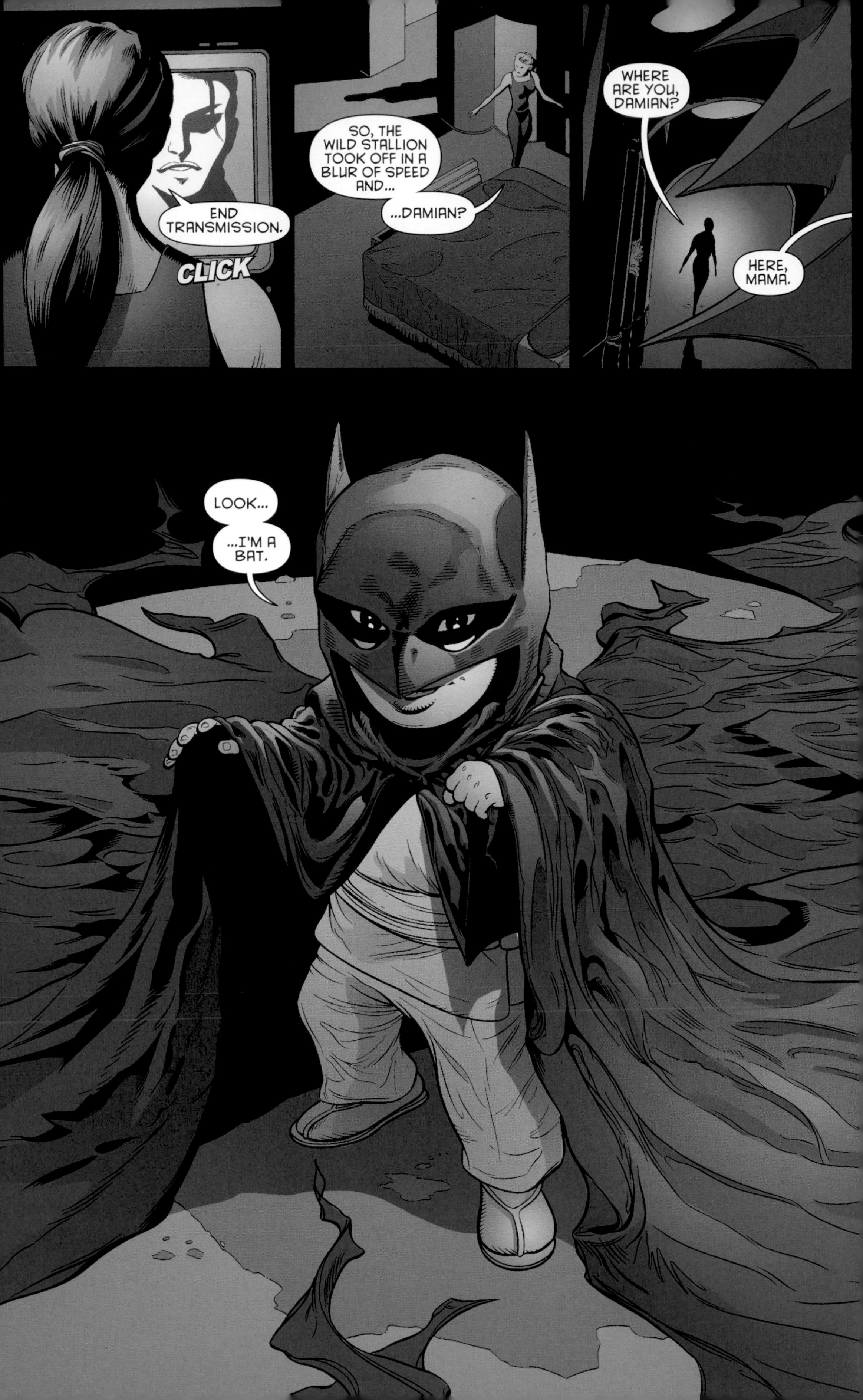
END TRANSMISSION.
CLICK
SO, THE WILD STALLION TOOK OFF IN A BLUR OF SPEED AND...
...DAMIAN?
WHERE ARE YOU, DAMIAN?
HERE, MAMA.
LOOK...
...I'M A BAT.

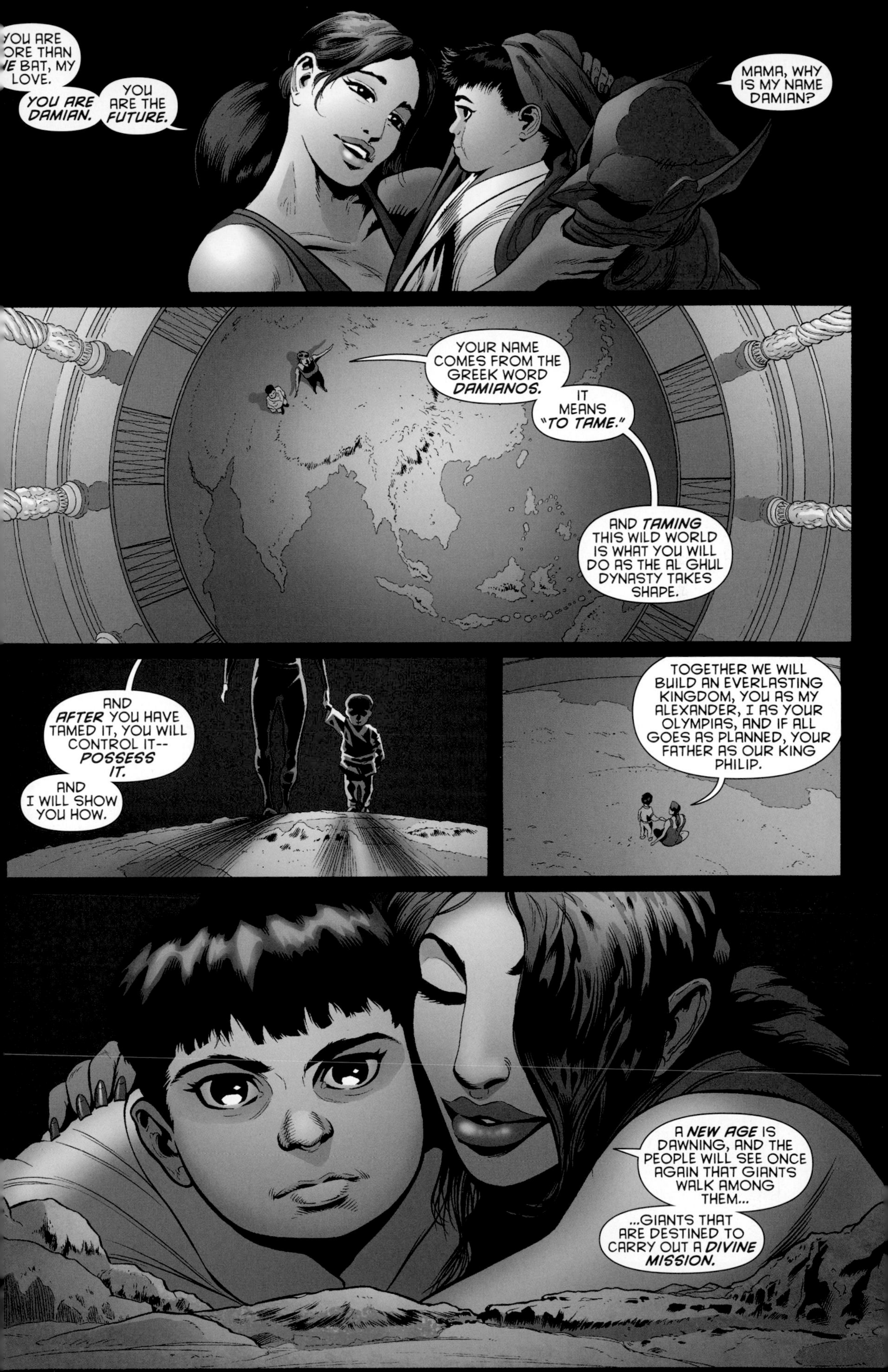
YOU ARE ORE THAN E BAT, MY LOVE.
YOU ARE DAMIAN.
YOU ARE THE FUTURE.
MAMA, WHY IS MY NAME DAMIAN?
YOUR NAME COMES FROM THE GREEK WORD DAMIANOS.
IT MEANS "TO TAME."
AND TAMING THIS WILD WORLD IS WHAT YOU WILL DO AS THE AL GHUL DYNASTY TAKES SHAPE.
AND AFTER YOU HAVE TAMED IT, YOU WILL CONTROL IT-- POSSESS IT.
AND I WILL SHOW YOU HOW.
TOGETHER WE WILL BUILD AN EVERLASTING KINGDOM, YOU AS MY ALEXANDER, I AS YOUR OLYMPIAS, AND IF ALL GOES AS PLANNED, YOUR FATHER AS OUR KING PHILIP.
A NEW AGE IS DAWNING, AND THE PEOPLE WILL SEE ONCE AGAIN THAT GIANTS WALK AMONG THEM...
...GIANTS THAT ARE DESTINED TO CARRY OUT A DIVINE MISSION.

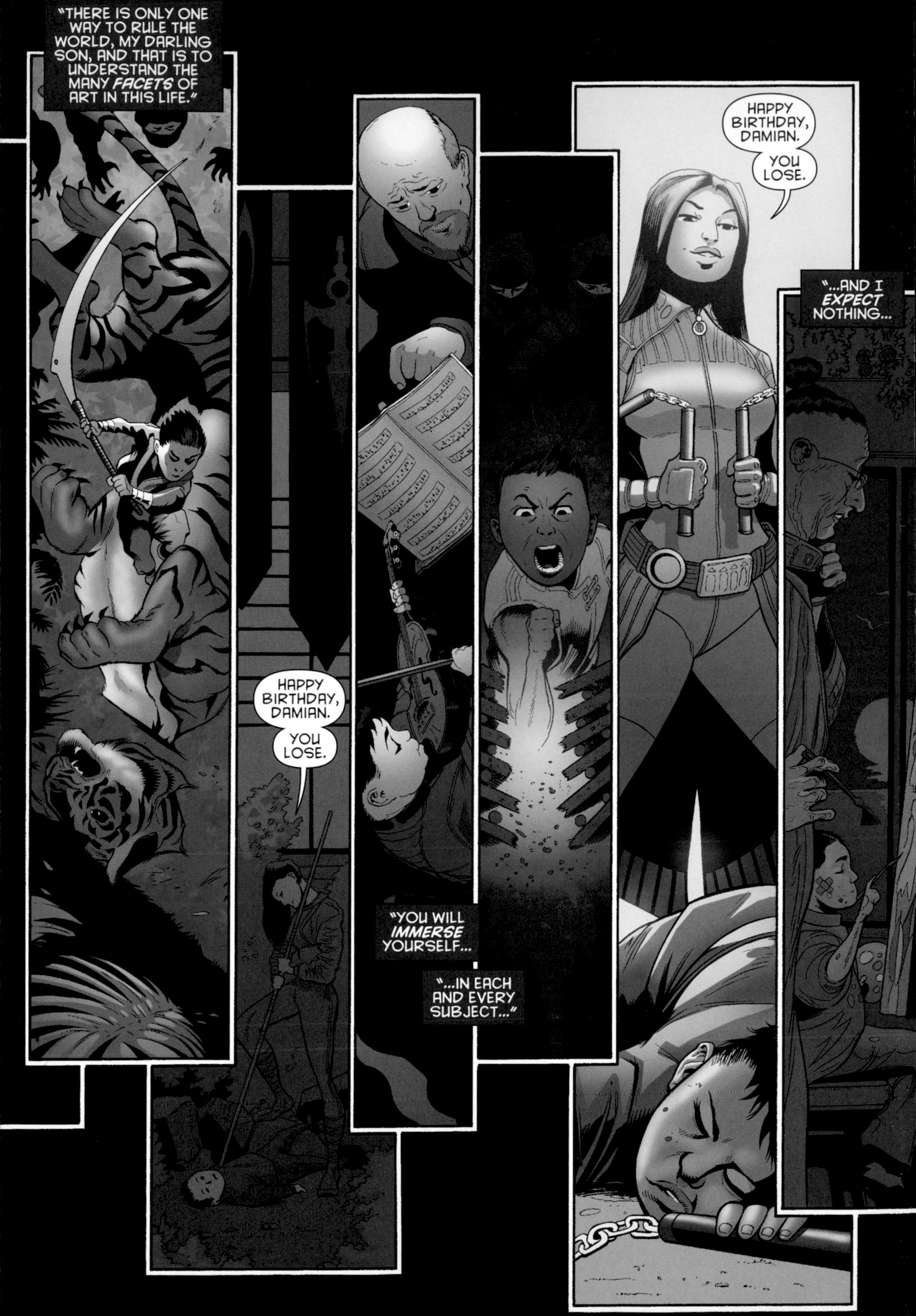
"THERE IS ONLY ONE WAY TO RULE THE WORLD, MY DARLING SON, AND THAT IS TO UNDERSTAND THE MANY *FACETS* OF ART IN THIS LIFE."
HAPPY BIRTHDAY, DAMIAN.
YOU LOSE.
"YOU WILL *IMMERSE* YOURSELF...
"...IN EACH AND EVERY SUBJECT..."
HAPPY BIRTHDAY, DAMIAN.
YOU LOSE.
"...AND I *EXPECT* NOTHING...

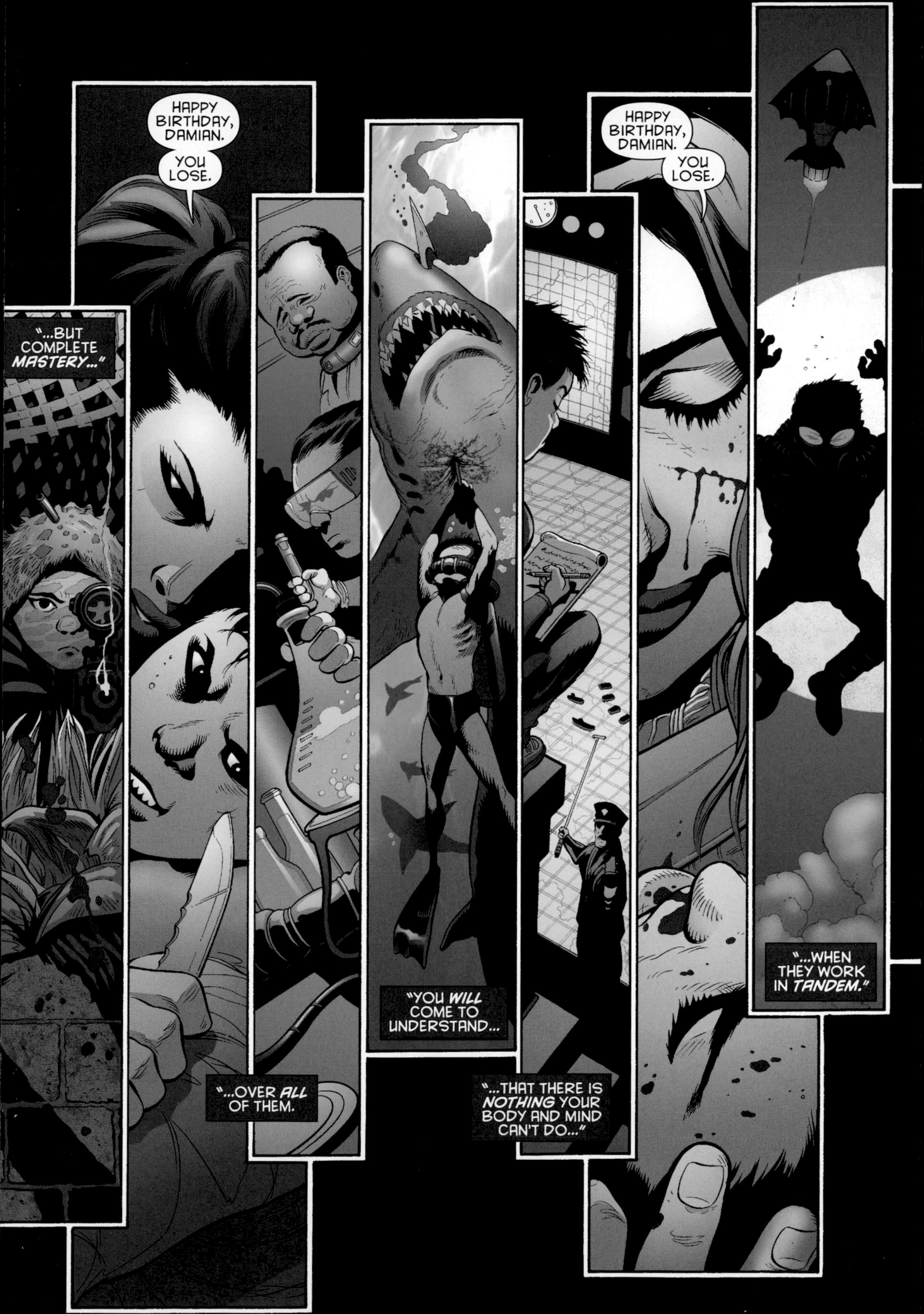
"...BUT COMPLETE MASTERY..."
HAPPY BIRTHDAY, DAMIAN.
YOU LOSE.
"...OVER ALL OF THEM.
"YOU WILL COME TO UNDERSTAND...
"...THAT THERE IS NOTHING YOUR BODY AND MIND CAN'T DO..."
HAPPY BIRTHDAY, DAMIAN.
YOU LOSE.
"...WHEN THEY WORK IN TANDEM."

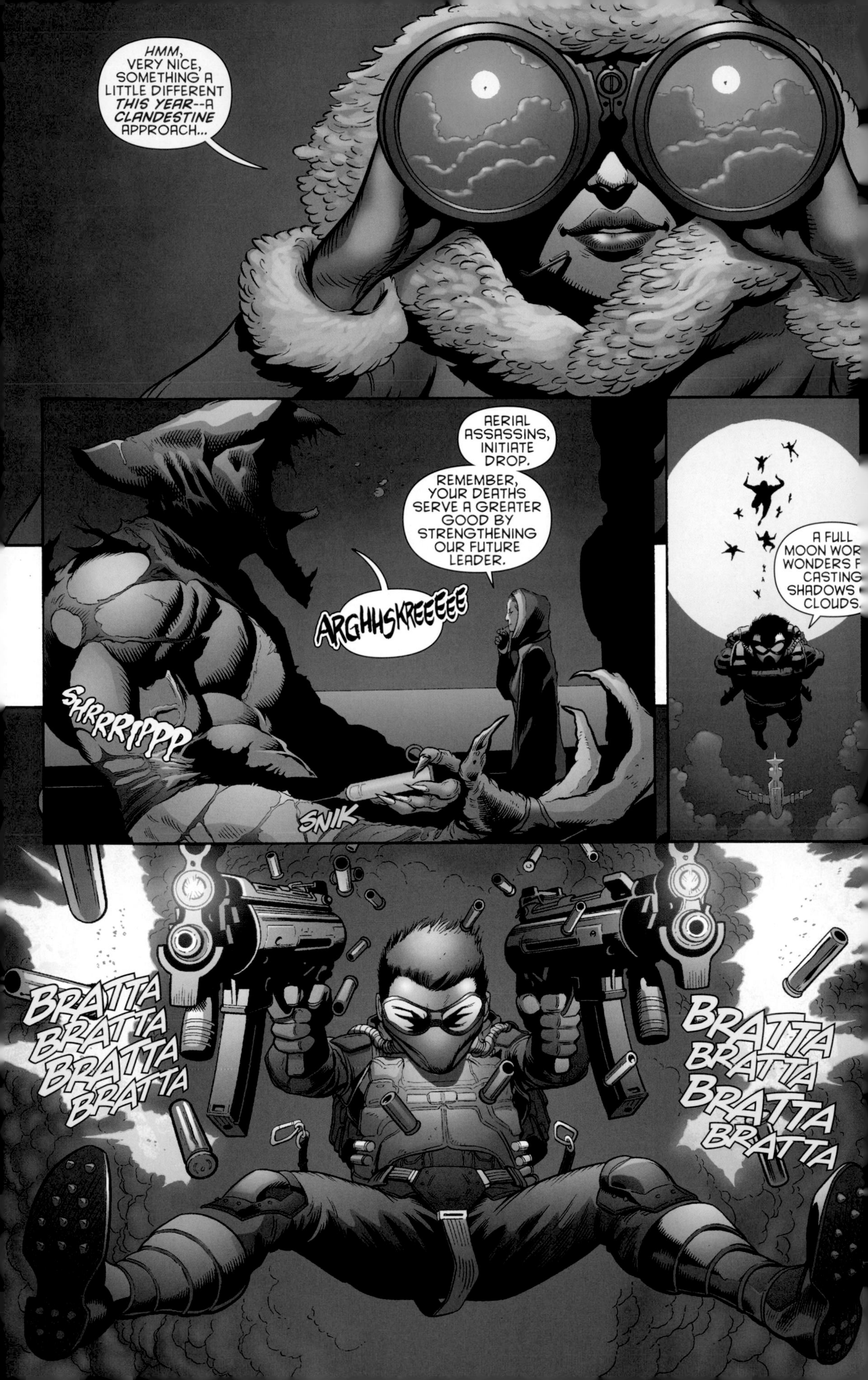

HMM, VERY NICE, SOMETHING A LITTLE DIFFERENT THIS YEAR--A CLANDESTINE APPROACH...
AERIAL ASSASSINS, INITIATE DROP.
REMEMBER, YOUR DEATHS SERVE A GREATER GOOD BY STRENGTHENING OUR FUTURE LEADER.
ARGHHSKREEEEEE
SHRRRIPPP
SNIK
BRATTA BRATTA BRATTA BRATTA
BRATTA BRATTA BRATTA BRATTA

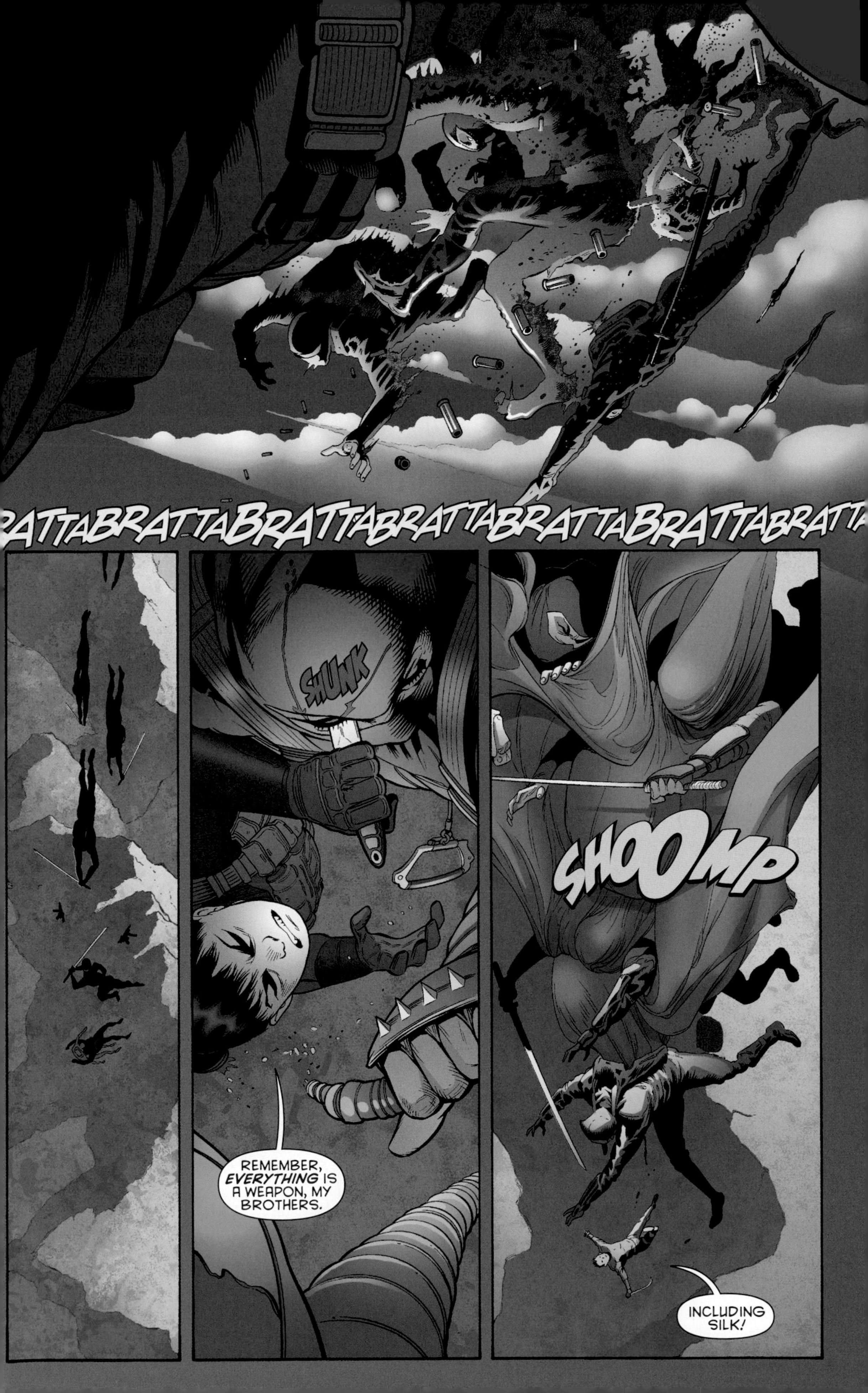
BRATTABRATTABRATTABRATTABRATTABRATTABRATTA
SHUNK
REMEMBER, EVERYTHING IS A WEAPON, MY BROTHERS.
SHOOOMP
INCLUDING SILK!

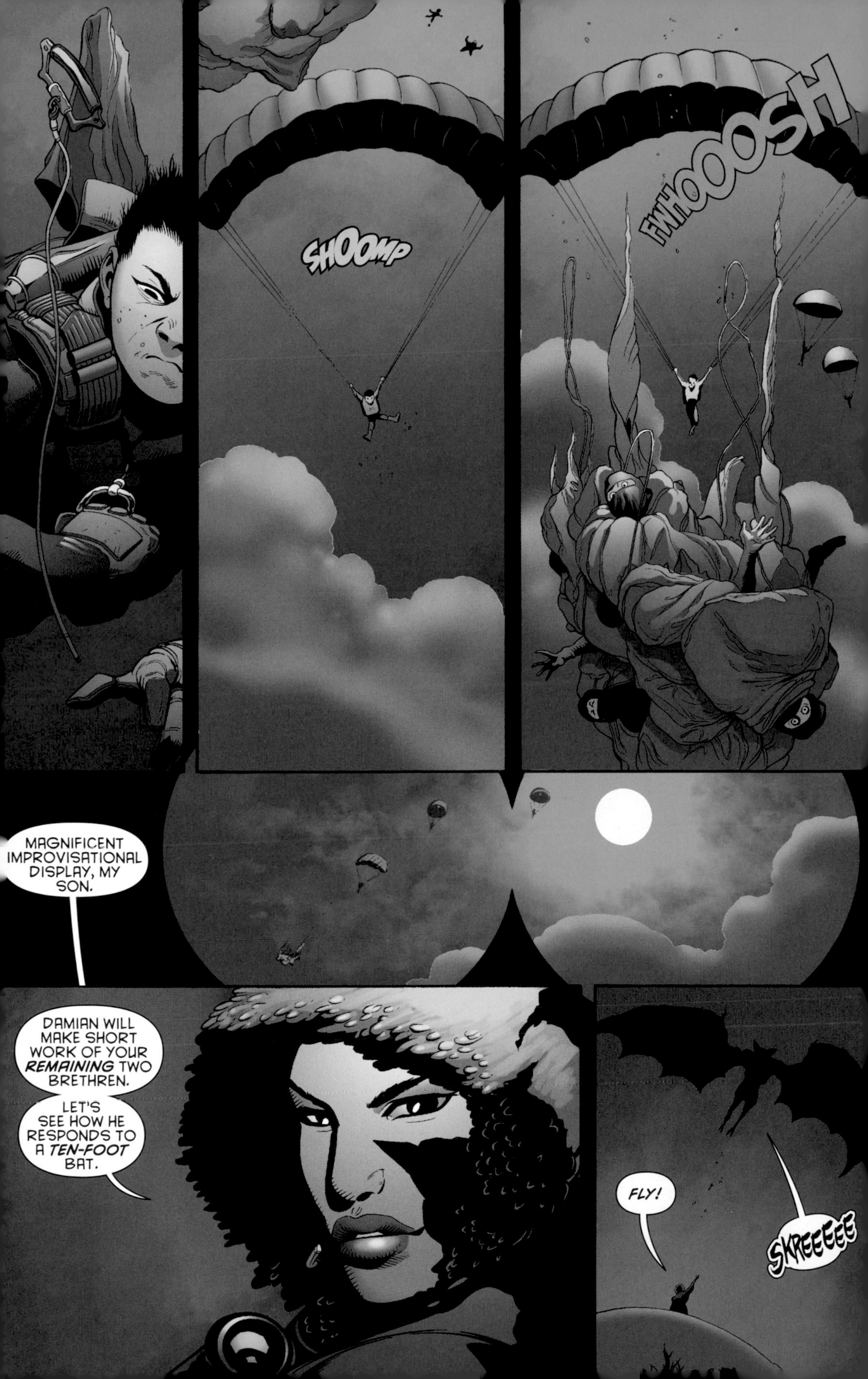
SHOOMP
FWHOOOOSH
MAGNIFICENT IMPROVISATIONAL DISPLAY, MY SON.
DAMIAN WILL MAKE SHORT WORK OF YOUR *REMAINING* TWO BRETHREN.
LET'S SEE HOW HE RESPONDS TO A *TEN-FOOT* BAT.
FLY!
SKREEEEE

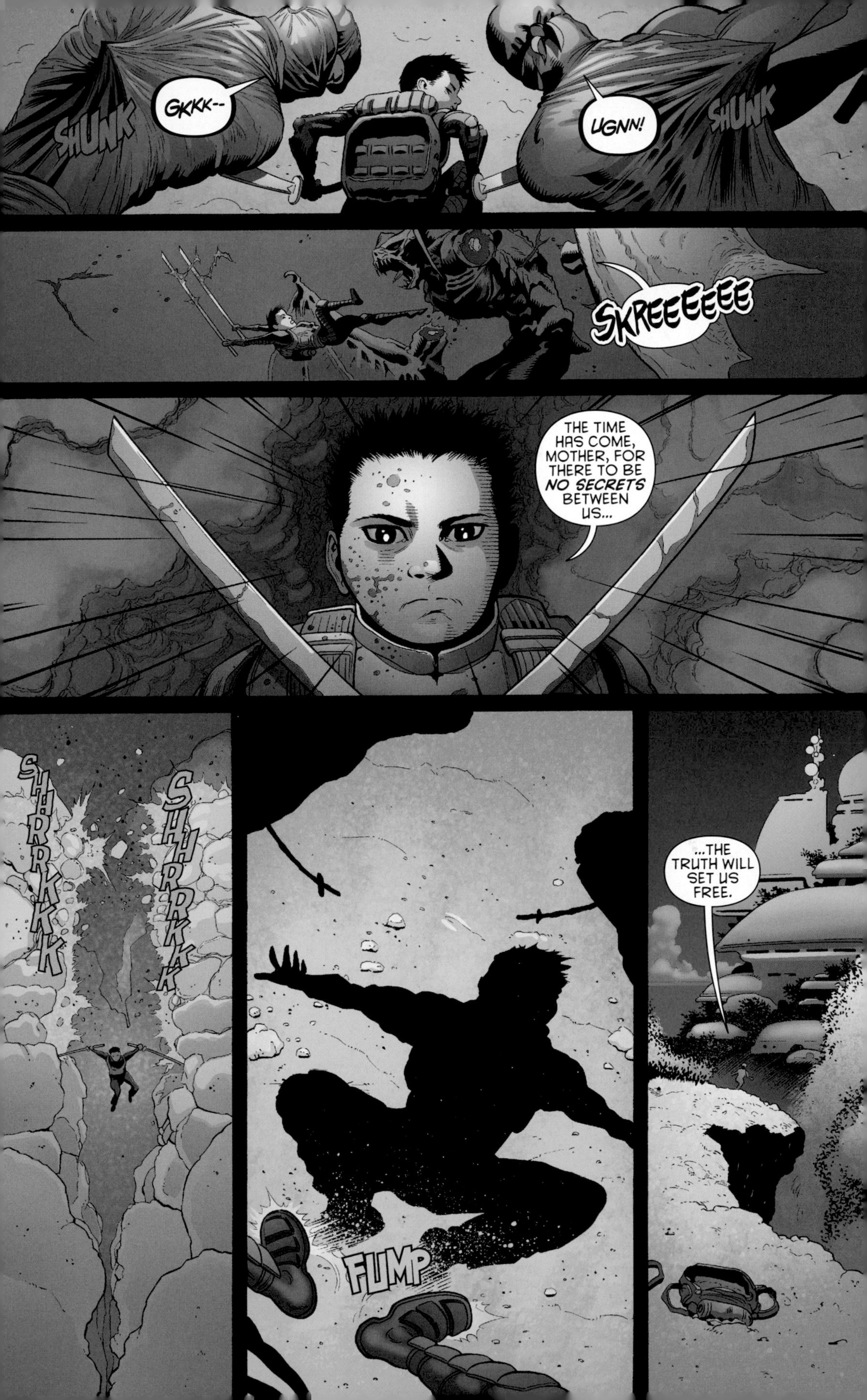
SHUNK
GKKK--
UGNN!
SHUNK
SKREEEEEE
THE TIME HAS COME, MOTHER, FOR THERE TO BE NO SECRETS BETWEEN US...
SHHRRKKK
SHHRRKKK
FUMP
...THE TRUTH WILL SET US FREE.

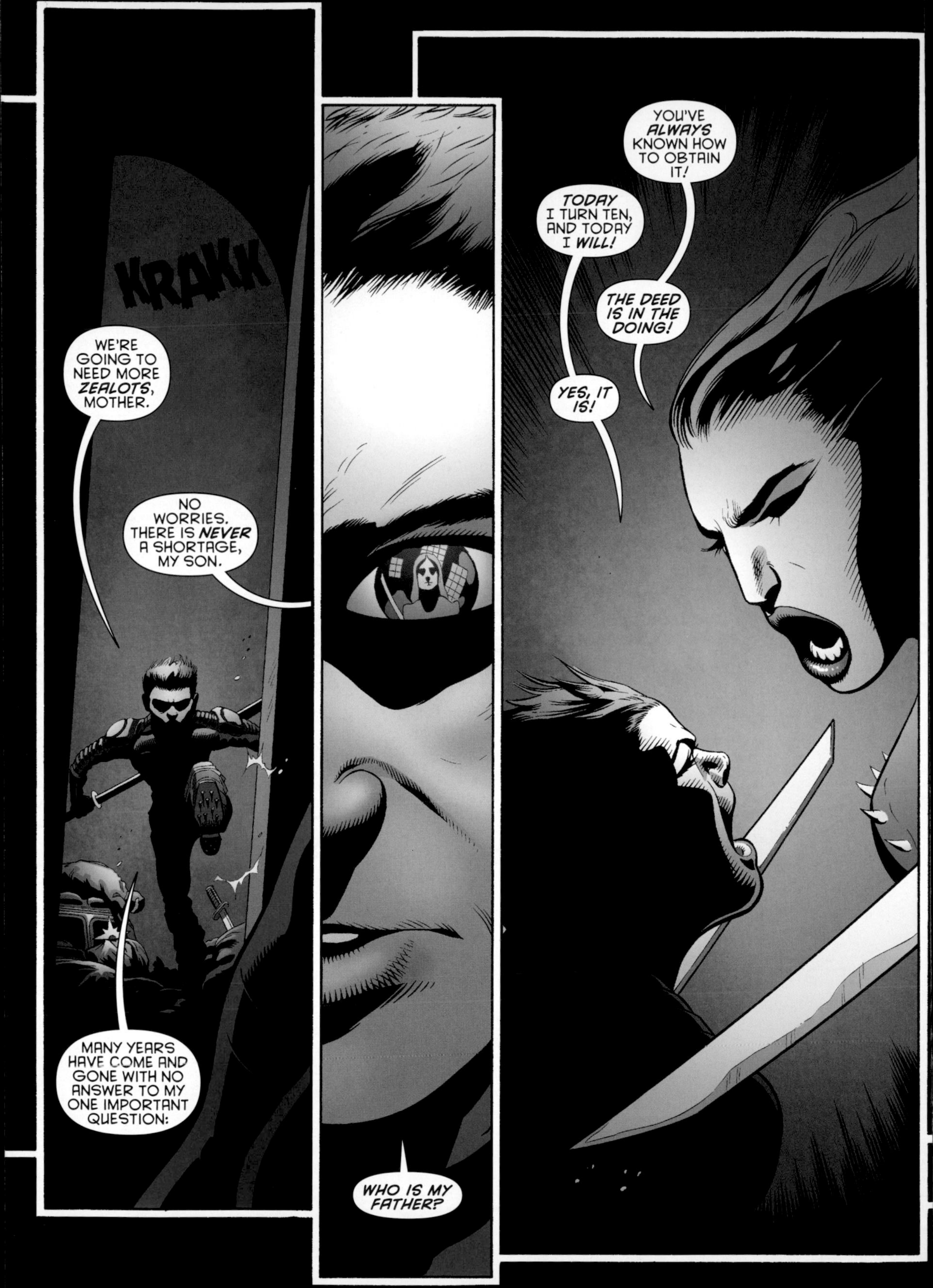
KRAKK
WE'RE GOING TO NEED MORE *ZEALOTS*, MOTHER.
NO WORRIES. THERE IS *NEVER* A SHORTAGE, MY SON.
MANY YEARS HAVE COME AND GONE WITH NO ANSWER TO MY ONE IMPORTANT QUESTION:
WHO IS MY FATHER?
YOU'VE *ALWAYS* KNOWN HOW TO OBTAIN IT!
TODAY I TURN TEN, AND TODAY I *WILL!*
THE DEED IS IN THE DOING!
YES, IT IS!

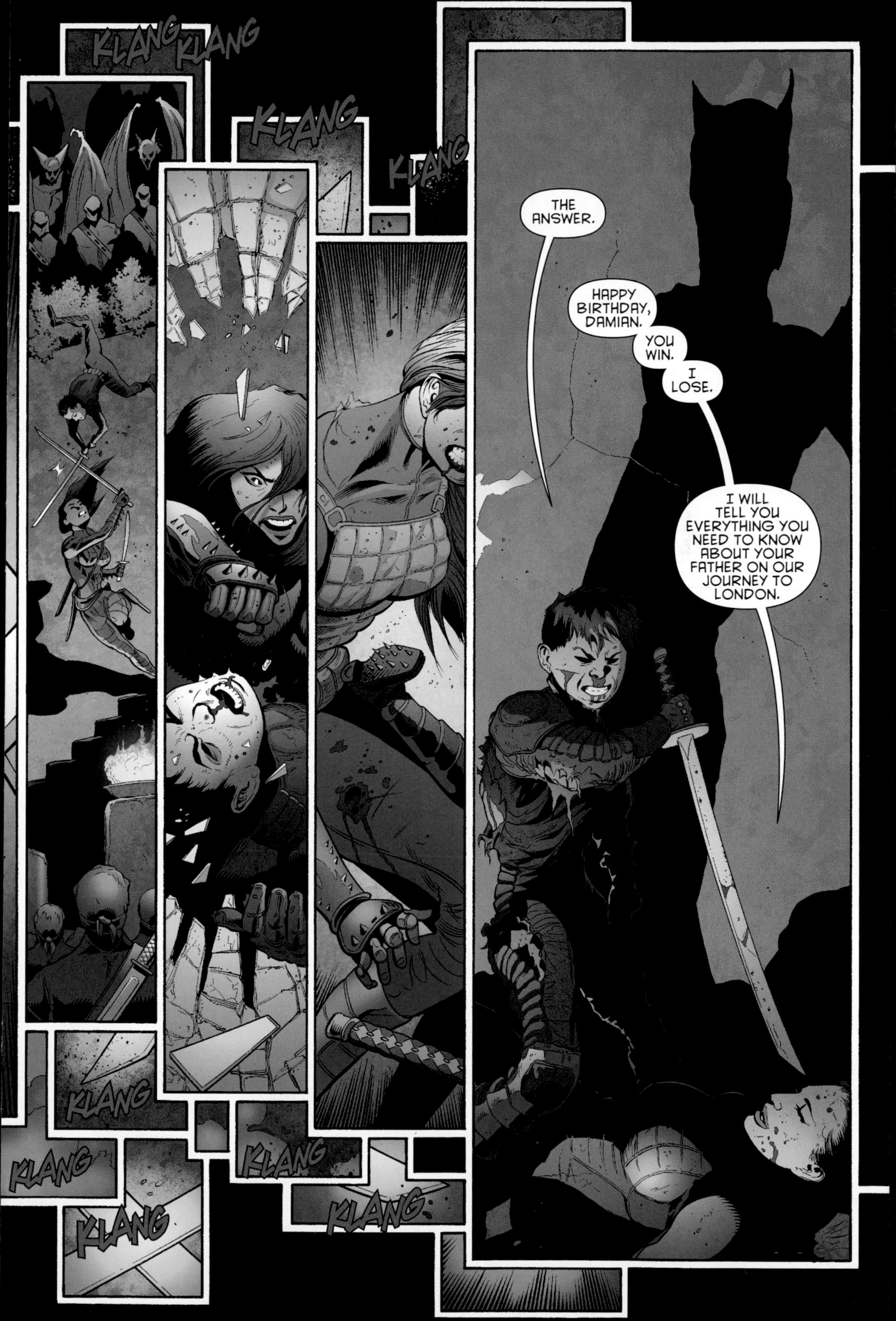
KLANG KLANG
KLANG
KLANG
THE ANSWER.
HAPPY BIRTHDAY, DAMIAN.
YOU WIN.
I LOSE.
I WILL TELL YOU EVERYTHING YOU NEED TO KNOW ABOUT YOUR FATHER ON OUR JOURNEY TO LONDON.
KLANG
KLANG
KLANG
KLANG
KLANG

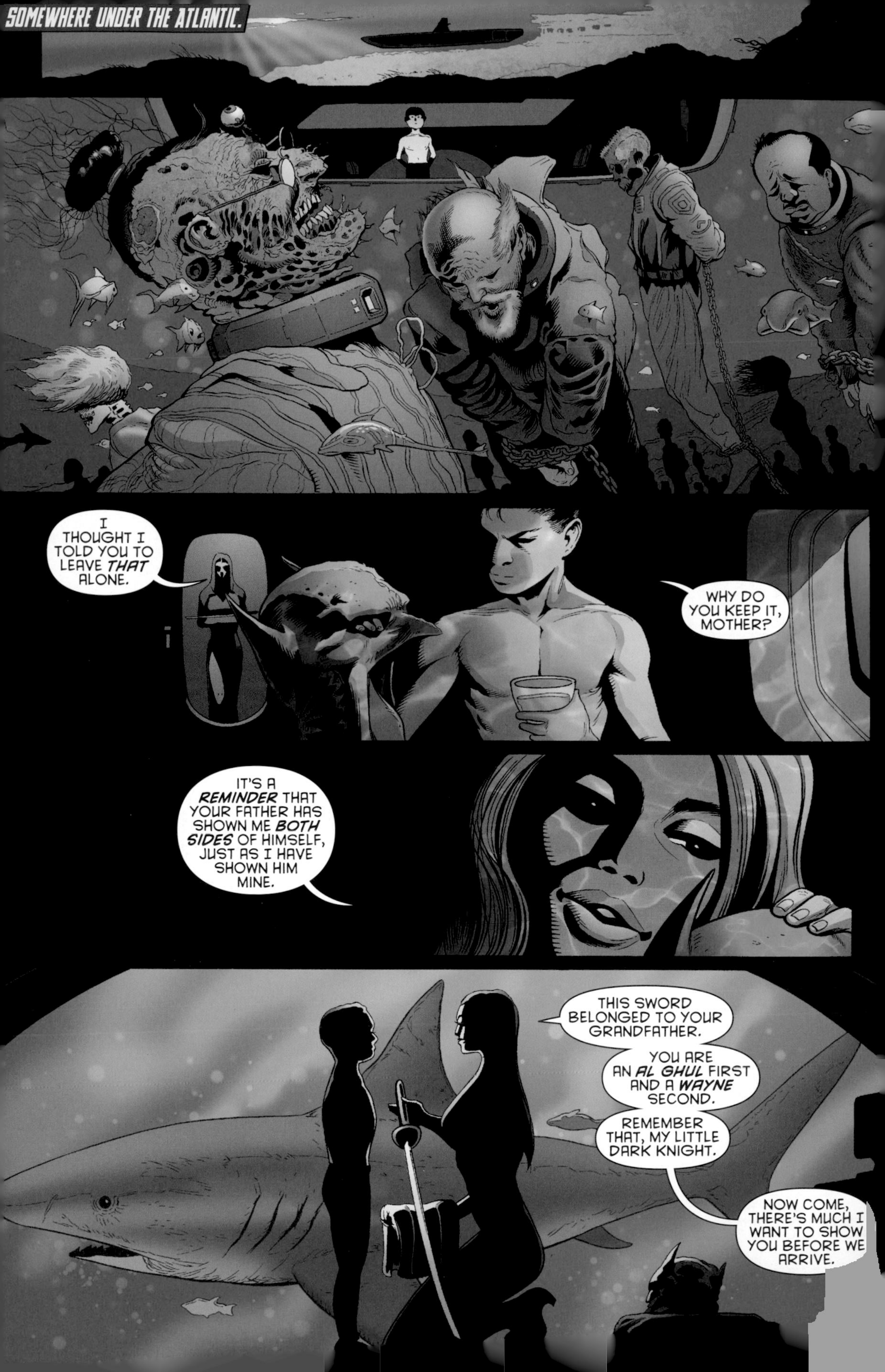
SOMEWHERE UNDER THE ATLANTIC.
I THOUGHT I TOLD YOU TO LEAVE THAT ALONE.
WHY DO YOU KEEP IT, MOTHER?
IT'S A REMINDER THAT YOUR FATHER HAS SHOWN ME BOTH SIDES OF HIMSELF, JUST AS I HAVE SHOWN HIM MINE.
THIS SWORD BELONGED TO YOUR GRANDFATHER.
YOU ARE AN AL GHUL FIRST AND A WAYNE SECOND.
REMEMBER THAT, MY LITTLE DARK KNIGHT.
NOW COME, THERE'S MUCH I WANT TO SHOW YOU BEFORE WE ARRIVE.

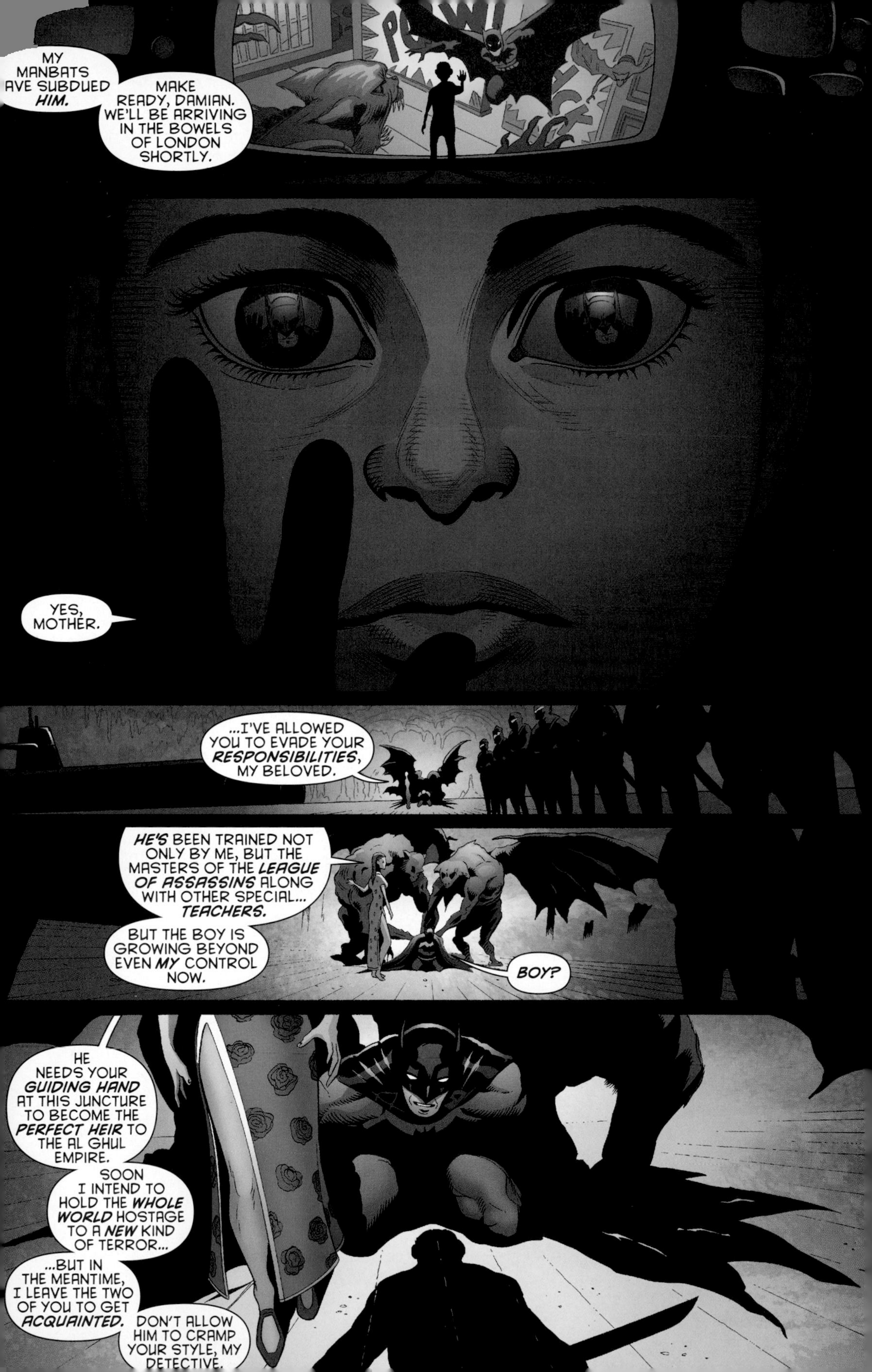
MY MANBATS AVE SUBDUED HIM.
MAKE READY, DAMIAN. WE'LL BE ARRIVING IN THE BOWELS OF LONDON SHORTLY.
YES, MOTHER.
...I'VE ALLOWED YOU TO EVADE YOUR RESPONSIBILITIES, MY BELOVED.
HE'S BEEN TRAINED NOT ONLY BY ME, BUT THE MASTERS OF THE LEAGUE OF ASSASSINS ALONG WITH OTHER SPECIAL... TEACHERS.
BUT THE BOY IS GROWING BEYOND EVEN MY CONTROL NOW.
BOY?
HE NEEDS YOUR GUIDING HAND AT THIS JUNCTURE TO BECOME THE PERFECT HEIR TO THE AL GHUL EMPIRE.
SOON I INTEND TO HOLD THE WHOLE WORLD HOSTAGE TO A NEW KIND OF TERROR...
...BUT IN THE MEANTIME, I LEAVE THE TWO OF YOU TO GET ACQUAINTED.
DON'T ALLOW HIM TO CRAMP YOUR STYLE, MY DETECTIVE.

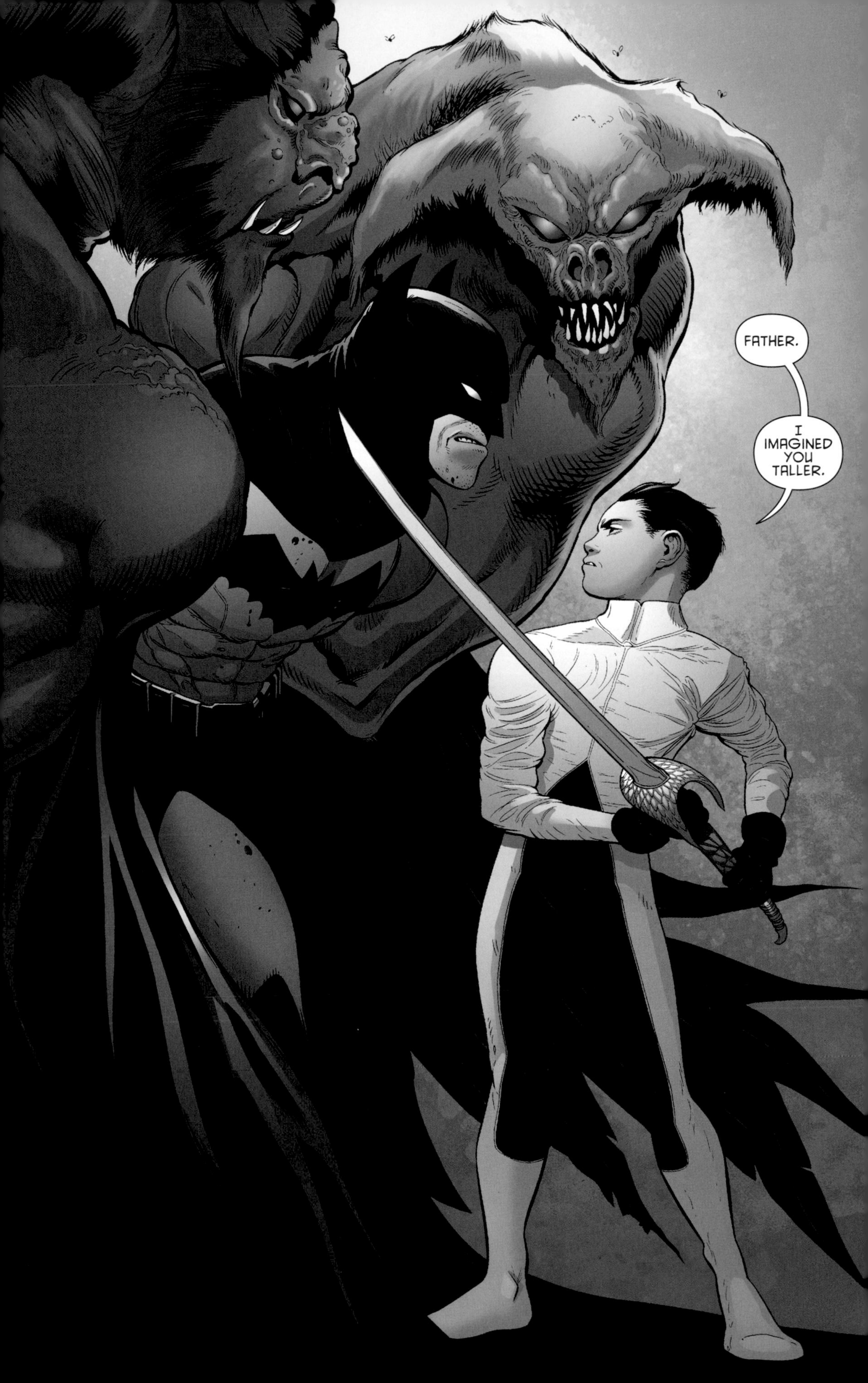
FATHER.
I IMAGINED YOU TALLER.

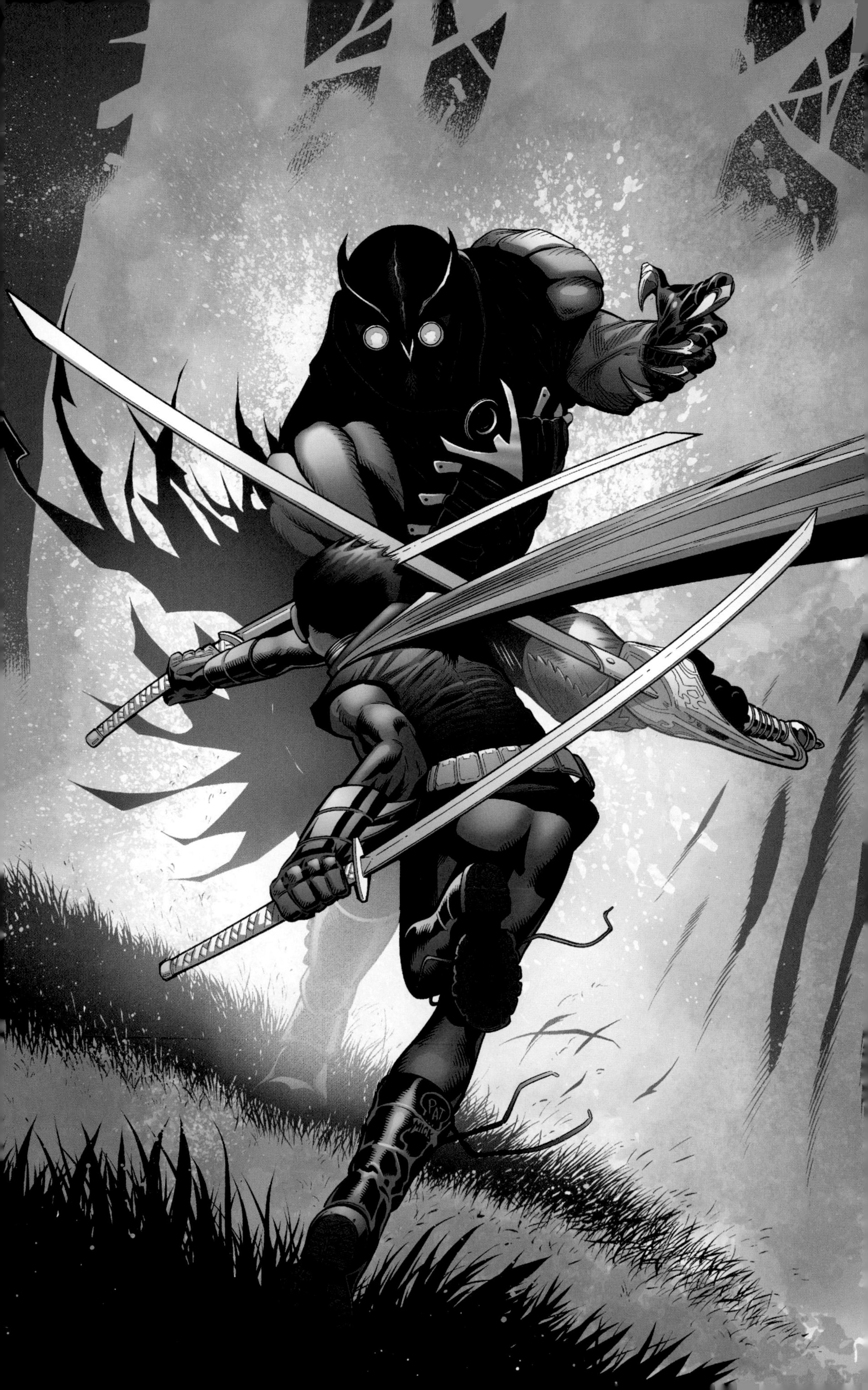

NIGHT OF THE OWLS: ROBIN HEARS A HOO

PETER J. TOMASI writer **LEE GARBETT** penciller **ANDY CLARKE** art, pages 16-17 **RAY MCCARTHY & KEITH CHAMPAGNE** inkers
cover by **GLEASON, GRAY & KALISZ**

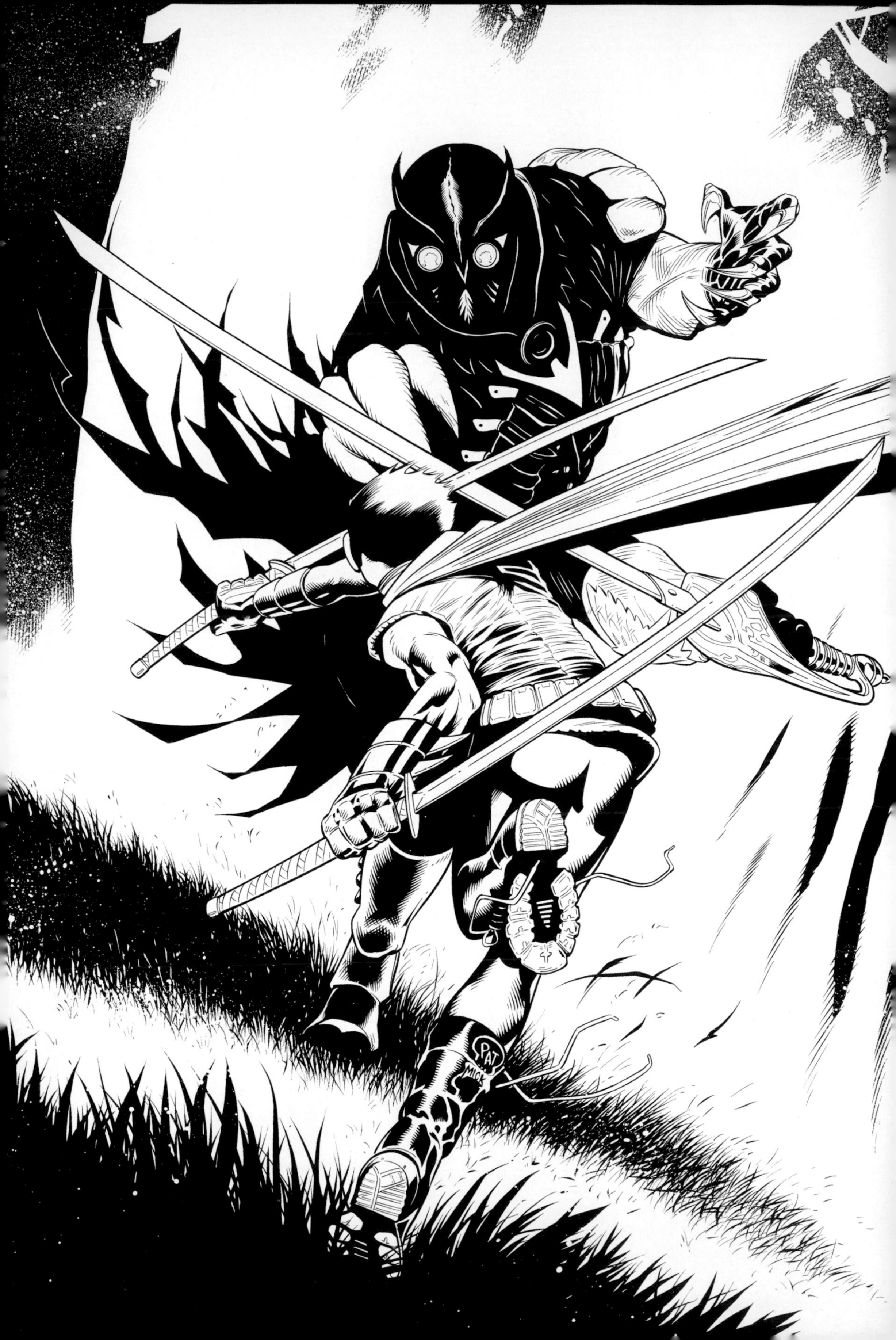

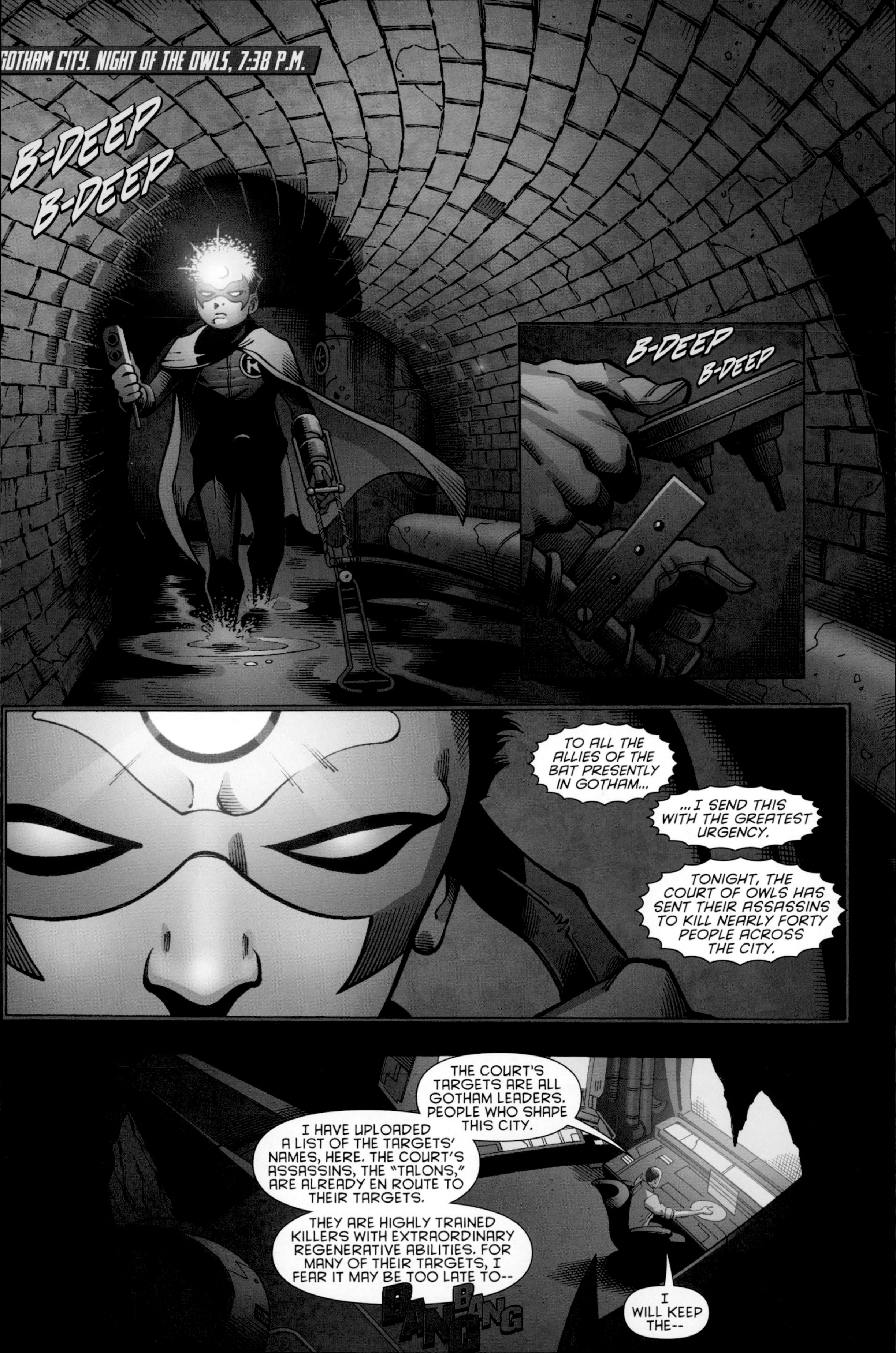
GOTHAM CITY. NIGHT OF THE OWLS, 7:38 P.M.
B-DEEP B-DEEP
B-DEEP B-DEEP
TO ALL THE ALLIES OF THE BAT PRESENTLY IN GOTHAM...
...I SEND THIS WITH THE GREATEST URGENCY.
TONIGHT, THE COURT OF OWLS HAS SENT THEIR ASSASSINS TO KILL NEARLY FORTY PEOPLE ACROSS THE CITY.
THE COURT'S TARGETS ARE ALL GOTHAM LEADERS. PEOPLE WHO SHAPE THIS CITY.
I HAVE UPLOADED A LIST OF THE TARGETS' NAMES, HERE. THE COURT'S ASSASSINS, THE "TALONS," ARE ALREADY EN ROUTE TO THEIR TARGETS.
THEY ARE HIGHLY TRAINED KILLERS WITH EXTRAORDINARY REGENERATIVE ABILITIES. FOR MANY OF THEIR TARGETS, I FEAR IT MAY BE TOO LATE TO--
BANG BANG BANG
I WILL KEEP THE--

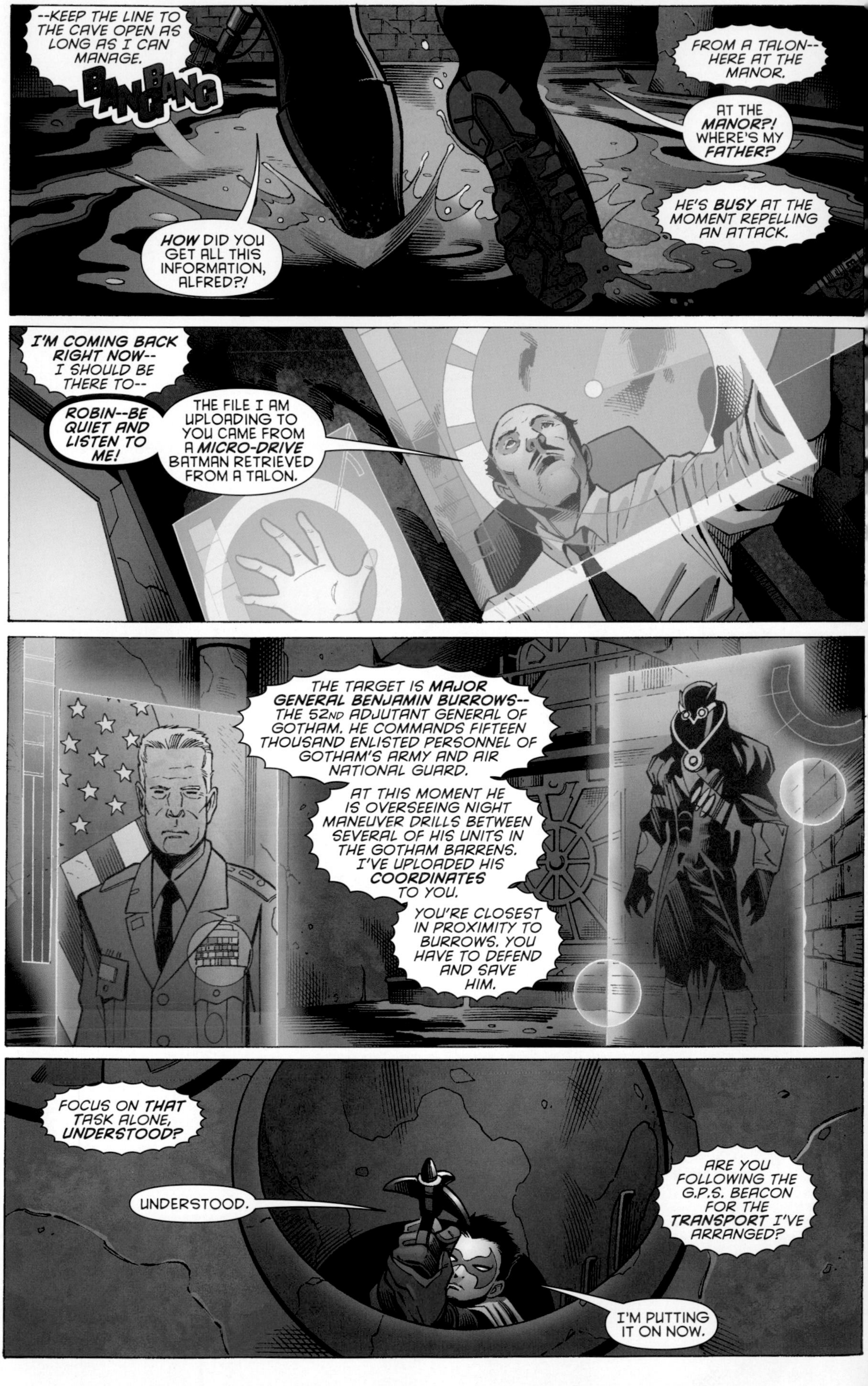

--KEEP THE LINE TO THE CAVE OPEN AS LONG AS I CAN MANAGE.
BANG BANG BANG
HOW DID YOU GET ALL THIS INFORMATION, ALFRED?!
FROM A TALON-- HERE AT THE MANOR.
AT THE MANOR?! WHERE'S MY FATHER?
HE'S BUSY AT THE MOMENT REPELLING AN ATTACK.
I'M COMING BACK RIGHT NOW-- I SHOULD BE THERE TO--
ROBIN--BE QUIET AND LISTEN TO ME!
THE FILE I AM UPLOADING TO YOU CAME FROM A MICRO-DRIVE BATMAN RETRIEVED FROM A TALON.
THE TARGET IS MAJOR GENERAL BENJAMIN BURROWS-- THE 52ND ADJUTANT GENERAL OF GOTHAM. HE COMMANDS FIFTEEN THOUSAND ENLISTED PERSONNEL OF GOTHAM'S ARMY AND AIR NATIONAL GUARD.
AT THIS MOMENT HE IS OVERSEEING NIGHT MANEUVER DRILLS BETWEEN SEVERAL OF HIS UNITS IN THE GOTHAM BARRENS. I'VE UPLOADED HIS COORDINATES TO YOU.
YOU'RE CLOSEST IN PROXIMITY TO BURROWS. YOU HAVE TO DEFEND AND SAVE HIM.
FOCUS ON THAT TASK ALONE, UNDERSTOOD?
UNDERSTOOD.
ARE YOU FOLLOWING THE G.P.S. BEACON FOR THE TRANSPORT I'VE ARRANGED?
I'M PUTTING IT ON NOW.

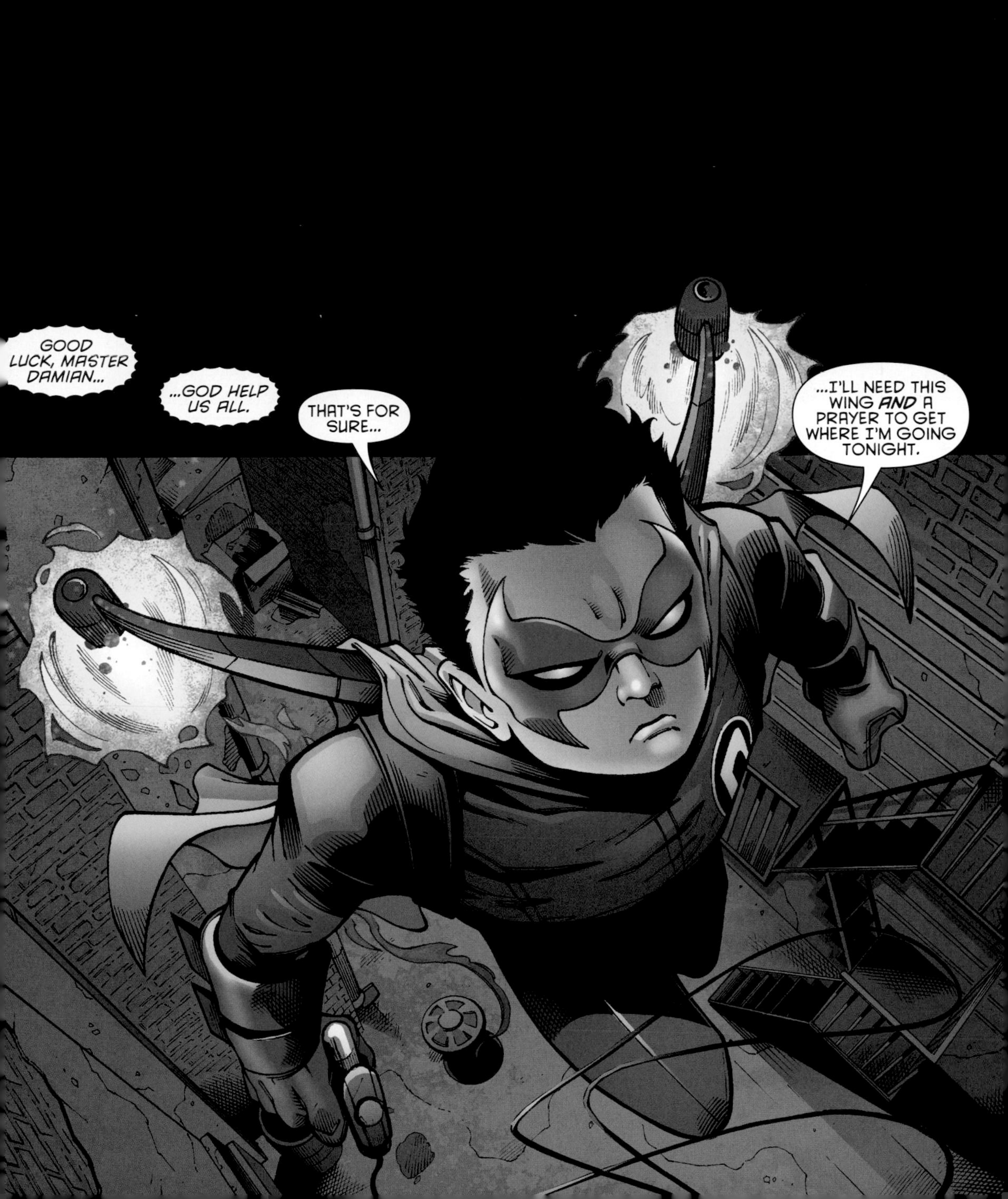
GOOD LUCK, MASTER DAMIAN...
...GOD HELP US ALL.
THAT'S FOR SURE...
...I'LL NEED THIS WING *AND* A PRAYER TO GET WHERE I'M GOING TONIGHT.

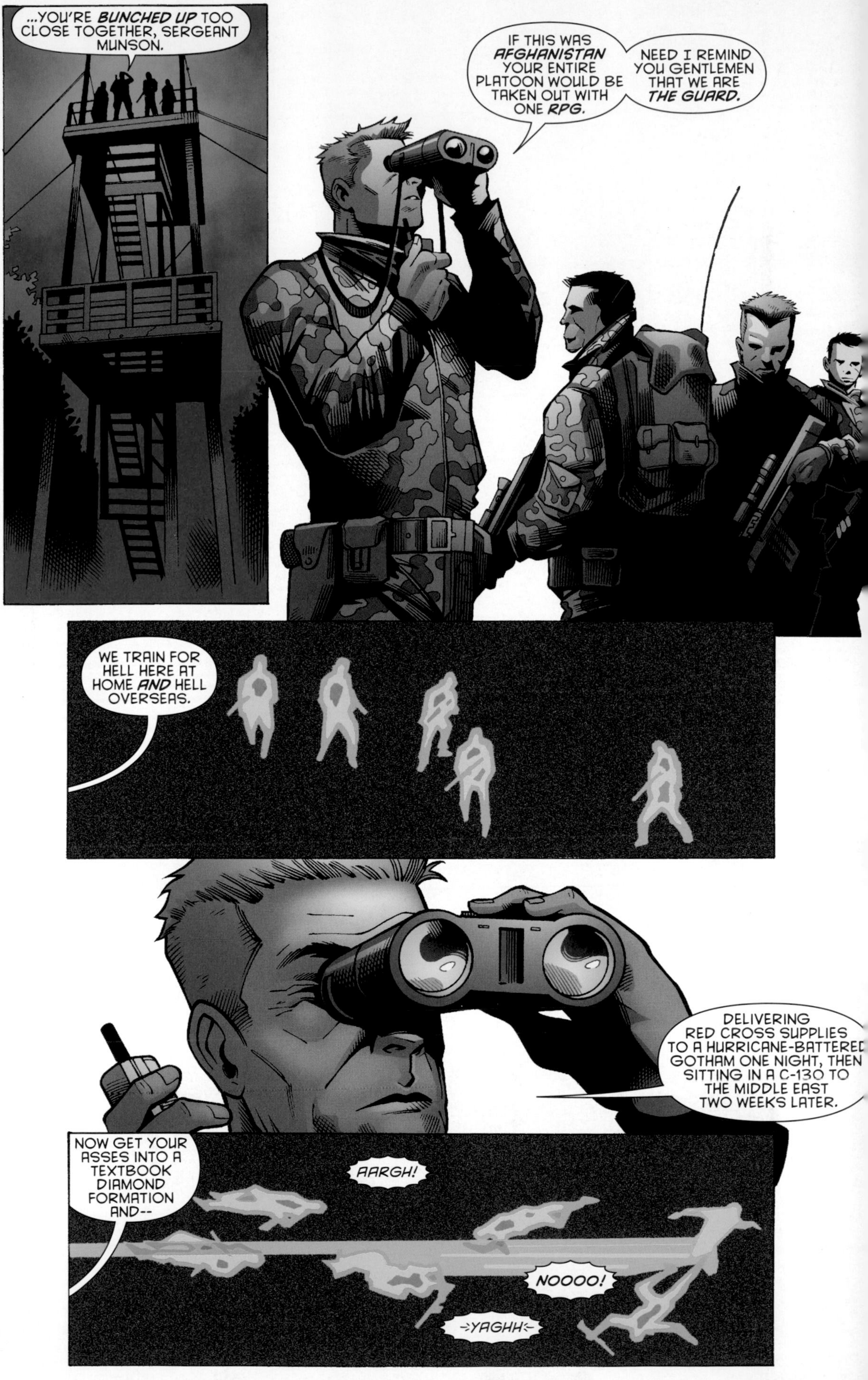

...YOU'RE BUNCHED UP TOO CLOSE TOGETHER, SERGEANT MUNSON.
IF THIS WAS AFGHANISTAN YOUR ENTIRE PLATOON WOULD BE TAKEN OUT WITH ONE RPG.
NEED I REMIND YOU GENTLEMEN THAT WE ARE THE GUARD.
WE TRAIN FOR HELL HERE AT HOME AND HELL OVERSEAS.
DELIVERING RED CROSS SUPPLIES TO A HURRICANE-BATTERED GOTHAM ONE NIGHT, THEN SITTING IN A C-130 TO THE MIDDLE EAST TWO WEEKS LATER.
NOW GET YOUR ASSES INTO A TEXTBOOK DIAMOND FORMATION AND--
AARGH!
NOOOO!
YAGHH

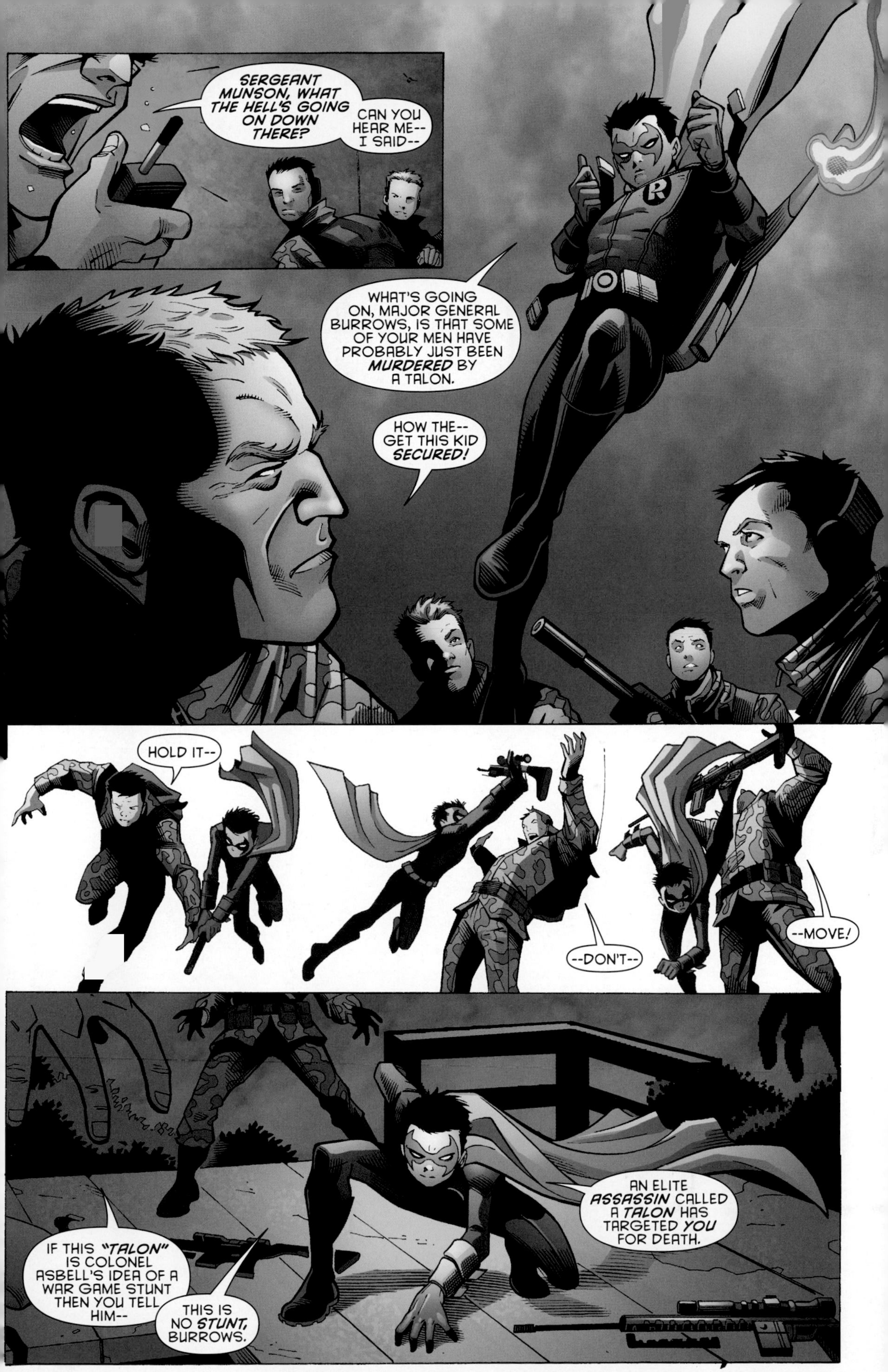
SERGEANT MUNSON, WHAT THE HELL'S GOING ON DOWN THERE?
CAN YOU HEAR ME-- I SAID--
WHAT'S GOING ON, MAJOR GENERAL BURROWS, IS THAT SOME OF YOUR MEN HAVE PROBABLY JUST BEEN MURDERED BY A TALON.
HOW THE-- GET THIS KID SECURED!
HOLD IT--
--DON'T--
--MOVE!
AN ELITE ASSASSIN CALLED A TALON HAS TARGETED YOU FOR DEATH.
IF THIS "TALON" IS COLONEL ASBELL'S IDEA OF A WAR GAME STUNT THEN YOU TELL HIM--
THIS IS NO STUNT, BURROWS.

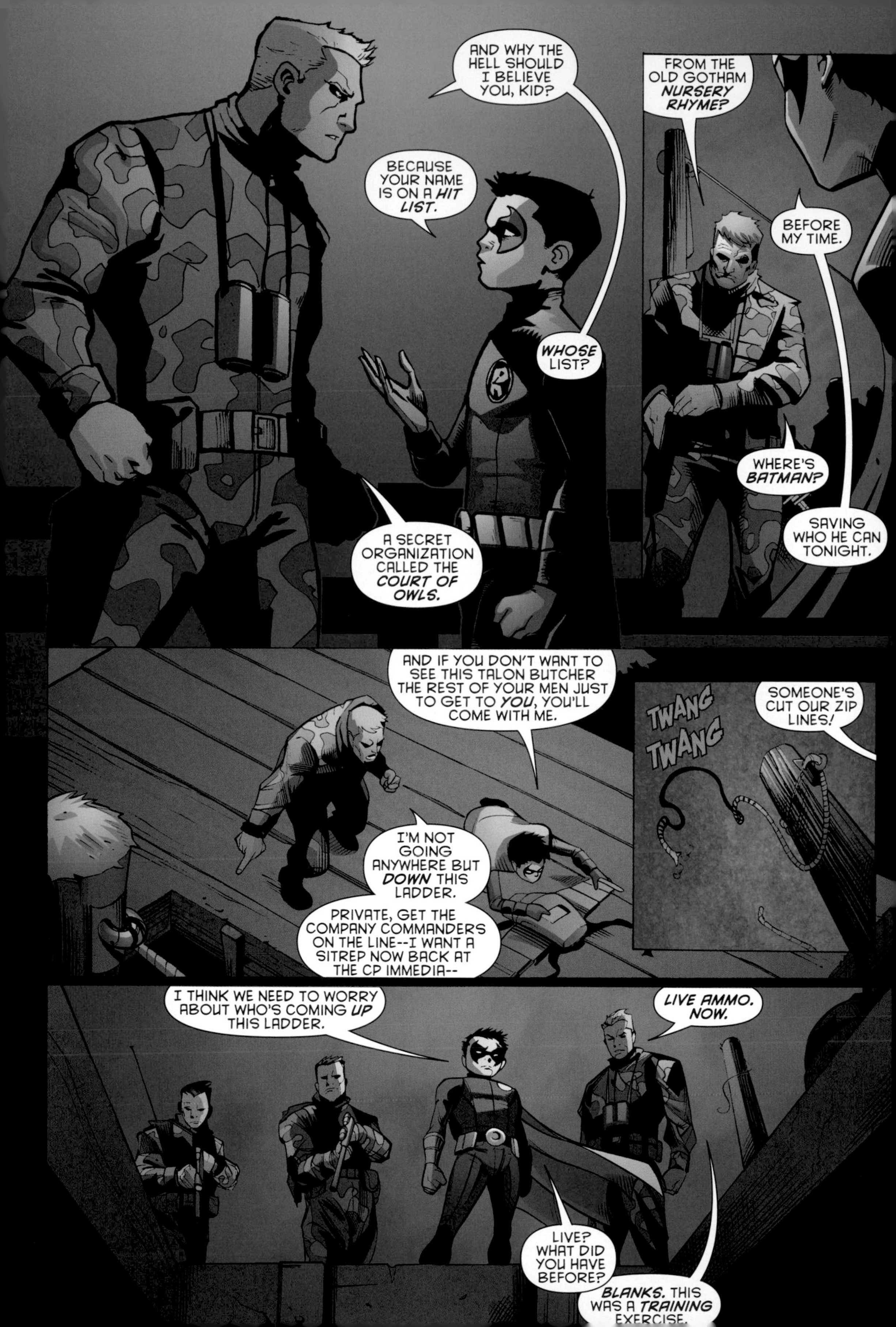
AND WHY THE HELL SHOULD I BELIEVE YOU, KID?
BECAUSE YOUR NAME IS ON A *HIT LIST*.
WHOSE LIST?
A SECRET ORGANIZATION CALLED THE *COURT OF OWLS*.
FROM THE OLD GOTHAM *NURSERY RHYME?*
BEFORE MY TIME.
WHERE'S *BATMAN?*
SAVING WHO HE CAN TONIGHT.
AND IF YOU DON'T WANT TO SEE THIS TALON BUTCHER THE REST OF YOUR MEN JUST TO GET TO *YOU*, YOU'LL COME WITH ME.
I'M NOT GOING ANYWHERE BUT *DOWN* THIS LADDER.
PRIVATE, GET THE COMPANY COMMANDERS ON THE LINE--I WANT A SITREP NOW BACK AT THE CP IMMEDIA--
TWANG
TWANG
SOMEONE'S CUT OUR ZIP LINES!
I THINK WE NEED TO WORRY ABOUT WHO'S COMING *UP* THIS LADDER.
LIVE AMMO. NOW.
LIVE? WHAT DID YOU HAVE BEFORE?
BLANKS. THIS WAS A *TRAINING* EXERCISE.

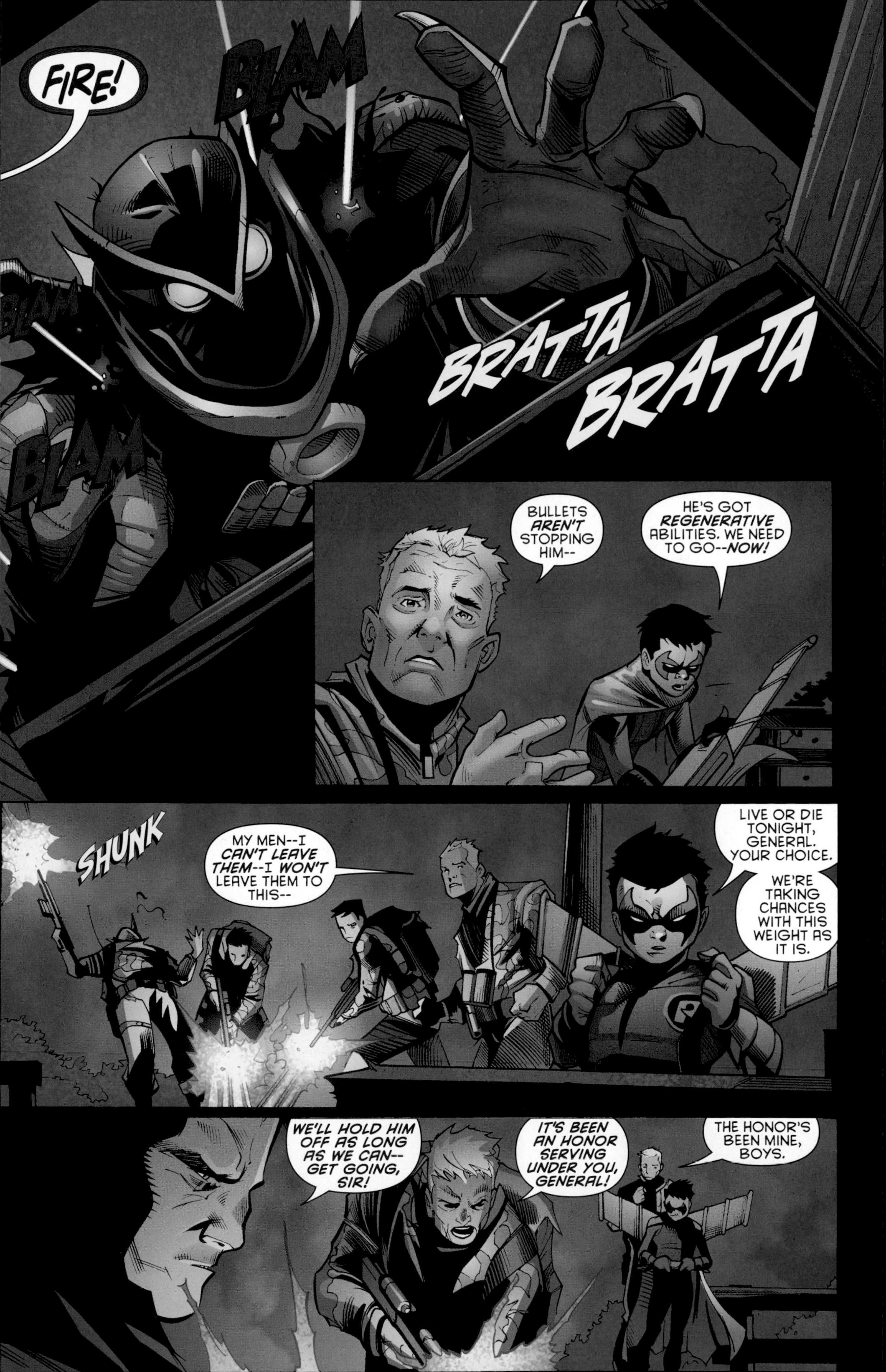
FIRE!
BLAM
BLAM
BLAM
BRATTA BRATTA
BULLETS AREN'T STOPPING HIM--
HE'S GOT REGENERATIVE ABILITIES. WE NEED TO GO--NOW!
SHUNK
MY MEN--I CAN'T LEAVE THEM--I WON'T LEAVE THEM TO THIS--
LIVE OR DIE TONIGHT, GENERAL. YOUR CHOICE.
WE'RE TAKING CHANCES WITH THIS WEIGHT AS IT IS.
WE'LL HOLD HIM OFF AS LONG AS WE CAN--GET GOING, SIR!
IT'S BEEN AN HONOR SERVING UNDER YOU, GENERAL!
THE HONOR'S BEEN MINE, BOYS.

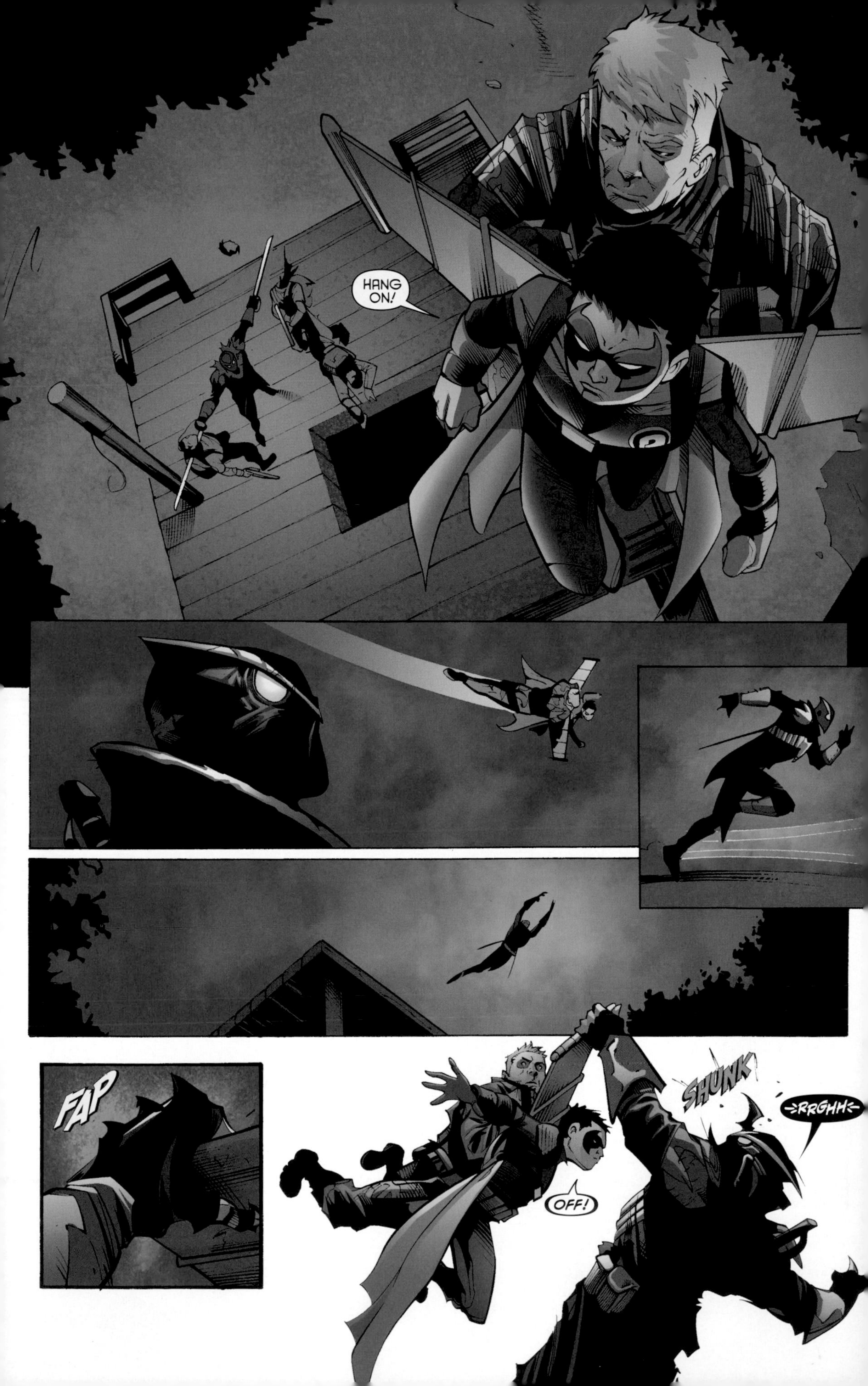
HANG ON!
FAP
SHUNK
RRGHH
OFF!

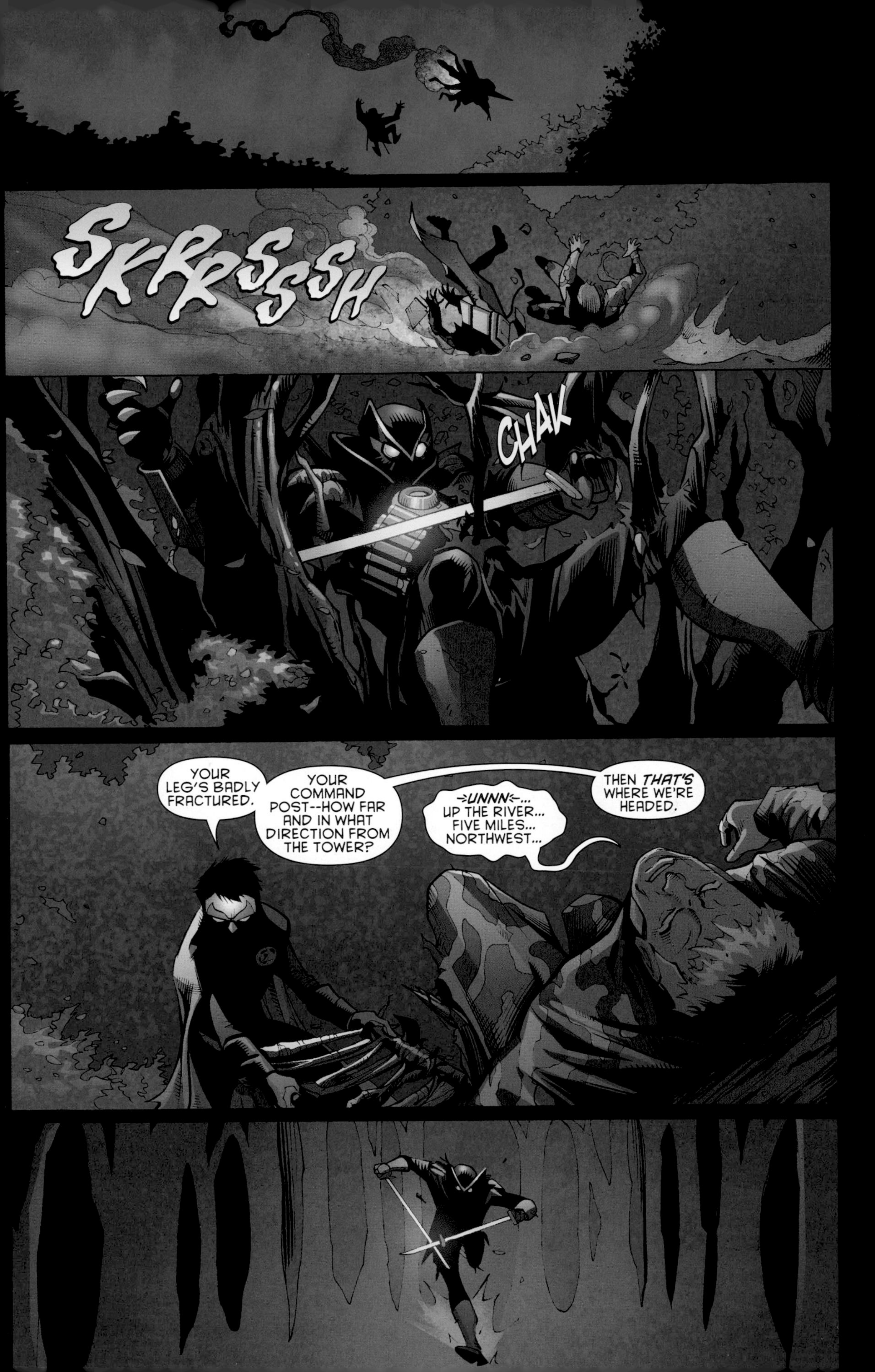
SKRSSSH
CHAK
YOUR LEG'S BADLY FRACTURED.
YOUR COMMAND POST--HOW FAR AND IN WHAT DIRECTION FROM THE TOWER?
UNNN... UP THE RIVER... FIVE MILES... NORTHWEST...
THEN THAT'S WHERE WE'RE HEADED.

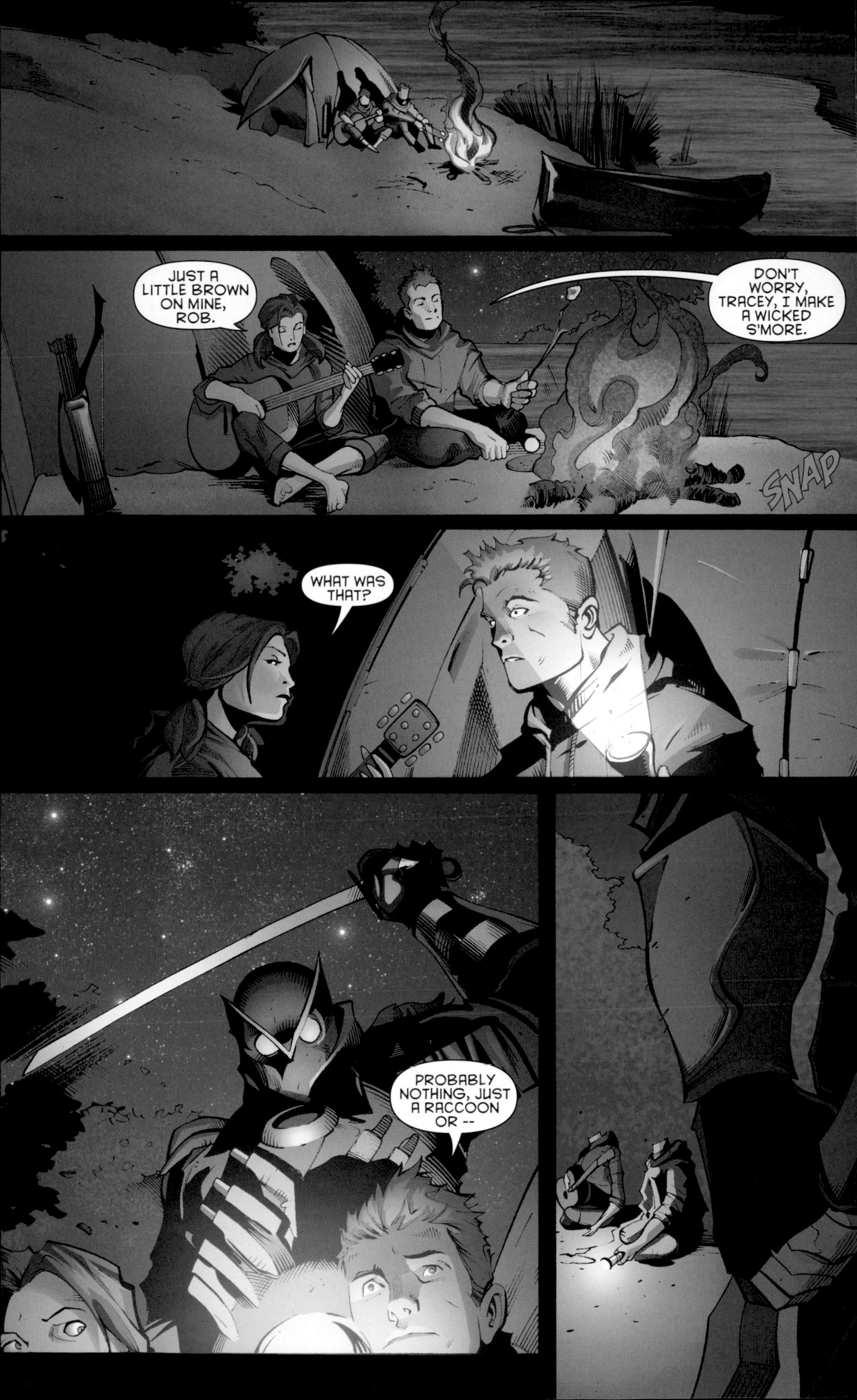
JUST A LITTLE BROWN ON MINE, ROB.
DON'T WORRY, TRACEY, I MAKE A WICKED S'MORE.
SNAP
WHAT WAS THAT?
PROBABLY NOTHING, JUST A RACCOON OR --

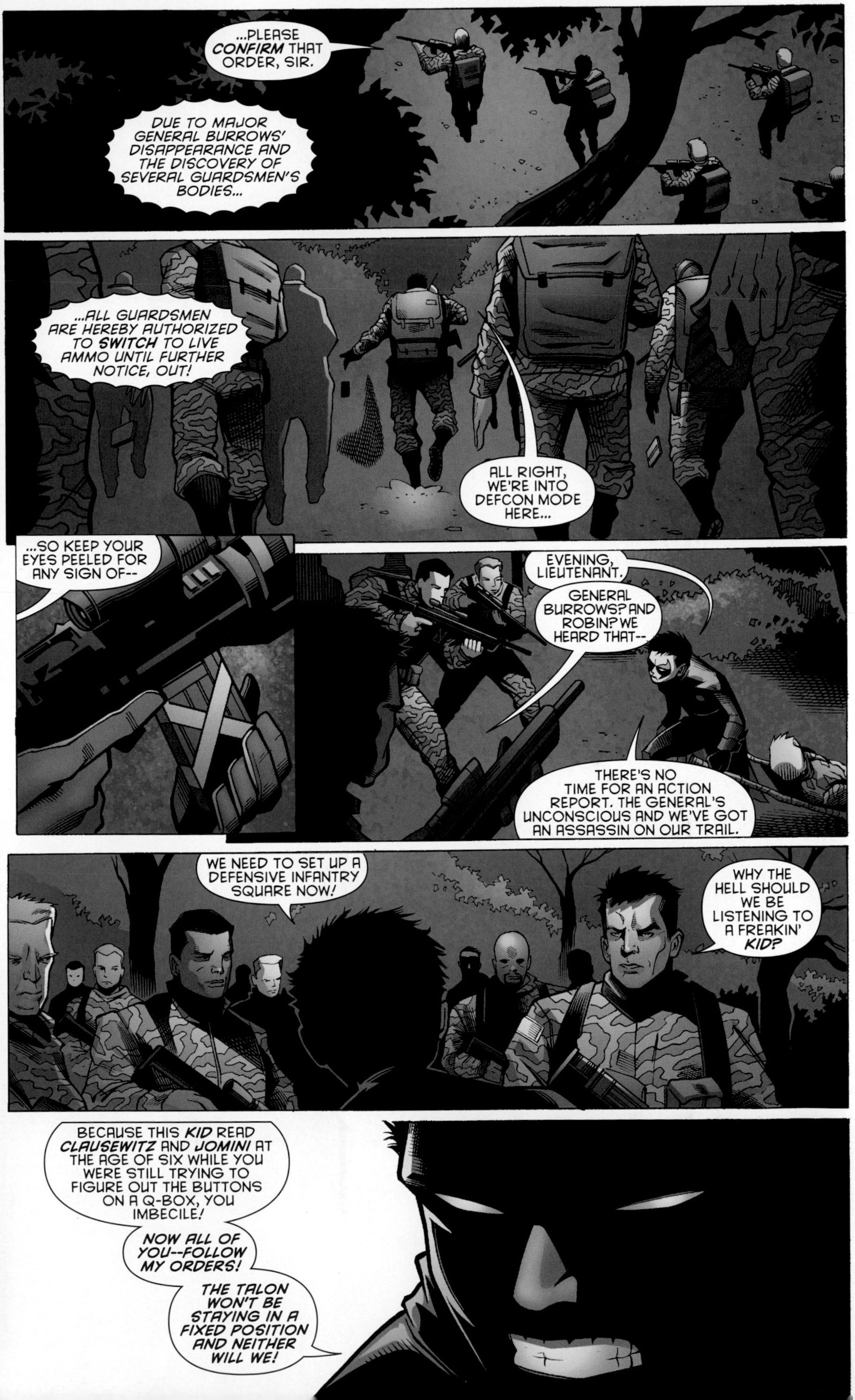
...PLEASE CONFIRM THAT ORDER, SIR.
DUE TO MAJOR GENERAL BURROWS' DISAPPEARANCE AND THE DISCOVERY OF SEVERAL GUARDSMEN'S BODIES...
...ALL GUARDSMEN ARE HEREBY AUTHORIZED TO SWITCH TO LIVE AMMO UNTIL FURTHER NOTICE, OUT!
ALL RIGHT, WE'RE INTO DEFCON MODE HERE...
...SO KEEP YOUR EYES PEELED FOR ANY SIGN OF--
EVENING, LIEUTENANT.
GENERAL BURROWS? AND ROBIN? WE HEARD THAT--
THERE'S NO TIME FOR AN ACTION REPORT. THE GENERAL'S UNCONSCIOUS AND WE'VE GOT AN ASSASSIN ON OUR TRAIL.
WE NEED TO SET UP A DEFENSIVE INFANTRY SQUARE NOW!
WHY THE HELL SHOULD WE BE LISTENING TO A FREAKIN' KID?
BECAUSE THIS KID READ CLAUSEWITZ AND JOMINI AT THE AGE OF SIX WHILE YOU WERE STILL TRYING TO FIGURE OUT THE BUTTONS ON A Q-BOX, YOU IMBECILE!
NOW ALL OF YOU--FOLLOW MY ORDERS!
THE TALON WON'T BE STAYING IN A FIXED POSITION AND NEITHER WILL WE!

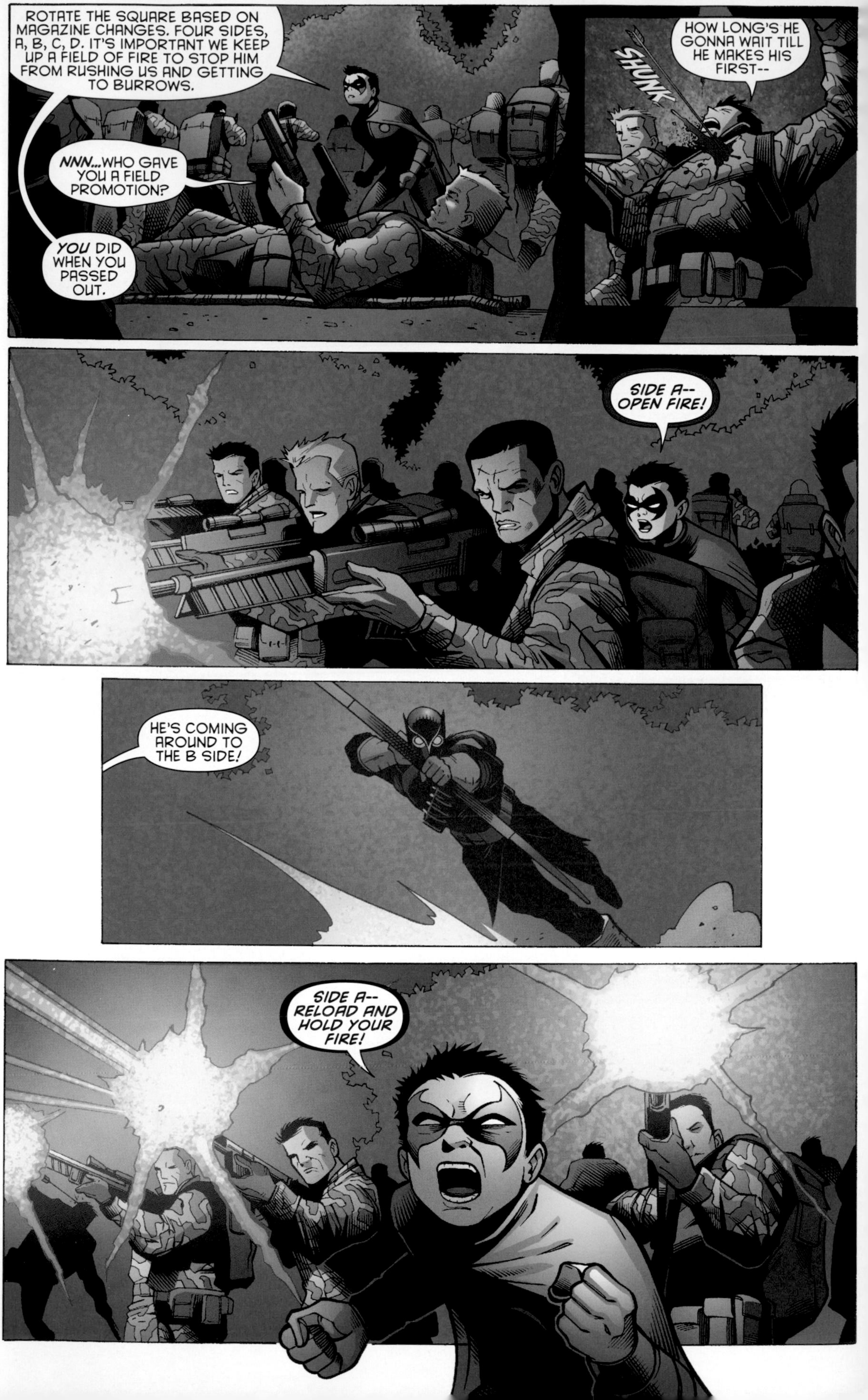
ROTATE THE SQUARE BASED ON MAGAZINE CHANGES. FOUR SIDES, A, B, C, D. IT'S IMPORTANT WE KEEP UP A FIELD OF FIRE TO STOP HIM FROM RUSHING US AND GETTING TO BURROWS.
NNN...WHO GAVE YOU A FIELD PROMOTION?
YOU DID WHEN YOU PASSED OUT.
HOW LONG'S HE GONNA WAIT TILL HE MAKES HIS FIRST--
SHUNK
SIDE A-- OPEN FIRE!
HE'S COMING AROUND TO THE B SIDE!
SIDE A-- RELOAD AND HOLD YOUR FIRE!

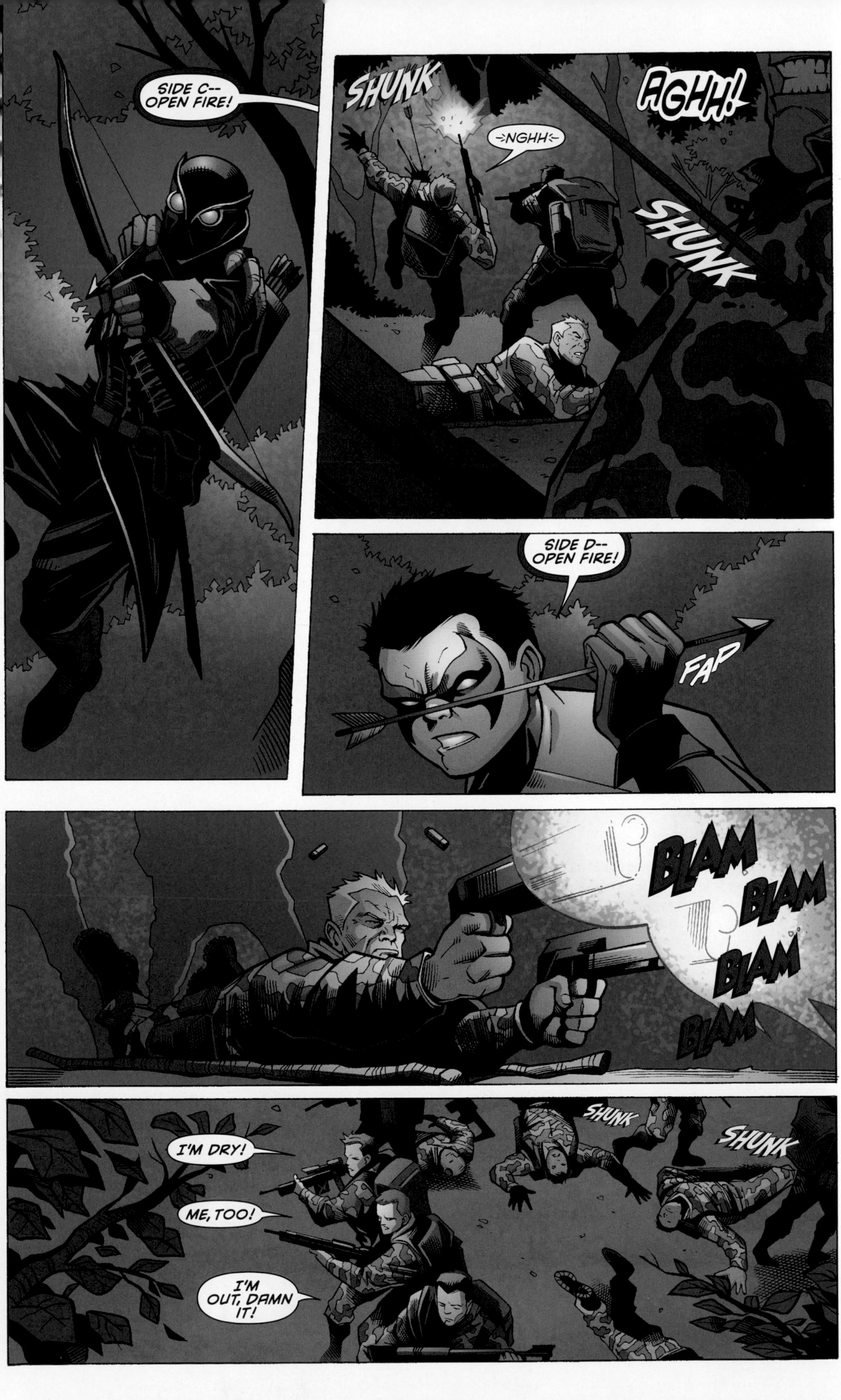
SIDE C-- OPEN FIRE!
SHUNK
-NGHH-
AGHH!
SHUNK
SIDE D-- OPEN FIRE!
FAP
BLAM
BLAM
BLAM
BLAM
I'M DRY!
ME, TOO!
I'M OUT, DAMN IT!
SHUNK
SHUNK

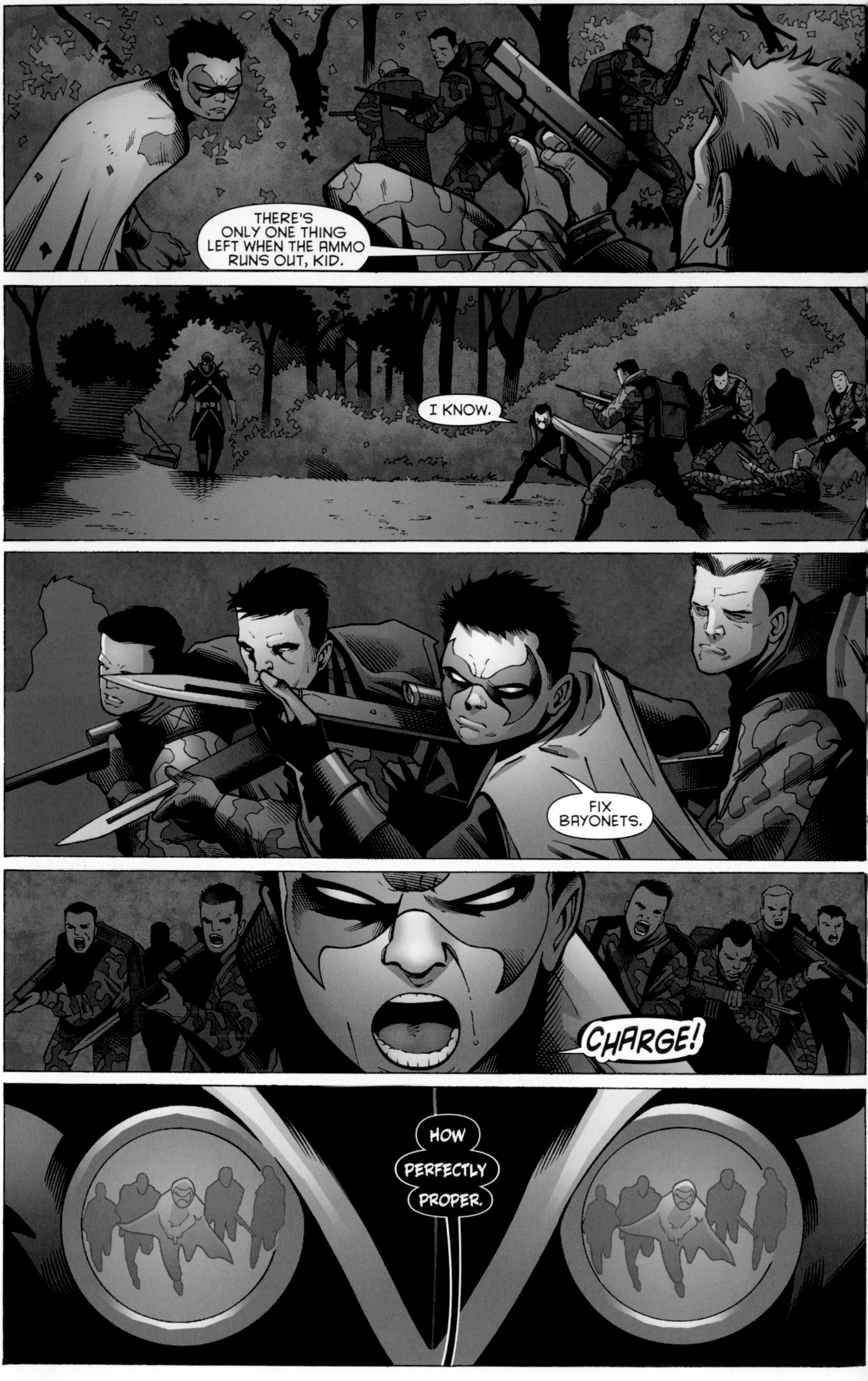
THERE'S ONLY ONE THING LEFT WHEN THE AMMO RUNS OUT, KID.
I KNOW.
FIX BAYONETS.
CHARGE!
HOW PERFECTLY PROPER.

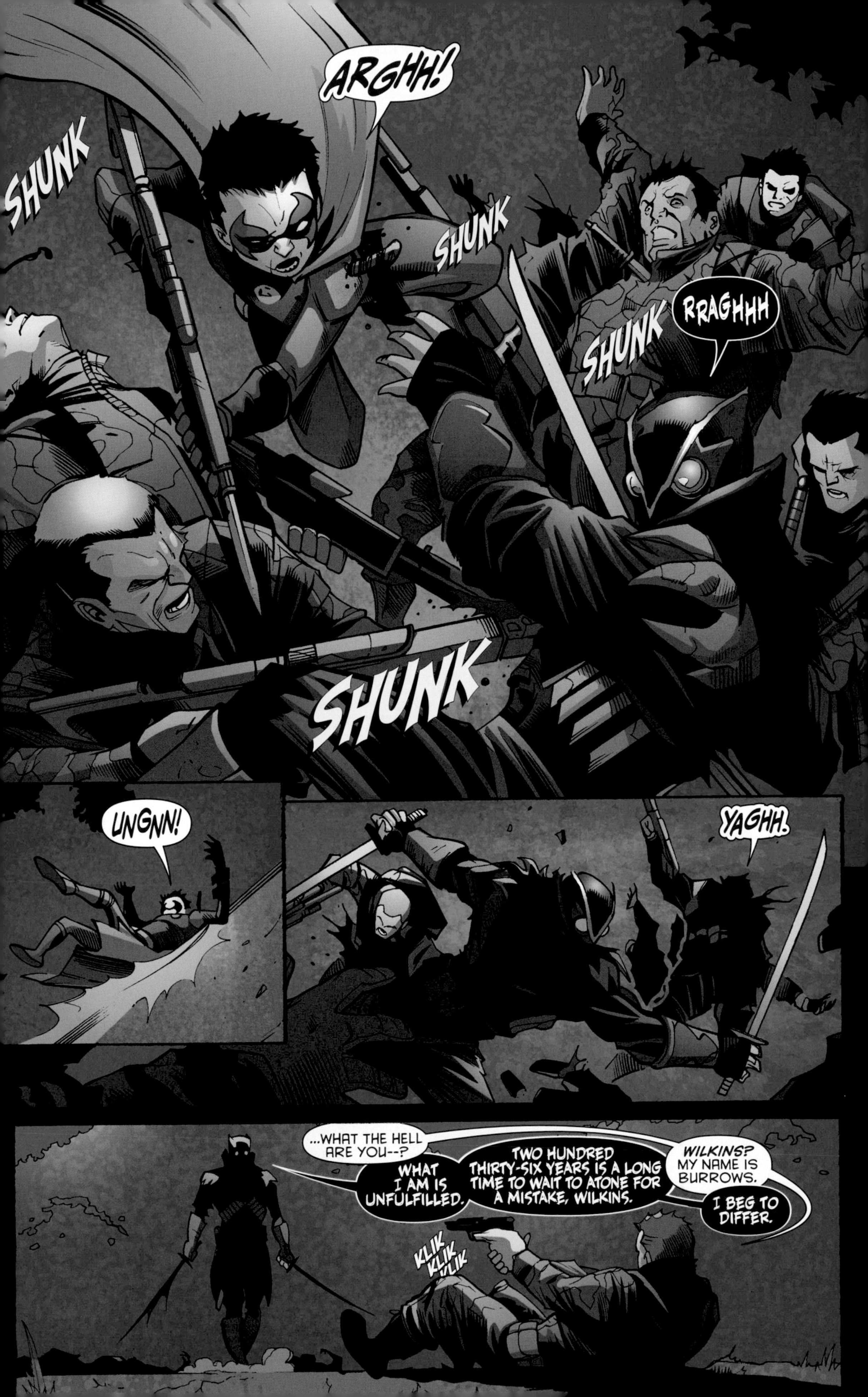
ARGHH!
SHUNK
SHUNK
SHUNK
RRAGHHH
SHUNK
UNGNN!
YAGHH.
...WHAT THE HELL ARE YOU--?
WHAT I AM IS UNFULFILLED.
TWO HUNDRED THIRTY-SIX YEARS IS A LONG TIME TO WAIT TO ATONE FOR A MISTAKE, WILKINS.
WILKINS? MY NAME IS BURROWS.
I BEG TO DIFFER.
KLIK KLIK KLIK

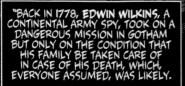
"BACK IN 1778, **EDWIN WILKINS,** A CONTINENTAL ARMY SPY, TOOK ON A DANGEROUS MISSION IN GOTHAM BUT ONLY ON THE CONDITION THAT HIS FAMILY BE TAKEN CARE OF IN CASE OF HIS DEATH, WHICH, EVERYONE ASSUMED, WAS LIKELY.

"**GENERAL WASHINGTON** HIMSELF PROMISED WILKINS THAT HIS LOVED ONES WOULD RECEIVE A SIGNIFICANT **LAND GRANT** FOR HIS SERVICE IF THEIR **WAR OF INDEPENDENCE** PROVED TRIUMPHANT.

"I WAS SUMMONED FROM MY NEST AND GIVEN AN ORDER BY THE COURT OF **OWLS** TO **ERADICATE** WILKINS AND ALL BLOOD RELATIVES...

"...SO THE LAND GRANT THAT WOULD PASS TO HIM AND HIS ANCESTORS IN THE UNLIKELY CASE OF A COLONIAL VICTORY COULD LATER BE BOUGHT WITHOUT DIFFICULTY BY A FAVORITE SON OF THE COURT AND DEVELOPED FOR THEIR OWN INTERESTS.

"AFTER SWIMMING UNDERWATER THROUGH SENTRY POINTS, I SECRETLY SLIPPED ONTO THE BRITISH PRISON FRIGATE AND **KILLED** EDWIN IN HIS SLEEP.

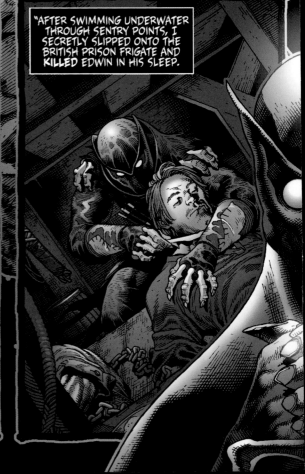

"WILKINS' MISSION WAS SUCCESSFUL AND HE MANAGED TO PASS THE INFORMATION HE HAD GLEANED TO CAPTAIN ALEXANDER HAMILTON ONLY MOMENTS PRIOR TO HIS **CAPTURE** BY THE BRITISH."

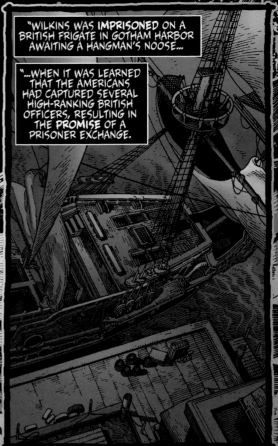

"WILKINS WAS **IMPRISONED** ON A BRITISH FRIGATE IN GOTHAM HARBOR AWAITING A HANGMAN'S NOOSE...

"...WHEN IT WAS LEARNED THAT THE AMERICANS HAD CAPTURED SEVERAL HIGH-RANKING BRITISH OFFICERS, RESULTING IN THE **PROMISE** OF A PRISONER EXCHANGE.

"I WAITED UNTIL 1783 TO **ELIMINATE** THE REST OF THE WILKINS FAMILY AFTER THEY LEGALLY TOOK HOLD OF THEIR LAND GRANT SO THERE WOULD BE **NO HEIRS.**

"EDWIN WILKINS' YOUNGEST SON, SAMUEL, SOMEHOW **SURVIVED** THE GRIEVOUS WOUNDS I INFLICTED UPON HIM.

"SAMUEL WAS APPARENTLY HIDDEN AWAY AND RAISED BY FRIENDS OF THE WILKINS FAMILY WHILE THE COURT OF OWLS EVENTUALLY TOOK CONTROL OF THE LAND.

"THIS FAMILY'S SURNAME WAS **BURROWS.**"

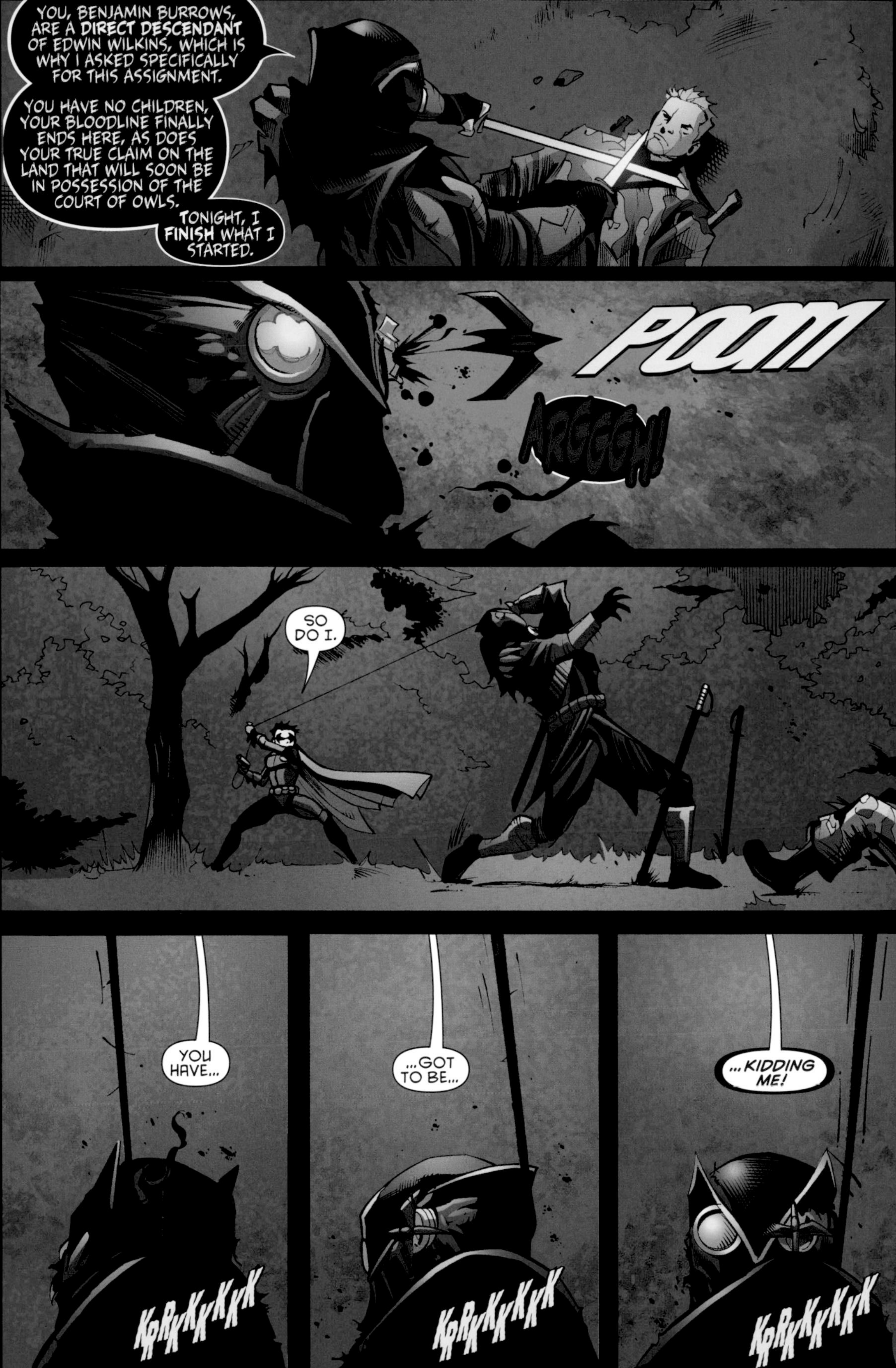
YOU, BENJAMIN BURROWS, ARE A DIRECT DESCENDANT OF EDWIN WILKINS, WHICH IS WHY I ASKED SPECIFICALLY FOR THIS ASSIGNMENT.
YOU HAVE NO CHILDREN, YOUR BLOODLINE FINALLY ENDS HERE, AS DOES YOUR TRUE CLAIM ON THE LAND THAT WILL SOON BE IN POSSESSION OF THE COURT OF OWLS.
TONIGHT, I FINISH WHAT I STARTED.
POOM
ARGGGH!
SO DO I.
YOU HAVE...
KRRKKKKKK
...GOT TO BE...
KRRKKKKKK
...KIDDING ME!
KRRKKKKKK

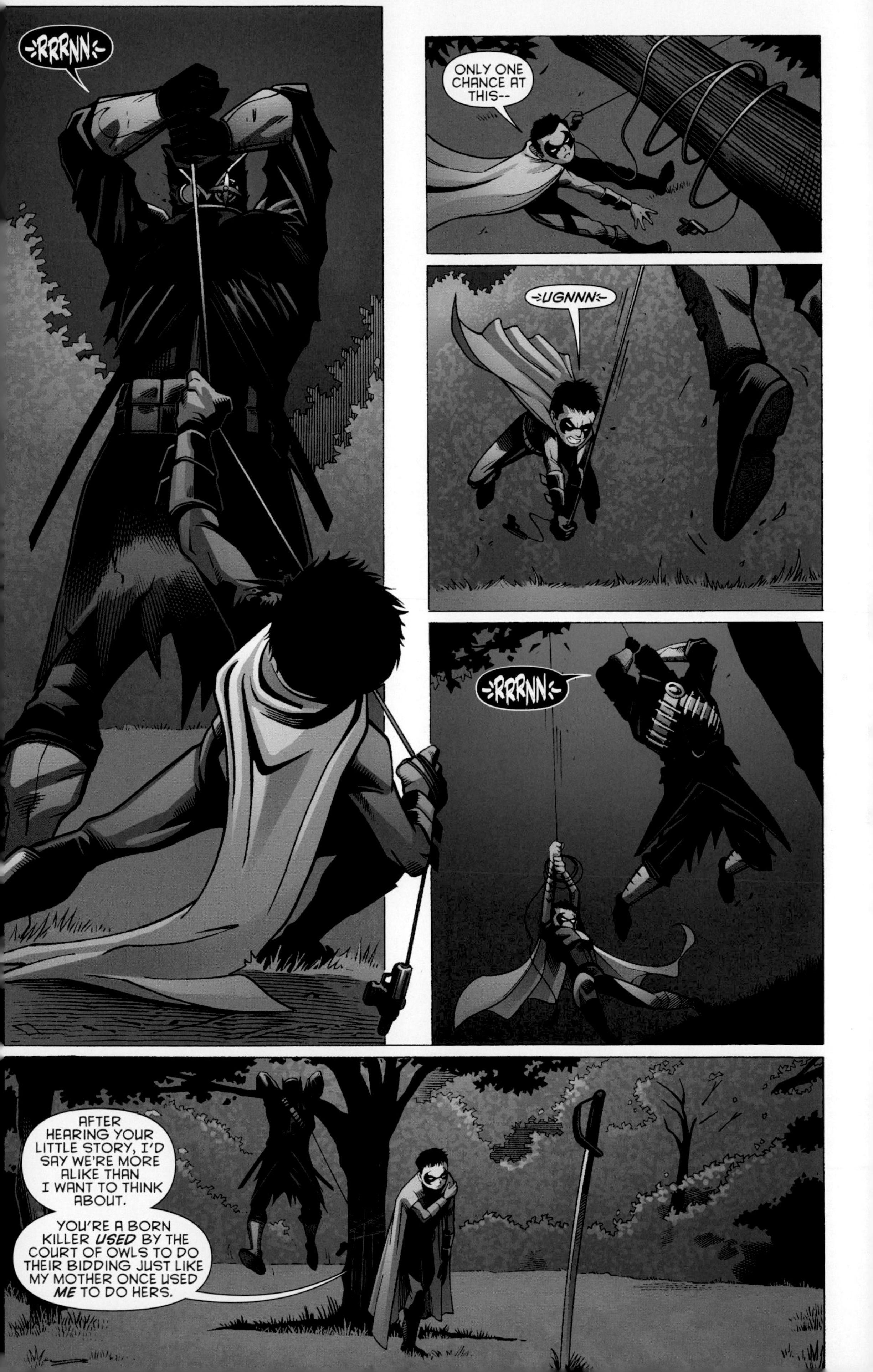
RRRNN
ONLY ONE CHANCE AT THIS--
UGNNN
RRRNN
AFTER HEARING YOUR LITTLE STORY, I'D SAY WE'RE MORE ALIKE THAN I WANT TO THINK ABOUT.
YOU'RE A BORN KILLER USED BY THE COURT OF OWLS TO DO THEIR BIDDING JUST LIKE MY MOTHER ONCE USED ME TO DO HERS.

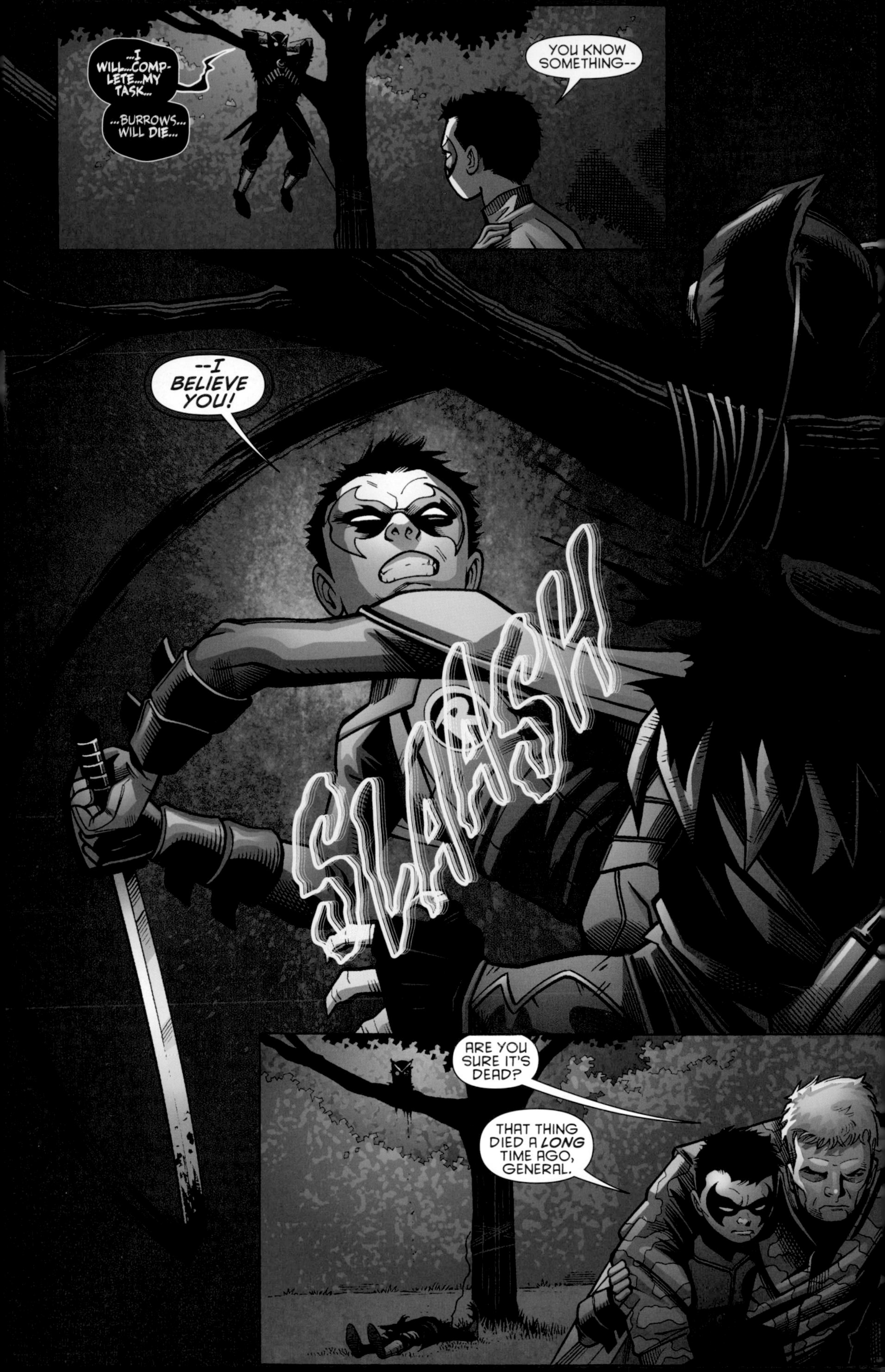
...I WILL...COMP-LETE...MY TASK...
...BURROWS... WILL DIE...
YOU KNOW SOMETHING--
--I BELIEVE YOU!
SLASH
ARE YOU SURE IT'S DEAD?
THAT THING DIED A LONG TIME AGO, GENERAL.

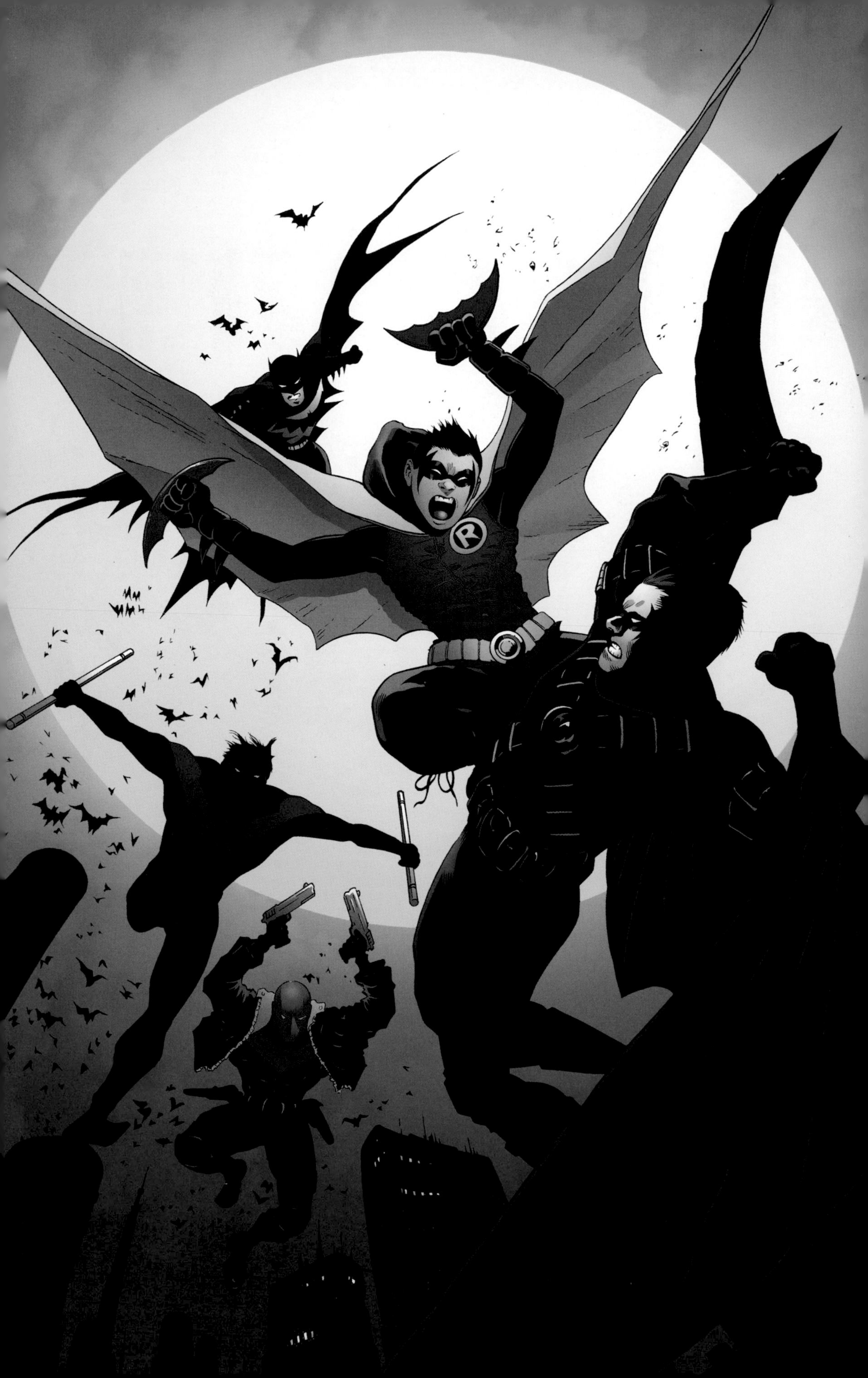

TERMINUS: SCAR OF THE BAT

PETER J. TOMASI writer **PATRICK GLEASON** penciller **MICK GRAY** inker
cover by **GLEASON, GRAY & KALISZ**

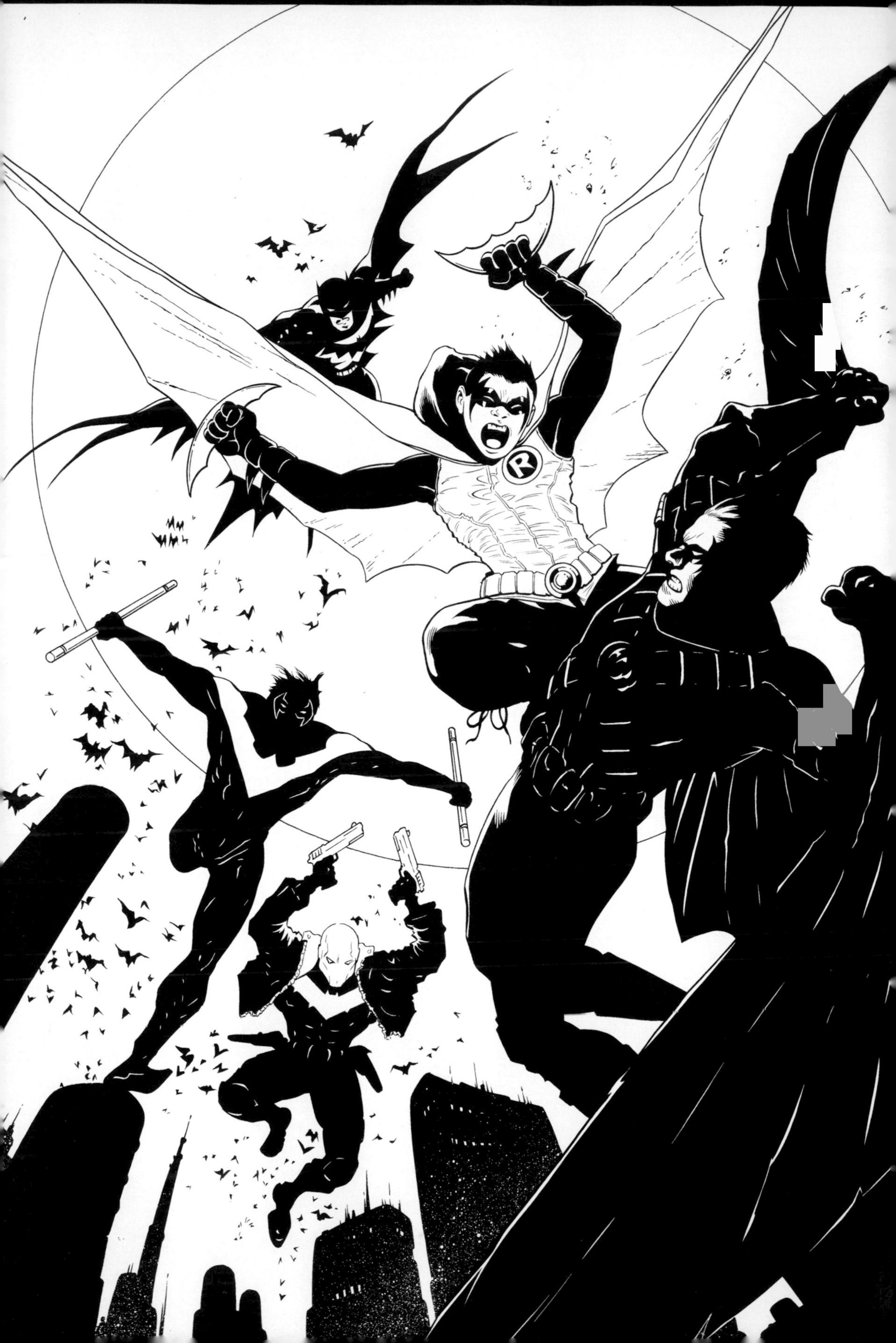

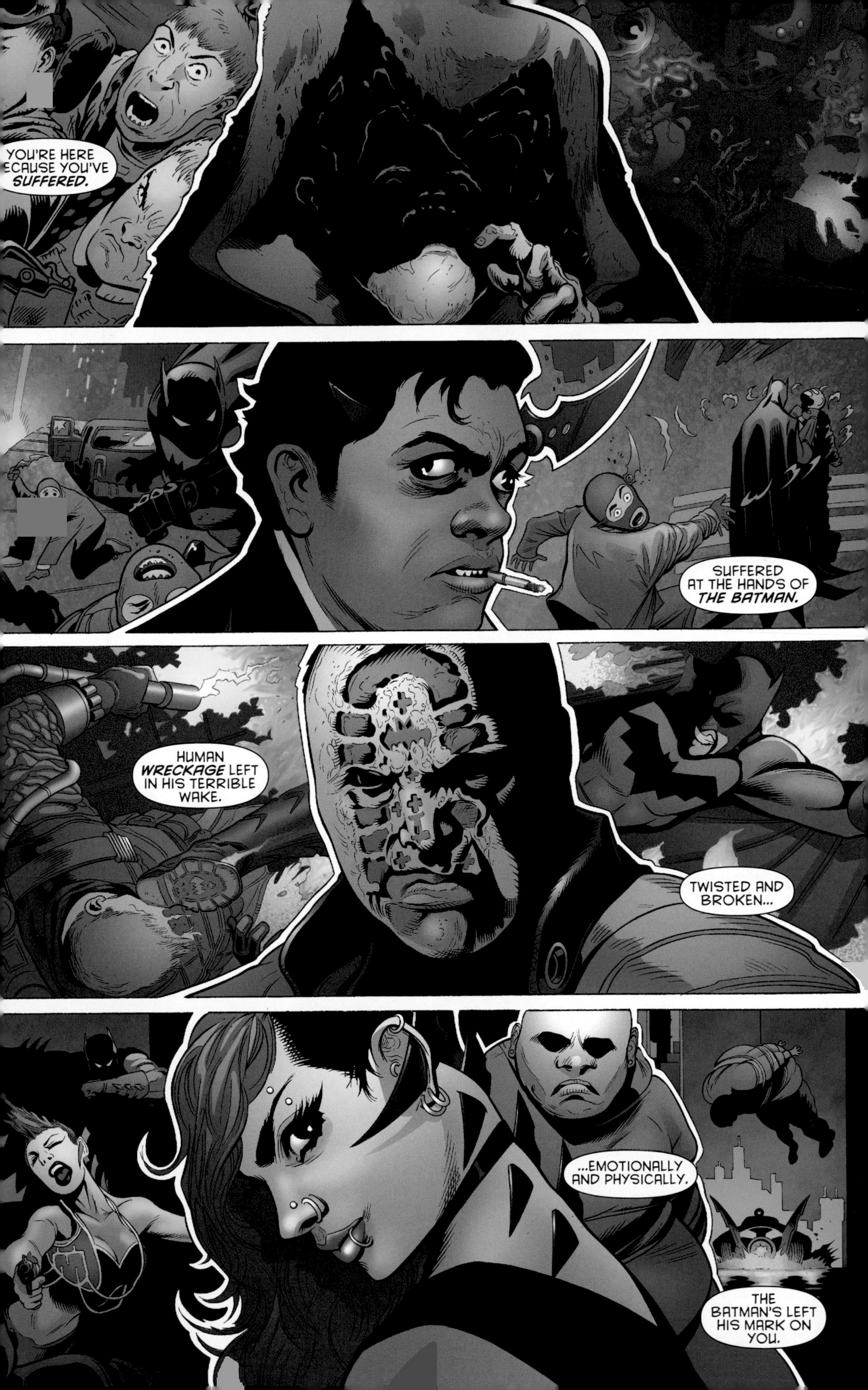
YOU'RE HERE
ECAUSE YOU'VE
SUFFERED.
SUFFERED
AT THE HANDS OF
THE BATMAN.
HUMAN
WRECKAGE LEFT
IN HIS TERRIBLE
WAKE.
TWISTED AND
BROKEN...
...EMOTIONALLY
AND PHYSICALLY.
THE
BATMAN'S LEFT
HIS MARK ON
YOU.

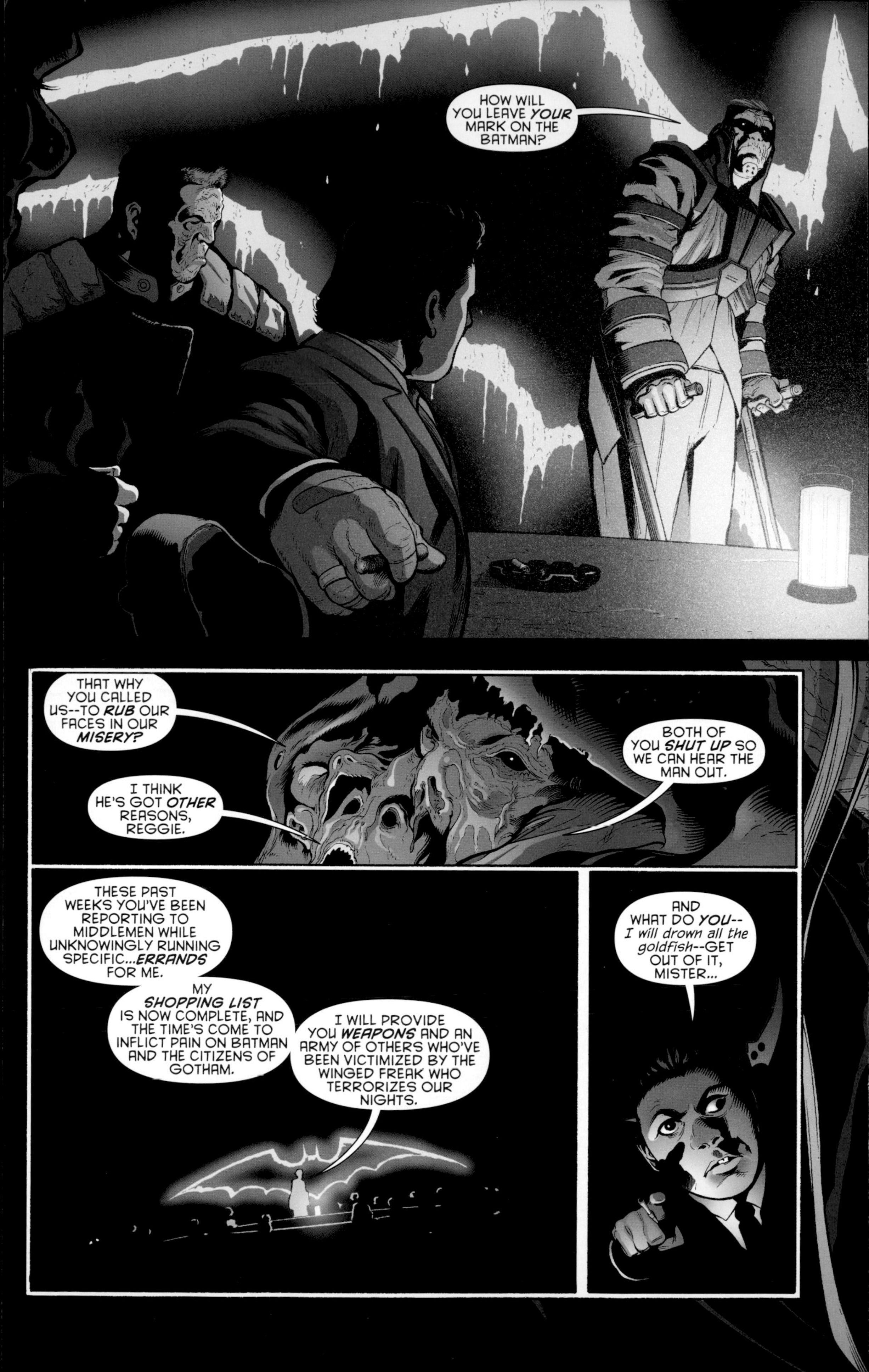
HOW WILL YOU LEAVE YOUR MARK ON THE BATMAN?
THAT WHY YOU CALLED US--TO RUB OUR FACES IN OUR MISERY?
I THINK HE'S GOT OTHER REASONS, REGGIE.
BOTH OF YOU SHUT UP SO WE CAN HEAR THE MAN OUT.
THESE PAST WEEKS YOU'VE BEEN REPORTING TO MIDDLEMEN WHILE UNKNOWINGLY RUNNING SPECIFIC...ERRANDS FOR ME.
MY SHOPPING LIST IS NOW COMPLETE, AND THE TIME'S COME TO INFLICT PAIN ON BATMAN AND THE CITIZENS OF GOTHAM.
I WILL PROVIDE YOU WEAPONS AND AN ARMY OF OTHERS WHO'VE BEEN VICTIMIZED BY THE WINGED FREAK WHO TERRORIZES OUR NIGHTS.
AND WHAT DO YOU-- I will drown all the goldfish--GET OUT OF IT, MISTER...

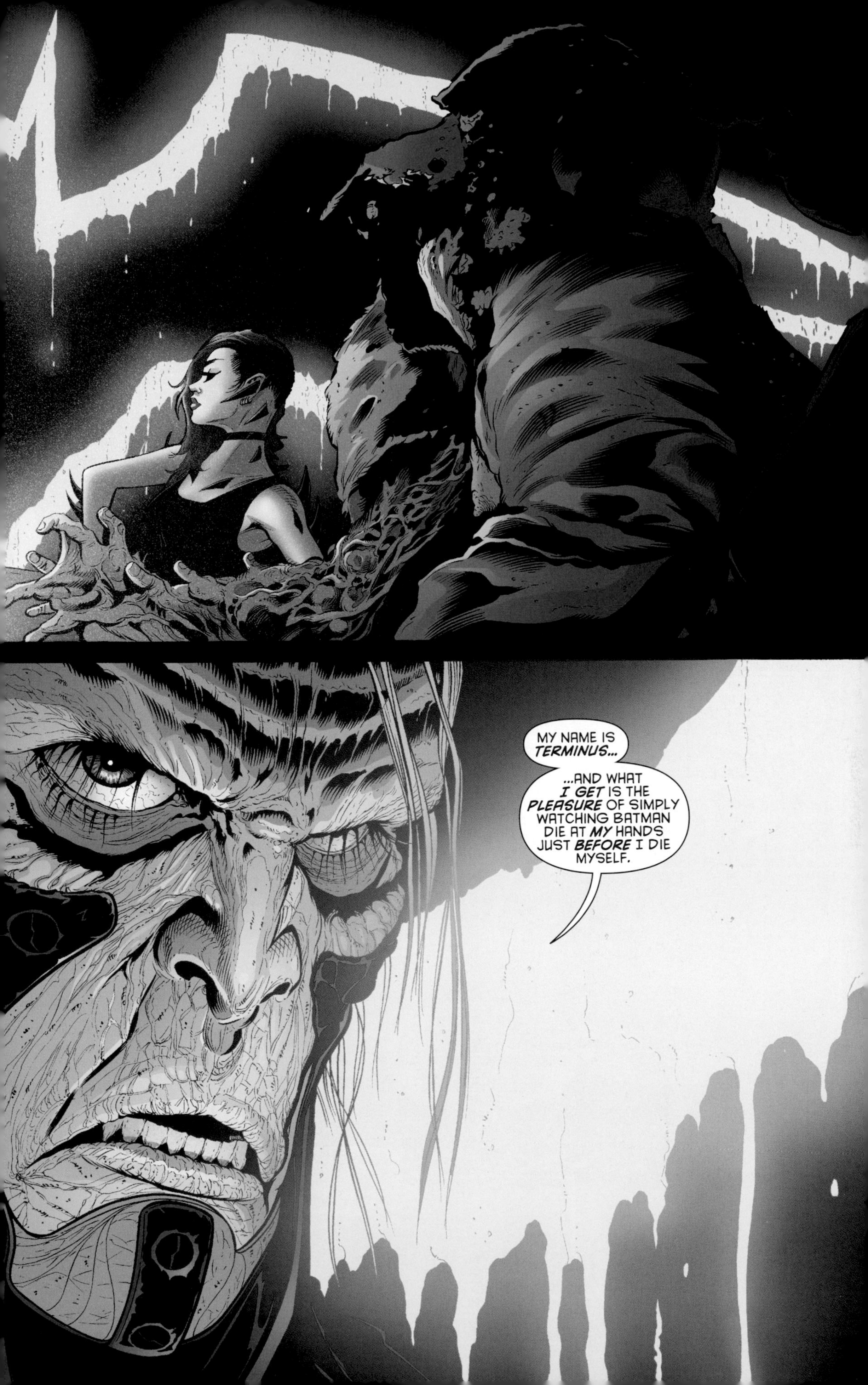
MY NAME IS TERMINUS...
...AND WHAT I GET IS THE PLEASURE OF SIMPLY WATCHING BATMAN DIE AT MY HANDS JUST BEFORE I DIE MYSELF.

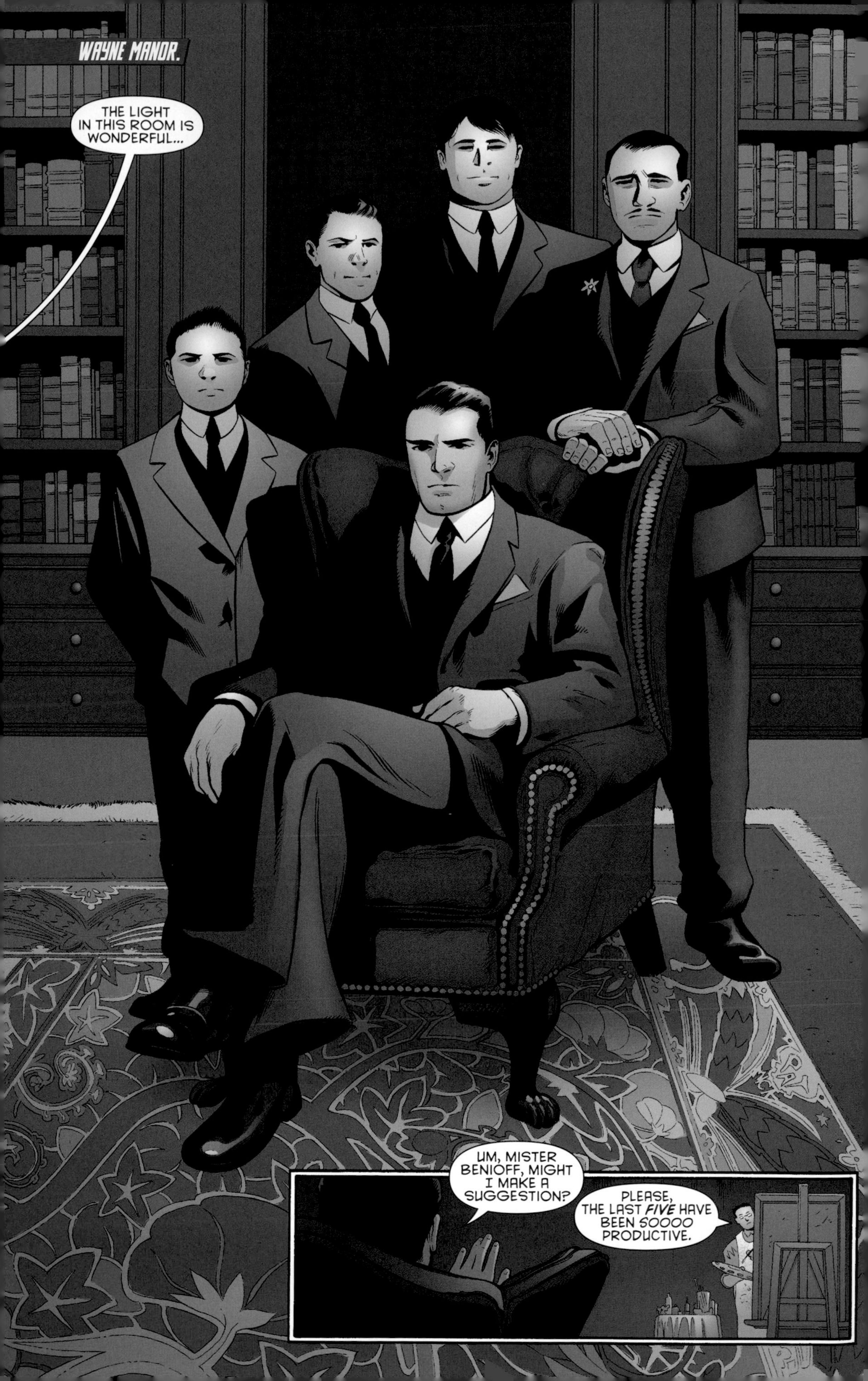
WAYNE MANOR.
THE LIGHT IN THIS ROOM IS WONDERFUL...
UM, MISTER BENIOFF, MIGHT I MAKE A SUGGESTION?
PLEASE, THE LAST FIVE HAVE BEEN SOOOO PRODUCTIVE.

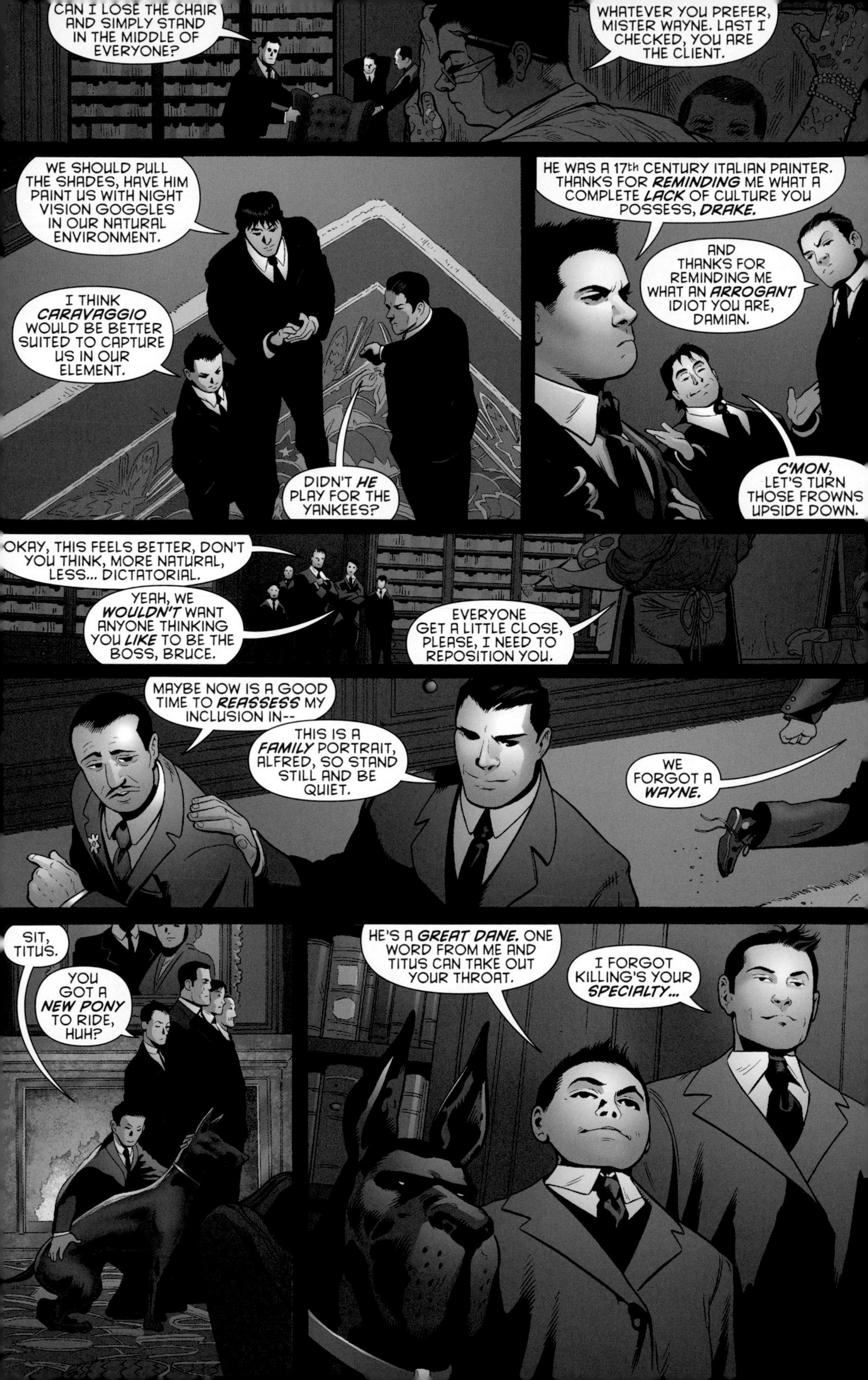
CAN I LOSE THE CHAIR AND SIMPLY STAND IN THE MIDDLE OF EVERYONE?
WHATEVER YOU PREFER, MISTER WAYNE. LAST I CHECKED, YOU ARE THE CLIENT.
WE SHOULD PULL THE SHADES, HAVE HIM PAINT US WITH NIGHT VISION GOGGLES IN OUR NATURAL ENVIRONMENT.
I THINK CARAVAGGIO WOULD BE BETTER SUITED TO CAPTURE US IN OUR ELEMENT.
DIDN'T HE PLAY FOR THE YANKEES?
HE WAS A 17th CENTURY ITALIAN PAINTER. THANKS FOR REMINDING ME WHAT A COMPLETE LACK OF CULTURE YOU POSSESS, DRAKE.
AND THANKS FOR REMINDING ME WHAT AN ARROGANT IDIOT YOU ARE, DAMIAN.
C'MON, LET'S TURN THOSE FROWNS UPSIDE DOWN.
OKAY, THIS FEELS BETTER, DON'T YOU THINK, MORE NATURAL, LESS... DICTATORIAL.
YEAH, WE WOULDN'T WANT ANYONE THINKING YOU LIKE TO BE THE BOSS, BRUCE.
EVERYONE GET A LITTLE CLOSE, PLEASE, I NEED TO REPOSITION YOU.
MAYBE NOW IS A GOOD TIME TO REASSESS MY INCLUSION IN--
THIS IS A FAMILY PORTRAIT, ALFRED, SO STAND STILL AND BE QUIET.
WE FORGOT A WAYNE.
SIT, TITUS.
YOU GOT A NEW PONY TO RIDE, HUH?
HE'S A GREAT DANE. ONE WORD FROM ME AND TITUS CAN TAKE OUT YOUR THROAT.
I FORGOT KILLING'S YOUR SPECIALTY...

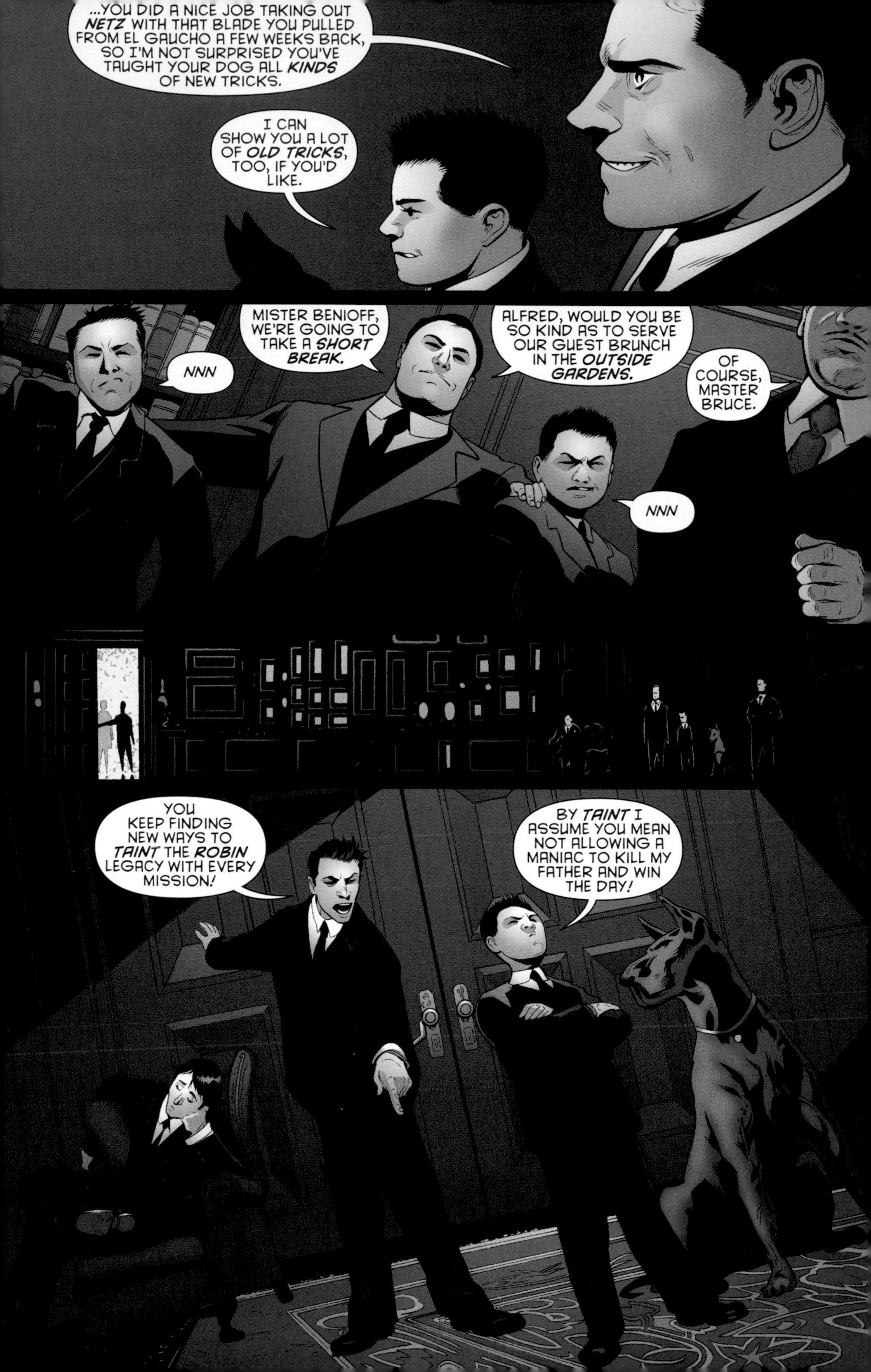
...YOU DID A NICE JOB TAKING OUT NETZ WITH THAT BLADE YOU PULLED FROM EL GAUCHO A FEW WEEKS BACK, SO I'M NOT SURPRISED YOU'VE TAUGHT YOUR DOG ALL KINDS OF NEW TRICKS.
I CAN SHOW YOU A LOT OF OLD TRICKS, TOO, IF YOU'D LIKE.
NNN
MISTER BENIOFF, WE'RE GOING TO TAKE A SHORT BREAK.
ALFRED, WOULD YOU BE SO KIND AS TO SERVE OUR GUEST BRUNCH IN THE OUTSIDE GARDENS.
OF COURSE, MASTER BRUCE.
NNN
YOU KEEP FINDING NEW WAYS TO TAINT THE ROBIN LEGACY WITH EVERY MISSION!
BY TAINT I ASSUME YOU MEAN NOT ALLOWING A MANIAC TO KILL MY FATHER AND WIN THE DAY!

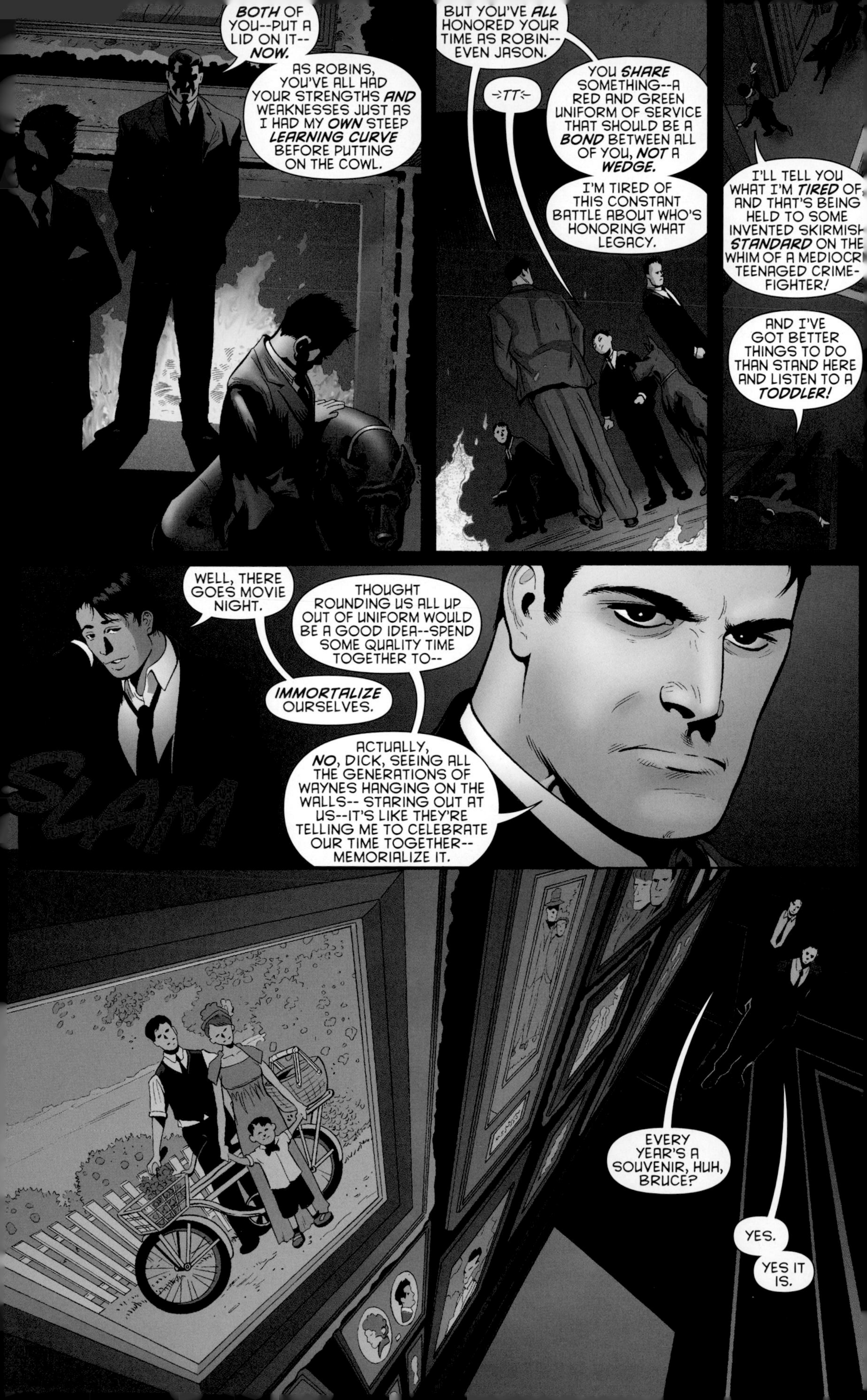

BOTH OF YOU--PUT A LID ON IT-- NOW.
AS ROBINS, YOU'VE ALL HAD YOUR STRENGTHS AND WEAKNESSES JUST AS I HAD MY OWN STEEP LEARNING CURVE BEFORE PUTTING ON THE COWL.
BUT YOU'VE ALL HONORED YOUR TIME AS ROBIN-- EVEN JASON.
-TT-
YOU SHARE SOMETHING--A RED AND GREEN UNIFORM OF SERVICE THAT SHOULD BE A BOND BETWEEN ALL OF YOU, NOT A WEDGE.
I'M TIRED OF THIS CONSTANT BATTLE ABOUT WHO'S HONORING WHAT LEGACY.
I'LL TELL YOU WHAT I'M TIRED OF, AND THAT'S BEING HELD TO SOME INVENTED SKIRMISH STANDARD ON THE WHIM OF A MEDIOCR TEENAGED CRIME-FIGHTER!
AND I'VE GOT BETTER THINGS TO DO THAN STAND HERE AND LISTEN TO A TODDLER!
SLAM
WELL, THERE GOES MOVIE NIGHT.
THOUGHT ROUNDING US ALL UP OUT OF UNIFORM WOULD BE A GOOD IDEA--SPEND SOME QUALITY TIME TOGETHER TO--
IMMORTALIZE OURSELVES.
ACTUALLY, NO, DICK, SEEING ALL THE GENERATIONS OF WAYNES HANGING ON THE WALLS-- STARING OUT AT US--IT'S LIKE THEY'RE TELLING ME TO CELEBRATE OUR TIME TOGETHER-- MEMORIALIZE IT.
EVERY YEAR'S A SOUVENIR, HUH, BRUCE?
YES.
YES IT IS.

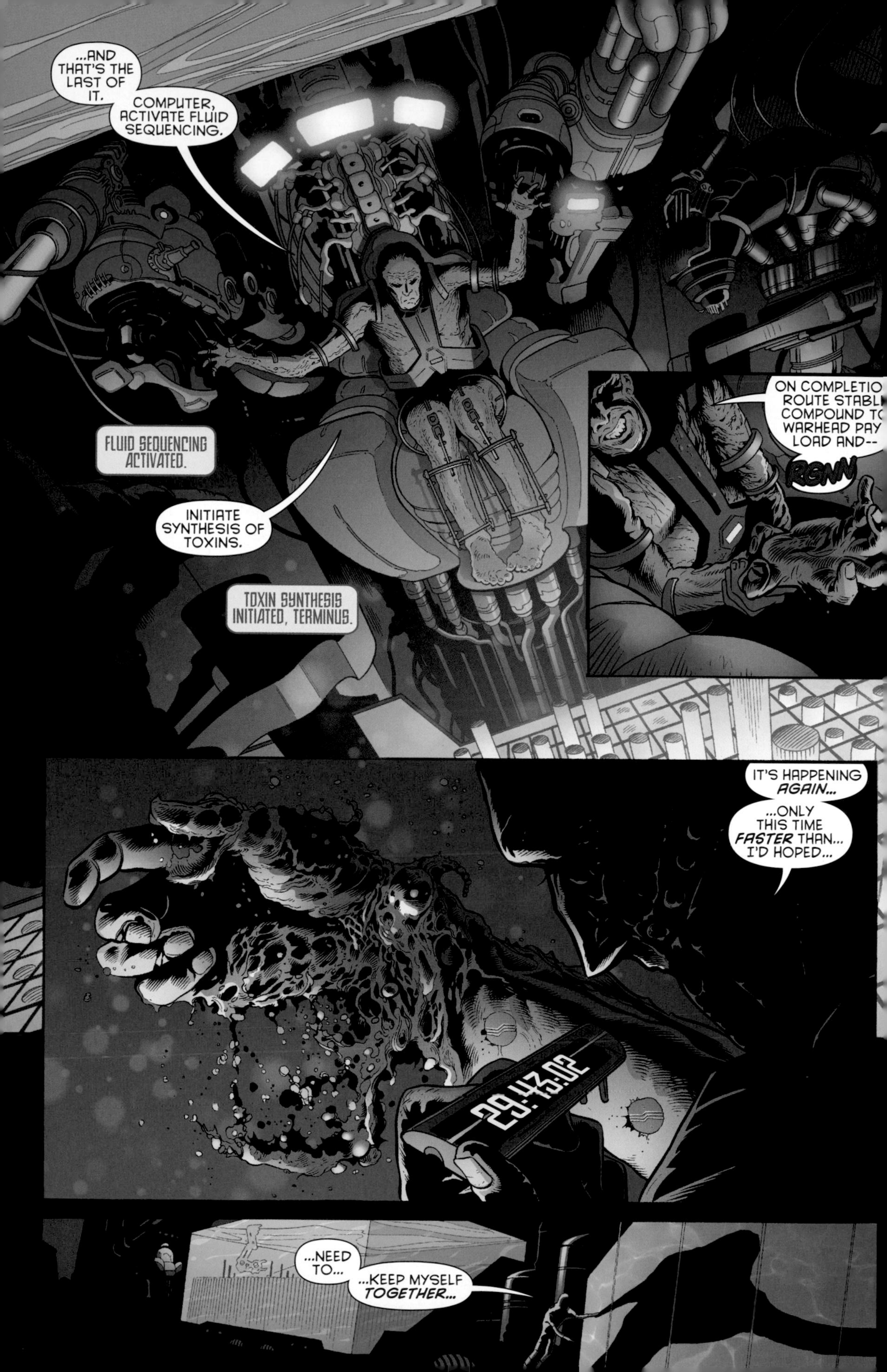
...AND THAT'S THE LAST OF IT.
COMPUTER, ACTIVATE FLUID SEQUENCING.
FLUID SEQUENCING ACTIVATED.
INITIATE SYNTHESIS OF TOXINS.
TOXIN SYNTHESIS INITIATED, TERMINUS.
ON COMPLETIO ROUTE STABL COMPOUND TO WARHEAD PAY LOAD AND--
RGNN
IT'S HAPPENING *AGAIN...*
...ONLY THIS TIME *FASTER* THAN... I'D HOPED...
29:43:02
...NEED TO...
...KEEP MYSELF *TOGETHER...*

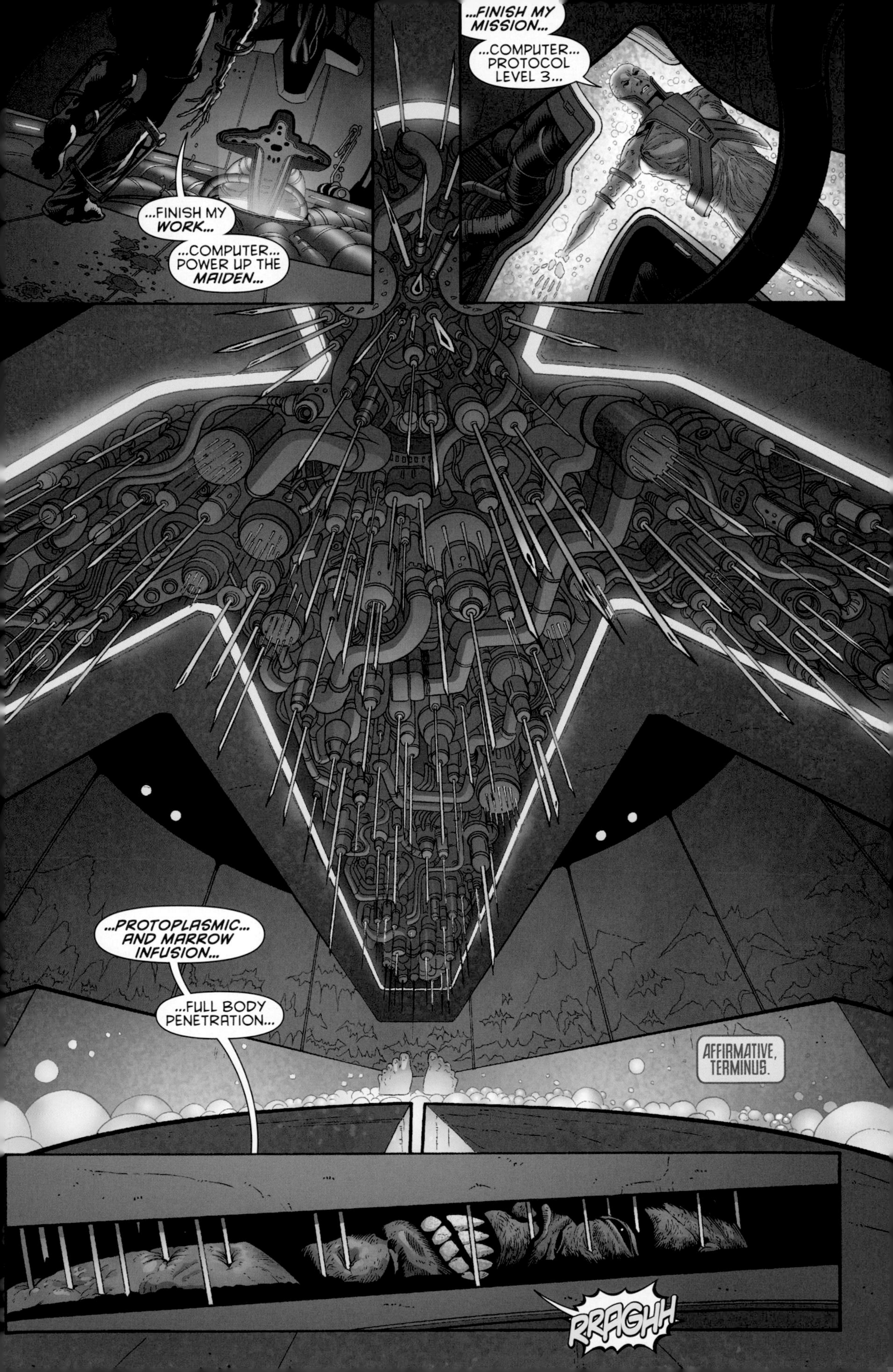
...FINISH MY WORK...
...COMPUTER... POWER UP THE MAIDEN...
...FINISH MY MISSION...
...COMPUTER... PROTOCOL LEVEL 3...
...PROTOPLASMIC... AND MARROW INFUSION...
...FULL BODY PENETRATION...
AFFIRMATIVE, TERMINUS.
RRAGHH

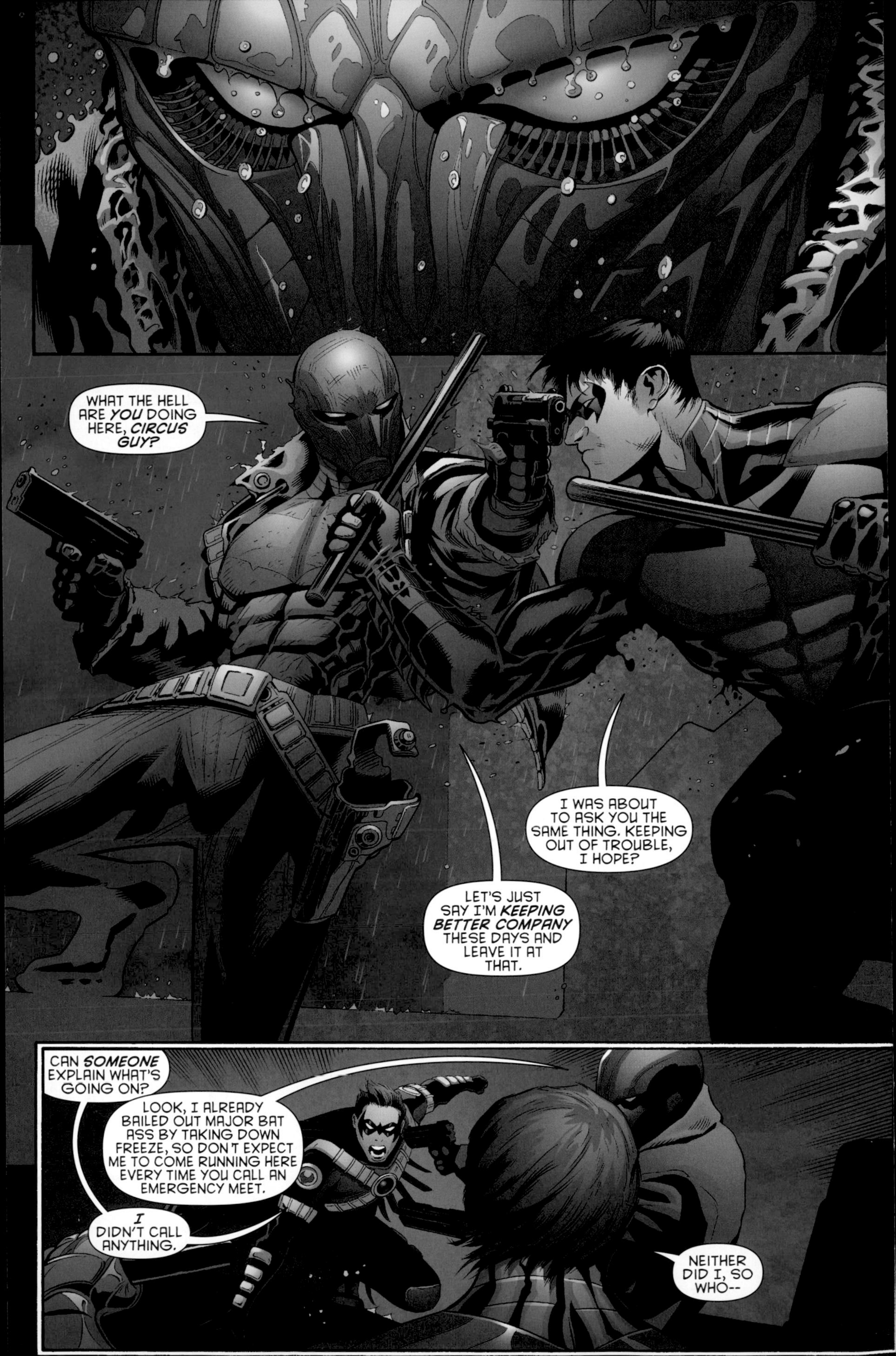
WHAT THE HELL ARE YOU DOING HERE, CIRCUS GUY?
I WAS ABOUT TO ASK YOU THE SAME THING. KEEPING OUT OF TROUBLE, I HOPE?
LET'S JUST SAY I'M KEEPING BETTER COMPANY THESE DAYS AND LEAVE IT AT THAT.
CAN SOMEONE EXPLAIN WHAT'S GOING ON?
LOOK, I ALREADY BAILED OUT MAJOR BAT ASS BY TAKING DOWN FREEZE, SO DON'T EXPECT ME TO COME RUNNING HERE EVERY TIME YOU CALL AN EMERGENCY MEET.
I DIDN'T CALL ANYTHING.
NEITHER DID I, SO WHO--

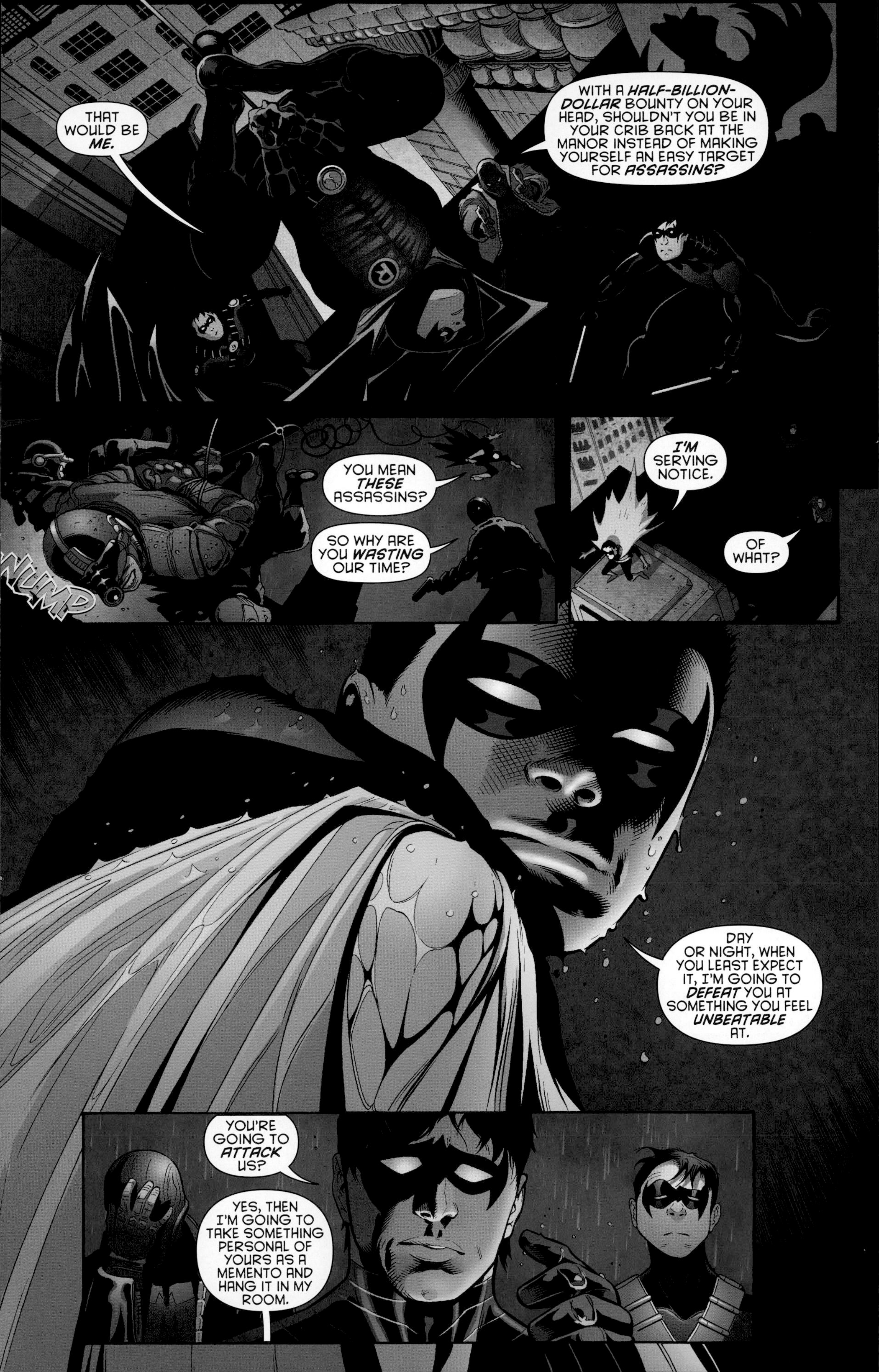
THAT WOULD BE *ME.*
WITH A *HALF-BILLION-DOLLAR* BOUNTY ON YOUR HEAD, SHOULDN'T YOU BE IN YOUR CRIB BACK AT THE MANOR INSTEAD OF MAKING YOURSELF AN EASY TARGET FOR *ASSASSINS?*
THUMP
YOU MEAN *THESE* ASSASSINS?
SO WHY ARE YOU *WASTING* OUR TIME?
I'M SERVING NOTICE.
OF WHAT?
DAY OR NIGHT, WHEN YOU LEAST EXPECT IT, I'M GOING TO *DEFEAT* YOU AT SOMETHING YOU FEEL *UNBEATABLE* AT.
YOU'RE GOING TO *ATTACK* US?
YES, THEN I'M GOING TO TAKE SOMETHING PERSONAL OF YOURS AS A MEMENTO AND HANG IT IN MY ROOM.

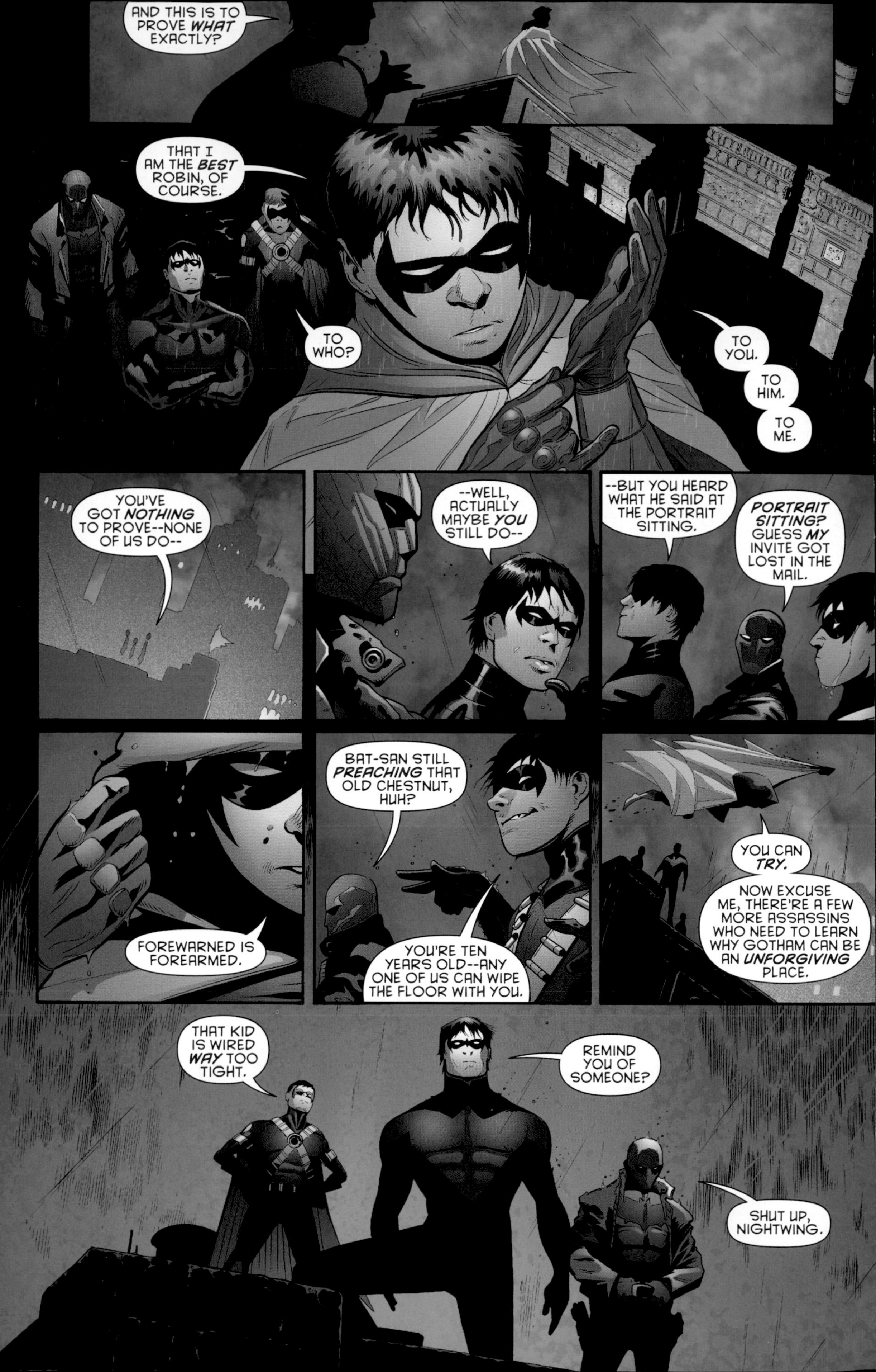

AND THIS IS TO PROVE *WHAT* EXACTLY?
THAT I AM THE *BEST* ROBIN, OF COURSE.
TO WHO?
TO YOU.
TO HIM.
TO ME.
YOU'VE GOT *NOTHING* TO PROVE--NONE OF US DO--
--WELL, ACTUALLY MAYBE *YOU* STILL DO--
--BUT YOU HEARD WHAT HE SAID AT THE PORTRAIT SITTING.
PORTRAIT SITTING? GUESS *MY* INVITE GOT LOST IN THE MAIL.
FOREWARNED IS FOREARMED.
BAT-SAN STILL *PREACHING* THAT OLD CHESTNUT, HUH?
YOU'RE TEN YEARS OLD--ANY ONE OF US CAN WIPE THE FLOOR WITH YOU.
YOU CAN *TRY.*
NOW EXCUSE ME, THERE'RE A FEW MORE ASSASSINS WHO NEED TO LEARN WHY GOTHAM CAN BE AN *UNFORGIVING* PLACE.
THAT KID IS WIRED *WAY* TOO TIGHT.
REMIND YOU OF SOMEONE?
SHUT UP, NIGHTWING.

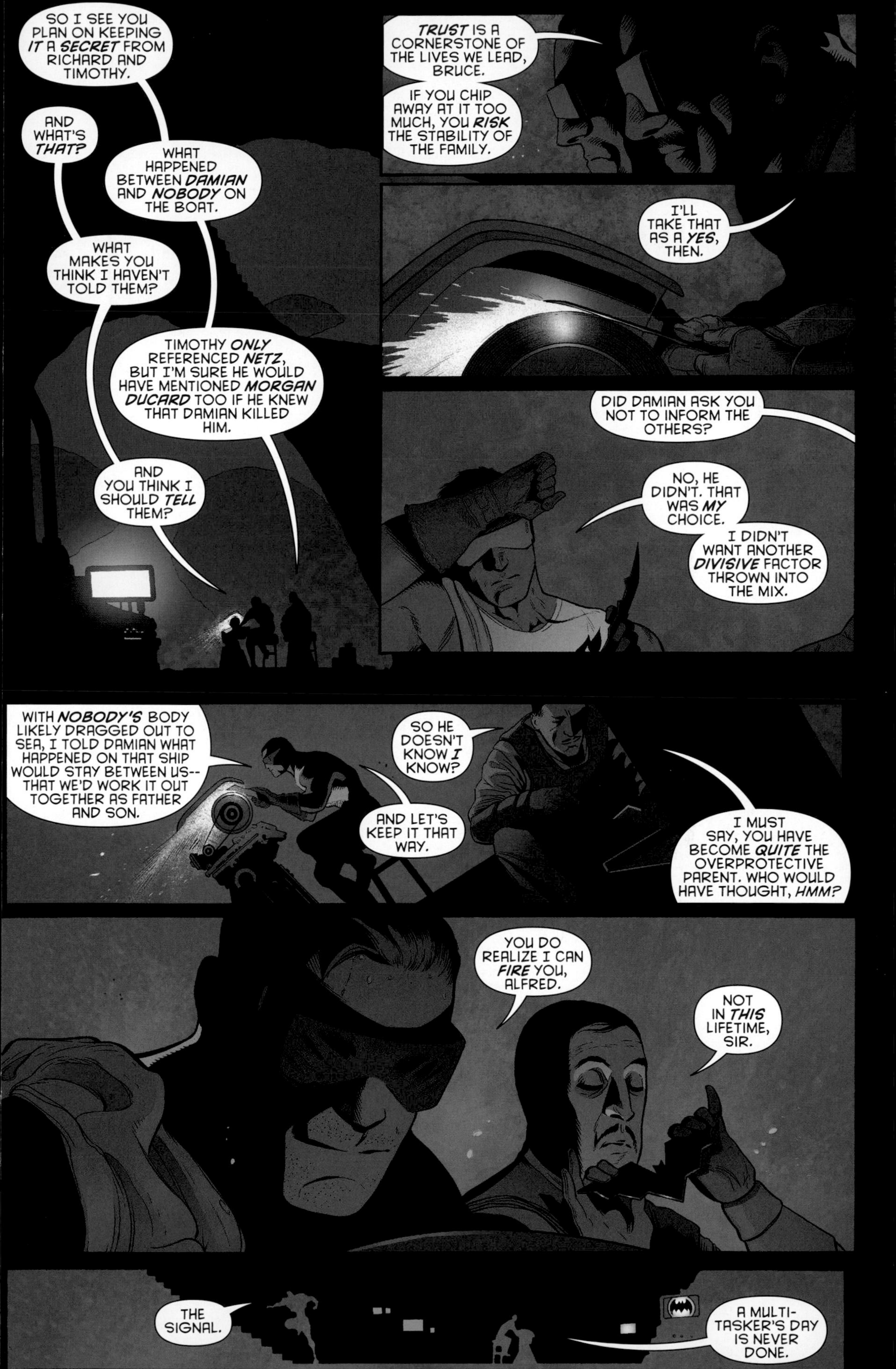
SO I SEE YOU PLAN ON KEEPING IT A SECRET FROM RICHARD AND TIMOTHY.
AND WHAT'S THAT?
WHAT HAPPENED BETWEEN DAMIAN AND NOBODY ON THE BOAT.
WHAT MAKES YOU THINK I HAVEN'T TOLD THEM?
TIMOTHY ONLY REFERENCED NETZ, BUT I'M SURE HE WOULD HAVE MENTIONED MORGAN DUCARD TOO IF HE KNEW THAT DAMIAN KILLED HIM.
AND YOU THINK I SHOULD TELL THEM?
TRUST IS A CORNERSTONE OF THE LIVES WE LEAD, BRUCE.
IF YOU CHIP AWAY AT IT TOO MUCH, YOU RISK THE STABILITY OF THE FAMILY.
I'LL TAKE THAT AS A YES, THEN.
DID DAMIAN ASK YOU NOT TO INFORM THE OTHERS?
NO, HE DIDN'T. THAT WAS MY CHOICE.
I DIDN'T WANT ANOTHER DIVISIVE FACTOR THROWN INTO THE MIX.
WITH NOBODY'S BODY LIKELY DRAGGED OUT TO SEA, I TOLD DAMIAN WHAT HAPPENED ON THAT SHIP WOULD STAY BETWEEN US--THAT WE'D WORK IT OUT TOGETHER AS FATHER AND SON.
SO HE DOESN'T KNOW I KNOW?
AND LET'S KEEP IT THAT WAY.
I MUST SAY, YOU HAVE BECOME QUITE THE OVERPROTECTIVE PARENT. WHO WOULD HAVE THOUGHT, HMM?
YOU DO REALIZE I CAN FIRE YOU, ALFRED.
NOT IN THIS LIFETIME, SIR.
THE SIGNAL.
A MULTI-TASKER'S DAY IS NEVER DONE.

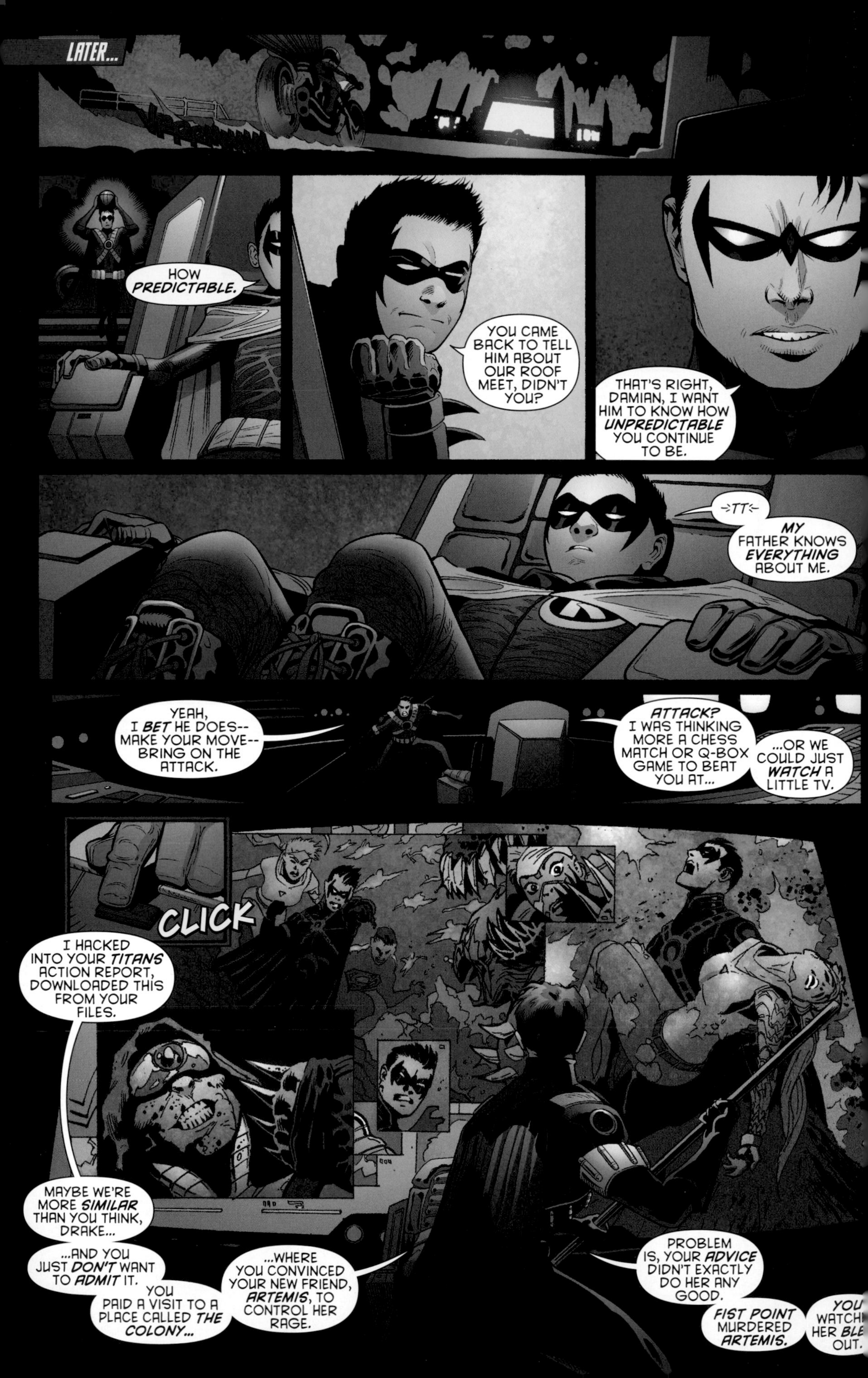
LATER...
HOW PREDICTABLE.
YOU CAME BACK TO TELL HIM ABOUT OUR ROOF MEET, DIDN'T YOU?
THAT'S RIGHT, DAMIAN, I WANT HIM TO KNOW HOW UNPREDICTABLE YOU CONTINUE TO BE.
TT
MY FATHER KNOWS EVERYTHING ABOUT ME.
YEAH, I BET HE DOES-- MAKE YOUR MOVE-- BRING ON THE ATTACK.
ATTACK? I WAS THINKING MORE A CHESS MATCH OR Q-BOX GAME TO BEAT YOU AT...
...OR WE COULD JUST WATCH A LITTLE TV.
CLICK
I HACKED INTO YOUR TITANS ACTION REPORT, DOWNLOADED THIS FROM YOUR FILES.
MAYBE WE'RE MORE SIMILAR THAN YOU THINK, DRAKE...
...AND YOU JUST DON'T WANT TO ADMIT IT.
YOU PAID A VISIT TO A PLACE CALLED THE COLONY...
...WHERE YOU CONVINCED YOUR NEW FRIEND, ARTEMIS, TO CONTROL HER RAGE.
PROBLEM IS, YOUR ADVICE DIDN'T EXACTLY DO HER ANY GOOD.
FIST POINT MURDERED ARTEMIS.
YOU WATCH HER BLE OUT.

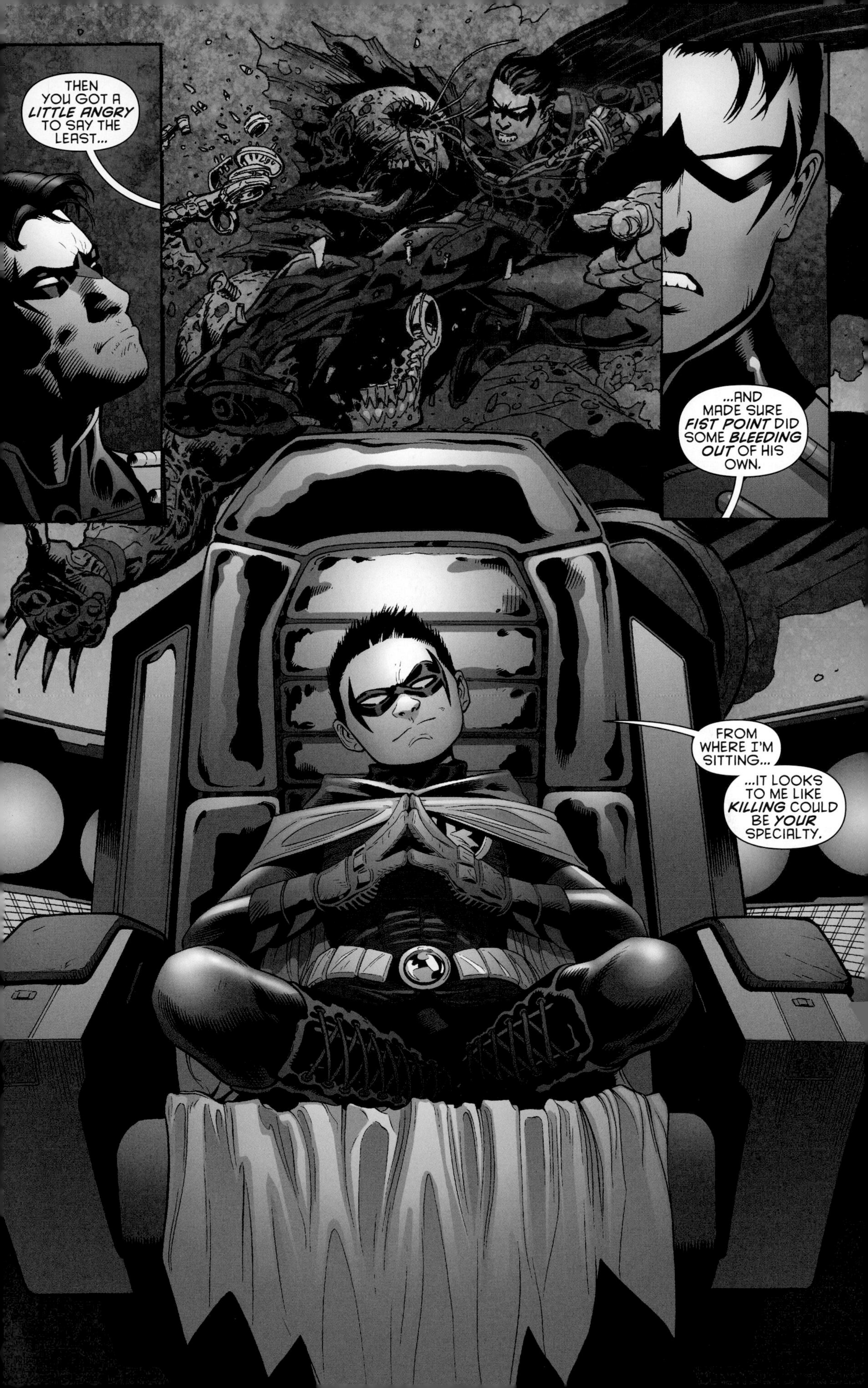
THEN YOU GOT A LITTLE ANGRY TO SAY THE LEAST...
...AND MADE SURE FIST POINT DID SOME BLEEDING OUT OF HIS OWN.
FROM WHERE I'M SITTING...
...IT LOOKS TO ME LIKE KILLING COULD BE YOUR SPECIALTY.

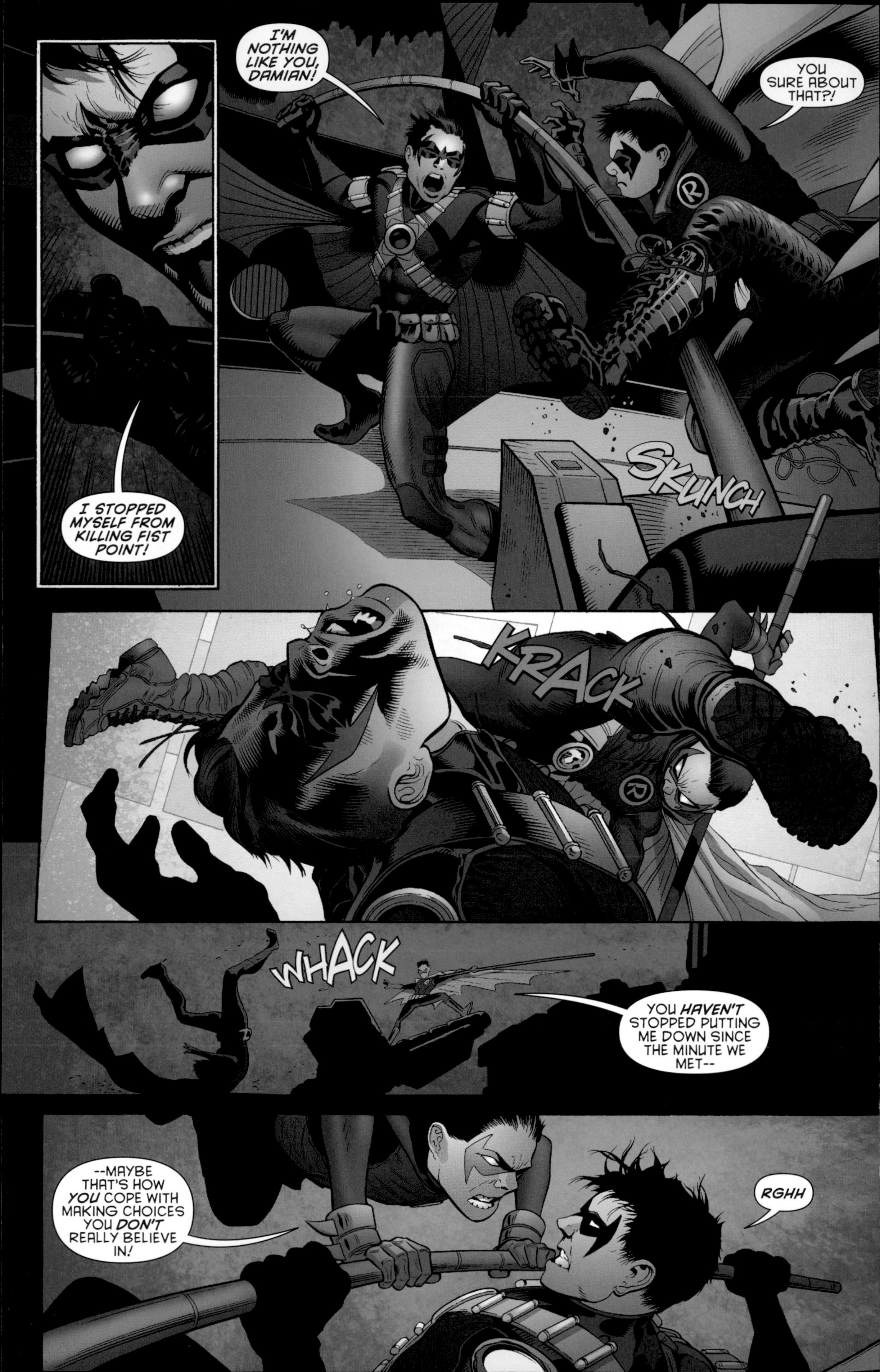
I'M NOTHING LIKE YOU, DAMIAN!
YOU SURE ABOUT THAT?!
I STOPPED MYSELF FROM KILLING FIST POINT!
SKUNCH
KRACK
WHACK
YOU HAVEN'T STOPPED PUTTING ME DOWN SINCE THE MINUTE WE MET--
--MAYBE THAT'S HOW YOU COPE WITH MAKING CHOICES YOU DON'T REALLY BELIEVE IN!
RGHH

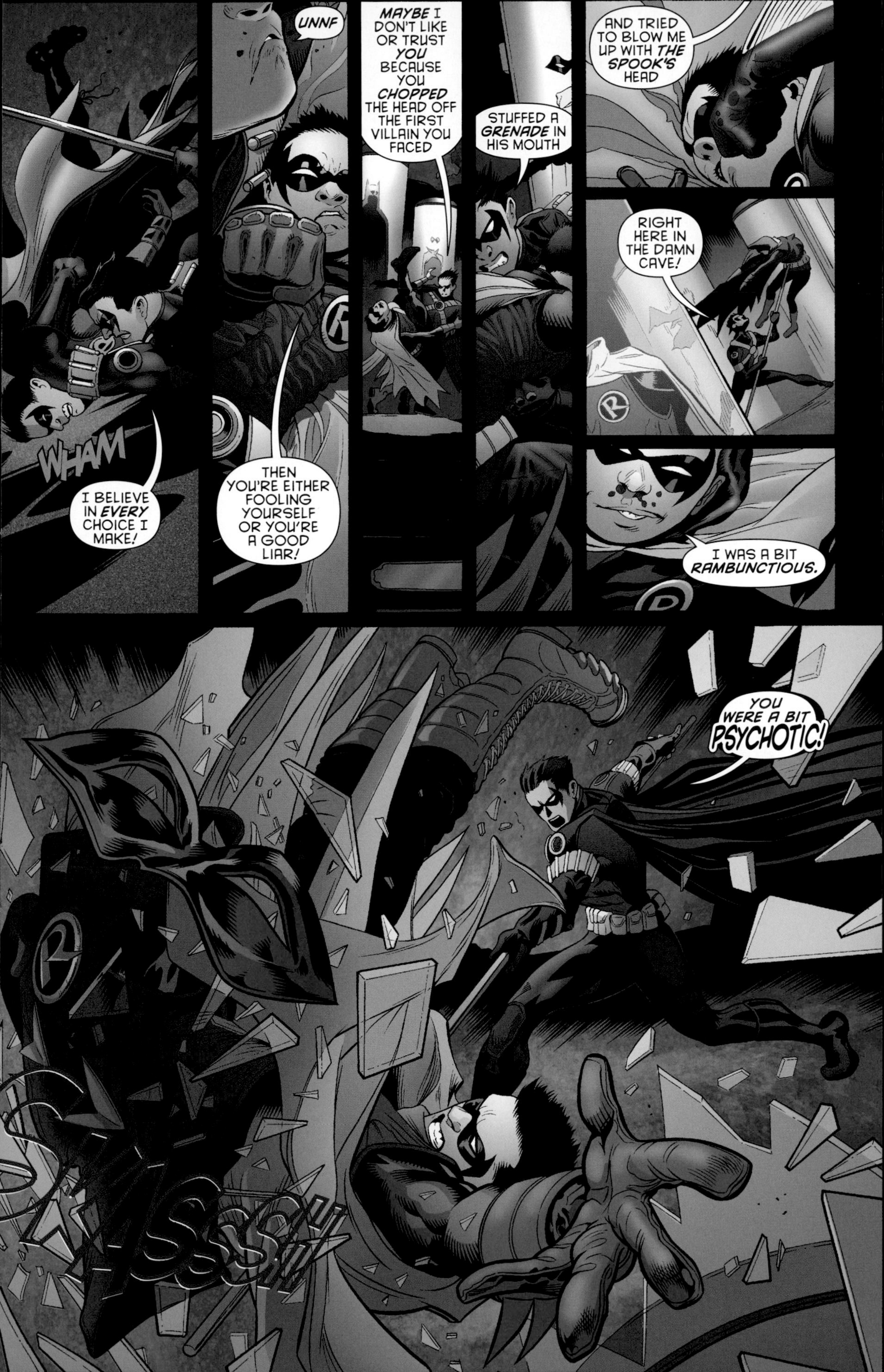

UNNF
MAYBE I DON'T LIKE OR TRUST YOU BECAUSE YOU CHOPPED THE HEAD OFF THE FIRST VILLAIN YOU FACED
STUFFED A GRENADE IN HIS MOUTH
AND TRIED TO BLOW ME UP WITH THE SPOOK'S HEAD
RIGHT HERE IN THE DAMN CAVE!
WHAM
I BELIEVE IN EVERY CHOICE I MAKE!
THEN YOU'RE EITHER FOOLING YOURSELF OR YOU'RE A GOOD LIAR!
I WAS A BIT RAMBUNCTIOUS.
YOU WERE A BIT PSYCHOTIC!

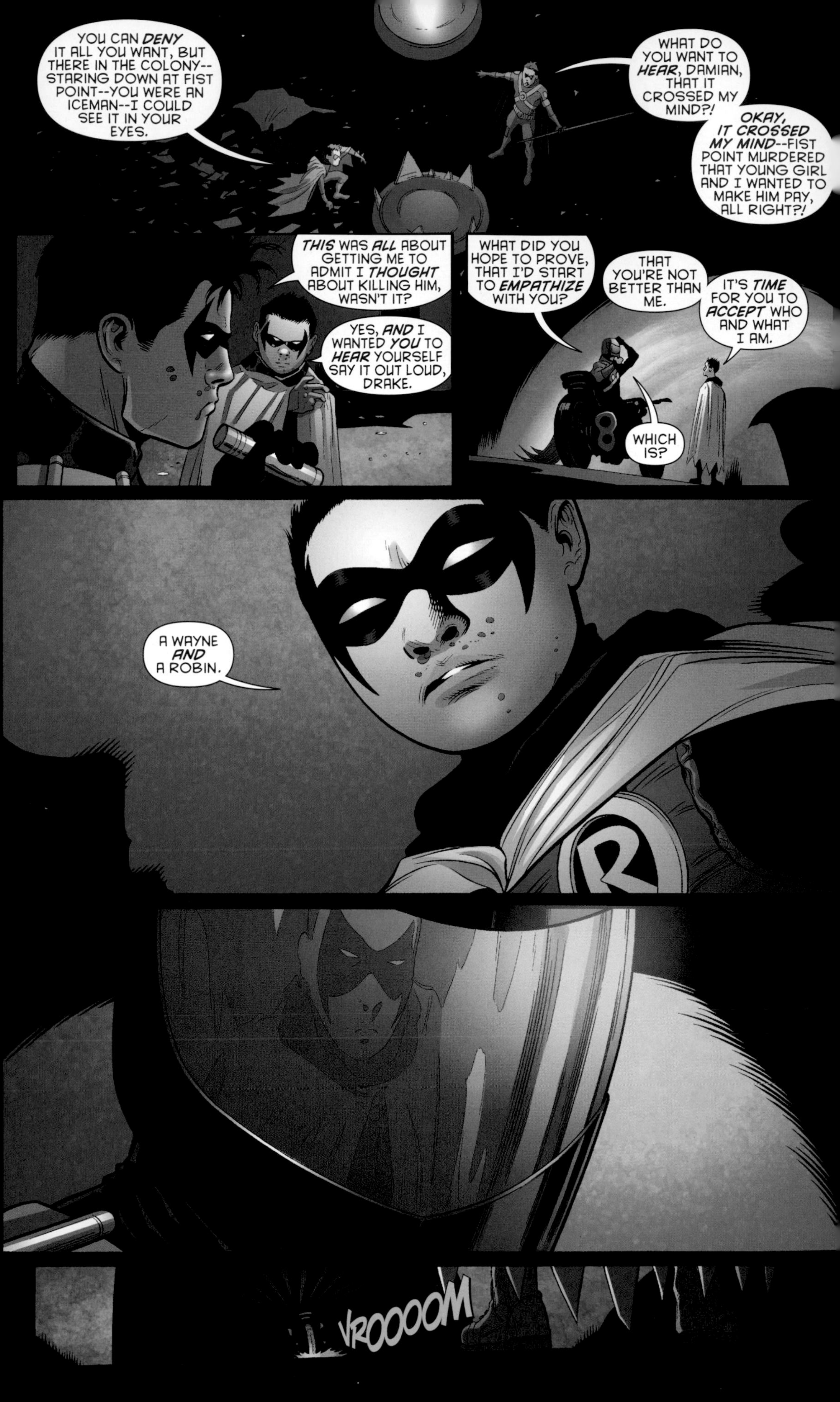
YOU CAN DENY IT ALL YOU WANT, BUT THERE IN THE COLONY--STARING DOWN AT FIST POINT--YOU WERE AN ICEMAN--I COULD SEE IT IN YOUR EYES.
WHAT DO YOU WANT TO HEAR, DAMIAN, THAT IT CROSSED MY MIND?!
OKAY, IT CROSSED MY MIND--FIST POINT MURDERED THAT YOUNG GIRL AND I WANTED TO MAKE HIM PAY, ALL RIGHT?!
THIS WAS ALL ABOUT GETTING ME TO ADMIT I THOUGHT ABOUT KILLING HIM, WASN'T IT?
YES, AND I WANTED YOU TO HEAR YOURSELF SAY IT OUT LOUD, DRAKE.
WHAT DID YOU HOPE TO PROVE, THAT I'D START TO EMPATHIZE WITH YOU?
THAT YOU'RE NOT BETTER THAN ME.
IT'S TIME FOR YOU TO ACCEPT WHO AND WHAT I AM.
WHICH IS?
A WAYNE AND A ROBIN.
VROOOOM

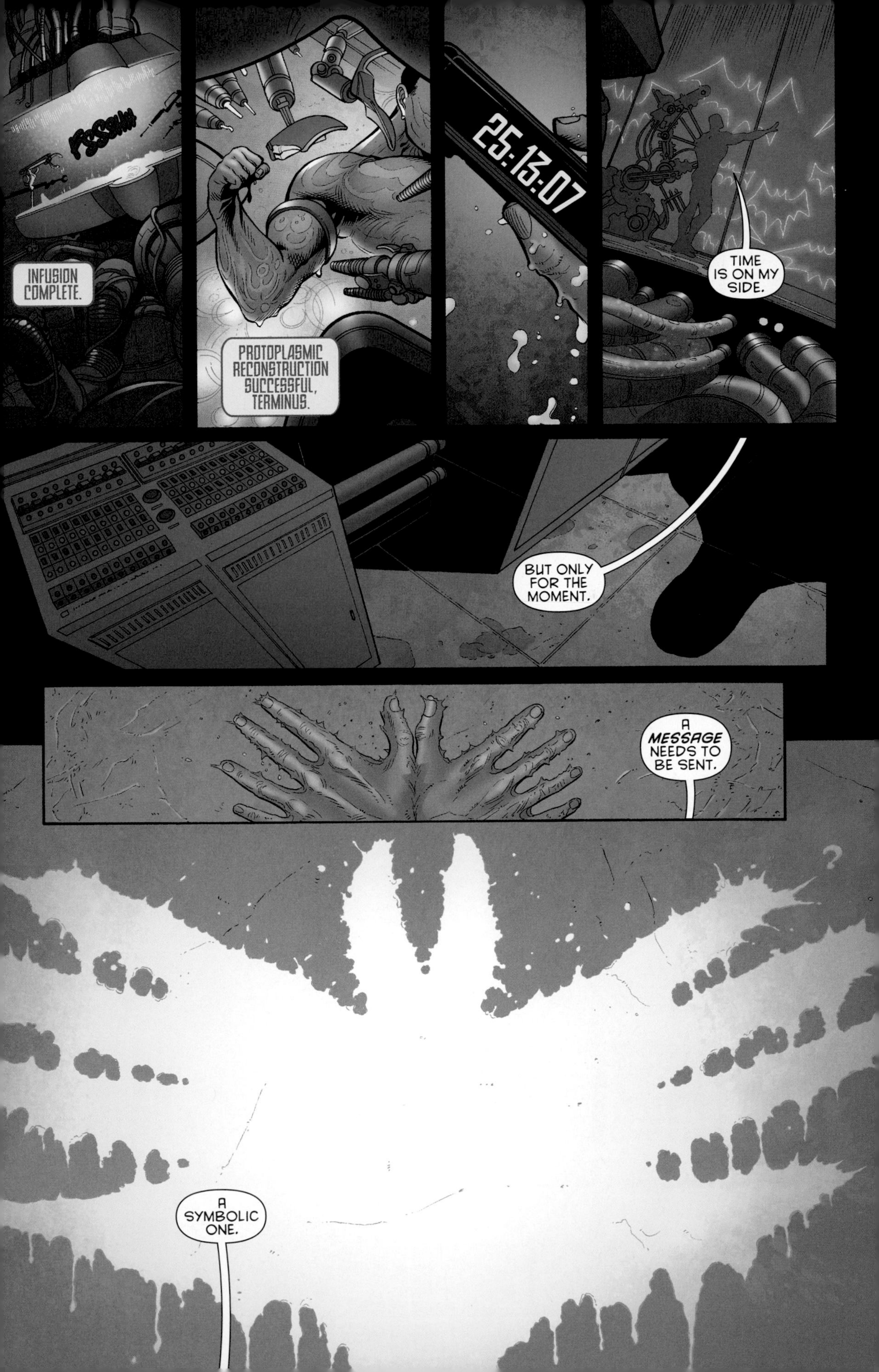
FSSSHH
INFUSION COMPLETE.
PROTOPLASMIC RECONSTRUCTION SUCCESSFUL, TERMINUS.
25:13:07
TIME IS ON MY SIDE.
BUT ONLY FOR THE MOMENT.
A MESSAGE NEEDS TO BE SENT.
A SYMBOLIC ONE.

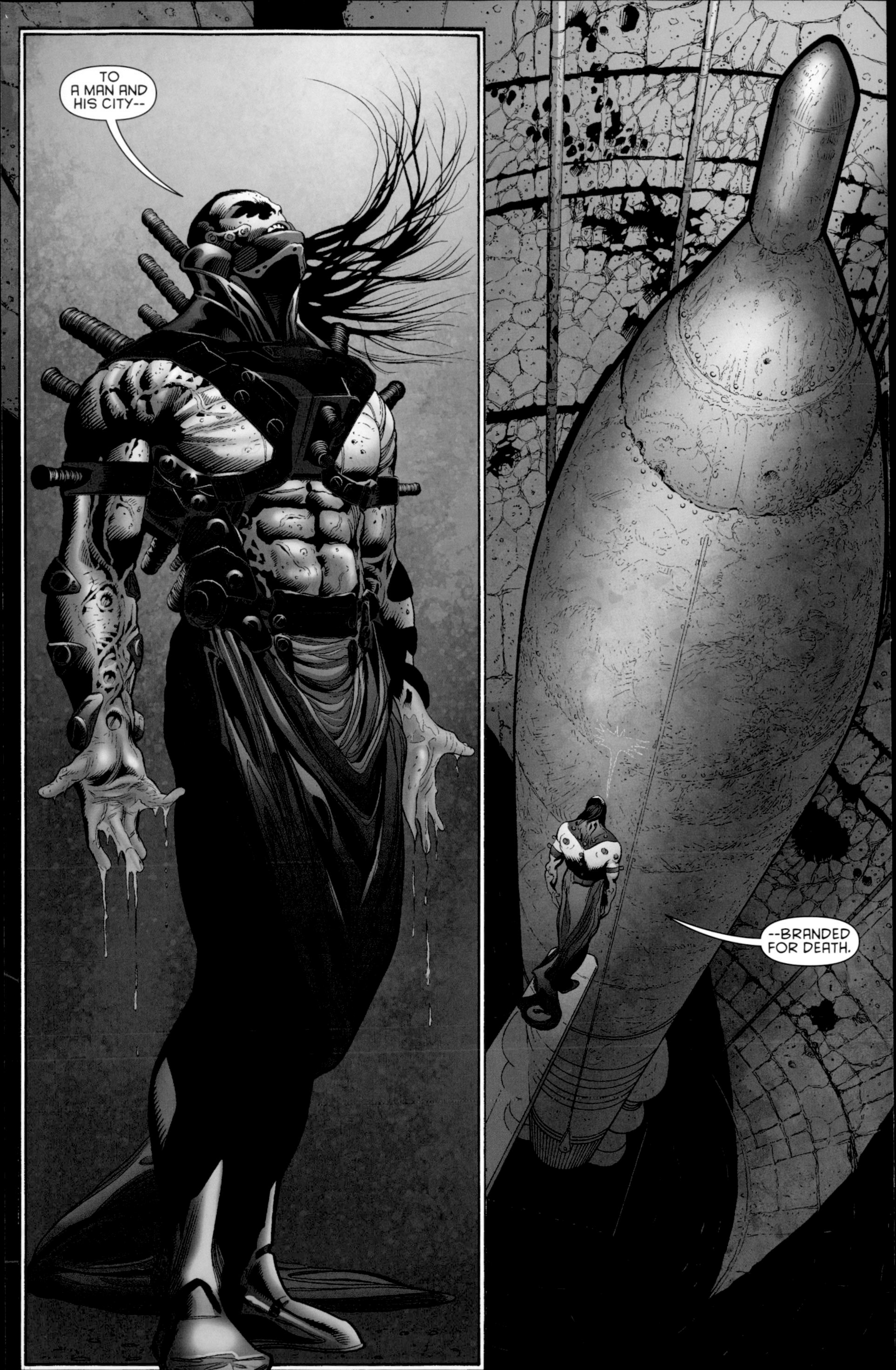
TO A MAN AND HIS CITY--
--BRANDED FOR DEATH.

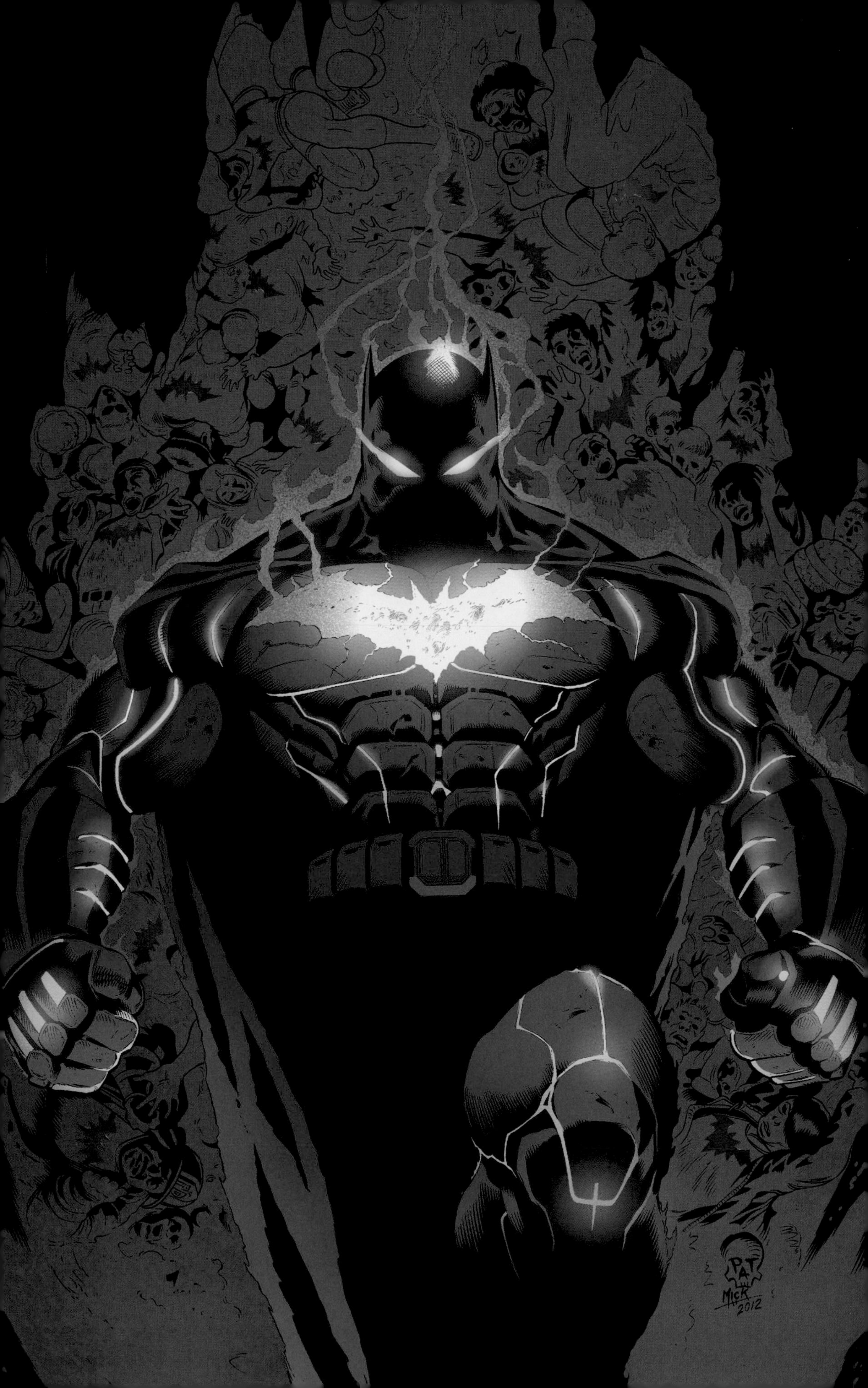
PAT
MICK
2012

TERMINUS: BRANDED

PETER J. TOMASI writer PATRICK GLEASON penciller MICK GRAY, KEITH CHAMPAGNE & TOM NGUYEN inkers
cover by GLEASON, GRAY & KALISZ

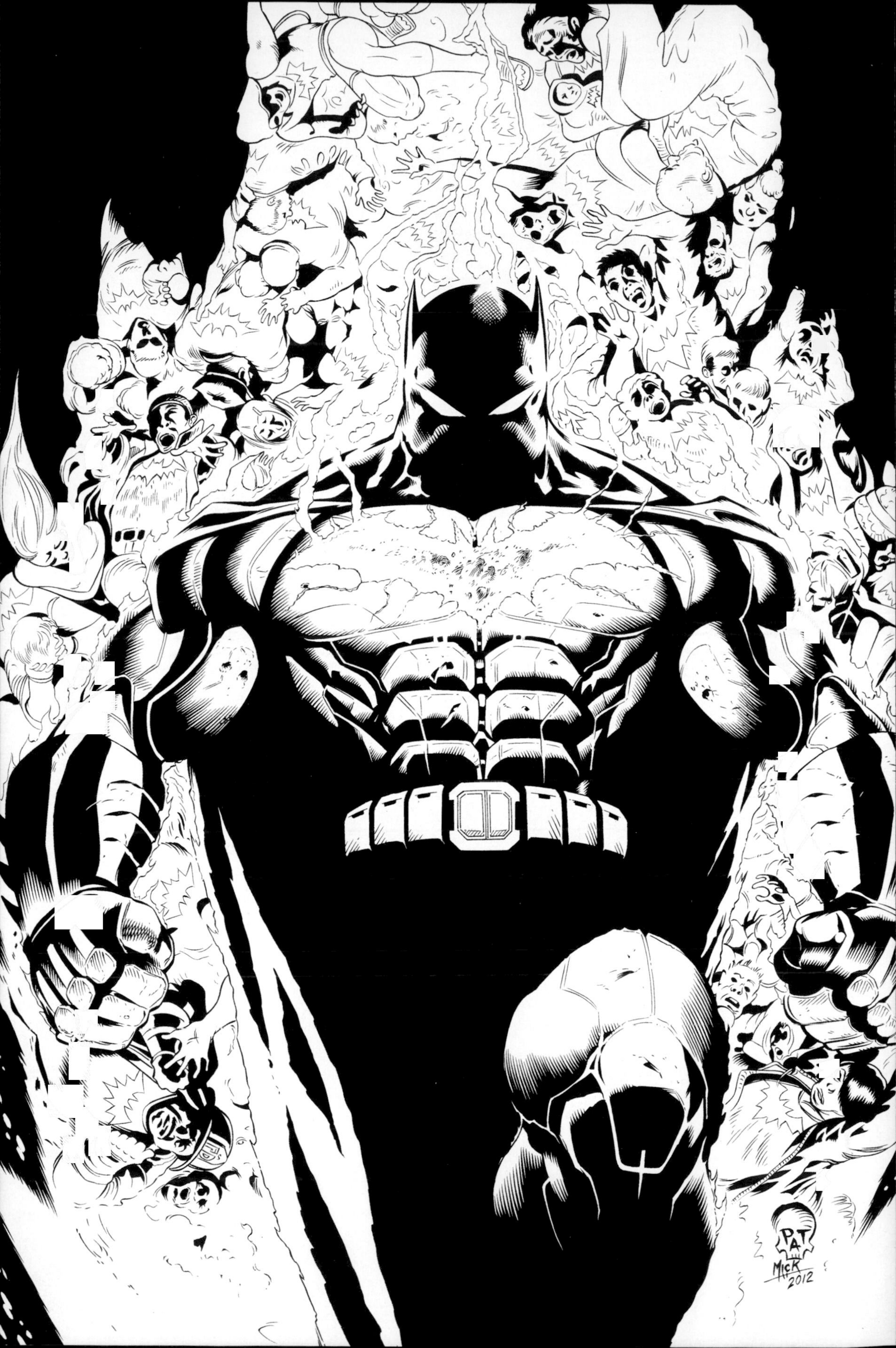

PAT
MICK
2012

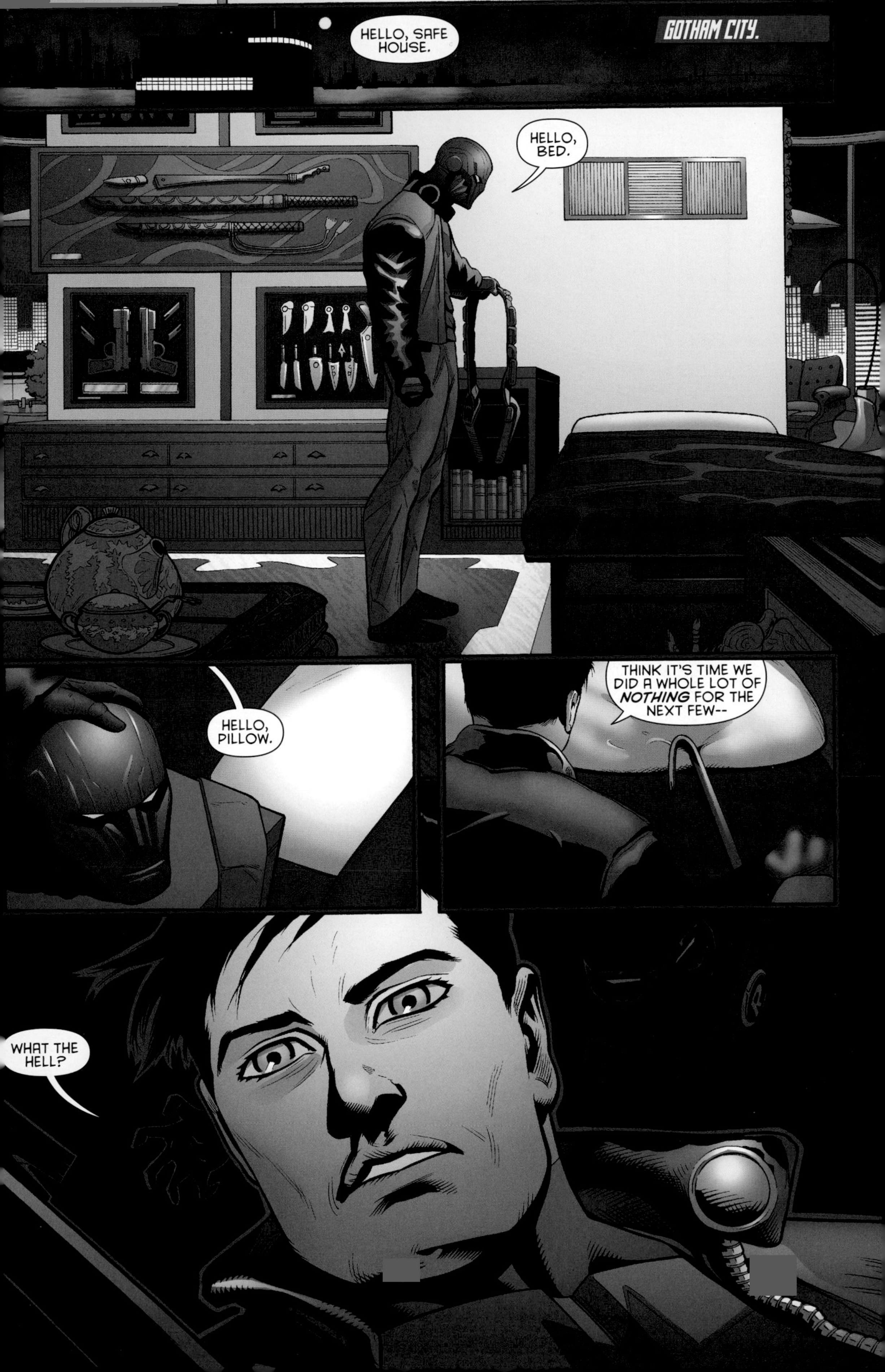
GOTHAM CITY.
HELLO, SAFE HOUSE.
HELLO, BED.
HELLO, PILLOW.
THINK IT'S TIME WE DID A WHOLE LOT OF *NOTHING* FOR THE NEXT FEW--
WHAT THE HELL?

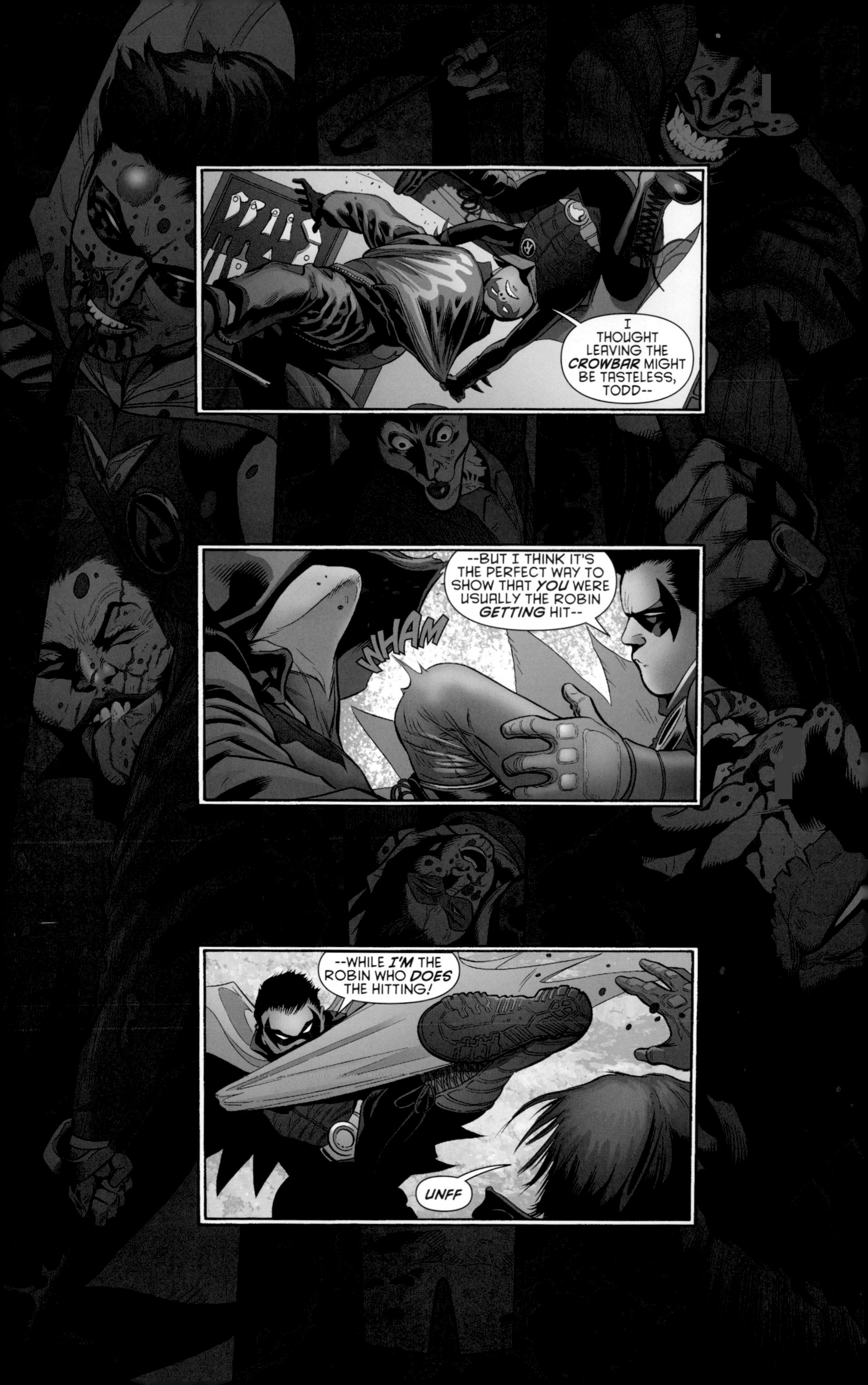
I THOUGHT LEAVING THE *CROWBAR* MIGHT BE TASTELESS, TODD--
--BUT I THINK IT'S THE PERFECT WAY TO SHOW THAT *YOU* WERE USUALLY THE ROBIN *GETTING* HIT--
WHAM
--WHILE *I'M* THE ROBIN WHO *DOES* THE HITTING!
UNFF

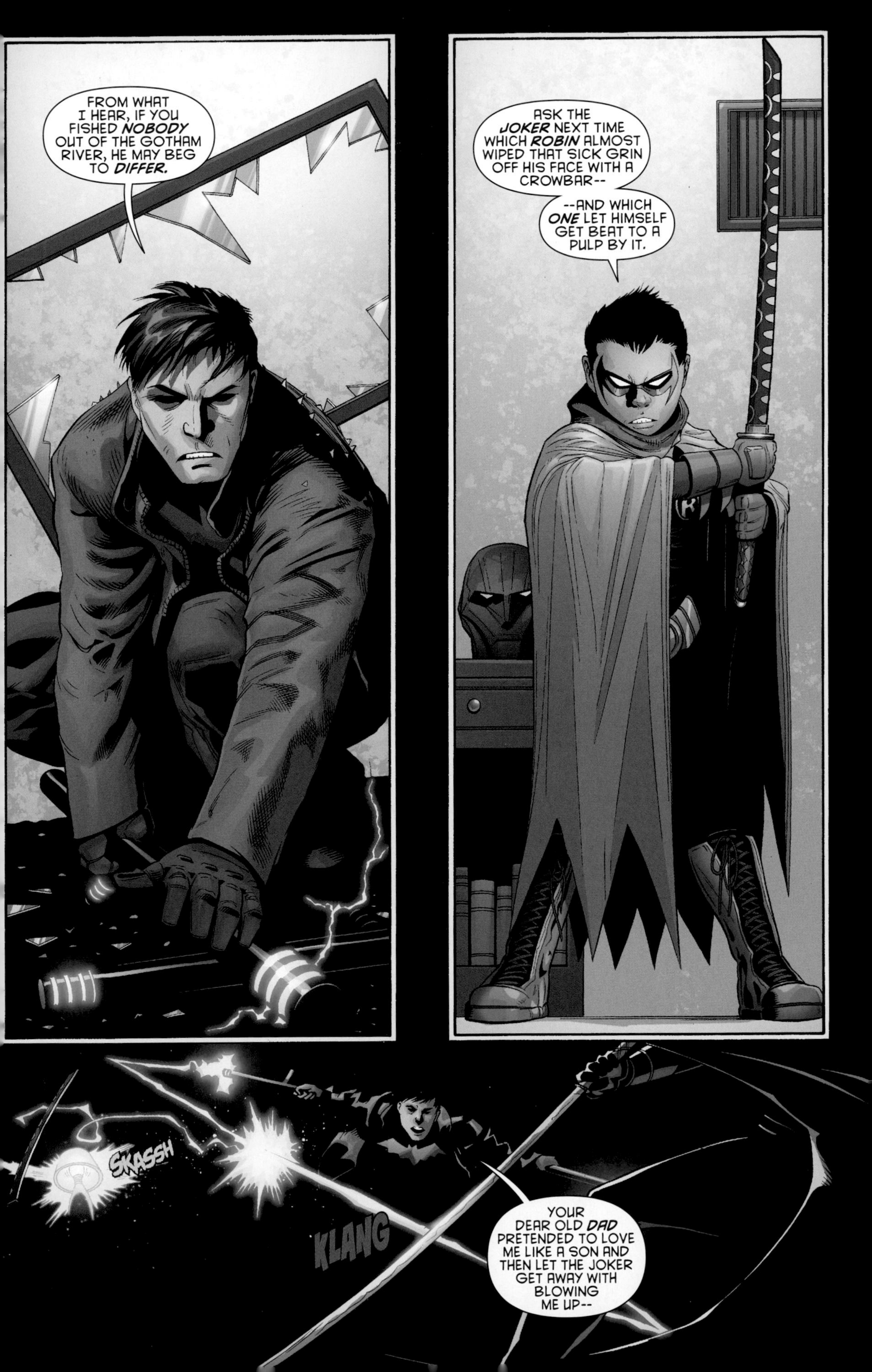
FROM WHAT I HEAR, IF YOU FISHED NOBODY OUT OF THE GOTHAM RIVER, HE MAY BEG TO DIFFER.
ASK THE JOKER NEXT TIME WHICH ROBIN ALMOST WIPED THAT SICK GRIN OFF HIS FACE WITH A CROWBAR--
--AND WHICH ONE LET HIMSELF GET BEAT TO A PULP BY IT.
SKASSH
KLANG
YOUR DEAR OLD DAD PRETENDED TO LOVE ME LIKE A SON AND THEN LET THE JOKER GET AWAY WITH BLOWING ME UP--

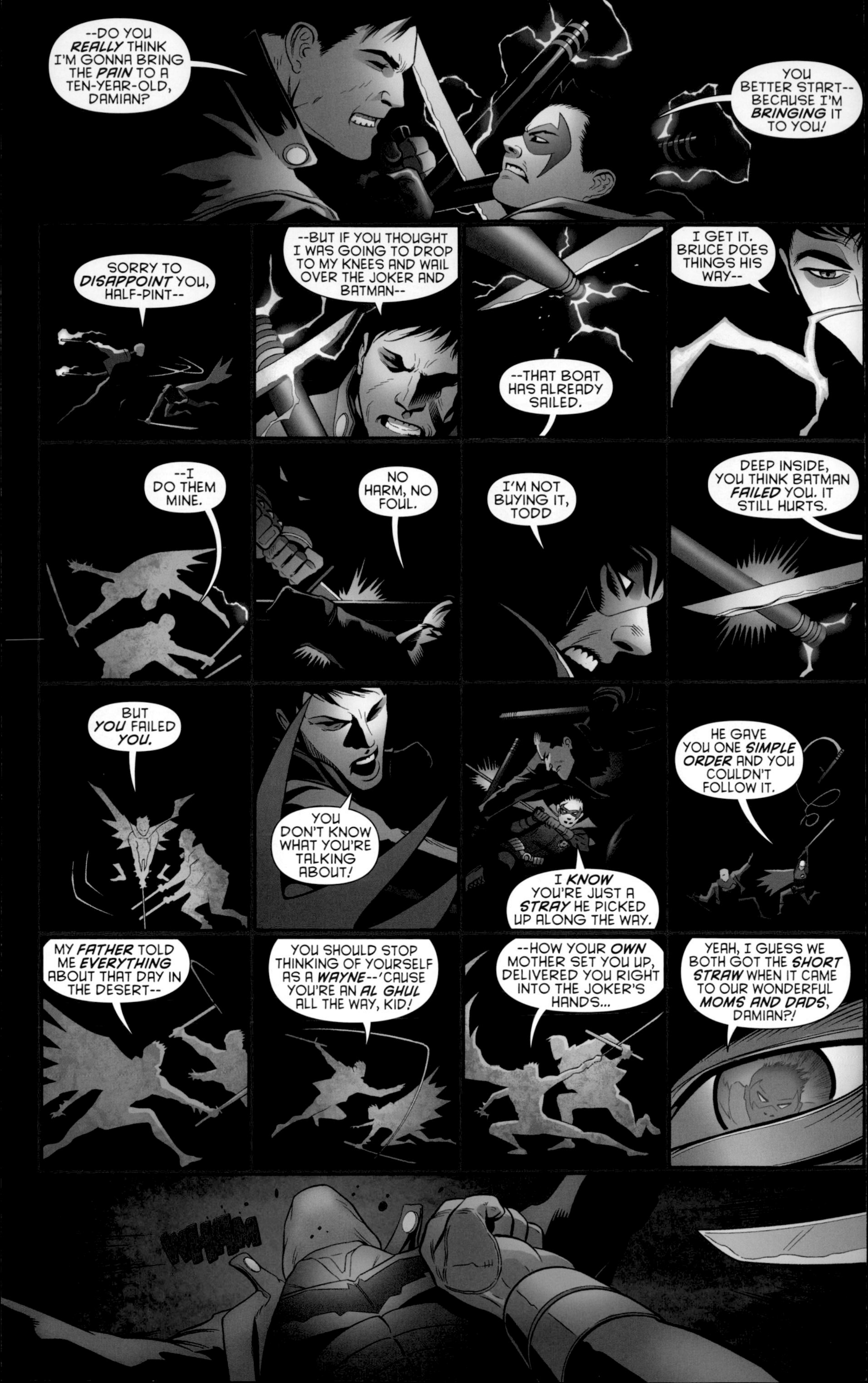
--DO YOU REALLY THINK I'M GONNA BRING THE PAIN TO A TEN-YEAR-OLD, DAMIAN?
YOU BETTER START-- BECAUSE I'M BRINGING IT TO YOU!
SORRY TO DISAPPOINT YOU, HALF-PINT--
--BUT IF YOU THOUGHT I WAS GOING TO DROP TO MY KNEES AND WAIL OVER THE JOKER AND BATMAN--
--THAT BOAT HAS ALREADY SAILED.
I GET IT. BRUCE DOES THINGS HIS WAY--
--I DO THEM MINE.
NO HARM, NO FOUL.
I'M NOT BUYING IT, TODD
DEEP INSIDE, YOU THINK BATMAN FAILED YOU. IT STILL HURTS.
BUT YOU FAILED YOU.
YOU DON'T KNOW WHAT YOU'RE TALKING ABOUT!
I KNOW YOU'RE JUST A STRAY HE PICKED UP ALONG THE WAY.
HE GAVE YOU ONE SIMPLE ORDER AND YOU COULDN'T FOLLOW IT.
MY FATHER TOLD ME EVERYTHING ABOUT THAT DAY IN THE DESERT--
YOU SHOULD STOP THINKING OF YOURSELF AS A WAYNE--'CAUSE YOU'RE AN AL GHUL ALL THE WAY, KID!
--HOW YOUR OWN MOTHER SET YOU UP, DELIVERED YOU RIGHT INTO THE JOKER'S HANDS...
YEAH, I GUESS WE BOTH GOT THE SHORT STRAW WHEN IT CAME TO OUR WONDERFUL MOMS AND DADS, DAMIAN?!

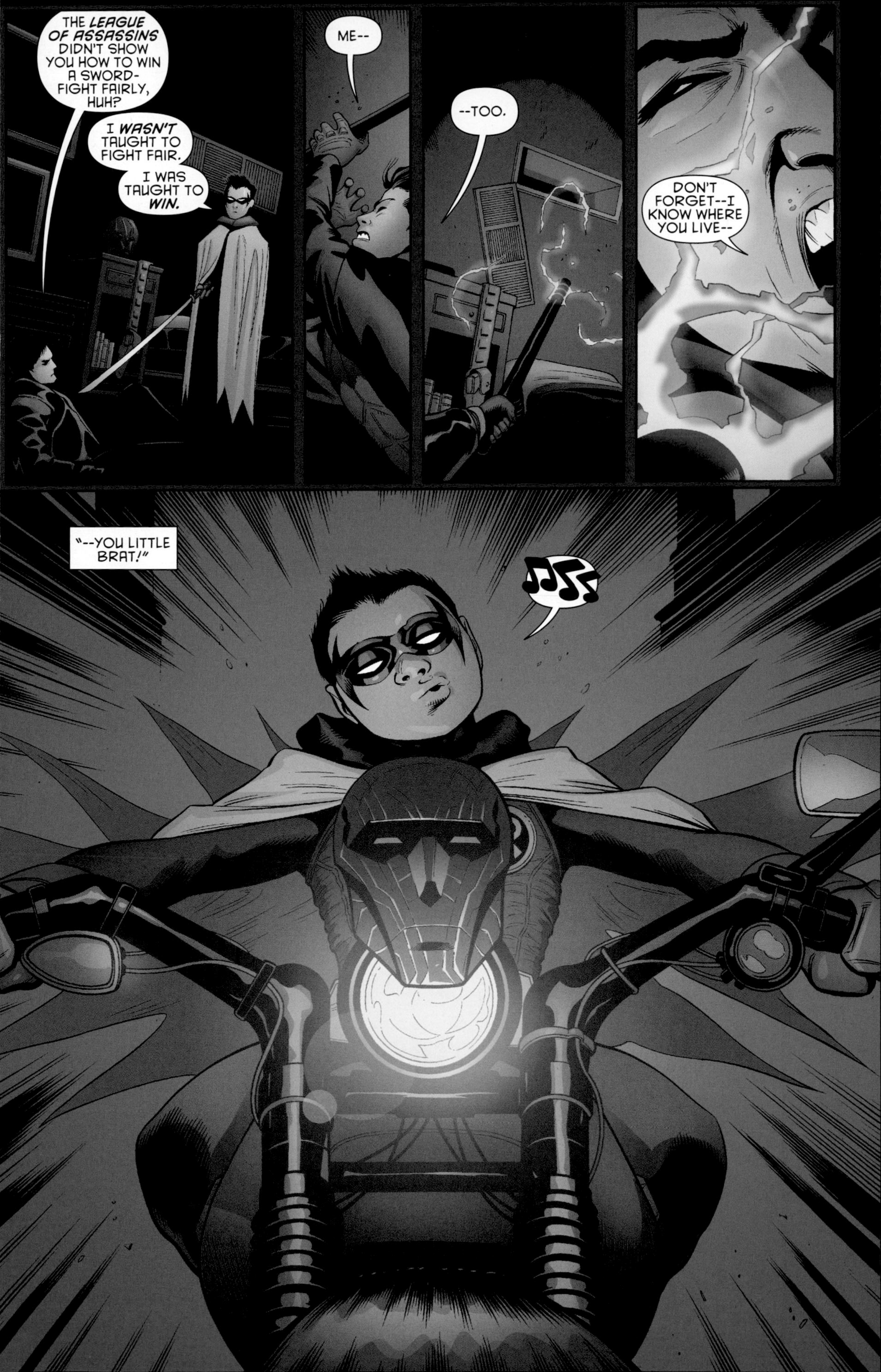
THE LEAGUE OF ASSASSINS DIDN'T SHOW YOU HOW TO WIN A SWORD-FIGHT FAIRLY, HUH?
I WASN'T TAUGHT TO FIGHT FAIR.
I WAS TAUGHT TO WIN.
ME--
--TOO.
DON'T FORGET--I KNOW WHERE YOU LIVE--
"--YOU LITTLE BRAT!"

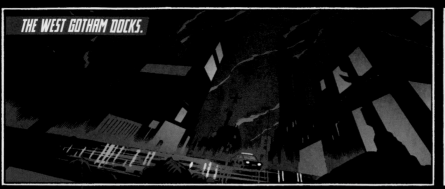

THE WEST GOTHAM DOCKS.

PROPERTY ALARM TRIGGERED--I'VE GOT A 211 AT DIECAST, REQUEST BACKUP.

COME OUT WITH YOUR HANDS UP!

PUT ANY WEAPONS YOU HAVE ON THE DECK NOW!

HOW ABOUT A PIGGYBACK RIDE-- *I forgot to floss today--* YOU STINKIN' COP?!

UNFF

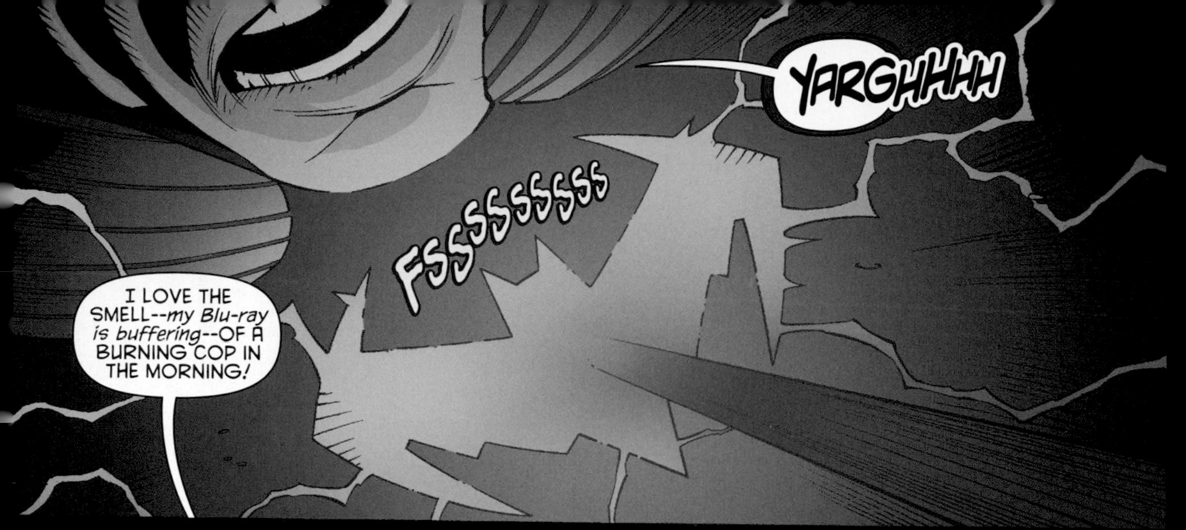
YARGHHHH
FSSSSSSSSS
I LOVE THE SMELL--*my Blu-ray is buffering*--OF A BURNING COP IN THE MORNING!

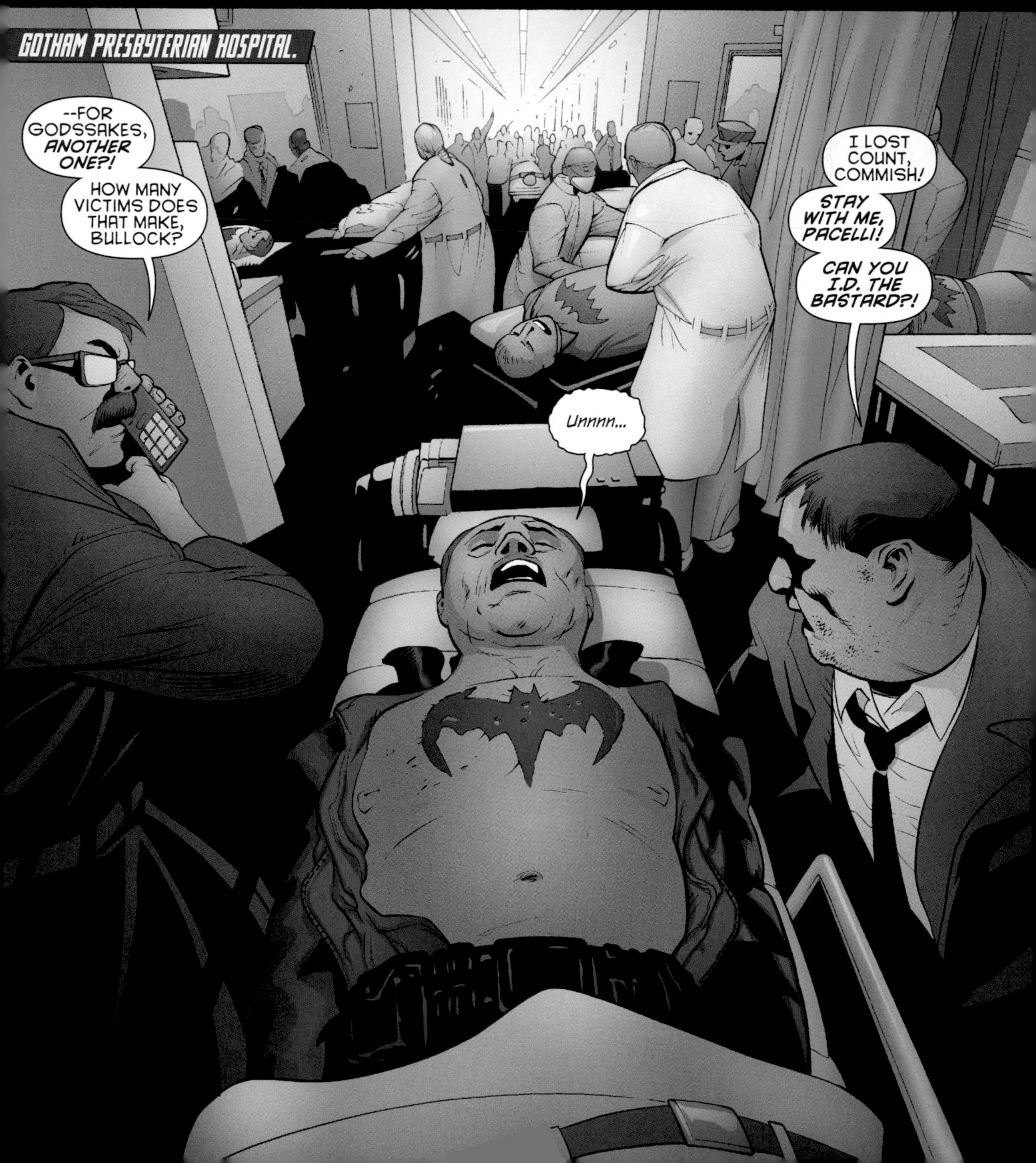
GOTHAM PRESBYTERIAN HOSPITAL.
--FOR GODSSAKES, ***ANOTHER ONE?!***
HOW MANY VICTIMS DOES THAT MAKE, BULLOCK?
I LOST COUNT, COMMISH!
STAY WITH ME, PACELLI!
CAN YOU I.D. THE BASTARD?!
Unnnn...

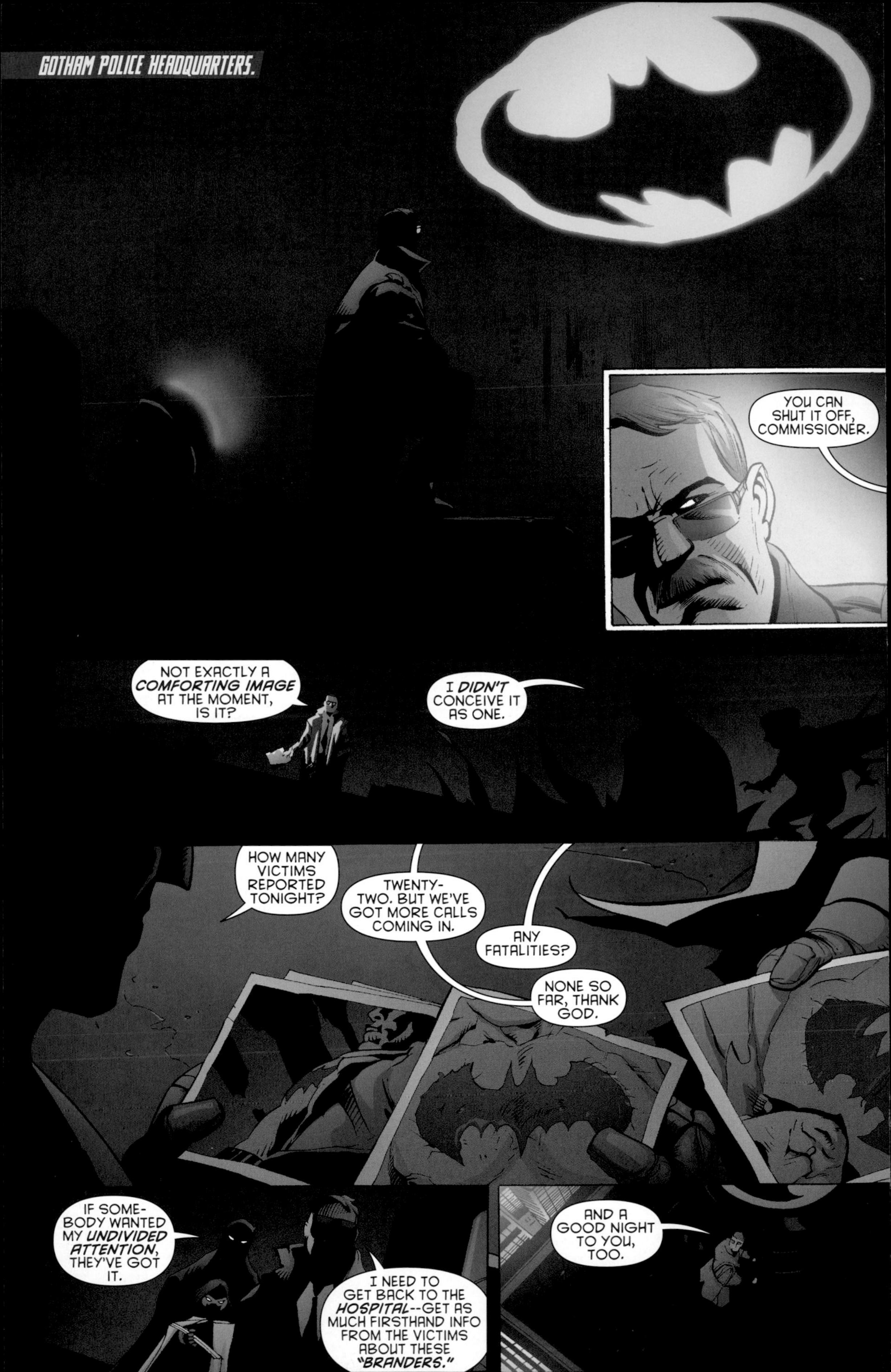
GOTHAM POLICE HEADQUARTERS.
YOU CAN SHUT IT OFF, COMMISSIONER.
NOT EXACTLY A *COMFORTING IMAGE* AT THE MOMENT, IS IT?
I *DIDN'T* CONCEIVE IT AS ONE.
HOW MANY VICTIMS REPORTED TONIGHT?
TWENTY-TWO. BUT WE'VE GOT MORE CALLS COMING IN.
ANY FATALITIES?
NONE SO FAR, THANK GOD.
IF SOMEBODY WANTED MY *UNDIVIDED ATTENTION*, THEY'VE GOT IT.
I NEED TO GET BACK TO THE *HOSPITAL*--GET AS MUCH FIRSTHAND INFO FROM THE VICTIMS ABOUT THESE *"BRANDERS."*
AND A GOOD NIGHT TO YOU, TOO.

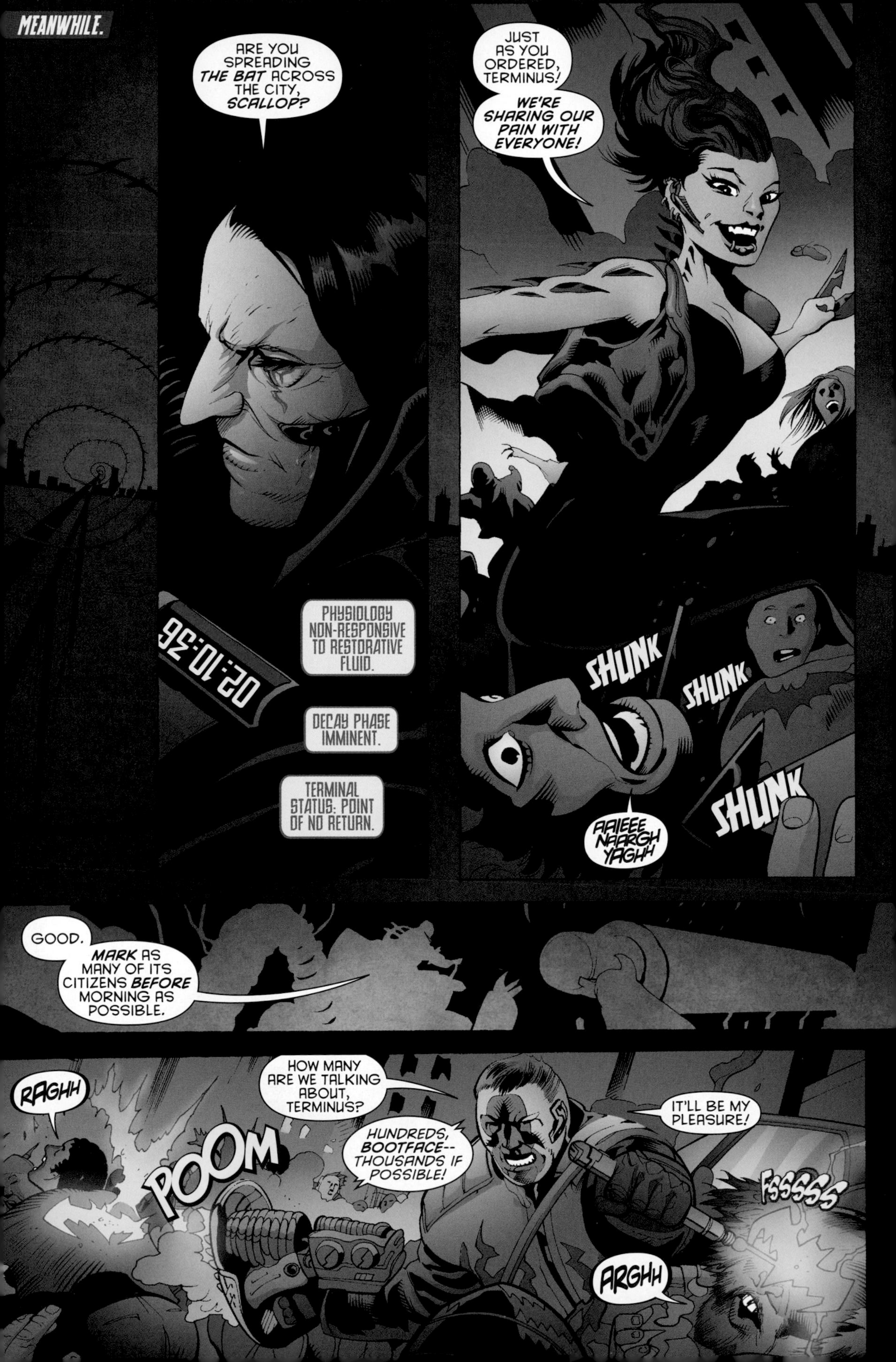
MEANWHILE.
ARE YOU SPREADING THE BAT ACROSS THE CITY, SCALLOP?
JUST AS YOU ORDERED, TERMINUS!
WE'RE SHARING OUR PAIN WITH EVERYONE!
02:10:36
PHYSIOLOGY NON-RESPONSIVE TO RESTORATIVE FLUID.
DECAY PHASE IMMINENT.
TERMINAL STATUS: POINT OF NO RETURN.
SHUNK
SHUNK
SHUNK
AAIEEE NAARGH YAGHH
GOOD. MARK AS MANY OF ITS CITIZENS BEFORE MORNING AS POSSIBLE.
RAGHH
POOM
HOW MANY ARE WE TALKING ABOUT, TERMINUS?
HUNDREDS, BOOTFACE-- THOUSANDS IF POSSIBLE!
IT'LL BE MY PLEASURE!
FSSSSS
ARGHH

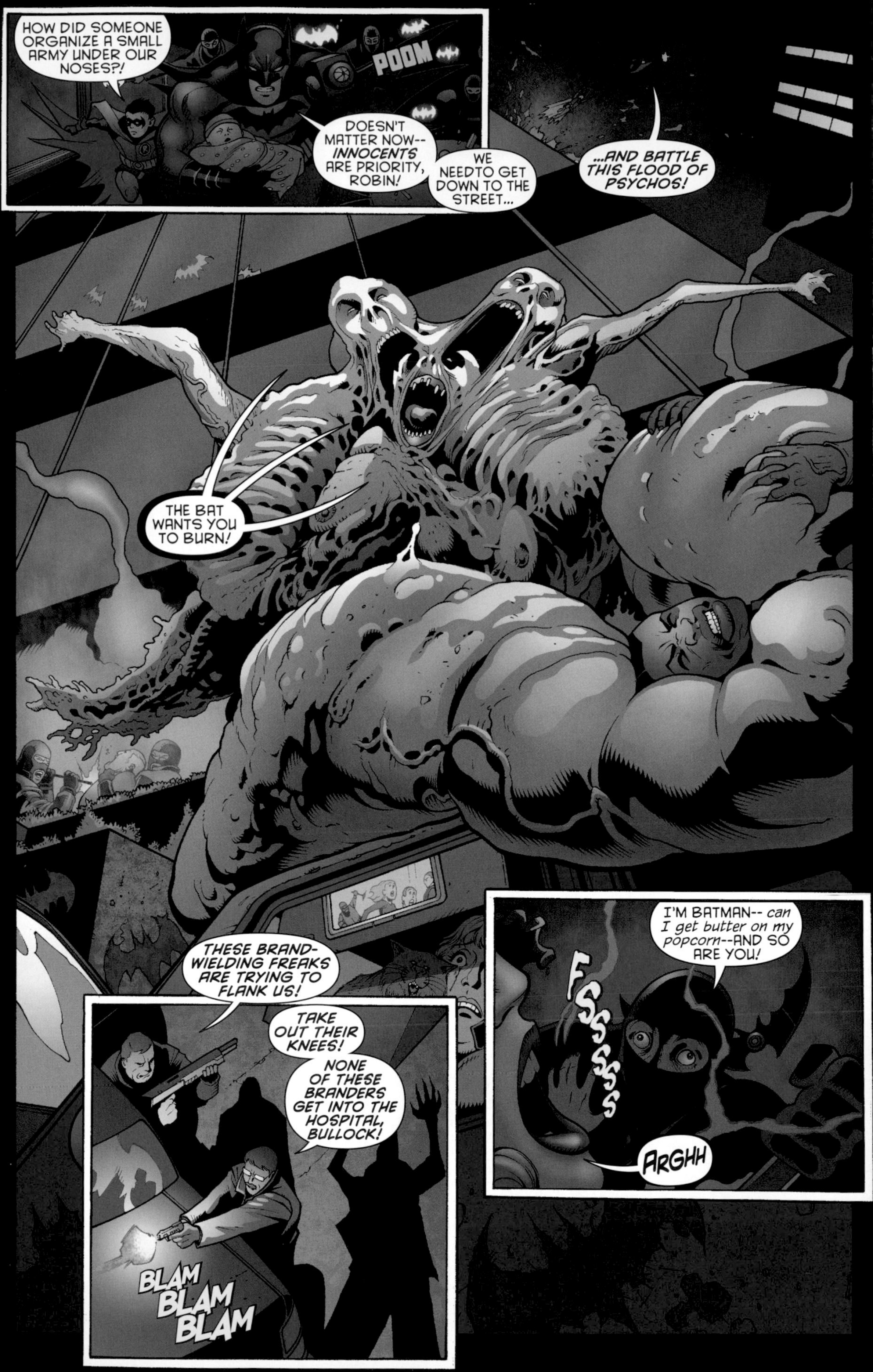
HOW DID SOMEONE ORGANIZE A SMALL ARMY UNDER OUR NOSES?!
POOM
DOESN'T MATTER NOW-- INNOCENTS ARE PRIORITY, ROBIN!
WE NEED TO GET DOWN TO THE STREET...
...AND BATTLE THIS FLOOD OF PSYCHOS!
THE BAT WANTS YOU TO BURN!
THESE BRAND-WIELDING FREAKS ARE TRYING TO FLANK US!
TAKE OUT THEIR KNEES!
NONE OF THESE BRANDERS GET INTO THE HOSPITAL, BULLOCK!
BLAM BLAM BLAM
I'M BATMAN-- can I get butter on my popcorn--AND SO ARE YOU!
FSSSSS
ARGHH

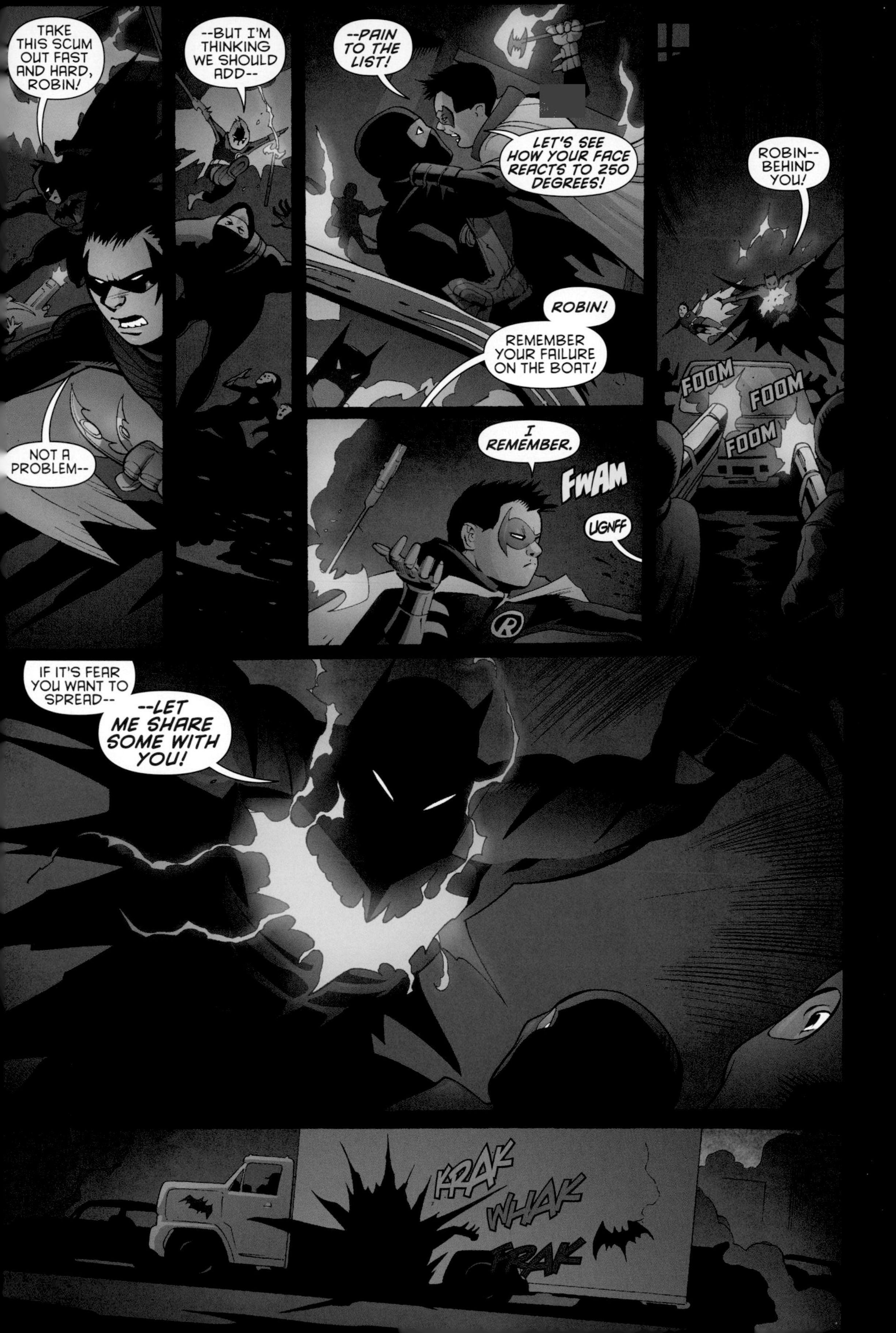
TAKE THIS SCUM OUT FAST AND HARD, ROBIN!
NOT A PROBLEM--
--BUT I'M THINKING WE SHOULD ADD--
--PAIN TO THE LIST!
LET'S SEE HOW YOUR FACE REACTS TO 250 DEGREES!
ROBIN!
REMEMBER YOUR FAILURE ON THE BOAT!
I REMEMBER.
FWAM
UGNFF
ROBIN-- BEHIND YOU!
FOOM
FOOM
FOOM
IF IT'S FEAR YOU WANT TO SPREAD--
--LET ME SHARE SOME WITH YOU!
KRAK
WHAK
KRAK

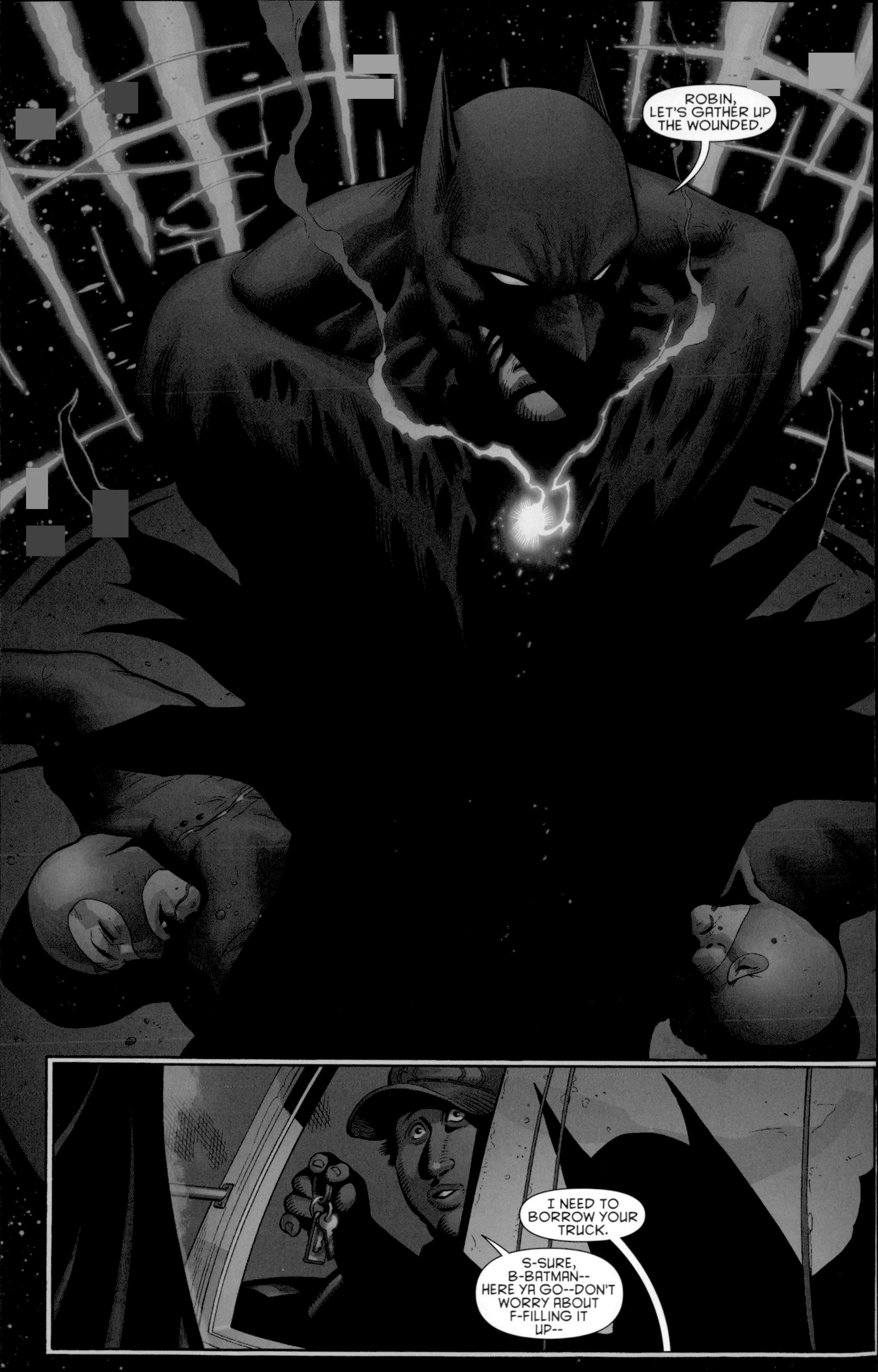
ROBIN, LET'S GATHER UP THE WOUNDED.
I NEED TO BORROW YOUR TRUCK.
S-SURE, B-BATMAN-- HERE YA GO--DON'T WORRY ABOUT F-FILLING IT UP--

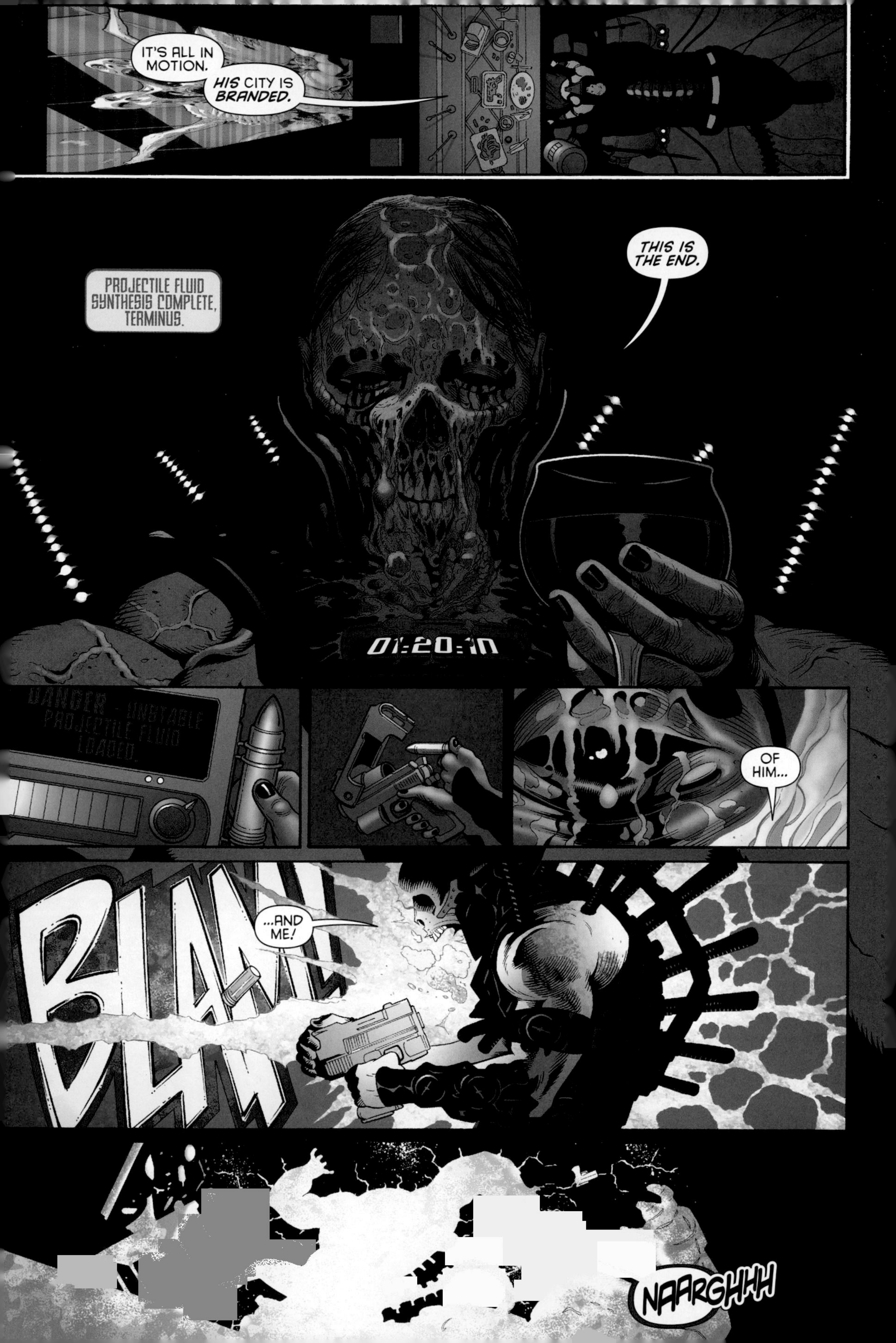
IT'S ALL IN MOTION.
HIS CITY IS BRANDED.
PROJECTILE FLUID SYNTHESIS COMPLETE, TERMINUS.
THIS IS THE END.
01:20:10
DANGER - UNSTABLE PROJECTILE FLUID LOADED.
OF HIM...
BLAM
...AND ME!
NAARGHHH

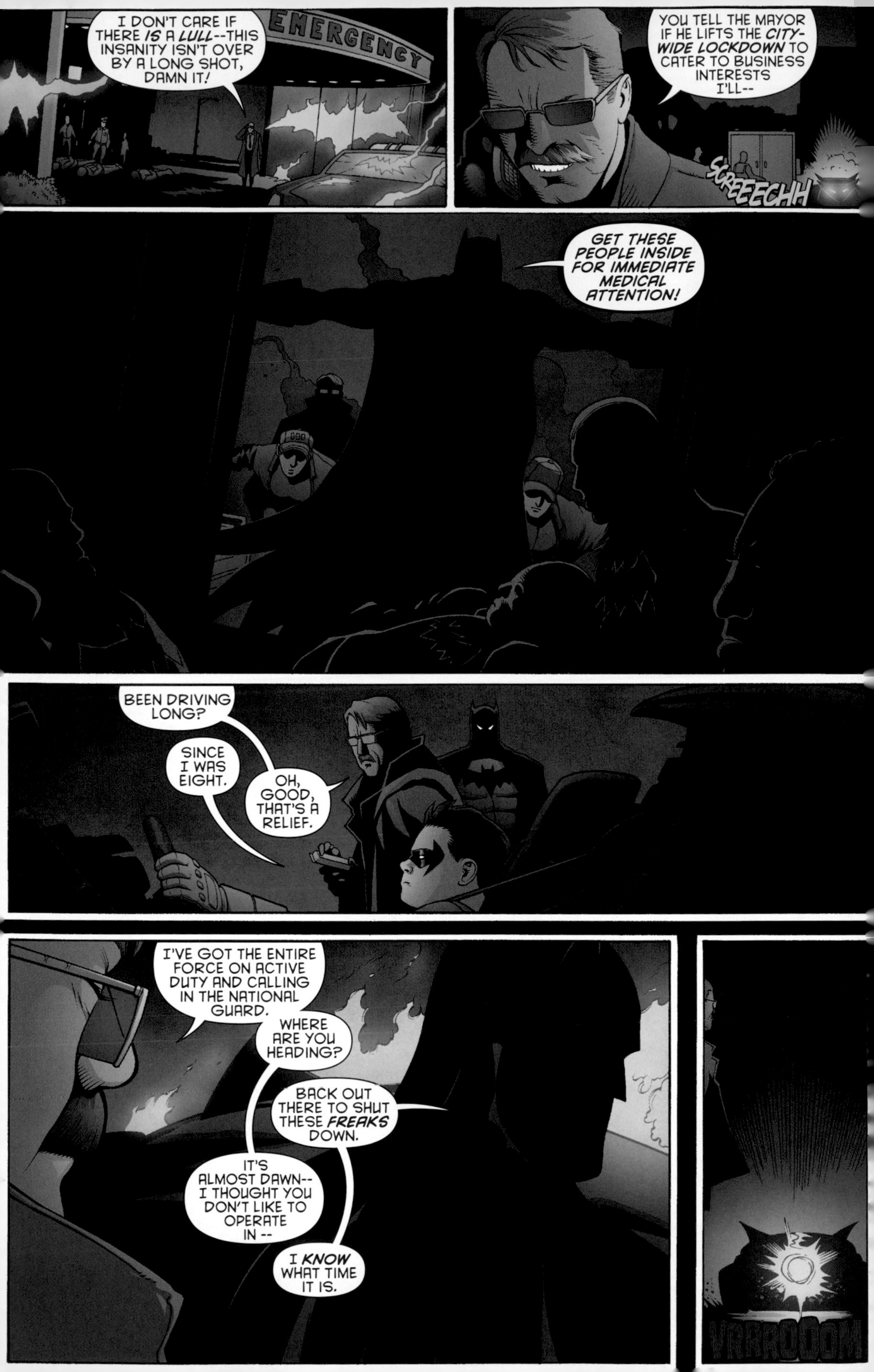
EMERGENCY
I DON'T CARE IF THERE *IS* A *LULL*--THIS INSANITY ISN'T OVER BY A LONG SHOT, DAMN IT!
YOU TELL THE MAYOR IF HE LIFTS THE *CITY-WIDE LOCKDOWN* TO CATER TO BUSINESS INTERESTS I'LL--
SCREEEECHH
GET THESE PEOPLE INSIDE FOR IMMEDIATE MEDICAL ATTENTION!
BEEN DRIVING LONG?
SINCE I WAS EIGHT.
OH, GOOD, THAT'S A RELIEF.
I'VE GOT THE ENTIRE FORCE ON ACTIVE DUTY AND CALLING IN THE NATIONAL GUARD.
WHERE ARE YOU HEADING?
BACK OUT THERE TO SHUT THESE *FREAKS* DOWN.
IT'S ALMOST DAWN--I THOUGHT YOU DON'T LIKE TO OPERATE IN --
I *KNOW* WHAT TIME IT IS.
VRRROOOM

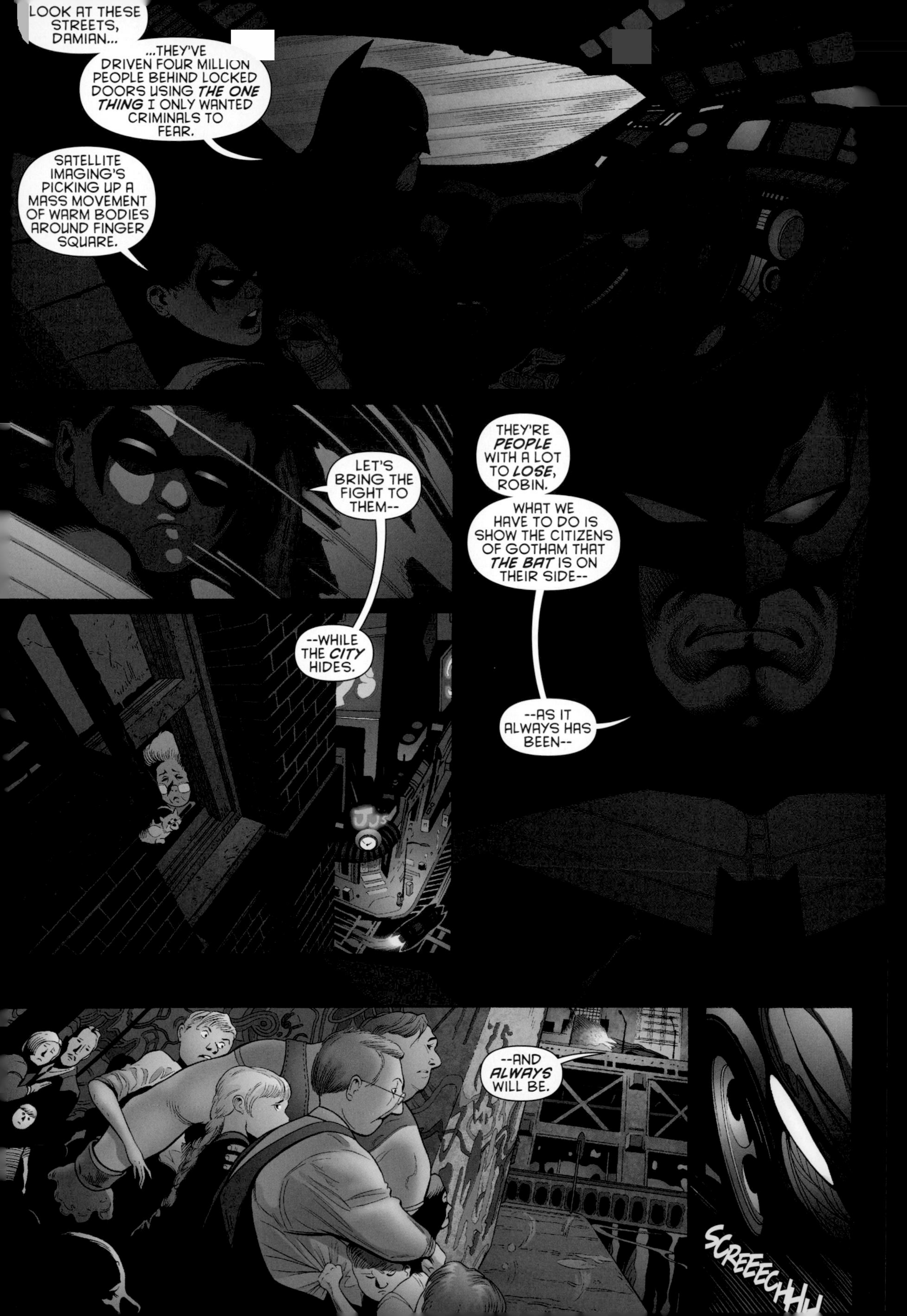
LOOK AT THESE STREETS, DAMIAN...
...THEY'VE DRIVEN FOUR MILLION PEOPLE BEHIND LOCKED DOORS USING *THE ONE THING* I ONLY WANTED CRIMINALS TO FEAR.
SATELLITE IMAGING'S PICKING UP A MASS MOVEMENT OF WARM BODIES AROUND FINGER SQUARE.
LET'S BRING THE FIGHT TO THEM--
--WHILE THE *CITY* HIDES.
THEY'RE *PEOPLE* WITH A LOT TO *LOSE*, ROBIN.
WHAT WE HAVE TO DO IS SHOW THE CITIZENS OF GOTHAM THAT *THE BAT* IS ON THEIR SIDE--
--AS IT ALWAYS HAS BEEN--
--AND *ALWAYS* WILL BE.
SCREEECHHH

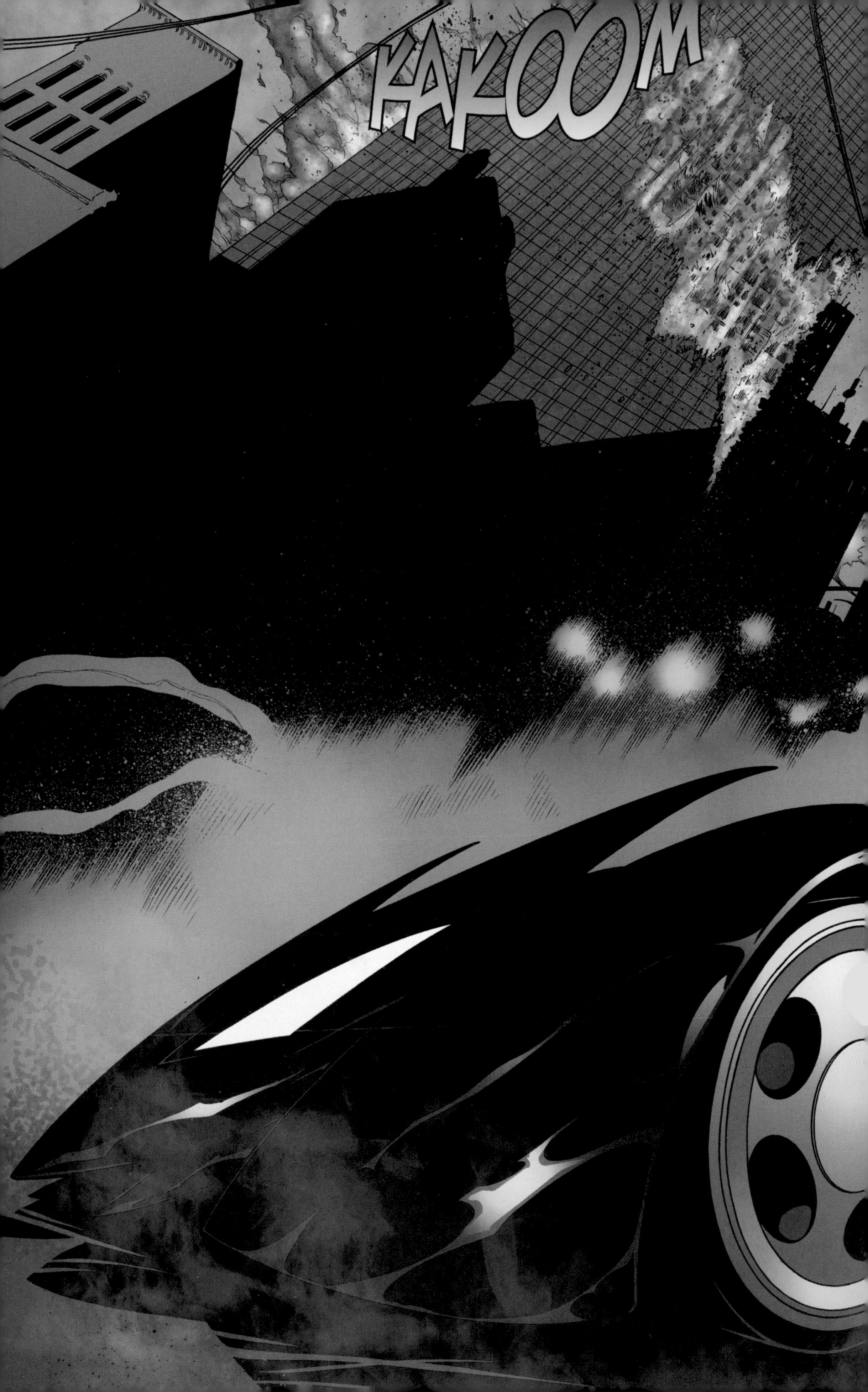
KAKOOM

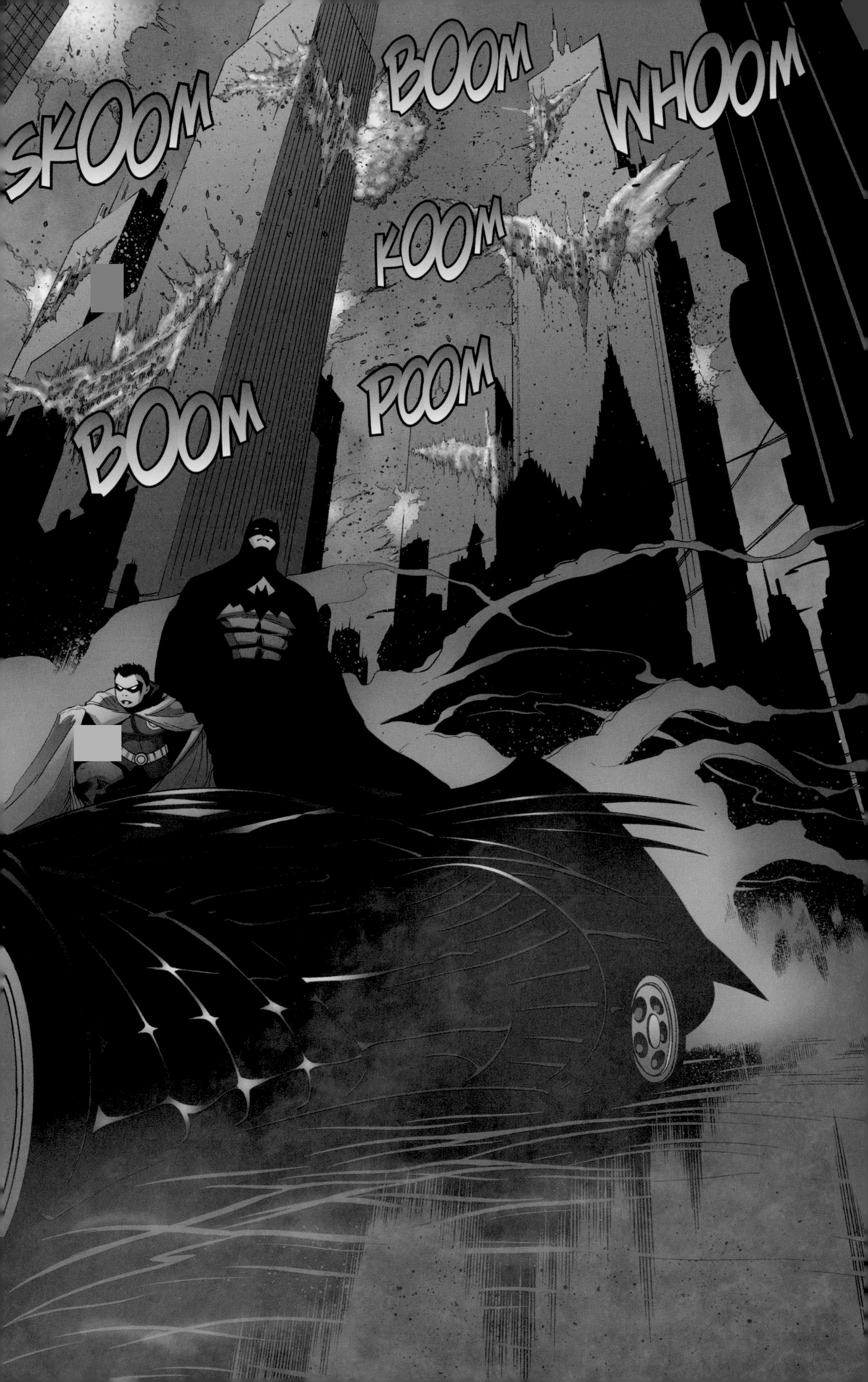
SKOOM
BOOM
WHOOM
KOOM
BOOM
POOM

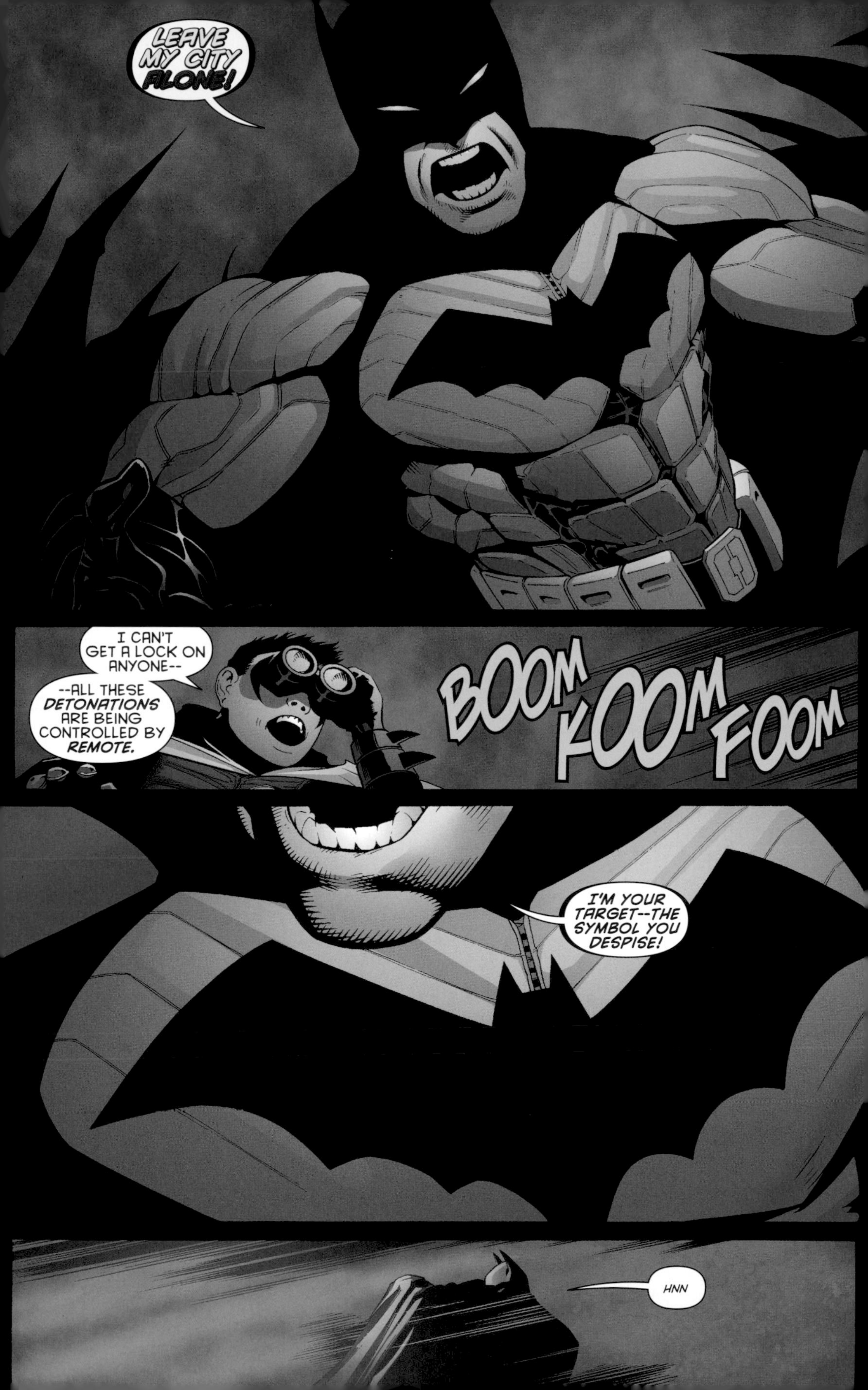
LEAVE MY CITY ALONE!
I CAN'T GET A LOCK ON ANYONE--
--ALL THESE DETONATIONS ARE BEING CONTROLLED BY REMOTE.
BOOM KOOM FOOM
I'M YOUR TARGET--THE SYMBOL YOU DESPISE!
HNN

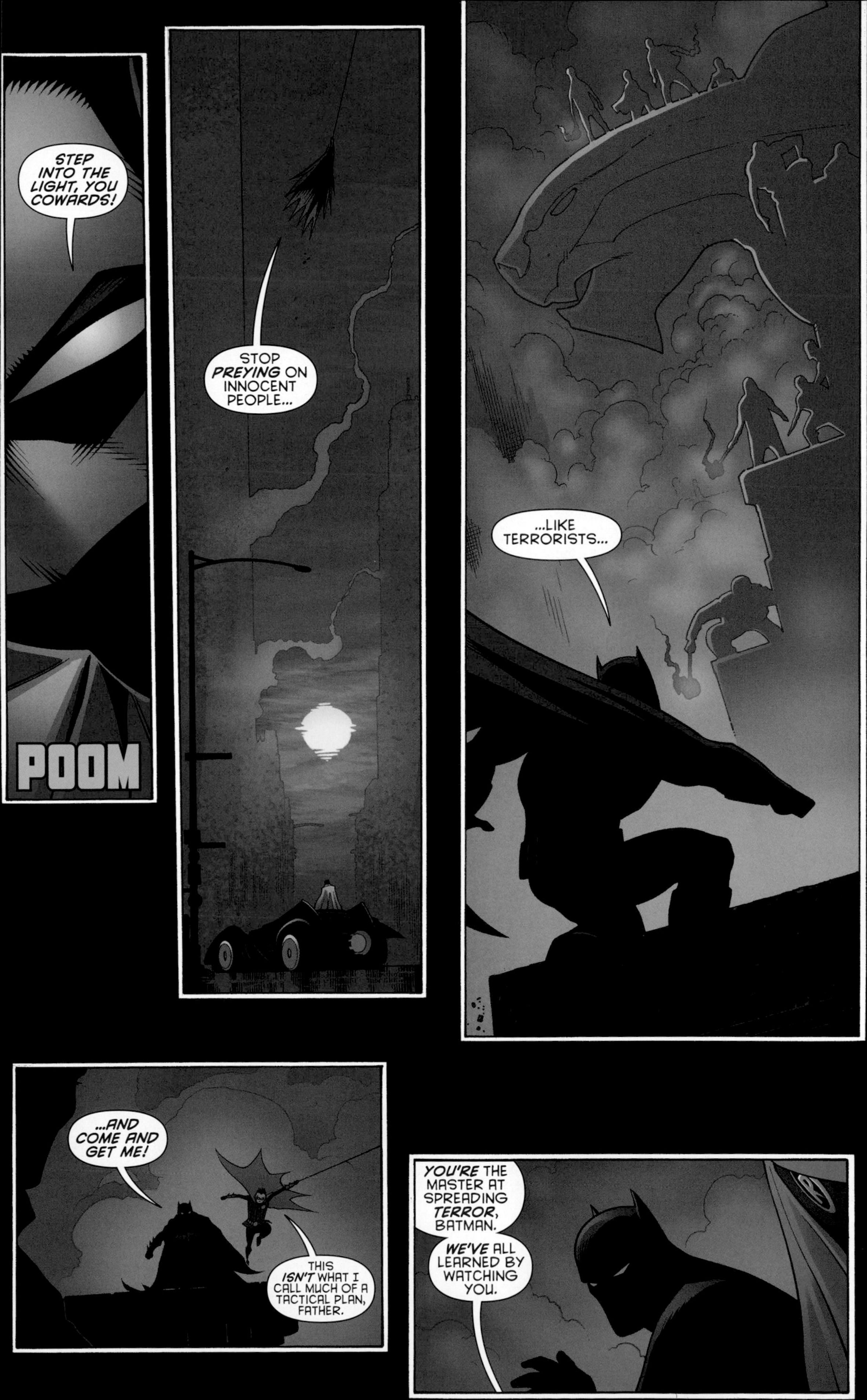
STEP INTO THE LIGHT, YOU COWARDS!
POOM
STOP PREYING ON INNOCENT PEOPLE...
...LIKE TERRORISTS...
...AND COME AND GET ME!
THIS ISN'T WHAT I CALL MUCH OF A TACTICAL PLAN, FATHER.
YOU'RE THE MASTER AT SPREADING TERROR, BATMAN.
WE'VE ALL LEARNED BY WATCHING YOU.

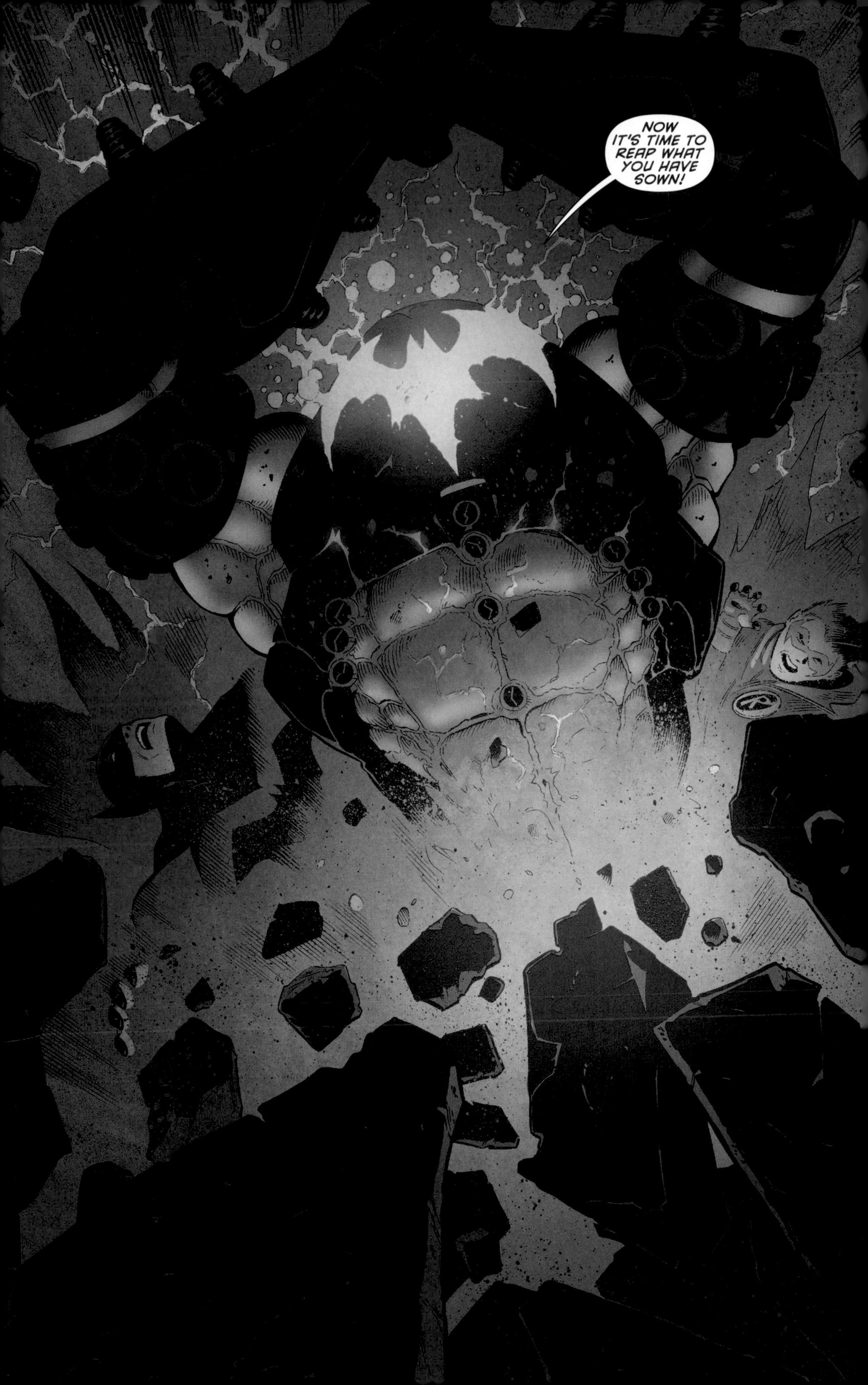
NOW IT'S TIME TO REAP WHAT YOU HAVE SOWN!

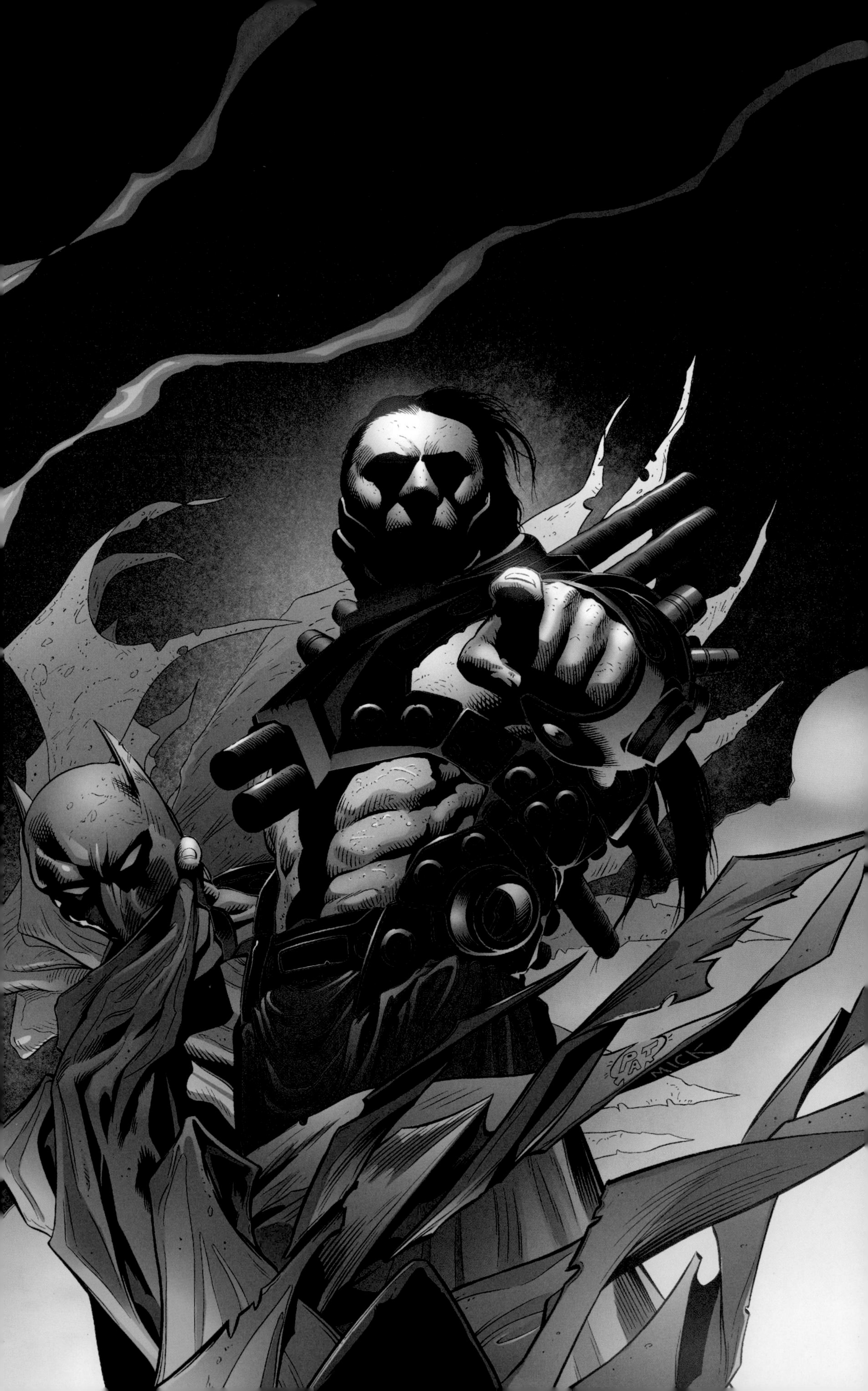

TERMINUS: LAST GASP

PETER J. TOMASI writer PATRICK GLEASON penciller MICK GRAY inker

cover by GLEASON, GRAY & KALISZ

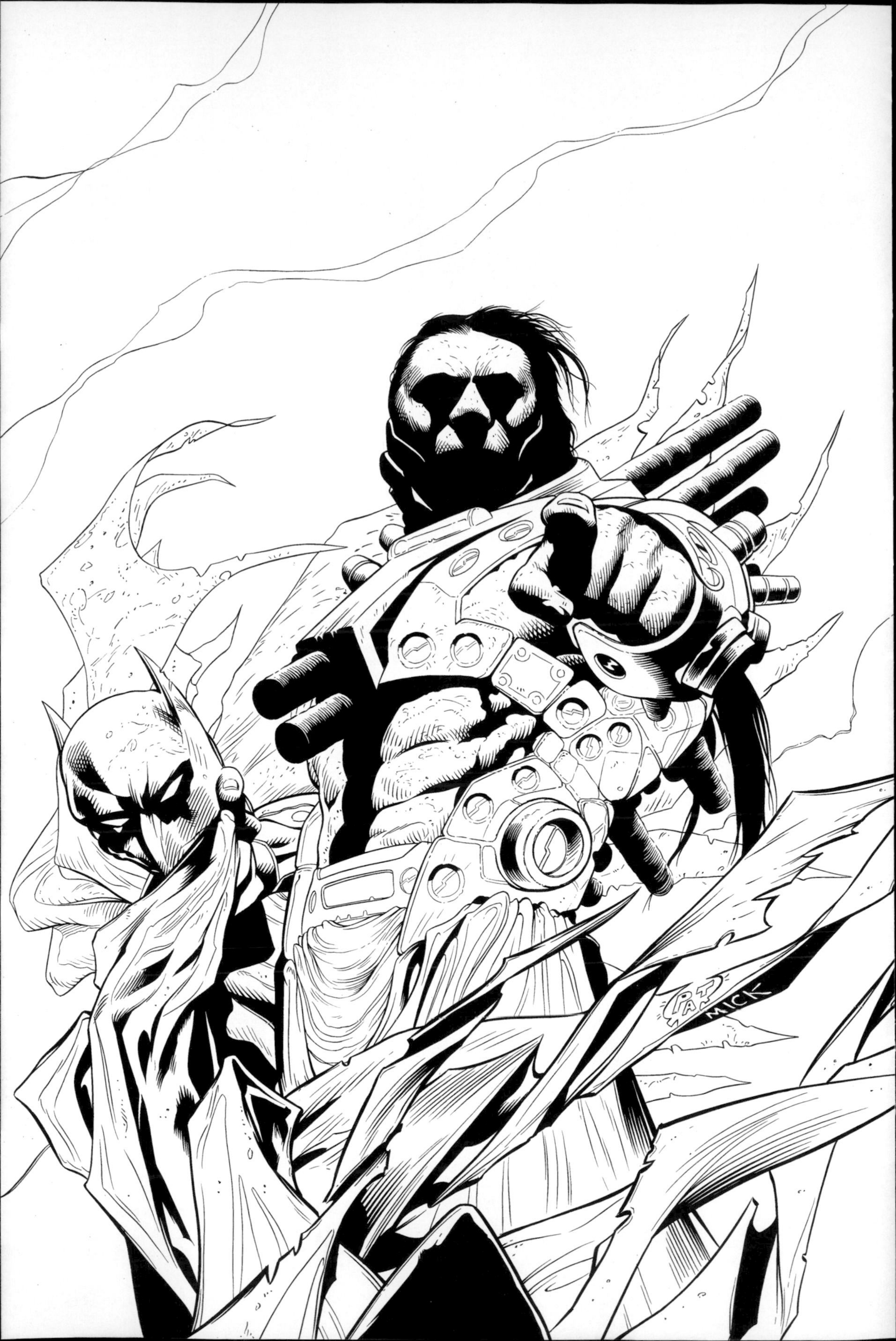

PAT
MICK

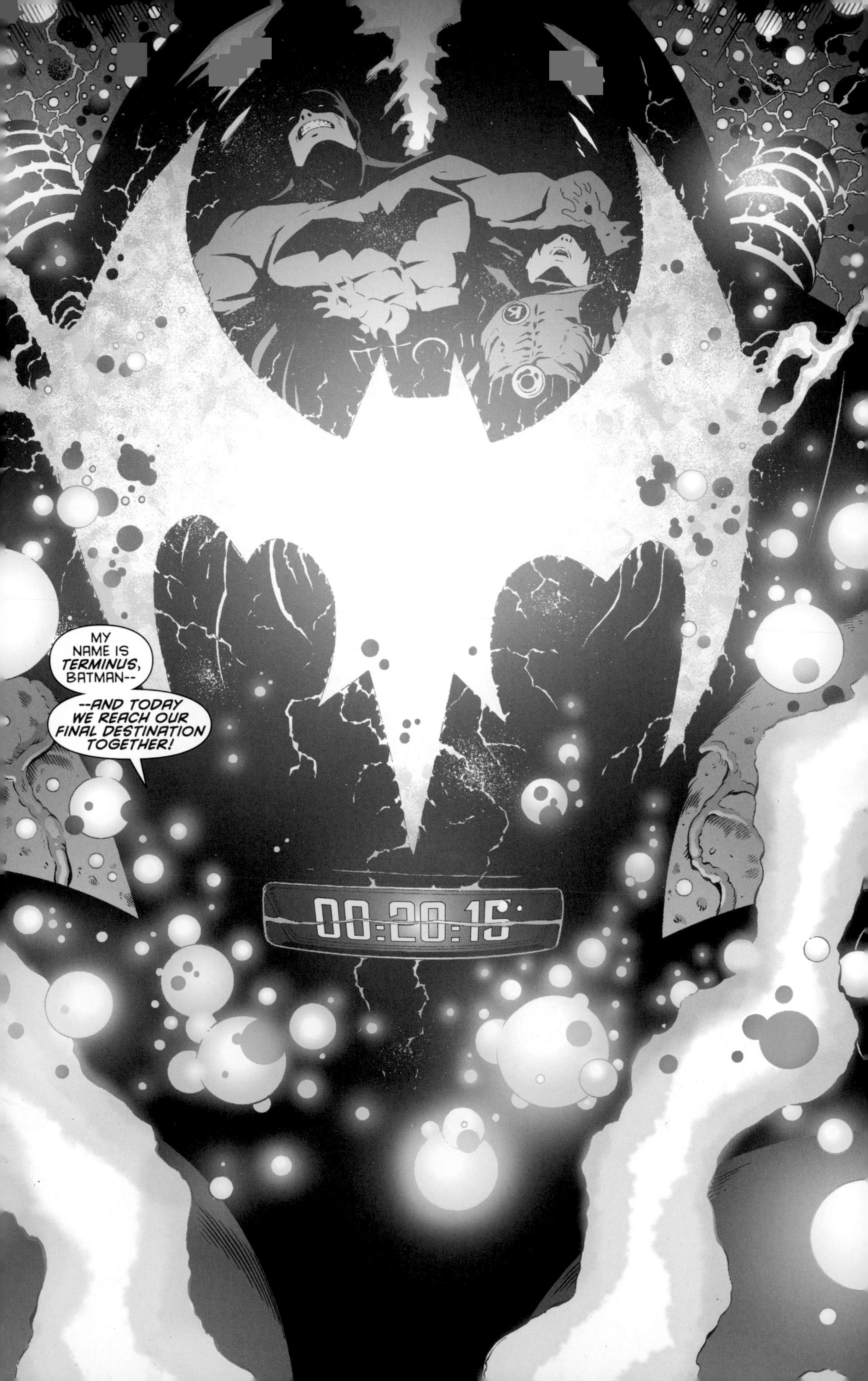
MY NAME IS TERMINUS, BATMAN--
--AND TODAY WE REACH OUR FINAL DESTINATION TOGETHER!
00:20:15

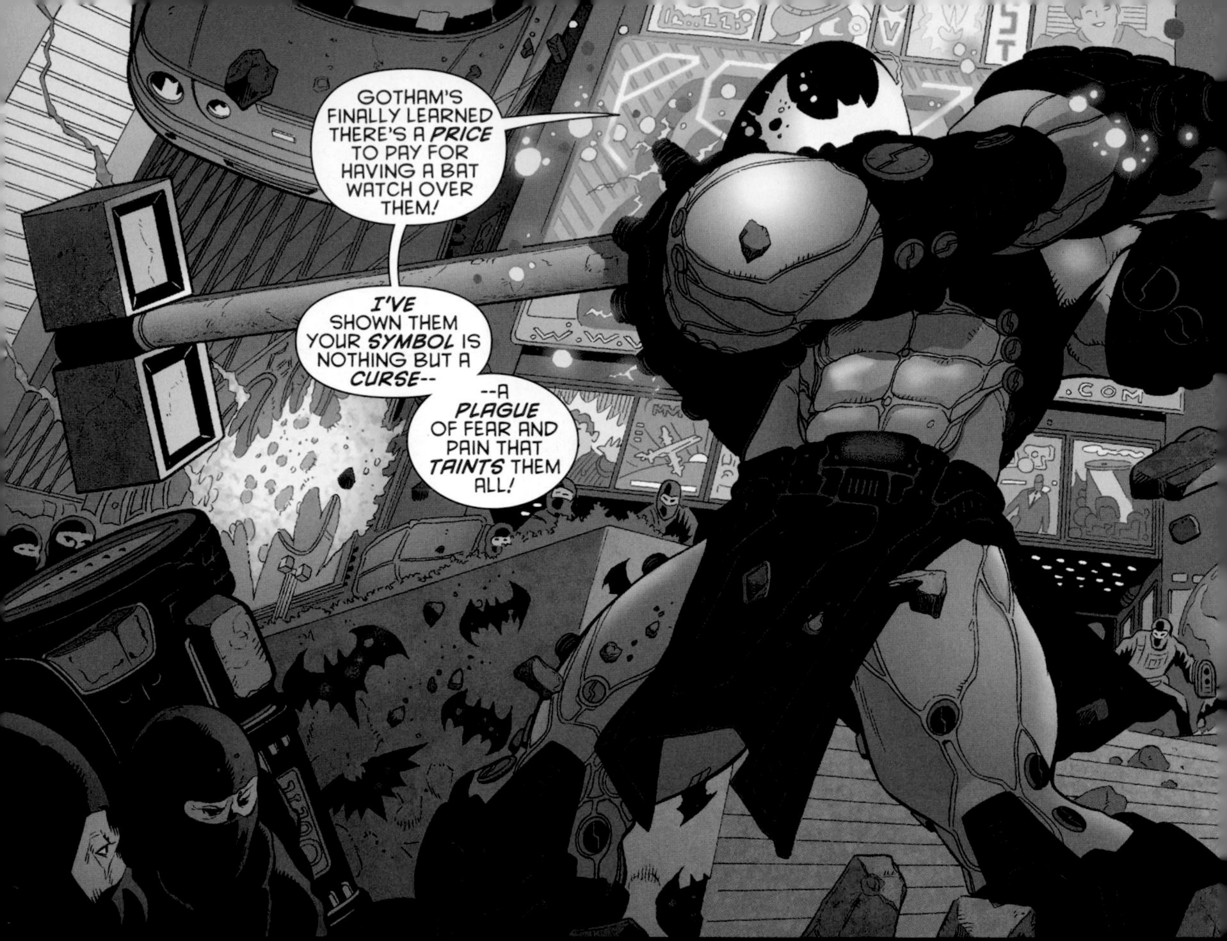
GOTHAM'S FINALLY LEARNED THERE'S A PRICE TO PAY FOR HAVING A BAT WATCH OVER THEM!
I'VE SHOWN THEM YOUR SYMBOL IS NOTHING BUT A CURSE--
--A PLAGUE OF FEAR AND PAIN THAT TAINTS THEM ALL!

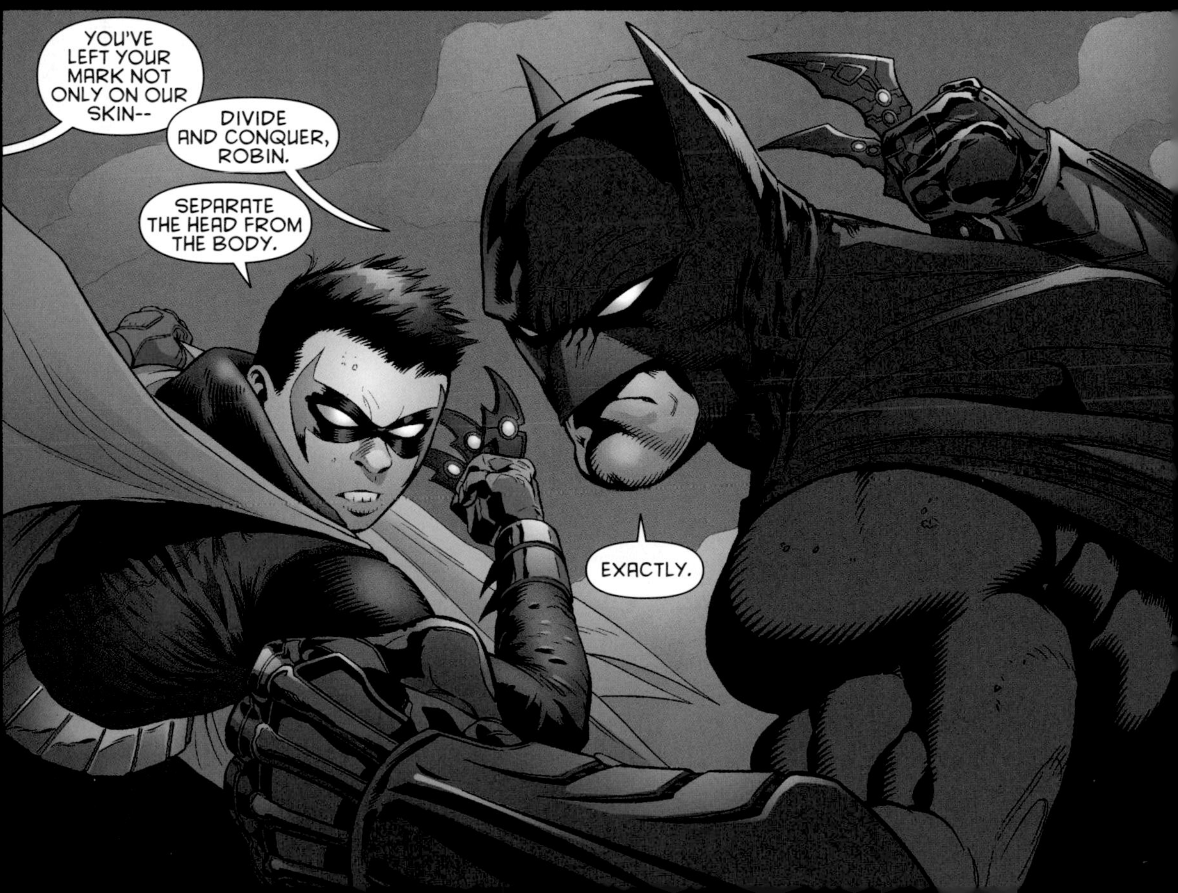
YOU'VE LEFT YOUR MARK NOT ONLY ON OUR SKIN--
DIVIDE AND CONQUER, ROBIN.
SEPARATE THE HEAD FROM THE BODY.
EXACTLY.

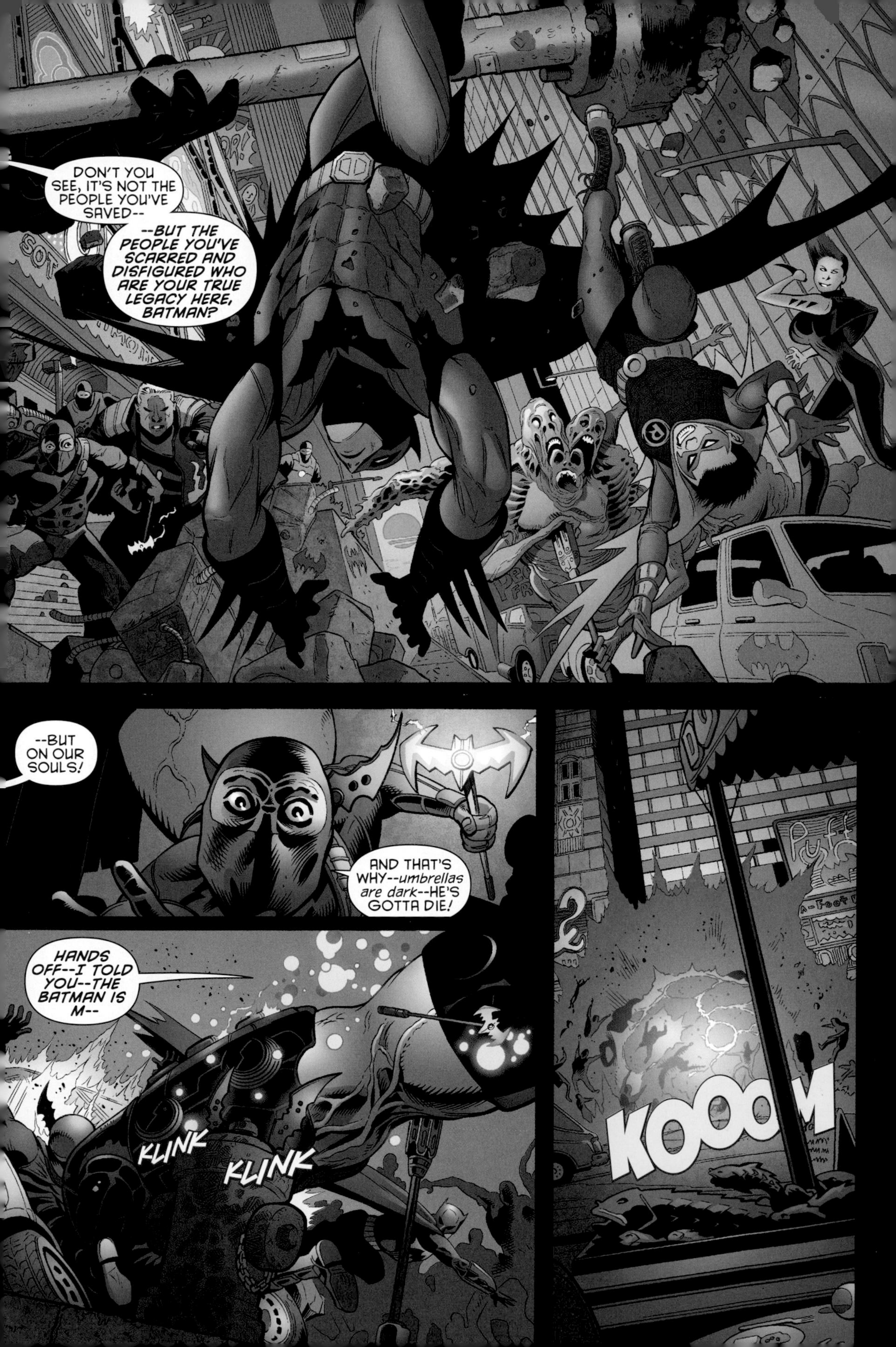
DON'T YOU SEE, IT'S NOT THE PEOPLE YOU'VE SAVED--
--BUT THE PEOPLE YOU'VE SCARRED AND DISFIGURED WHO ARE YOUR TRUE LEGACY HERE, BATMAN?
--BUT ON OUR SOULS!
AND THAT'S WHY--*umbrellas are dark*--HE'S GOTTA DIE!
HANDS OFF--I TOLD YOU--THE BATMAN IS M--
KLINK
KLINK
KOOOM

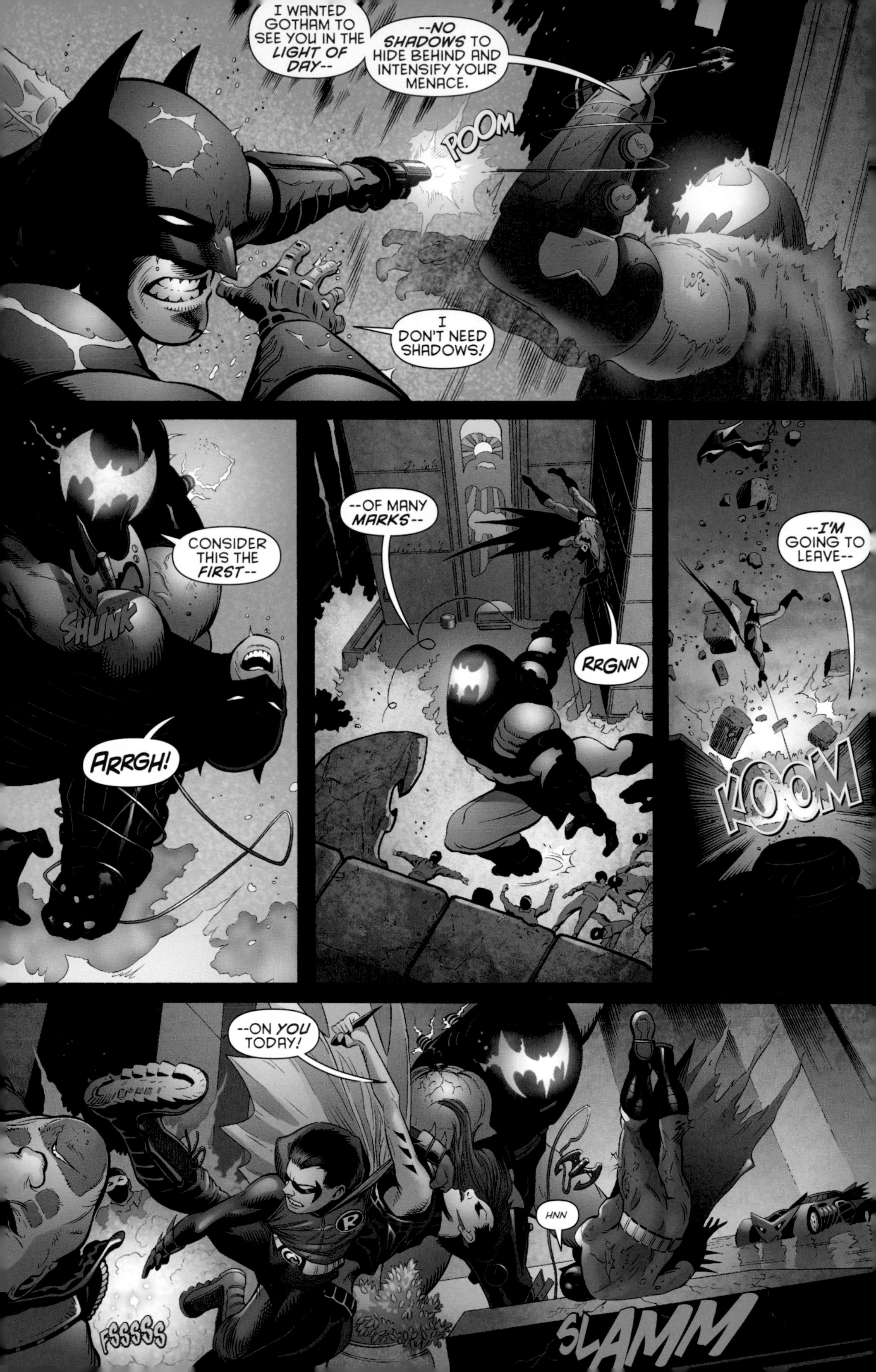
I WANTED GOTHAM TO SEE YOU IN THE LIGHT OF DAY--
--NO SHADOWS TO HIDE BEHIND AND INTENSIFY YOUR MENACE.
POOM
I DON'T NEED SHADOWS!
CONSIDER THIS THE FIRST--
SHUNK
ARRGH!
--OF MANY MARKS--
RRGNN
--I'M GOING TO LEAVE--
KOOM
--ON YOU TODAY!
HNN
FSSSSS
SLAMM

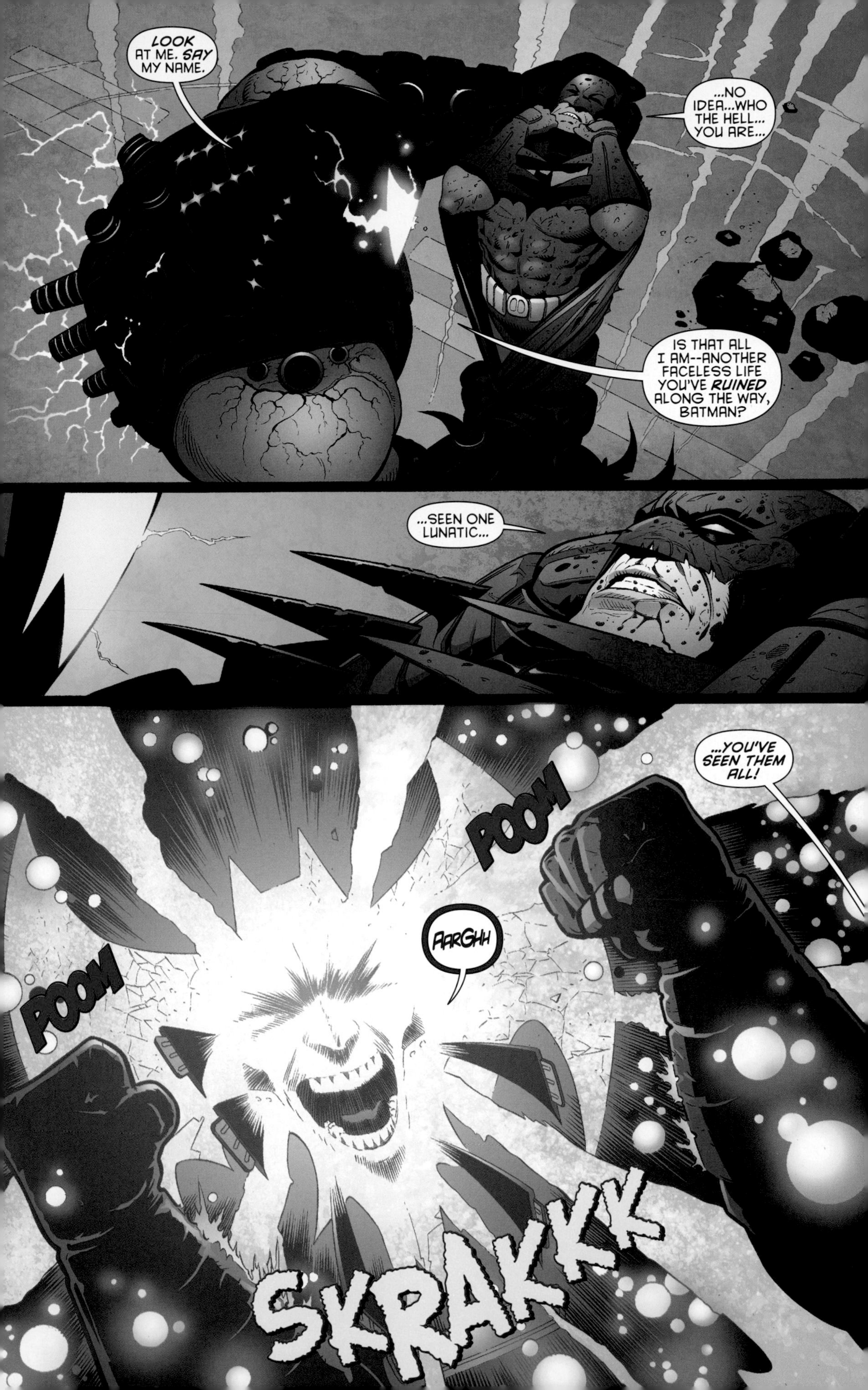
LOOK AT ME. SAY MY NAME.
...NO IDEA...WHO THE HELL... YOU ARE...
IS THAT ALL I AM--ANOTHER FACELESS LIFE YOU'VE RUINED ALONG THE WAY, BATMAN?
...SEEN ONE LUNATIC...
...YOU'VE SEEN THEM ALL!
POOM
AARGHH
POOM
SKRAKK

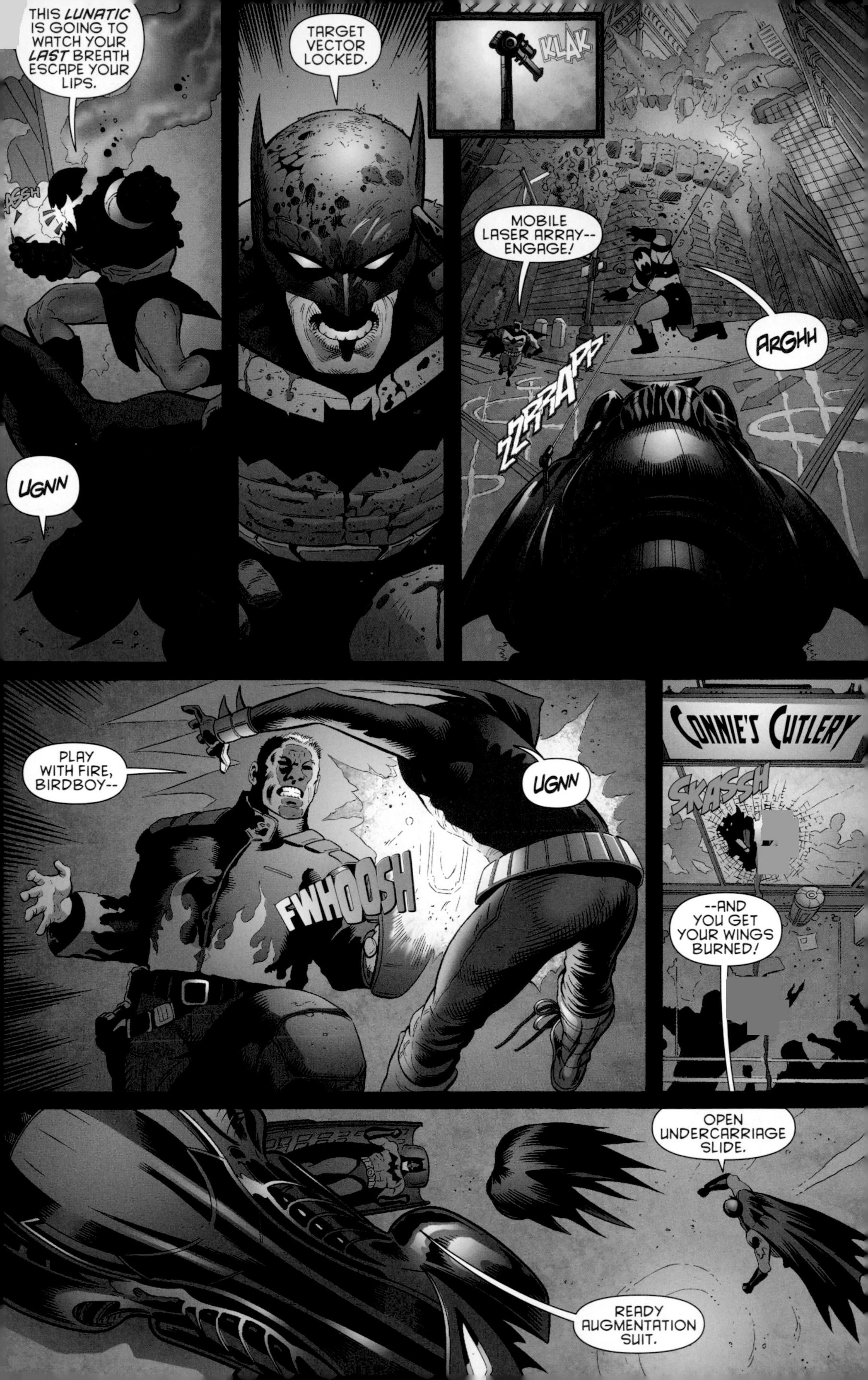
THIS *LUNATIC* IS GOING TO WATCH YOUR *LAST* BREATH ESCAPE YOUR LIPS.
UGNN
TARGET VECTOR LOCKED.
KLAK
MOBILE LASER ARRAY-- ENGAGE!
ZZRRRAPP
ARGHH
PLAY WITH FIRE, BIRDBOY--
UGNN
FWHOOSH
CONNIE'S CUTLERY
SKASSH
--AND YOU GET YOUR WINGS BURNED!
OPEN UNDERCARRIAGE SLIDE.
READY AUGMENTATION SUIT.

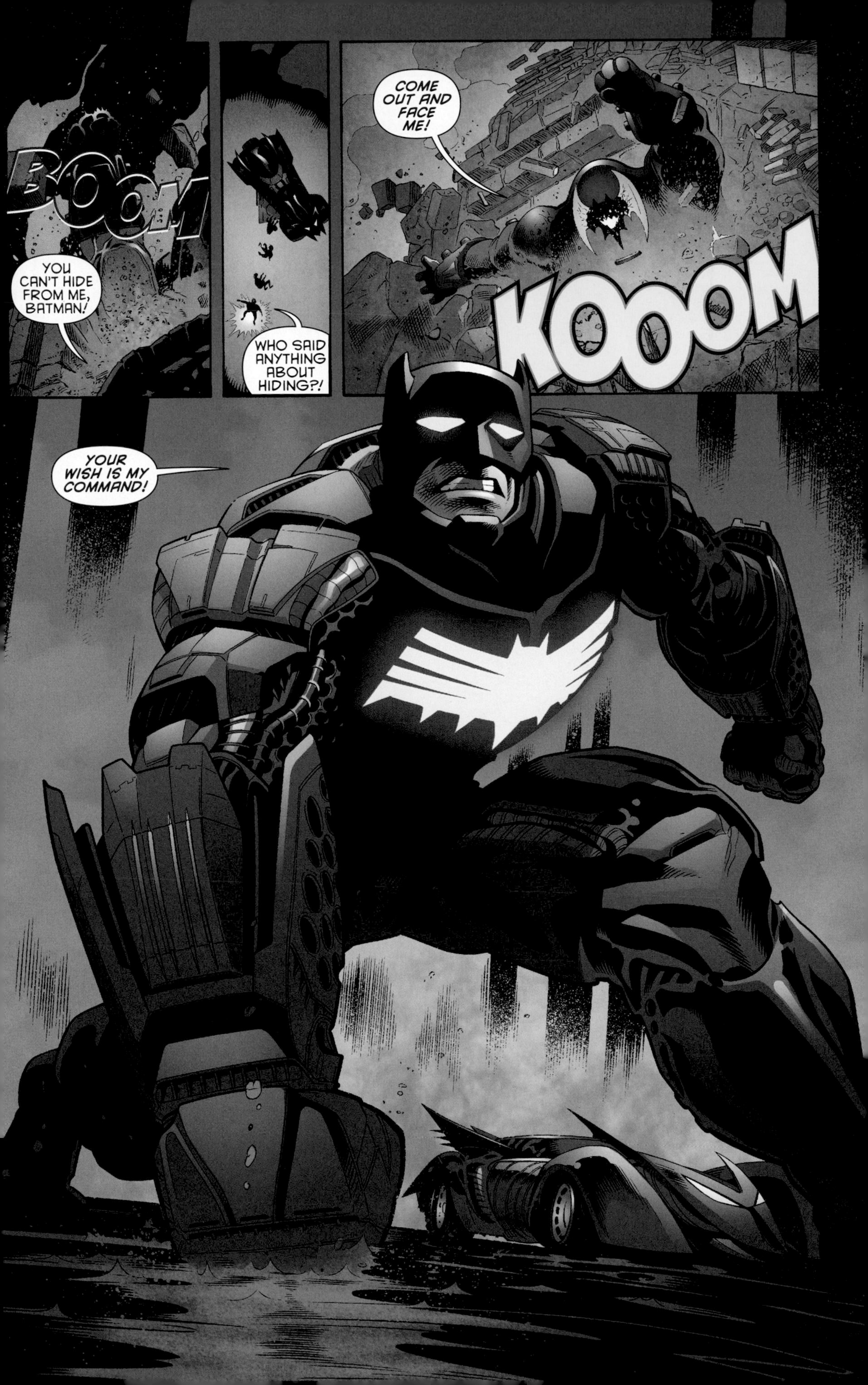
BOOM
YOU CAN'T HIDE FROM ME, BATMAN!
WHO SAID ANYTHING ABOUT HIDING?!
COME OUT AND FACE ME!
KOOOM
YOUR WISH IS MY COMMAND!

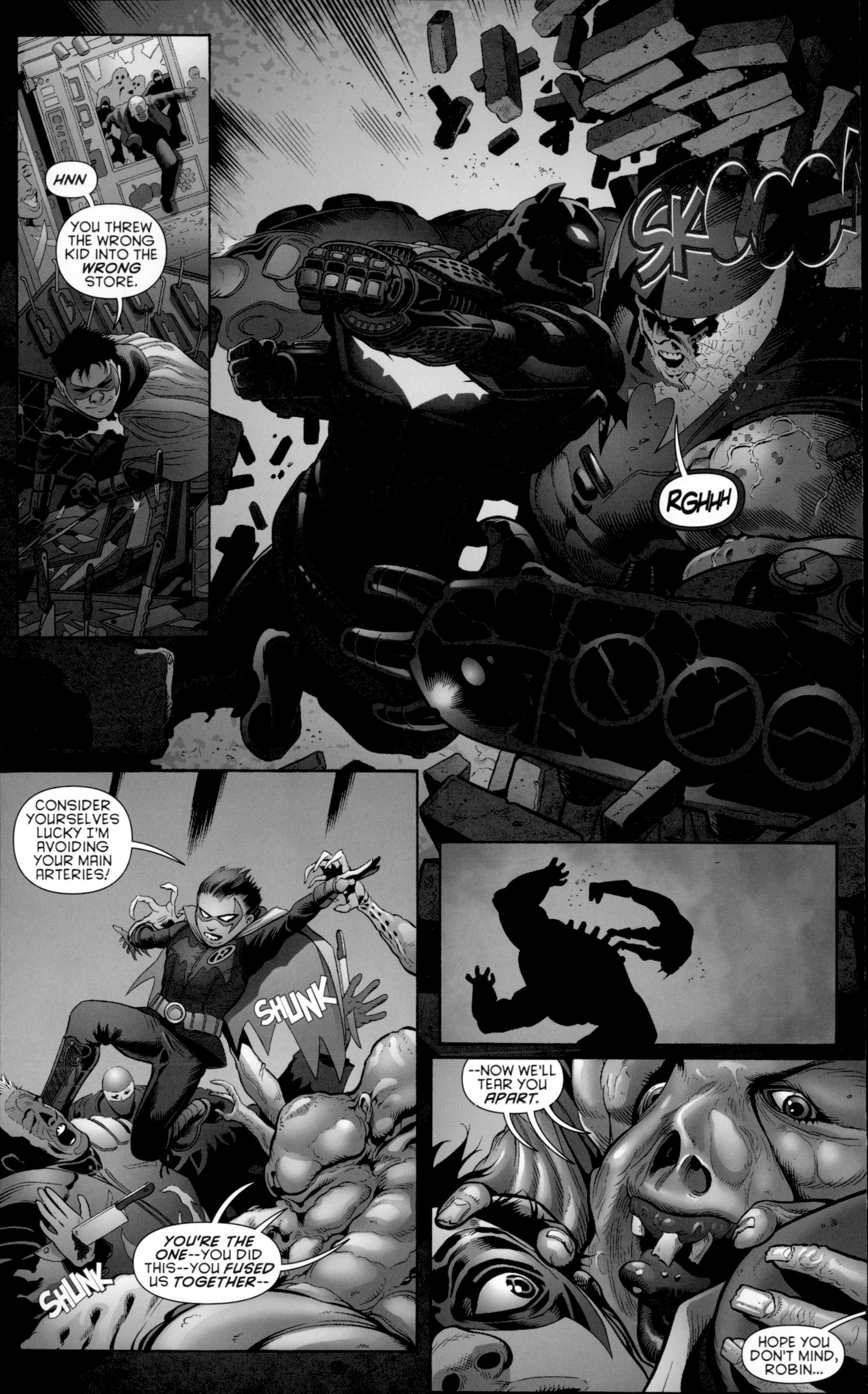
HNN
YOU THREW THE WRONG KID INTO THE WRONG STORE.
SKOOOCR
RGHHH
CONSIDER YOURSELVES LUCKY I'M AVOIDING YOUR MAIN ARTERIES!
SHUNK
YOU'RE THE ONE--YOU DID THIS--YOU FUSED US TOGETHER--
SHUNK
--NOW WE'LL TEAR YOU APART.
HOPE YOU DON'T MIND, ROBIN...

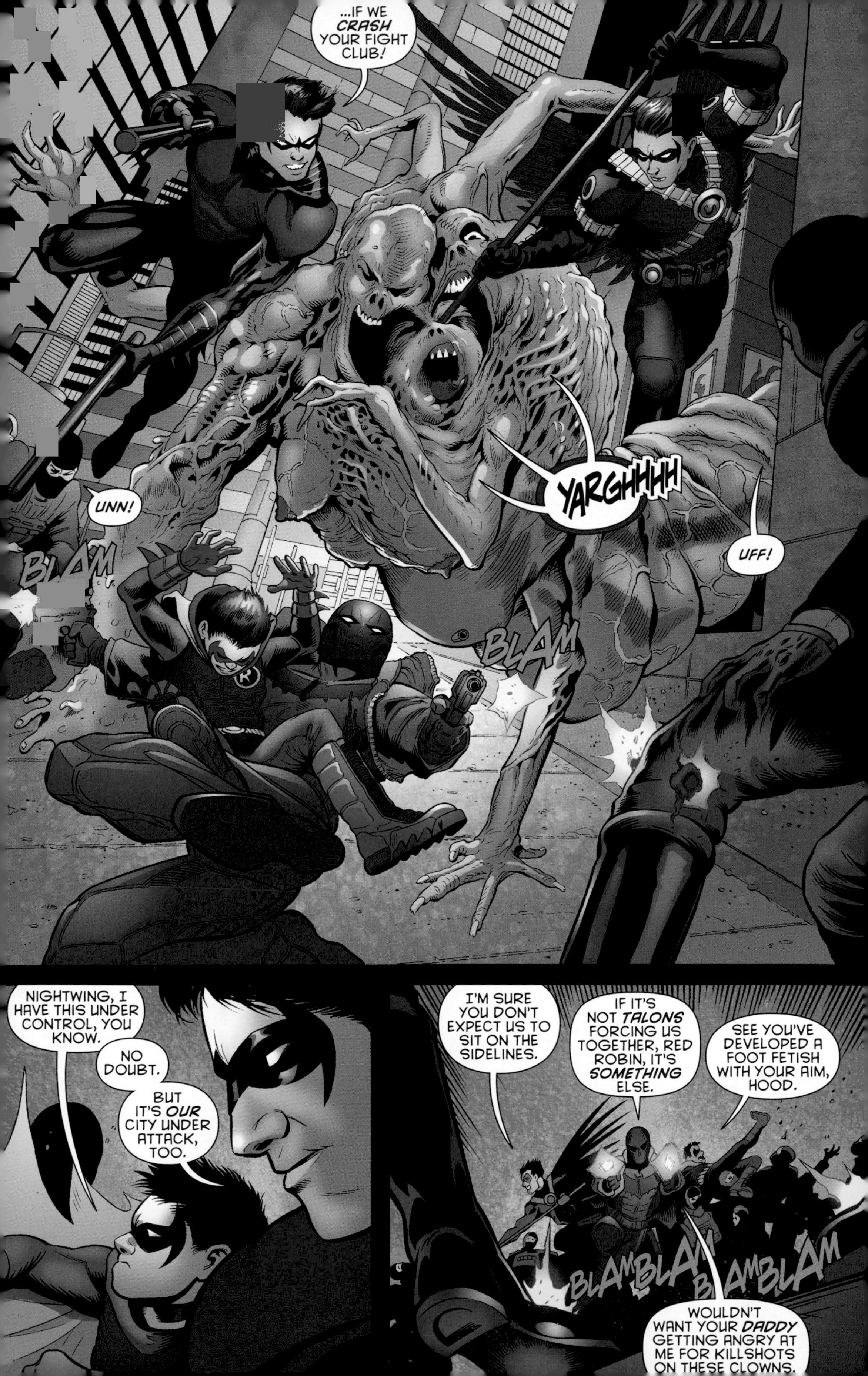
...IF WE CRASH YOUR FIGHT CLUB!
YARGHHHH
UNN!
BLAM
UFF!
BLAM
NIGHTWING, I HAVE THIS UNDER CONTROL, YOU KNOW.
NO DOUBT.
BUT IT'S OUR CITY UNDER ATTACK, TOO.
I'M SURE YOU DON'T EXPECT US TO SIT ON THE SIDELINES.
IF IT'S NOT TALONS FORCING US TOGETHER, RED ROBIN, IT'S SOMETHING ELSE.
SEE YOU'VE DEVELOPED A FOOT FETISH WITH YOUR AIM, HOOD.
BLAMBLAM BLAMBLAM
WOULDN'T WANT YOUR DADDY GETTING ANGRY AT ME FOR KILLSHOTS ON THESE CLOWNS.

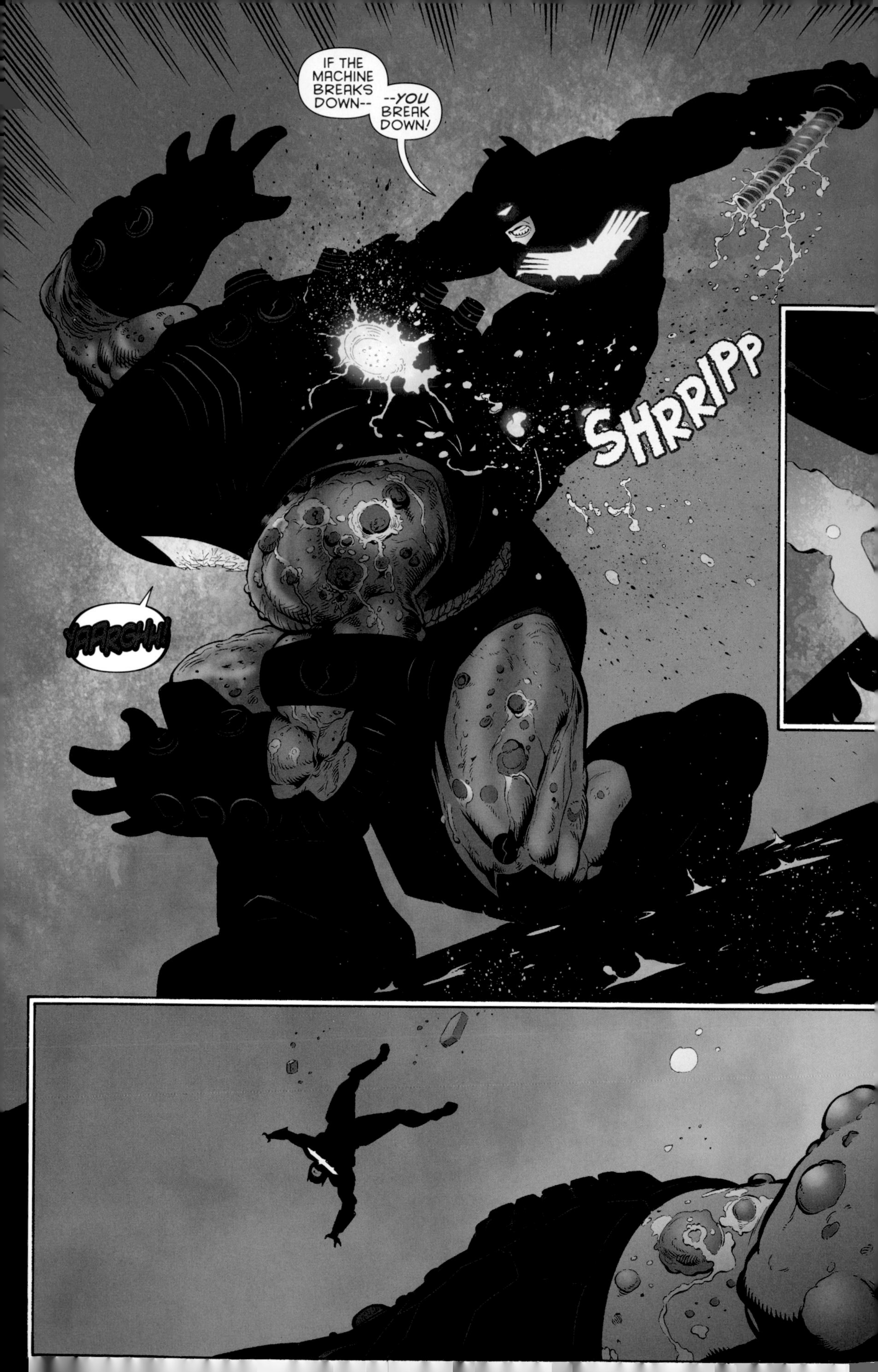
IF THE MACHINE BREAKS DOWN--
--YOU BREAK DOWN!
SHRRIPP
YAARGHH!

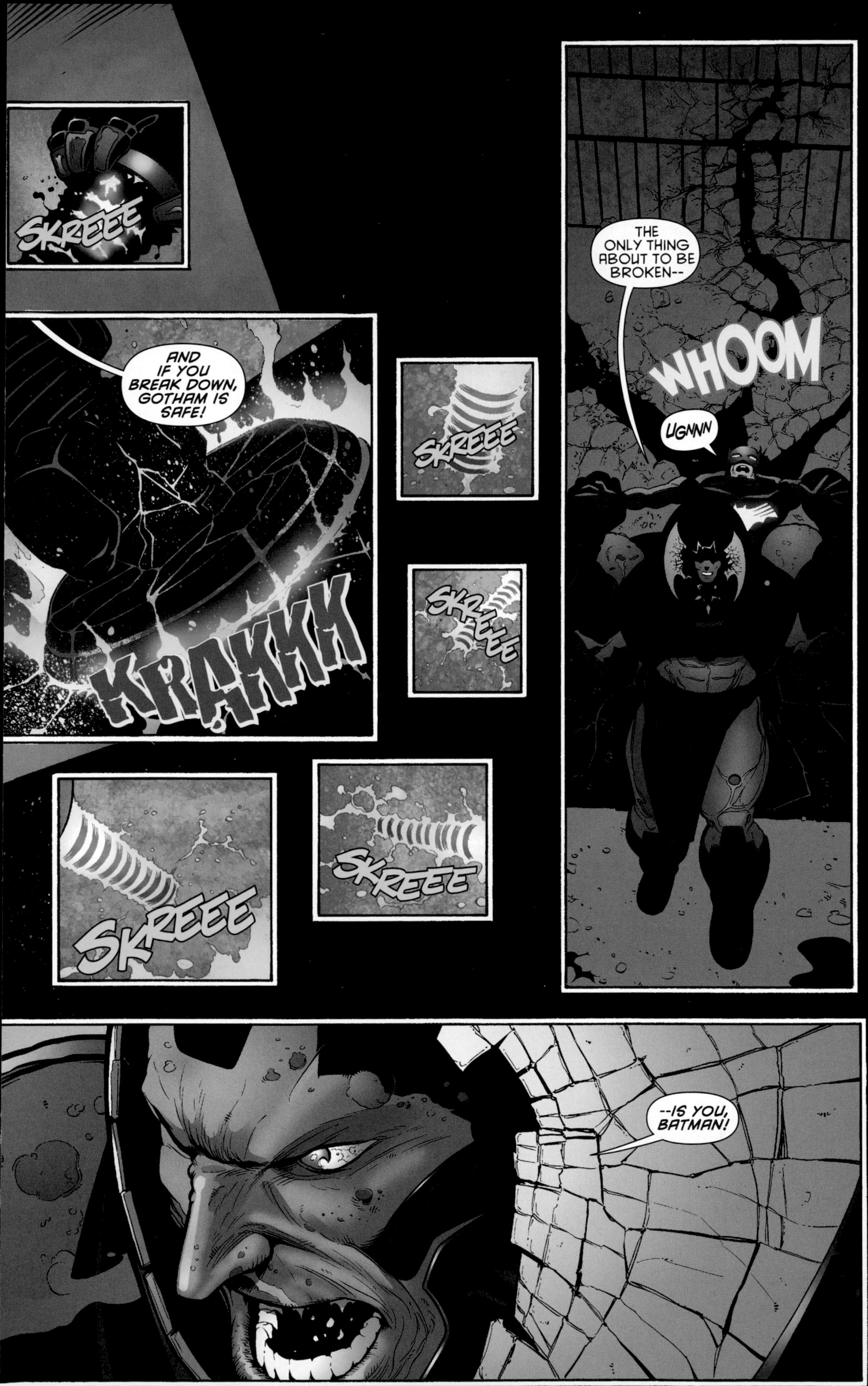
SKREEE
AND IF YOU BREAK DOWN, GOTHAM IS SAFE!
KRAKKK
SKREEE
SKREEE
SKREEE
SKREEE
THE ONLY THING ABOUT TO BE BROKEN--
WHOOM
UGNNN
--IS YOU, BATMAN!

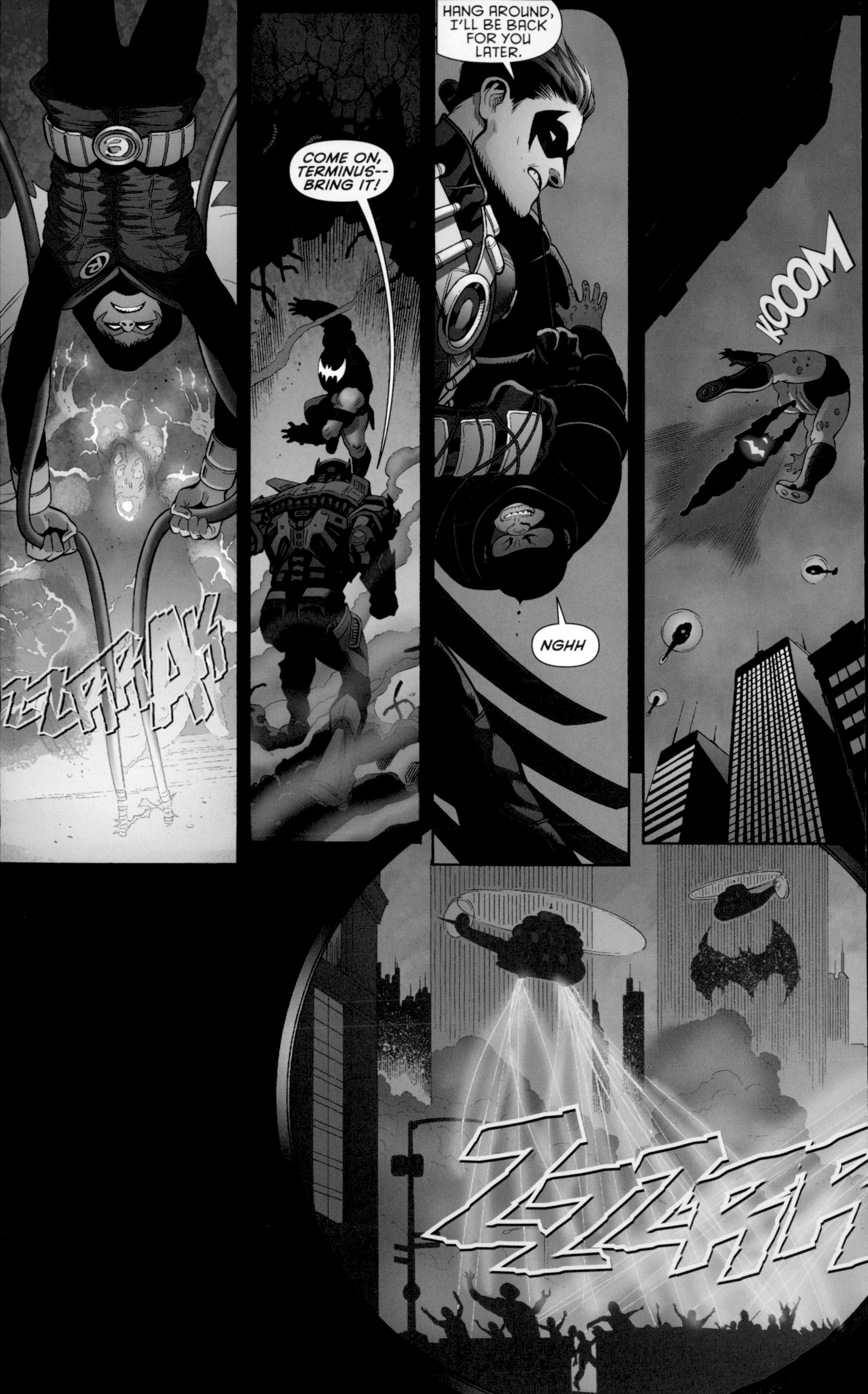
COME ON, TERMINUS-- BRING IT!
HANG AROUND, I'LL BE BACK FOR YOU LATER.
NGHH
KOOOM

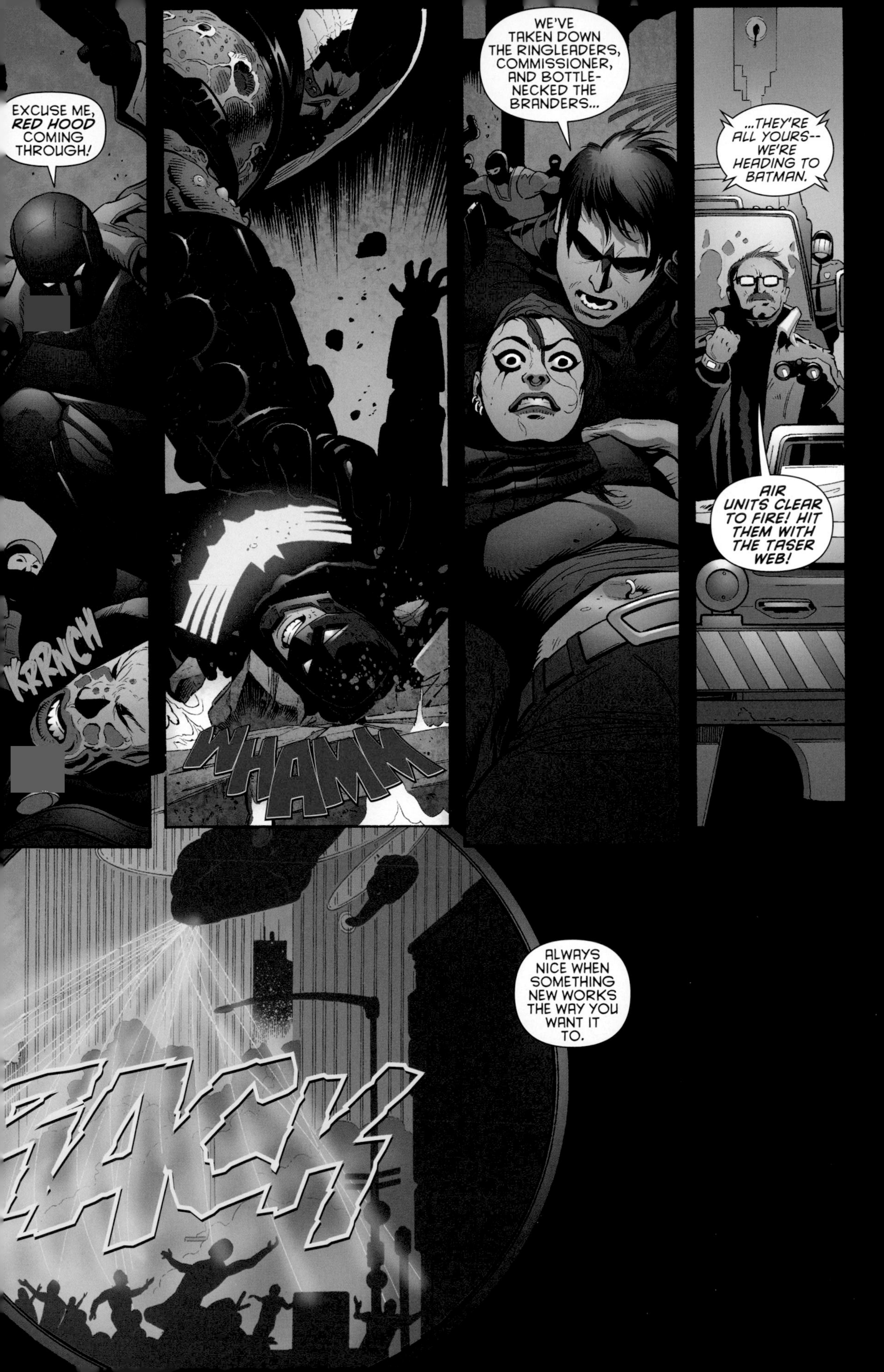

EXCUSE ME, RED HOOD COMING THROUGH!
KRRNCH
WHAMM
WE'VE TAKEN DOWN THE RINGLEADERS, COMMISSIONER, AND BOTTLE-NECKED THE BRANDERS...
...THEY'RE ALL YOURS-- WE'RE HEADING TO BATMAN.
AIR UNITS CLEAR TO FIRE! HIT THEM WITH THE TASER WEB!
ZACK
ALWAYS NICE WHEN SOMETHING NEW WORKS THE WAY YOU WANT IT TO.

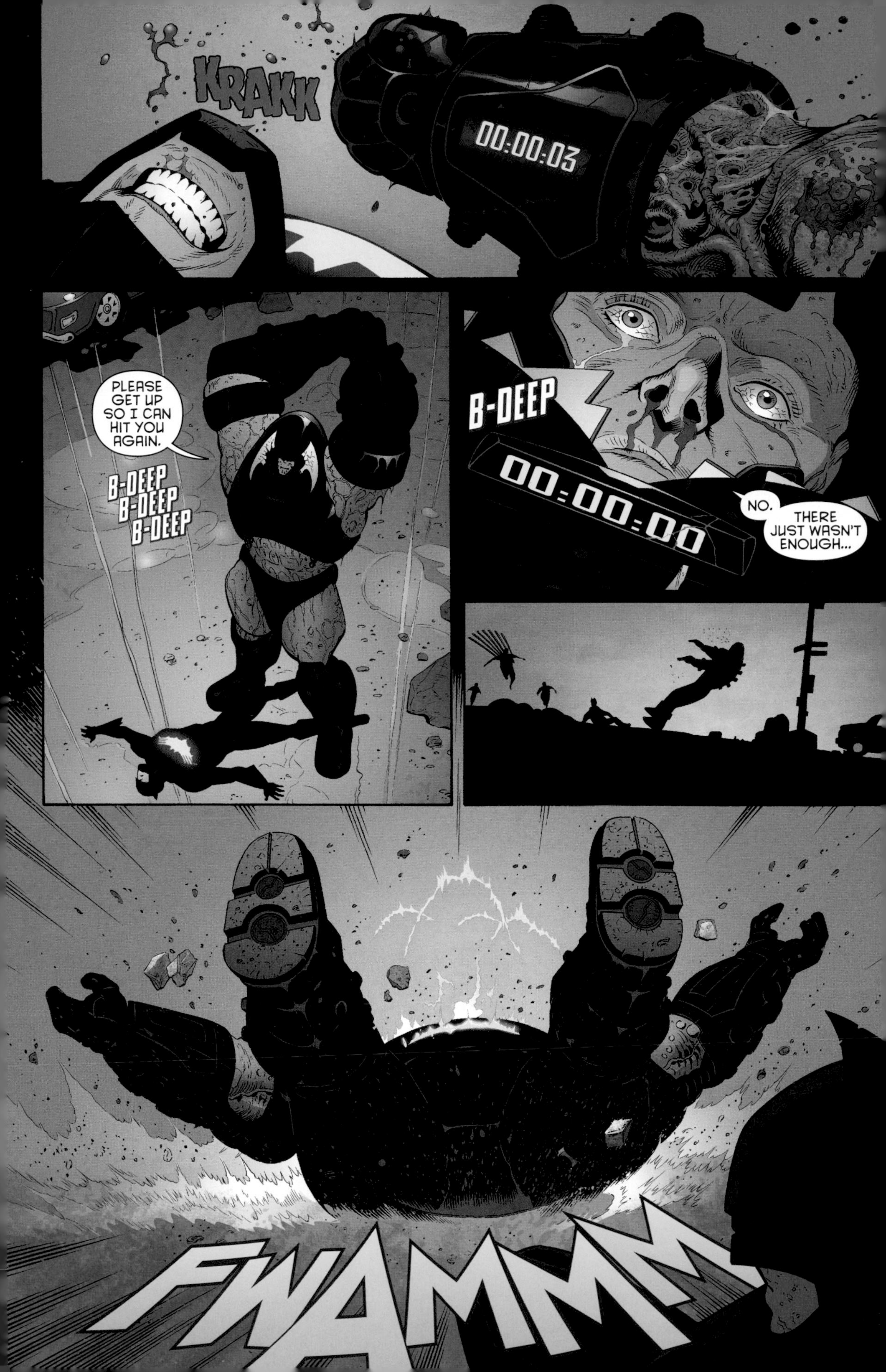
KRAKK
00:00:03
PLEASE GET UP SO I CAN HIT YOU AGAIN.
B-DEEP B-DEEP B-DEEP
B-DEEP
00:00:00
NO.
THERE JUST WASN'T ENOUGH...
FWAMMM

YOU STOPPED WHEN *THIS* CLOCK STOPPED.

...EVERY-ONE'S CLOCK IS TICKING DOWN...ONLY DIFFERENCE IS...

...I KNEW WHEN MY TIME WAS UP...RIGHT DOWN TO THE MINUTE...

...A BLESSING... AND A CURSE...

WHY DID YOU DO THIS?

THIS IS NOTHING... BUT THE *OPENING SALVO,* BATMAN...

...THAT CLOCK NOT ONLY COUNTED DOWN WHAT LITTLE LIFE I HAD LEFT-- IT WAS ALSO *SYNCHRONIZED* TO LAUNCH A *WARHEAD* FROM KANE COUNTY...

"...A WARHEAD THAT WHEN IT DETONATES WILL RELEASE A *WEAPONS GRADE TOXIN* THAT'LL ~~F~~ALL OVER YOUR CITY AND RENDER IT *LIFELESS* IN A WEEK WITH A *BLACK RAIN OF DECAY.*

"...I DIDN'T EXPECT TO BEAT YOU... I JUST WANTED TO BE HERE IN THE FRONT ROW WHEN THE PEOPLE AND CITY YOU'VE DEVOTED YOUR LIFE TO TURNED *MALIGNANT*...

"...I WANTED TO SEE YOU DIE INSIDE A LITTLE RIGHT BEFORE I DO."

WHAT ARE YOU DOING?!

STOPPING THAT ROCKET.

THRUSTERS AT MAXIMUM!

FWHOOOOOOSSH

...THERE'S NOTHING WORSE IN THIS LIFE THAN *FUTILITY,* BATMAN...

...YOUR *LAST MARK* ON GOTHAM WILL BE *DEVASTATION*...

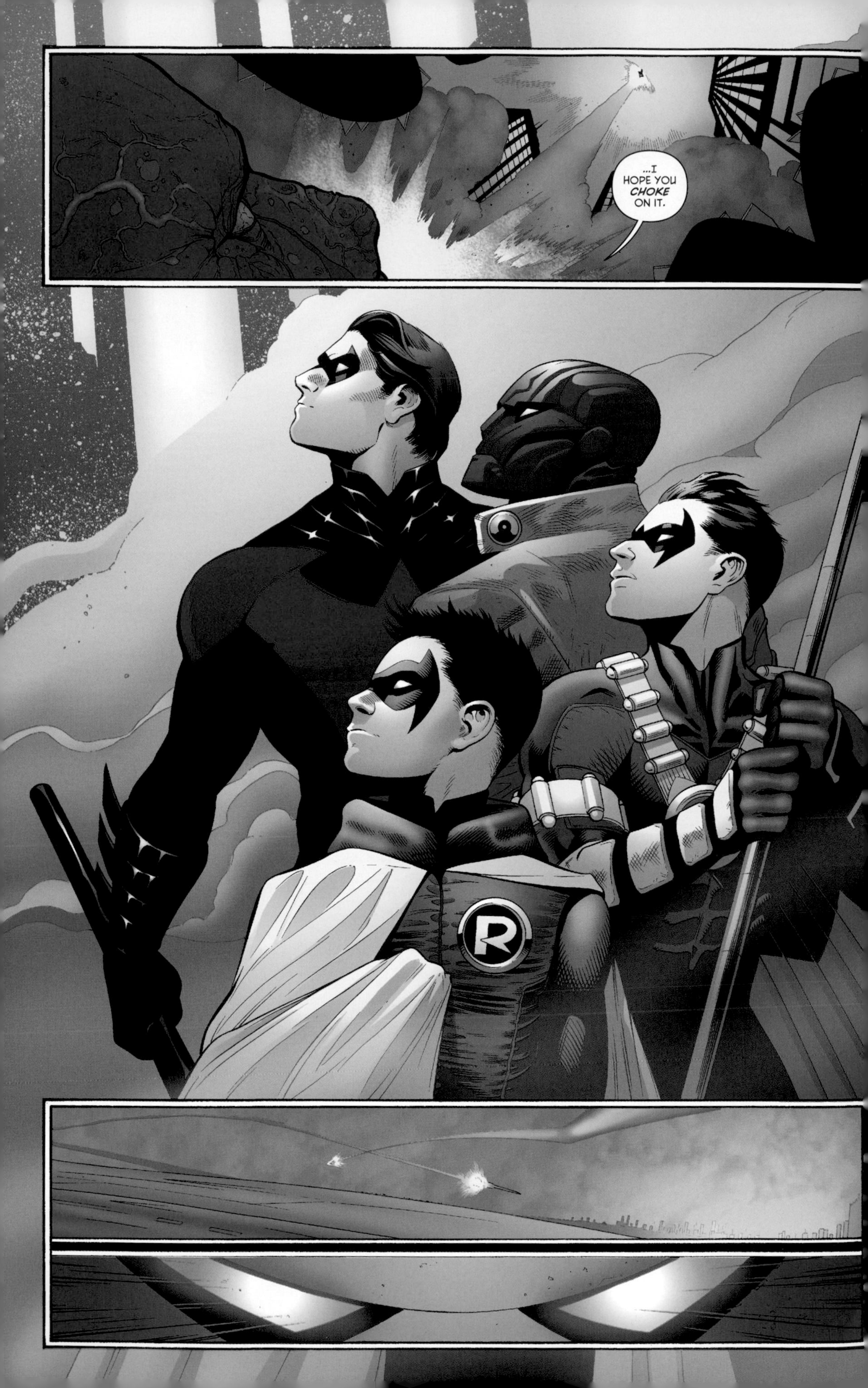
...I HOPE YOU CHOKE ON IT.

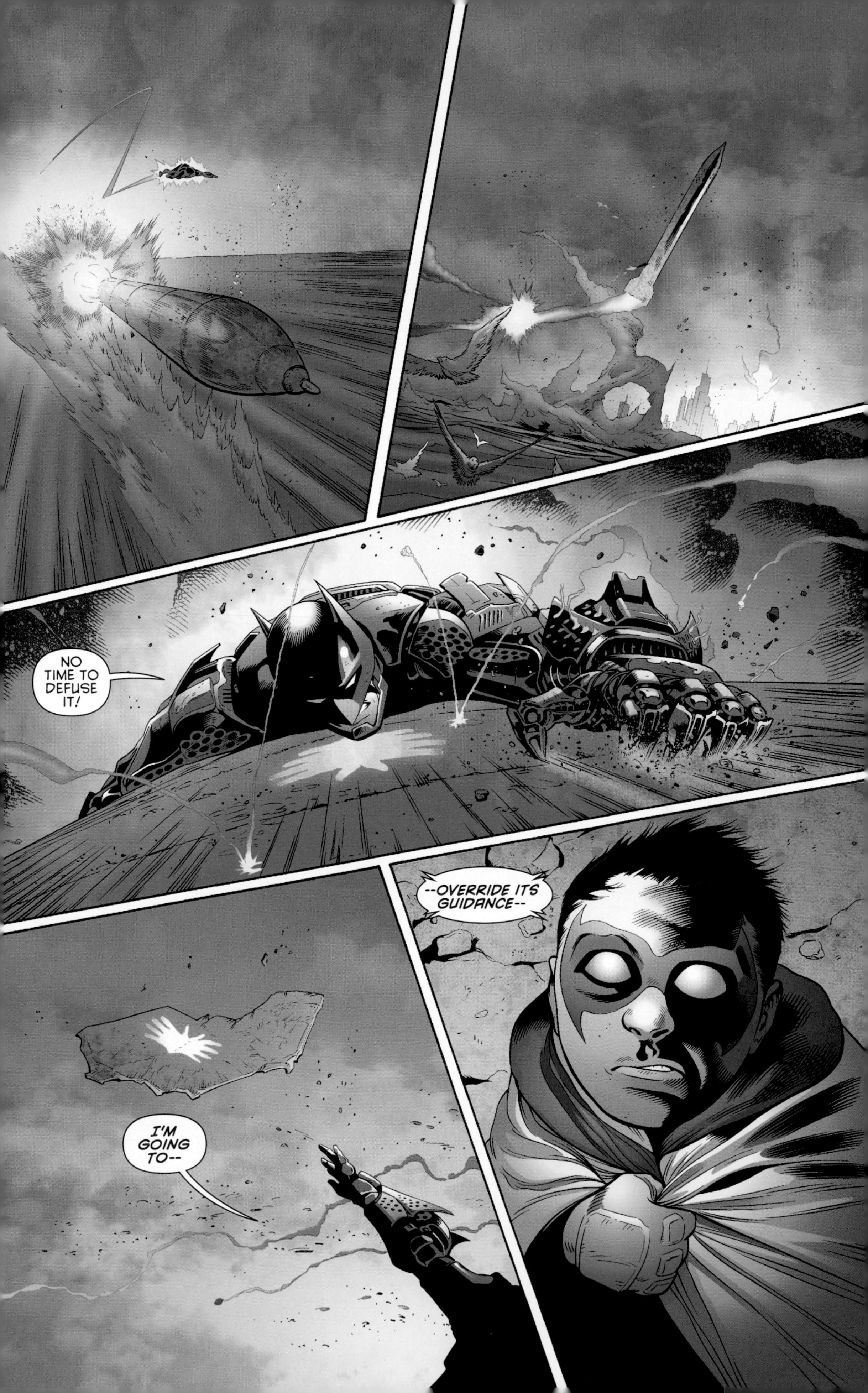
NO TIME TO DEFUSE IT!
I'M GOING TO--
--OVERRIDE ITS GUIDANCE--

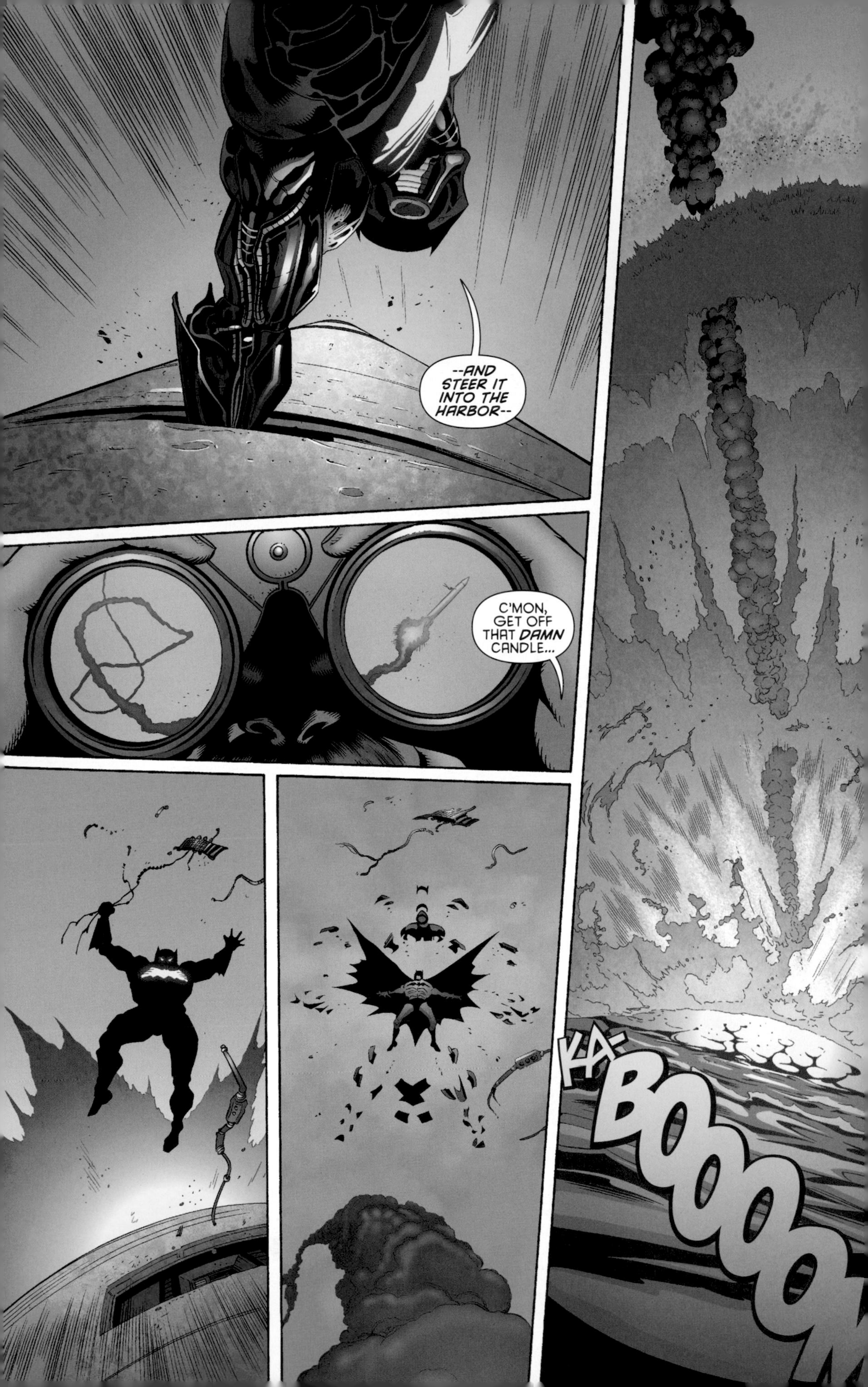
--AND STEER IT INTO THE HARBOR--
C'MON, GET OFF THAT *DAMN* CANDLE...
KA-BOOOOOM

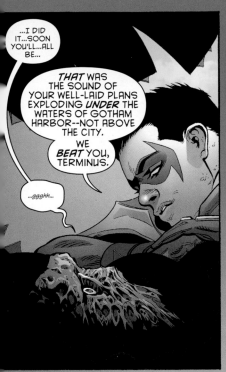

...I DID IT...SOON YOU'LL...ALL BE...

THAT WAS THE SOUND OF YOUR WELL-LAID PLANS EXPLODING *UNDER* THE WATERS OF GOTHAM HARBOR--NOT ABOVE THE CITY. WE *BEAT* YOU, TERMINUS.

...ggghh...

TAKE THAT *THOUGHT* WITH YOU INTO THE DARK.

WANT A RIDE?

SURE.

I THINK I CAN FIND MY WAY HOME, THANKS.

TWO'S COMPANY, FOUR'S A PAIN IN THE BUTT.

HEARD YOU ALREADY PAID A VISIT TO TIM AND JASON...

NO NEED FOR US TO TANGLE. HERE, HANG *THIS* ON YOUR WALL.

FAP

YOU DON'T NEED TO TRY SO HARD, DAMIAN.

IF YOU HAVEN'T NOTICED, KID, YOU'RE ALREADY *WEARING* THE "R" ON YOUR CHEST.

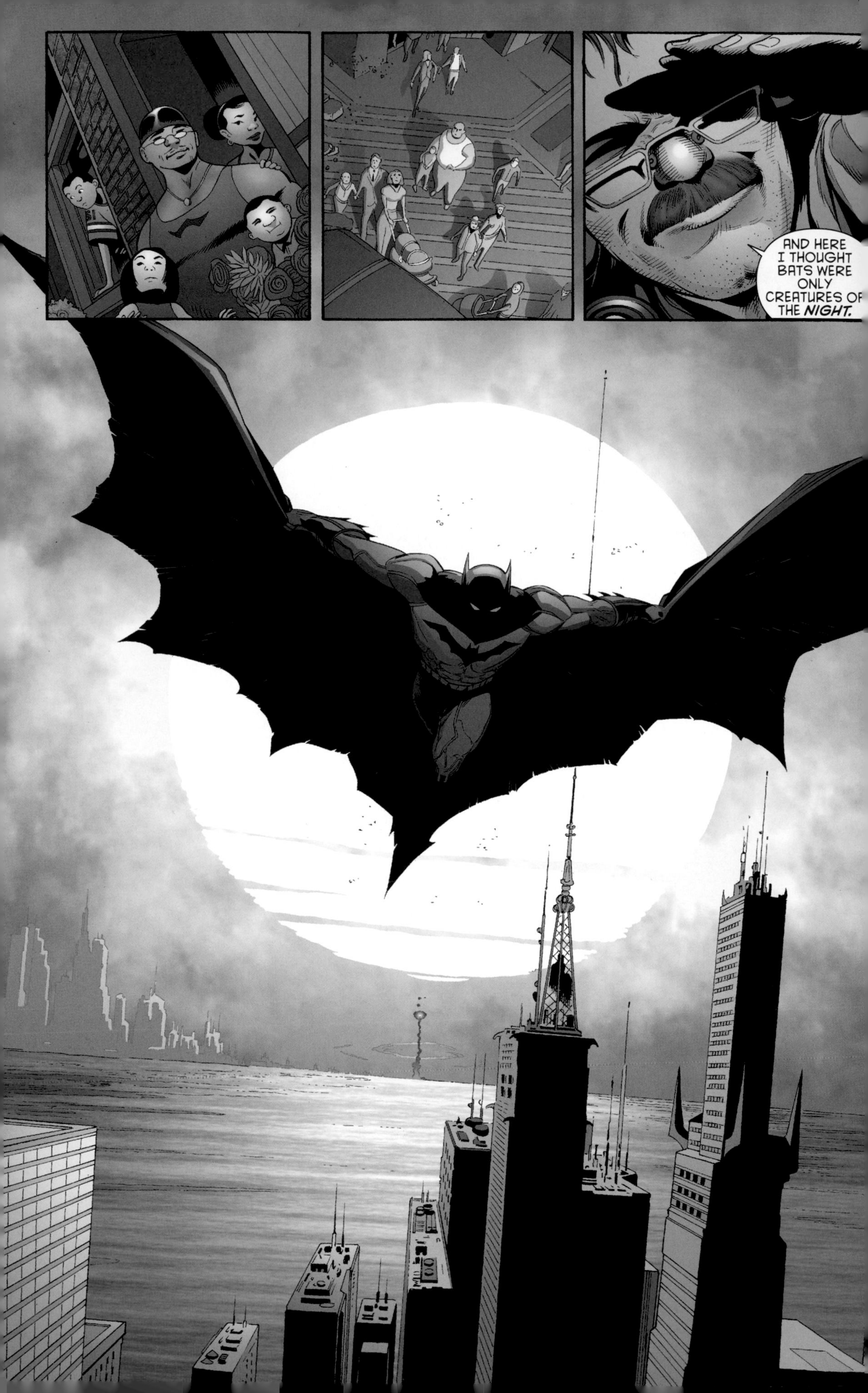
AND HERE I THOUGHT BATS WERE ONLY CREATURES OF THE NIGHT.

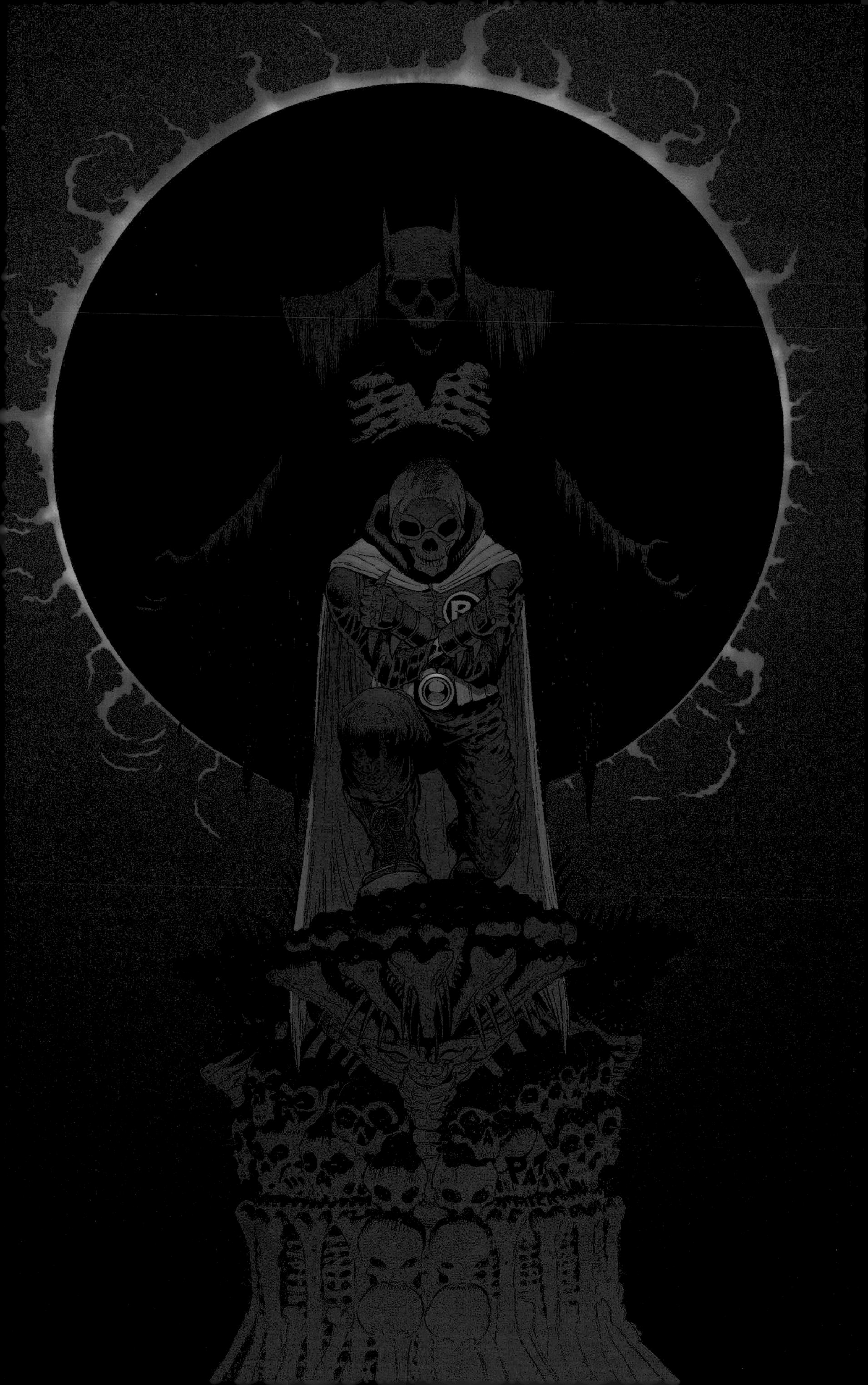

ECLIPSED

PETER J. TOMASI writer **PATRICK GLEASON** penciller, pages 1-15 **TOMAS GIORELLO** artist, pages 16-20 **MICK GRAY** inker, pages 1-15
cover by **GLEASON, GRAY & KALISZ**

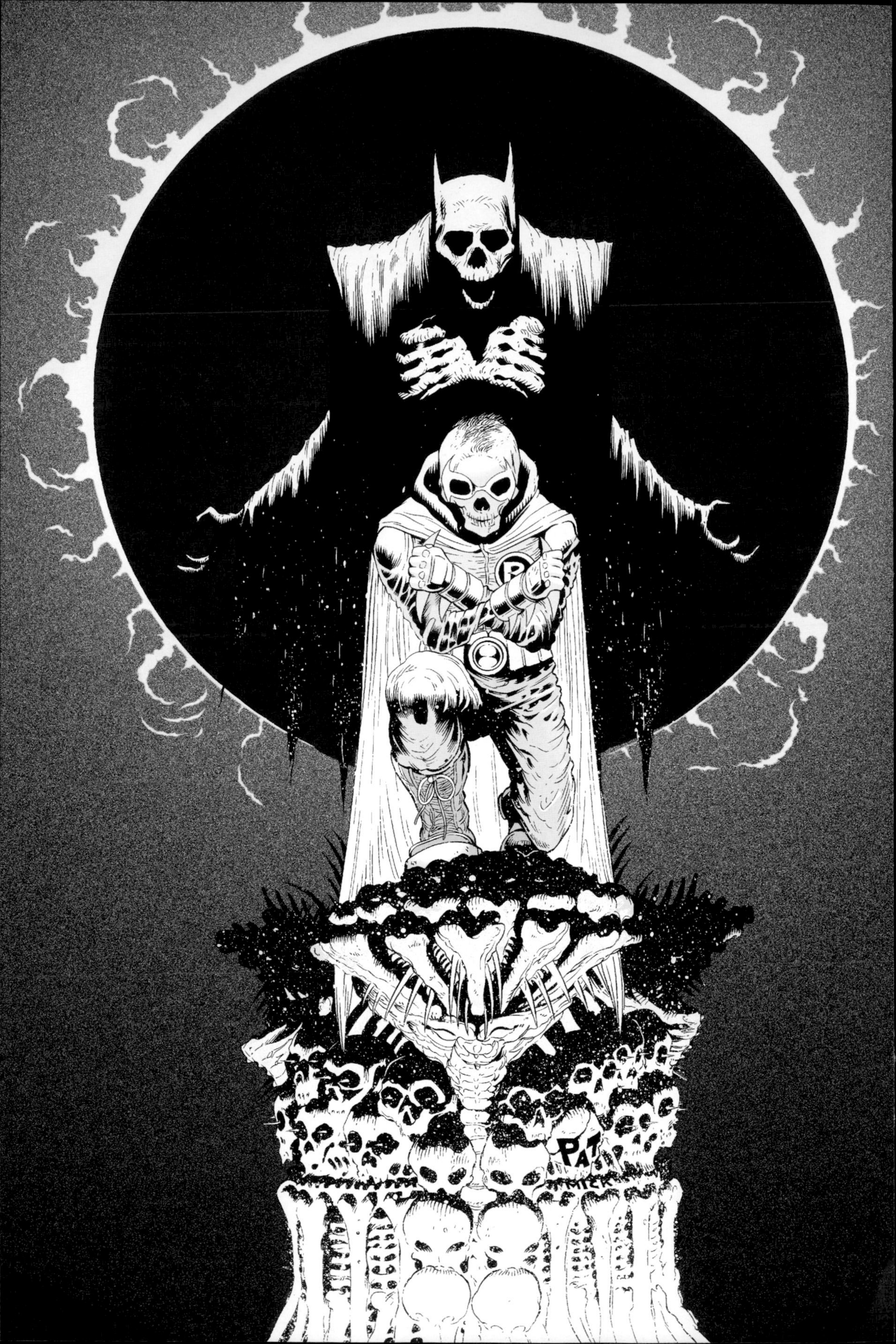
PAT
MICK

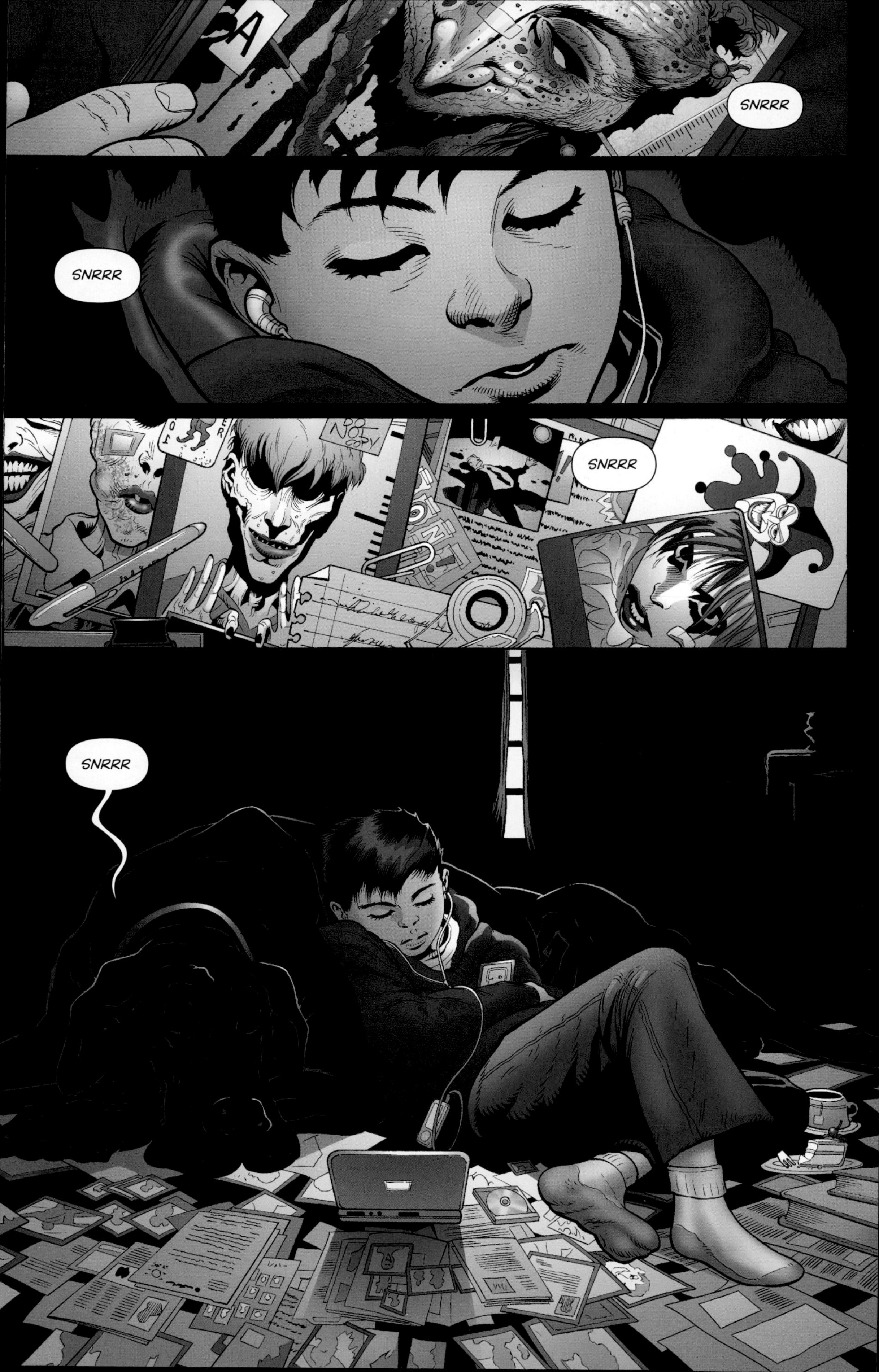
SNRRR
SNRRR
SNRRR
SNRRR

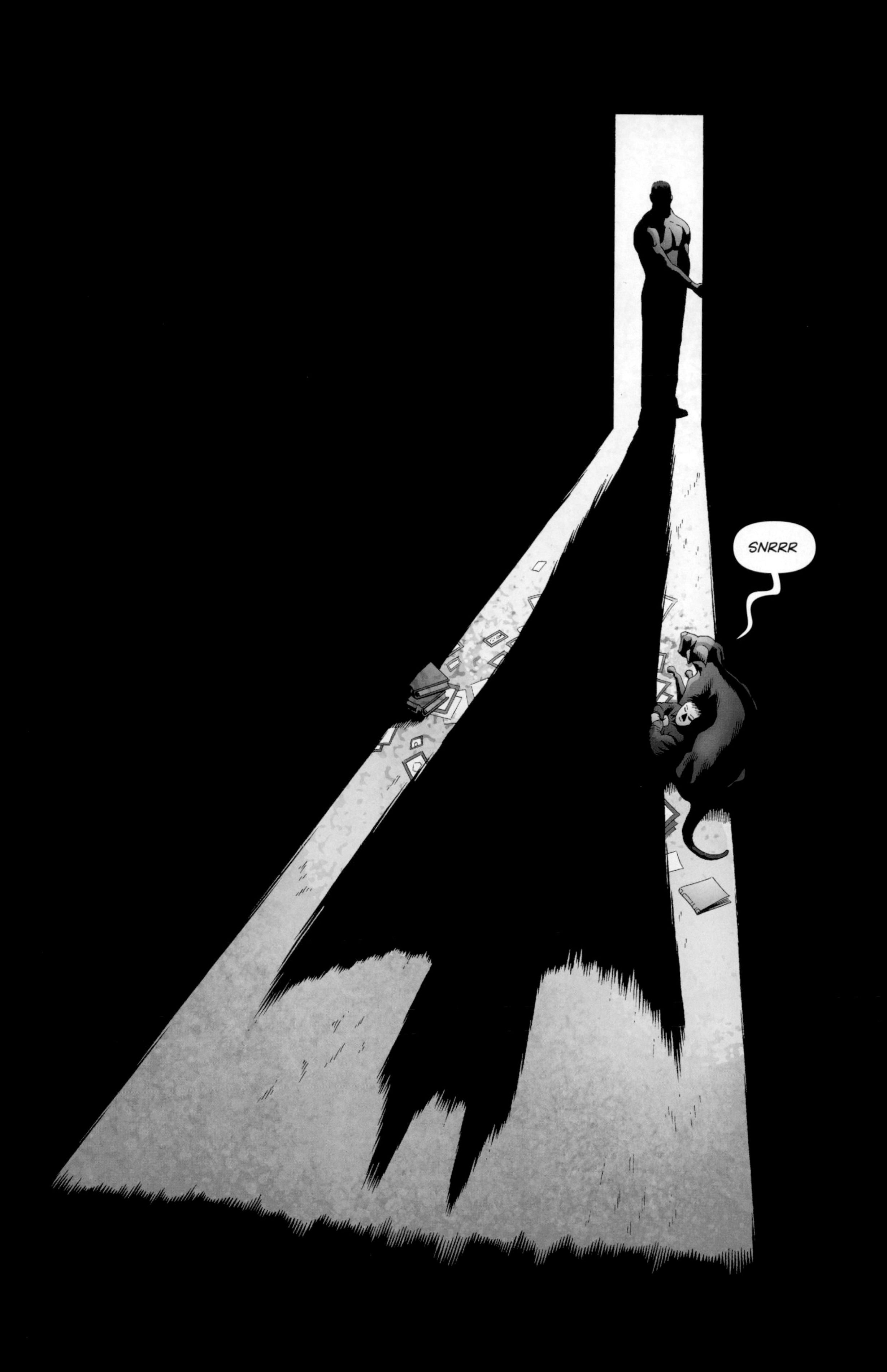
SNRRR

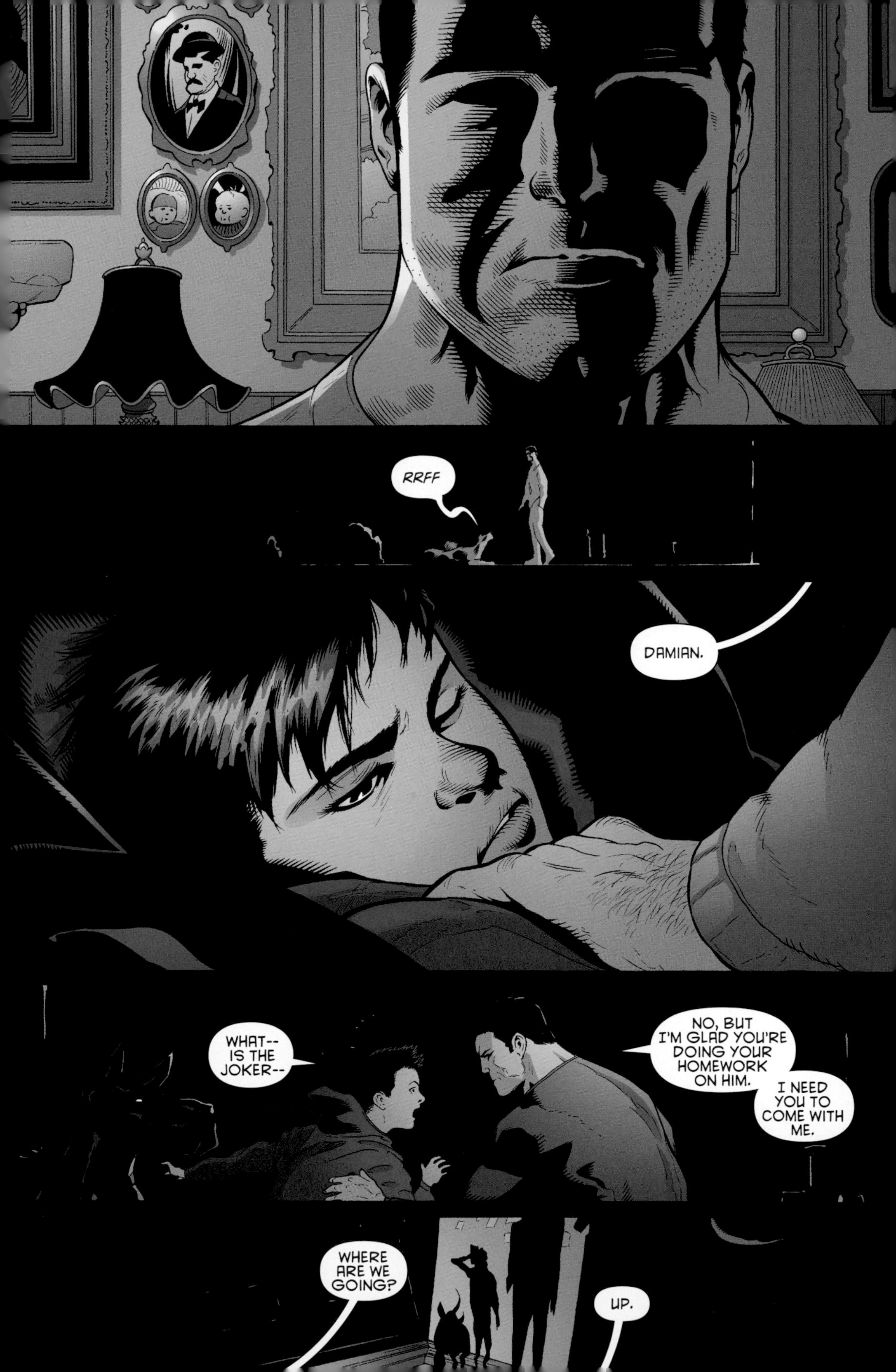
RRFF
DAMIAN.
WHAT-- IS THE JOKER--
NO, BUT I'M GLAD YOU'RE DOING YOUR HOMEWORK ON HIM.
I NEED YOU TO COME WITH ME.
WHERE ARE WE GOING?
UP.

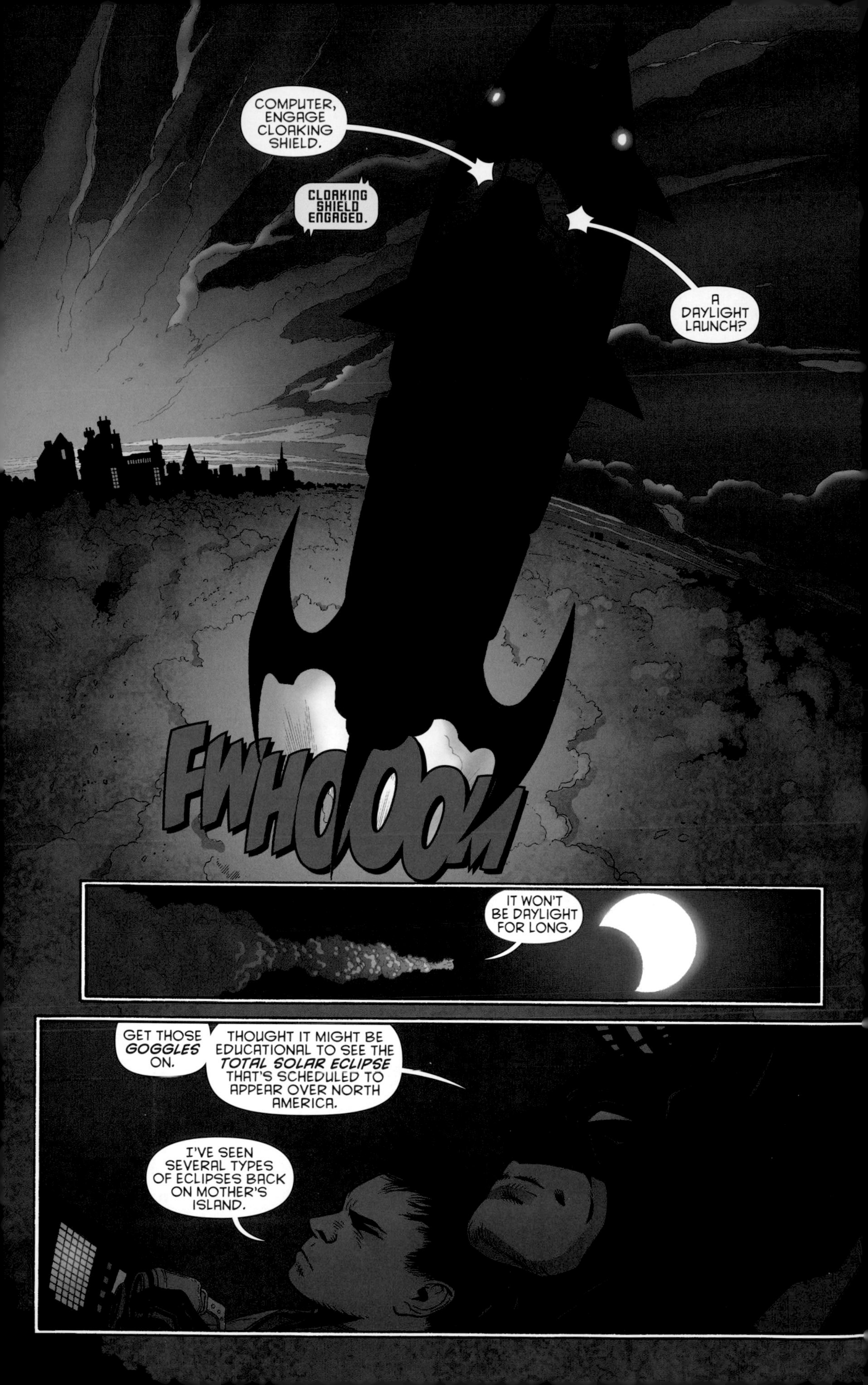
COMPUTER, ENGAGE CLOAKING SHIELD.
CLOAKING SHIELD ENGAGED.
A DAYLIGHT LAUNCH?
FWHOOOM
IT WON'T BE DAYLIGHT FOR LONG.
GET THOSE GOGGLES ON.
THOUGHT IT MIGHT BE EDUCATIONAL TO SEE THE TOTAL SOLAR ECLIPSE THAT'S SCHEDULED TO APPEAR OVER NORTH AMERICA.
I'VE SEEN SEVERAL TYPES OF ECLIPSES BACK ON MOTHER'S ISLAND.

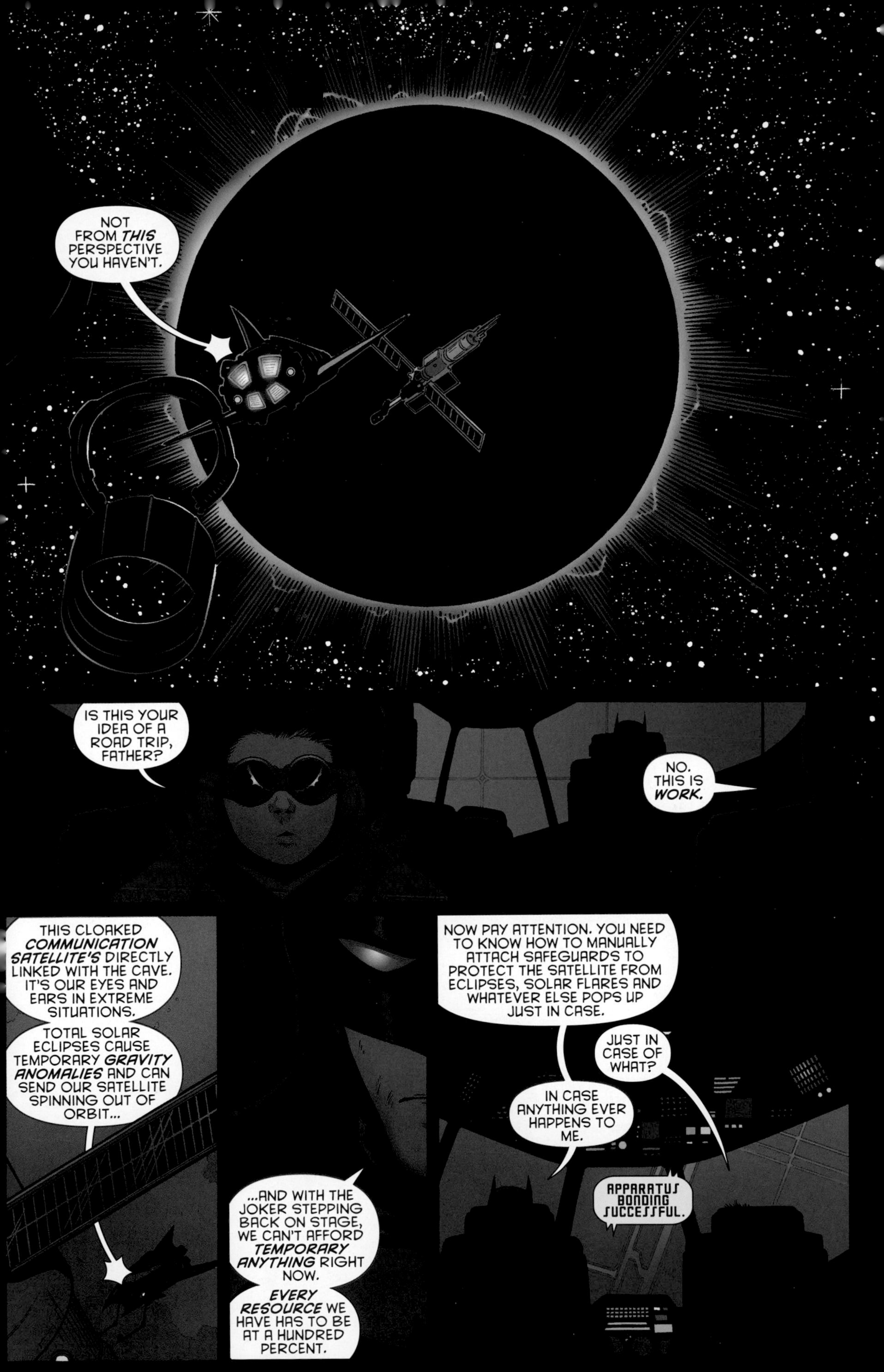
NOT FROM THIS PERSPECTIVE YOU HAVEN'T.
IS THIS YOUR IDEA OF A ROAD TRIP, FATHER?
NO. THIS IS WORK.
THIS CLOAKED COMMUNICATION SATELLITE'S DIRECTLY LINKED WITH THE CAVE. IT'S OUR EYES AND EARS IN EXTREME SITUATIONS.
TOTAL SOLAR ECLIPSES CAUSE TEMPORARY GRAVITY ANOMALIES AND CAN SEND OUR SATELLITE SPINNING OUT OF ORBIT...
...AND WITH THE JOKER STEPPING BACK ON STAGE, WE CAN'T AFFORD TEMPORARY ANYTHING RIGHT NOW.
EVERY RESOURCE WE HAVE HAS TO BE AT A HUNDRED PERCENT.
NOW PAY ATTENTION. YOU NEED TO KNOW HOW TO MANUALLY ATTACH SAFEGUARDS TO PROTECT THE SATELLITE FROM ECLIPSES, SOLAR FLARES AND WHATEVER ELSE POPS UP JUST IN CASE.
JUST IN CASE OF WHAT?
IN CASE ANYTHING EVER HAPPENS TO ME.
APPARATUS BONDING SUCCESSFUL.

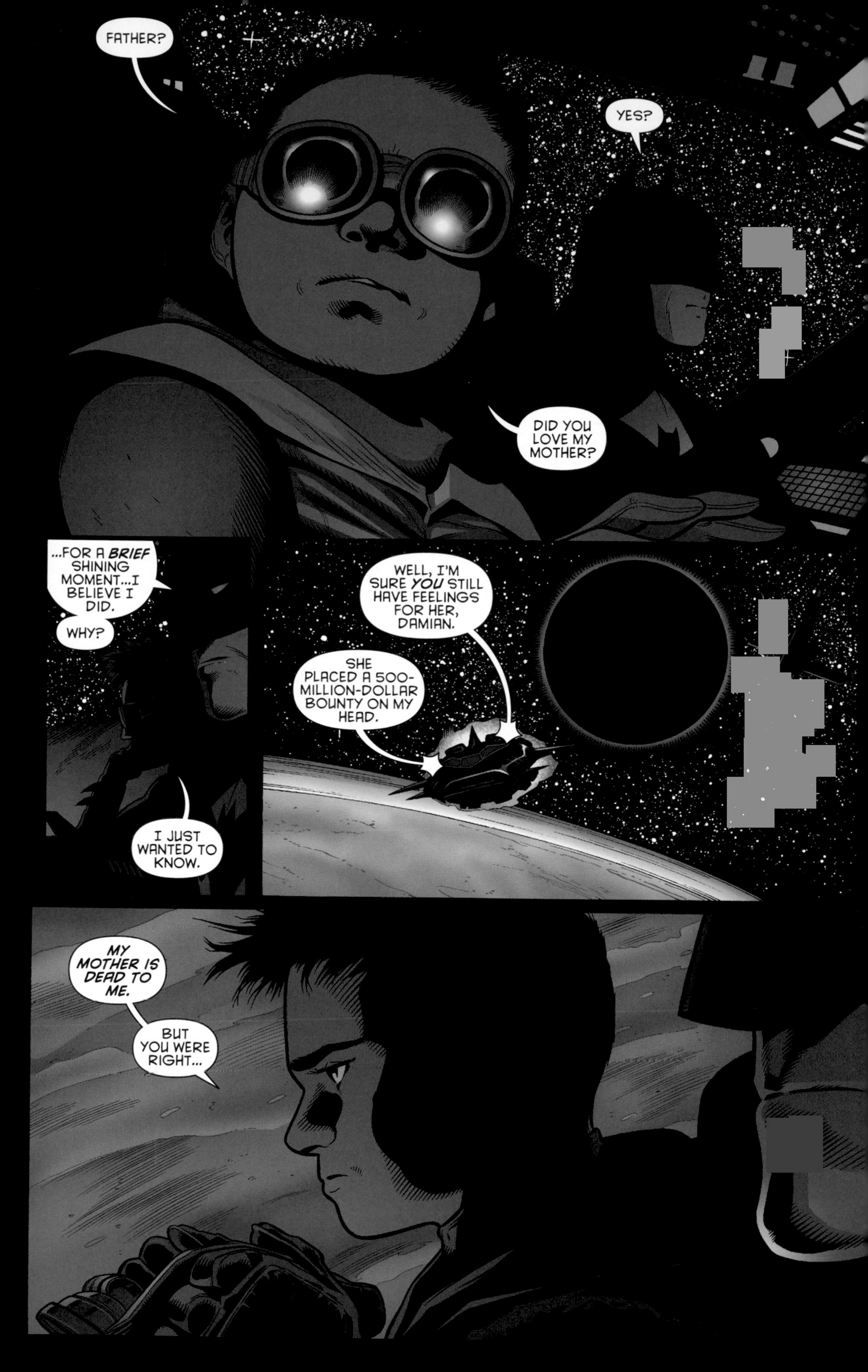
FATHER?
YES?
DID YOU LOVE MY MOTHER?
...FOR A BRIEF SHINING MOMENT...I BELIEVE I DID.
WHY?
I JUST WANTED TO KNOW.
WELL, I'M SURE YOU STILL HAVE FEELINGS FOR HER, DAMIAN.
SHE PLACED A 500-MILLION-DOLLAR BOUNTY ON MY HEAD.
MY MOTHER IS DEAD TO ME.
BUT YOU WERE RIGHT...

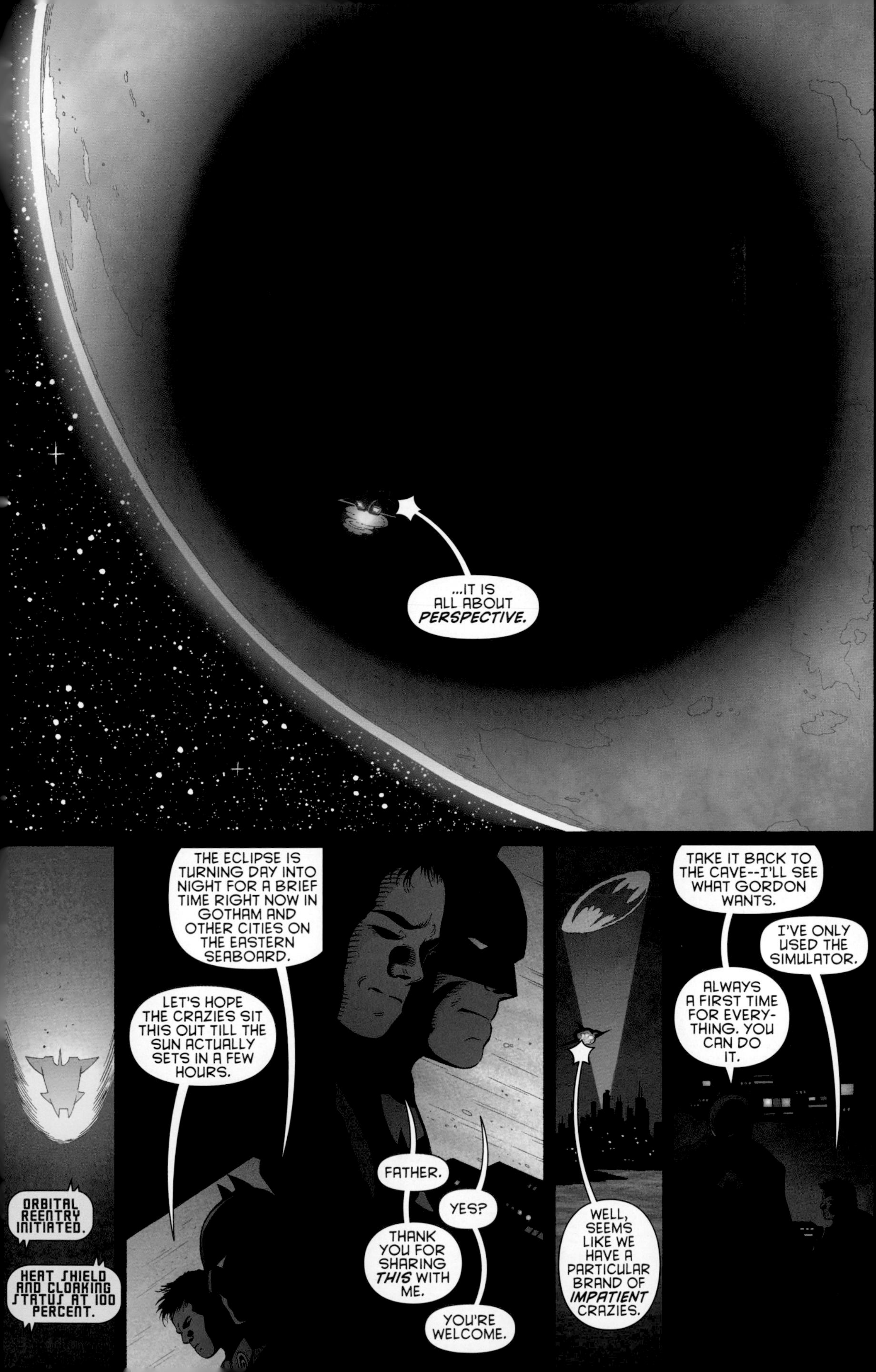
...IT IS ALL ABOUT *PERSPECTIVE.*
ORBITAL REENTRY INITIATED.
HEAT SHIELD AND CLOAKING STATUS AT 100 PERCENT.
THE ECLIPSE IS TURNING DAY INTO NIGHT FOR A BRIEF TIME RIGHT NOW IN GOTHAM AND OTHER CITIES ON THE EASTERN SEABOARD.
LET'S HOPE THE CRAZIES SIT THIS OUT TILL THE SUN ACTUALLY SETS IN A FEW HOURS.
FATHER.
YES?
THANK YOU FOR SHARING *THIS* WITH ME.
YOU'RE WELCOME.
WELL, SEEMS LIKE WE HAVE A PARTICULAR BRAND OF *IMPATIENT* CRAZIES.
TAKE IT BACK TO THE CAVE--I'LL SEE WHAT GORDON WANTS.
I'VE ONLY USED THE SIMULATOR.
ALWAYS A FIRST TIME FOR EVERY-THING. YOU CAN DO IT.

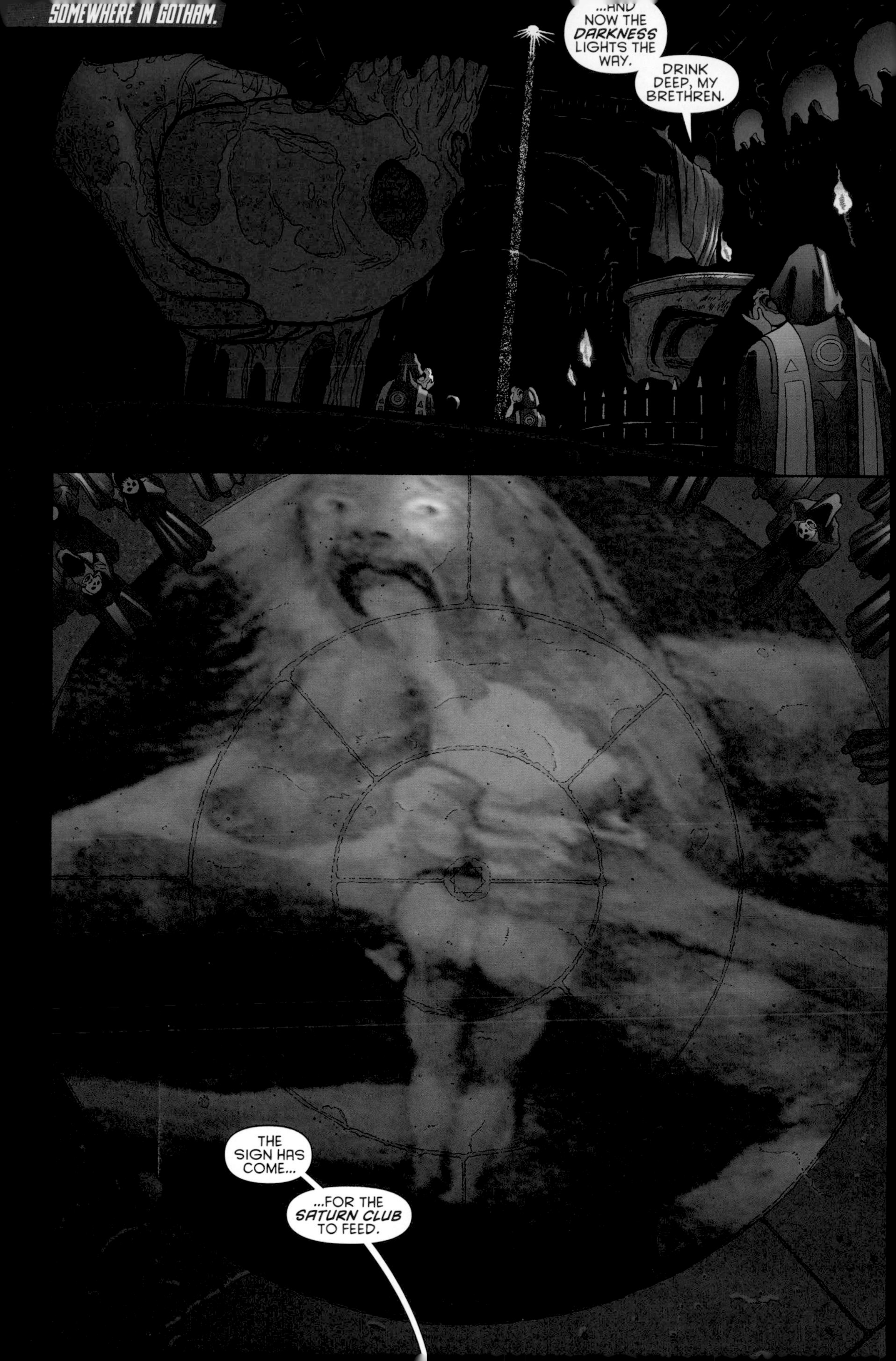
SOMEWHERE IN GOTHAM.
...AND NOW THE DARKNESS LIGHTS THE WAY.
DRINK DEEP, MY BRETHREN.
THE SIGN HAS COME...
...FOR THE SATURN CLUB TO FEED.

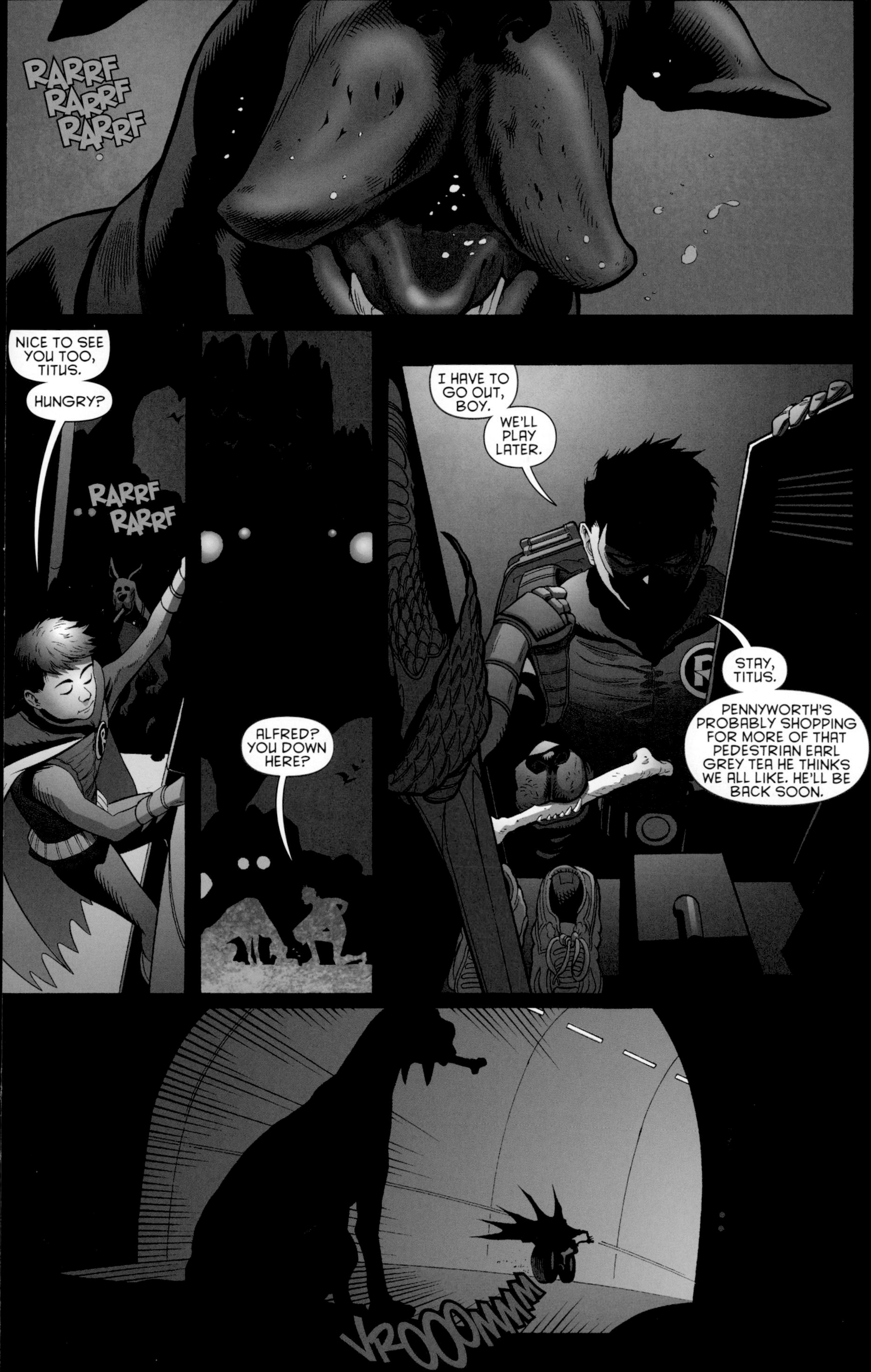
RARRF RARRF RARRF
NICE TO SEE YOU TOO, TITUS.
HUNGRY?
RARRF RARRF
ALFRED? YOU DOWN HERE?
I HAVE TO GO OUT, BOY.
WE'LL PLAY LATER.
STAY, TITUS.
PENNYWORTH'S PROBABLY SHOPPING FOR MORE OF THAT PEDESTRIAN EARL GREY TEA HE THINKS WE ALL LIKE. HE'LL BE BACK SOON.
VROOOMMM

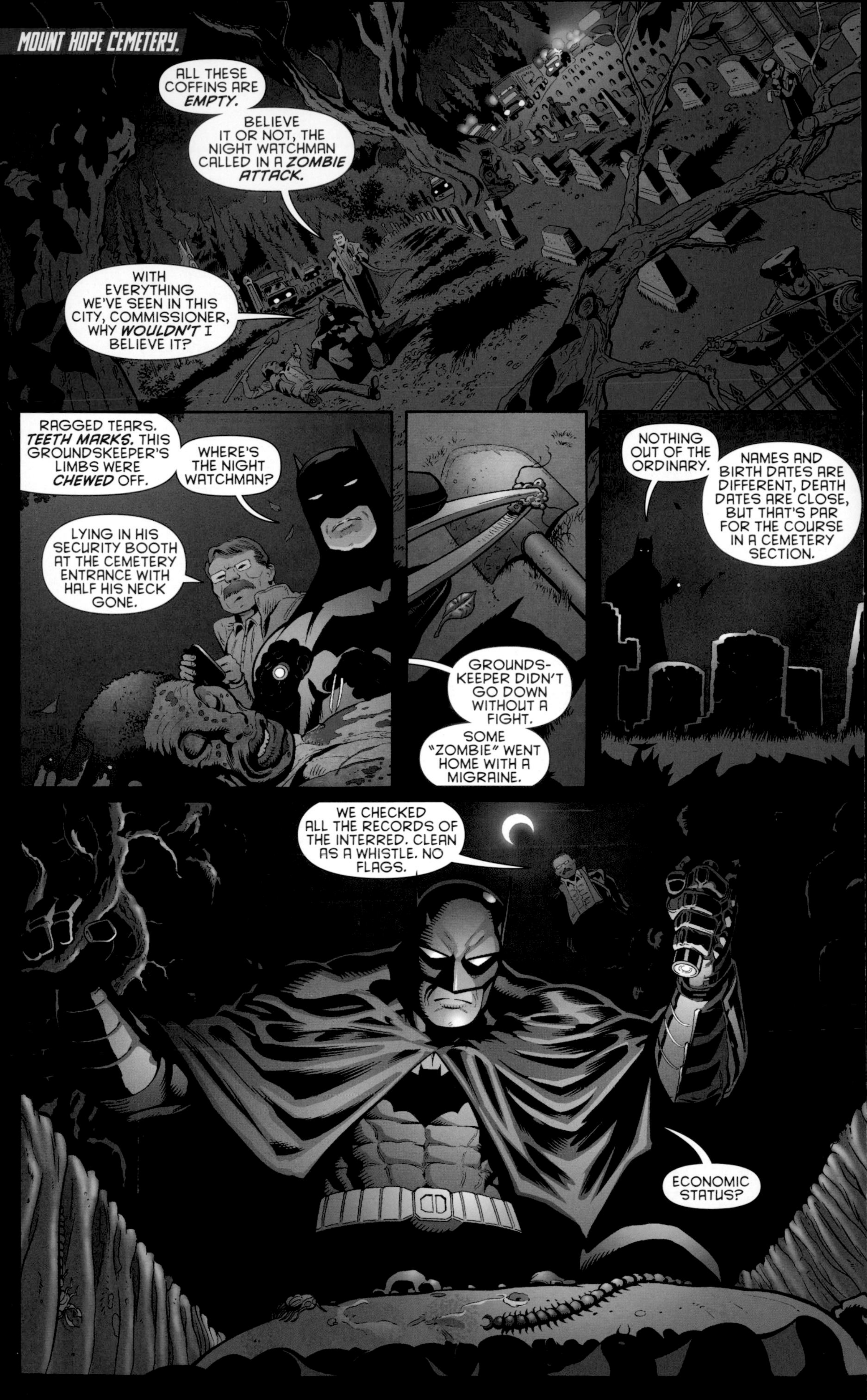
MOUNT HOPE CEMETERY.
ALL THESE COFFINS ARE EMPTY.
BELIEVE IT OR NOT, THE NIGHT WATCHMAN CALLED IN A ZOMBIE ATTACK.
WITH EVERYTHING WE'VE SEEN IN THIS CITY, COMMISSIONER, WHY WOULDN'T I BELIEVE IT?
RAGGED TEARS. TEETH MARKS. THIS GROUNDSKEEPER'S LIMBS WERE CHEWED OFF.
WHERE'S THE NIGHT WATCHMAN?
LYING IN HIS SECURITY BOOTH AT THE CEMETERY ENTRANCE WITH HALF HIS NECK GONE.
GROUNDS-KEEPER DIDN'T GO DOWN WITHOUT A FIGHT.
SOME "ZOMBIE" WENT HOME WITH A MIGRAINE.
NOTHING OUT OF THE ORDINARY.
NAMES AND BIRTH DATES ARE DIFFERENT, DEATH DATES ARE CLOSE, BUT THAT'S PAR FOR THE COURSE IN A CEMETERY SECTION.
WE CHECKED ALL THE RECORDS OF THE INTERRED. CLEAN AS A WHISTLE. NO FLAGS.
ECONOMIC STATUS?

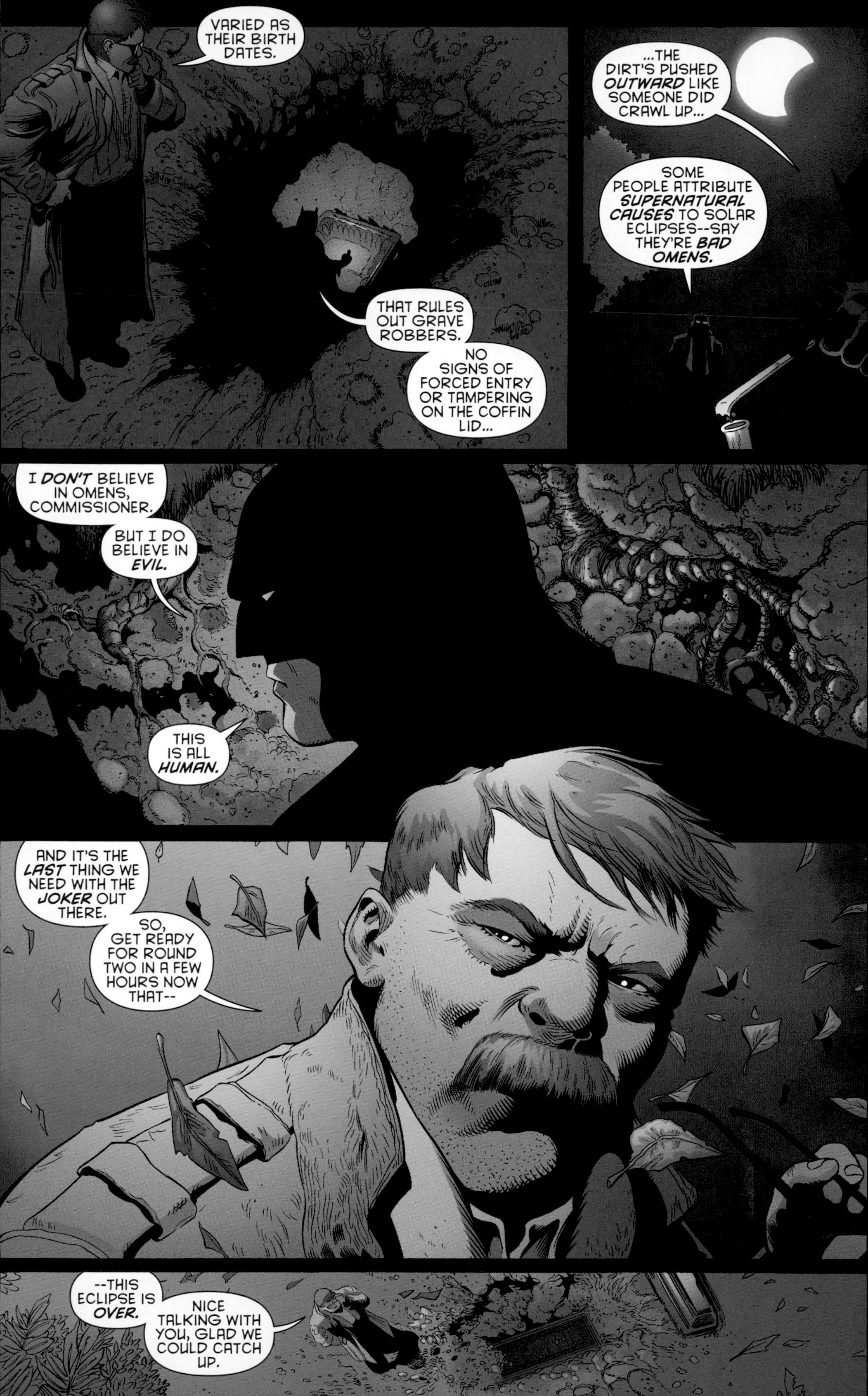
VARIED AS THEIR BIRTH DATES.
THAT RULES OUT GRAVE ROBBERS.
NO SIGNS OF FORCED ENTRY OR TAMPERING ON THE COFFIN LID...
...THE DIRT'S PUSHED OUTWARD LIKE SOMEONE DID CRAWL UP...
SOME PEOPLE ATTRIBUTE SUPERNATURAL CAUSES TO SOLAR ECLIPSES--SAY THEY'RE BAD OMENS.
I DON'T BELIEVE IN OMENS, COMMISSIONER.
BUT I DO BELIEVE IN EVIL.
THIS IS ALL HUMAN.
AND IT'S THE LAST THING WE NEED WITH THE JOKER OUT THERE.
SO, GET READY FOR ROUND TWO IN A FEW HOURS NOW THAT--
--THIS ECLIPSE IS OVER.
NICE TALKING WITH YOU, GLAD WE COULD CATCH UP.

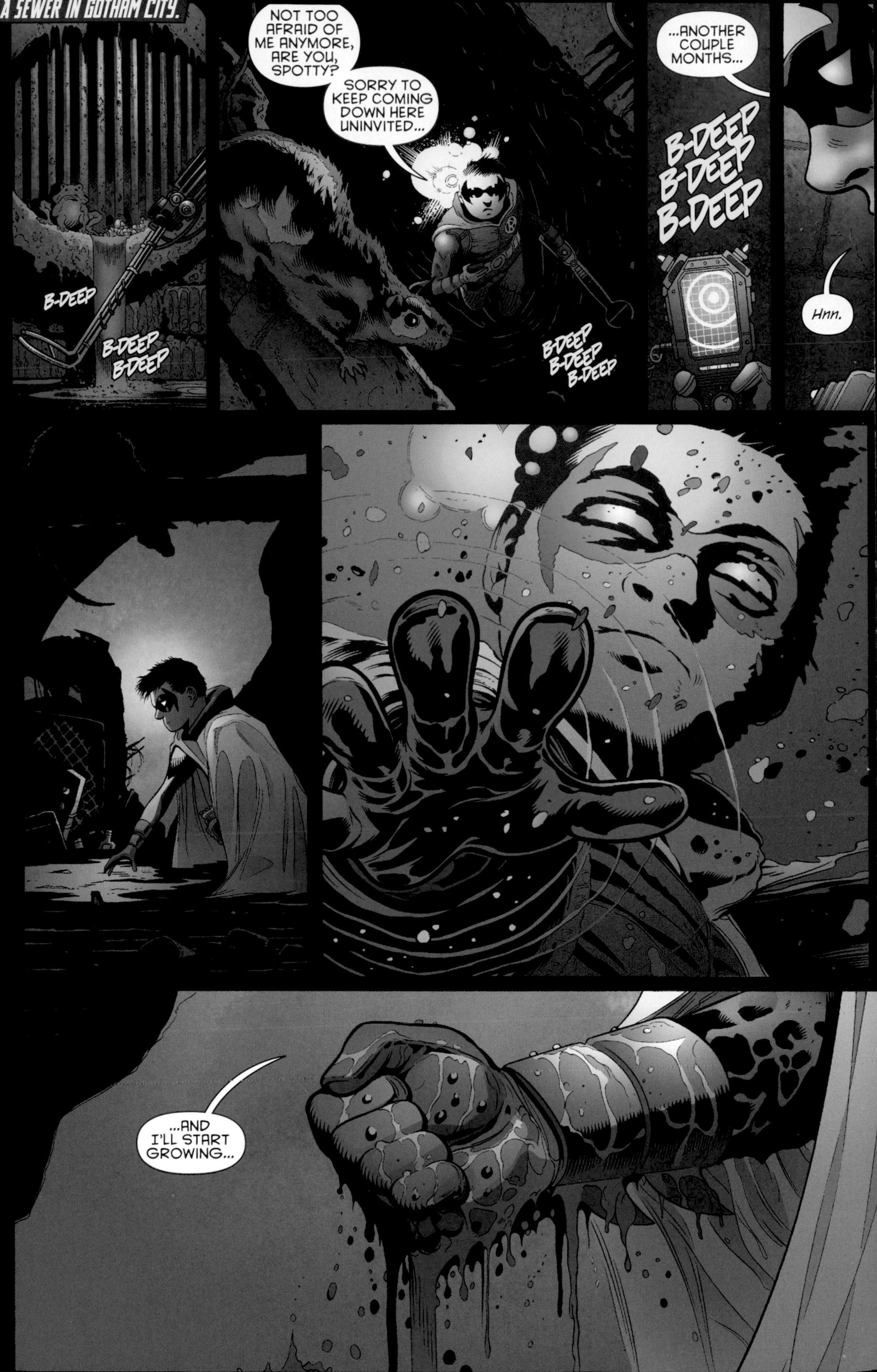
A SEWER IN GOTHAM CITY.
B-DEEP
B-DEEP B-DEEP
NOT TOO AFRAID OF ME ANYMORE, ARE YOU, SPOTTY?
SORRY TO KEEP COMING DOWN HERE UNINVITED...
B-DEEP B-DEEP B-DEEP
...ANOTHER COUPLE MONTHS...
B-DEEP B-DEEP B-DEEP
Hnn.
...AND I'LL START GROWING...

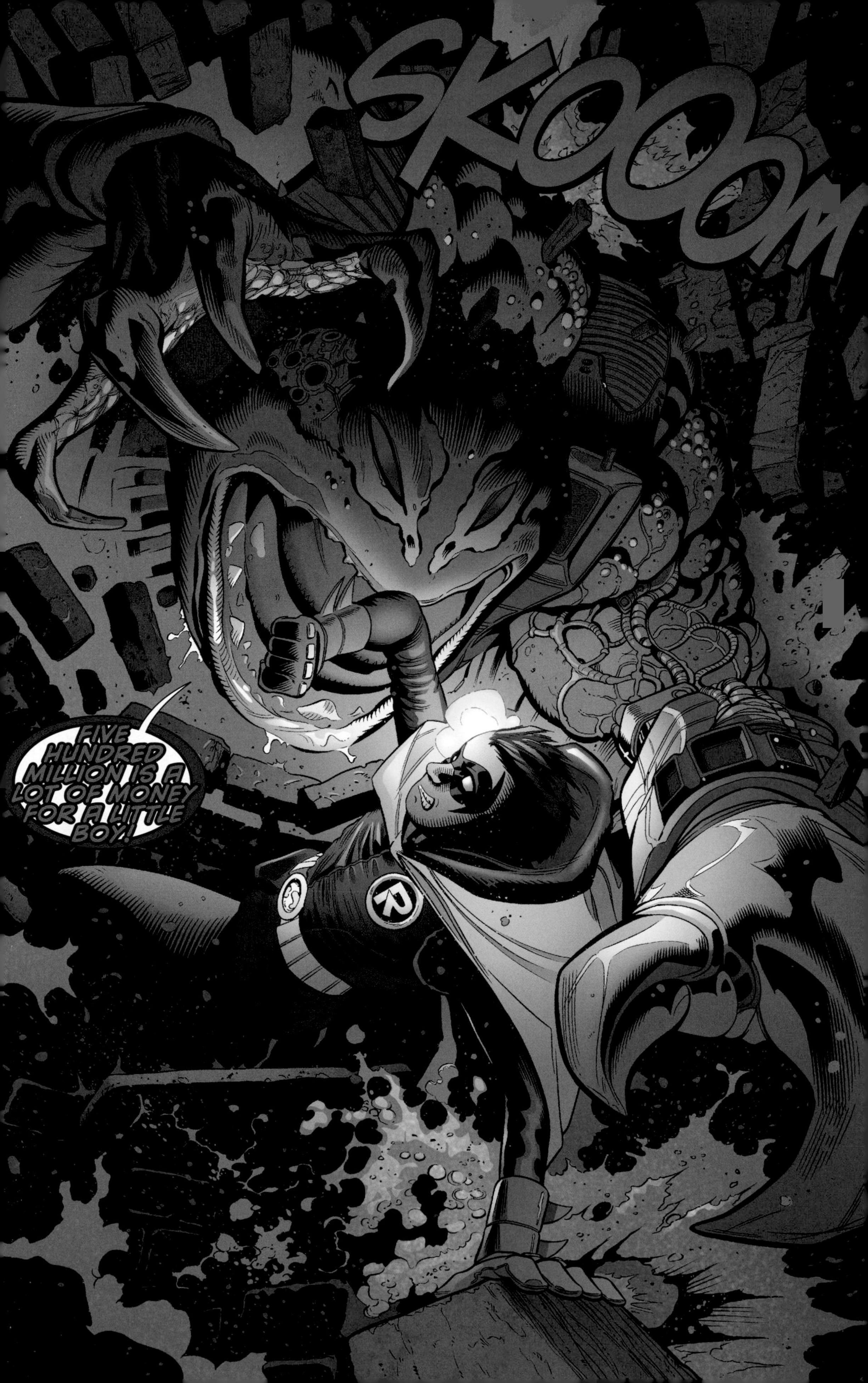
SKOOOM
FIVE HUNDRED MILLION IS A LOT OF MONEY FOR A LITTLE BOY!

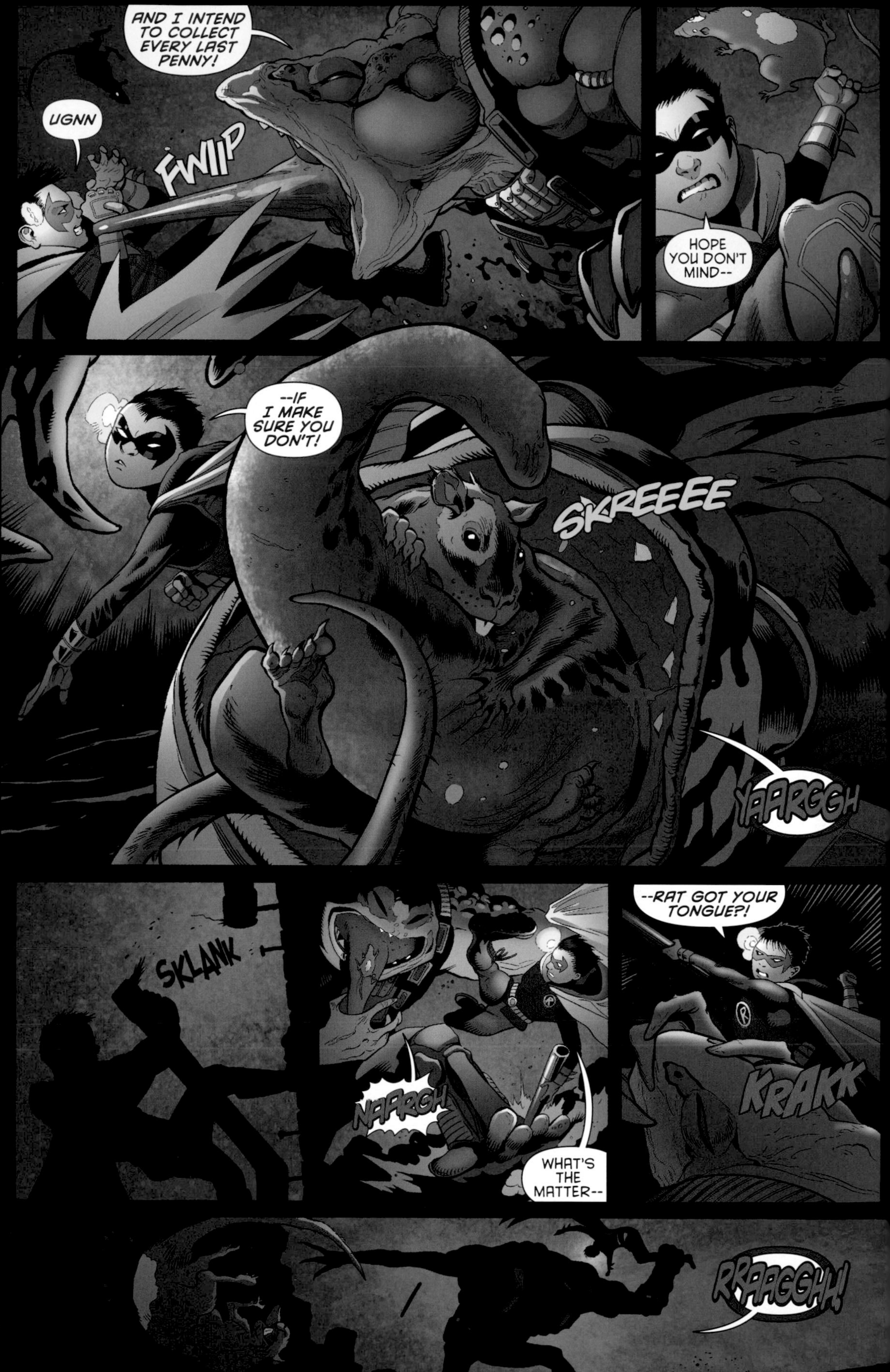
AND I INTEND TO COLLECT EVERY LAST PENNY!
UGNN
FWIIP
HOPE YOU DON'T MIND--
--IF I MAKE SURE YOU DON'T!
SKREEEEE
YAARGGH
SKLANK
NAARGH
WHAT'S THE MATTER--
--RAT GOT YOUR TONGUE?!
KRAKK
RRAAGGHH!

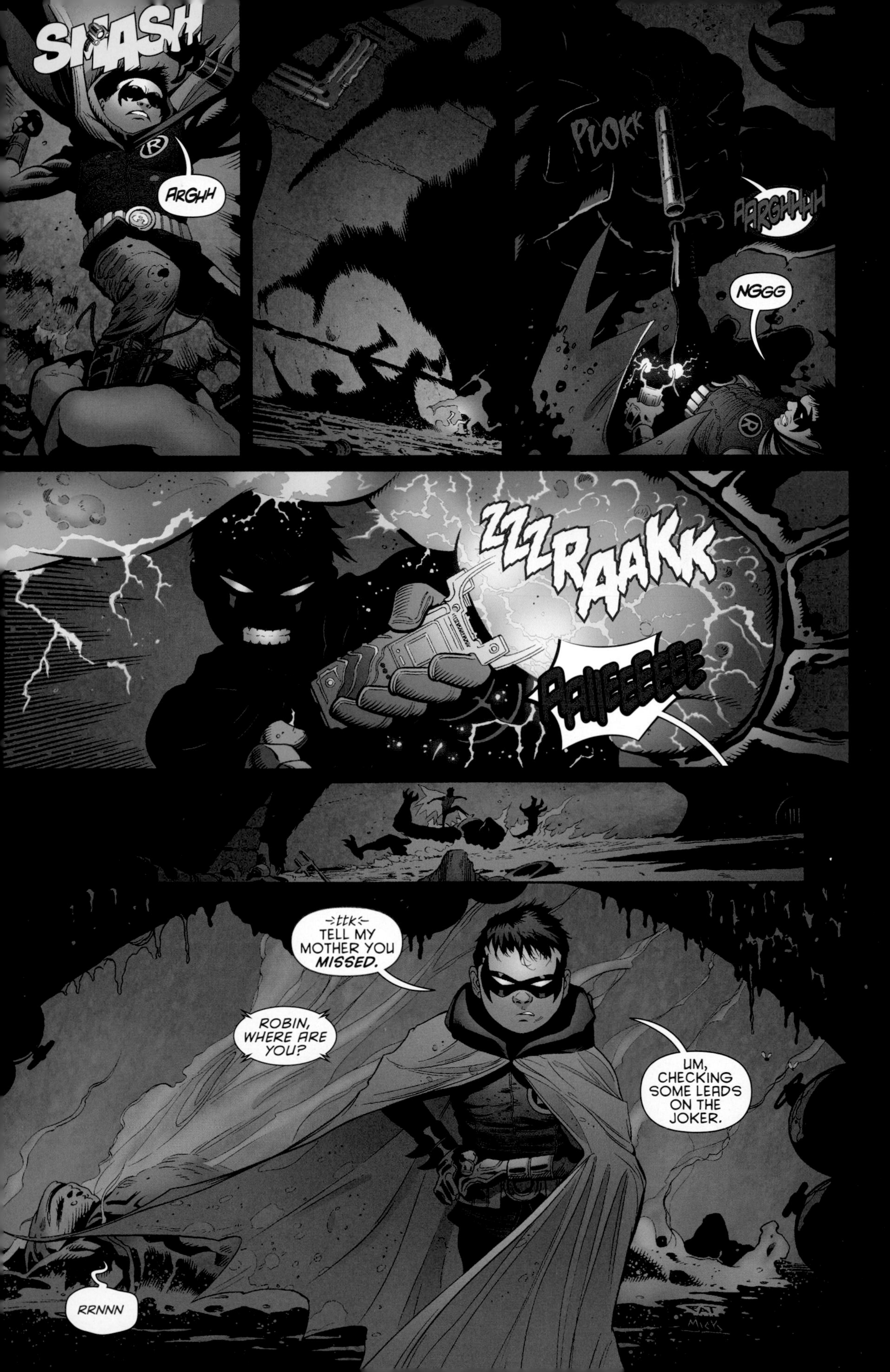
SMASH
ARGHH
PLOKK
AARGHHHH
NGGG
ZZZRAAKK
AAIIEEEEEE
ttk
TELL MY MOTHER YOU MISSED.
ROBIN, WHERE ARE YOU?
UM, CHECKING SOME LEADS ON THE JOKER.
RRNNN

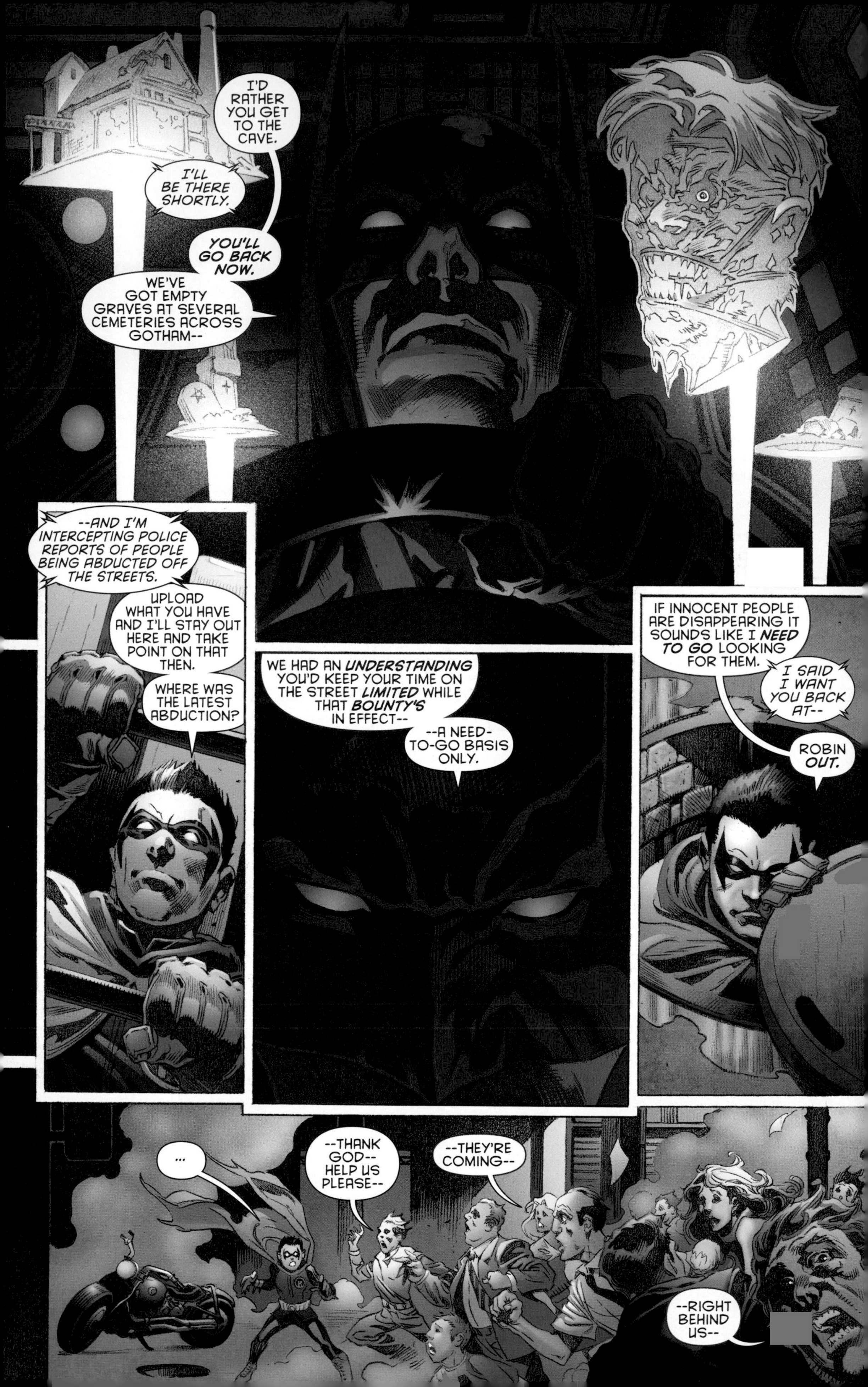
I'D RATHER YOU GET TO THE CAVE.
I'LL BE THERE SHORTLY.
YOU'LL GO BACK NOW.
WE'VE GOT EMPTY GRAVES AT SEVERAL CEMETERIES ACROSS GOTHAM--
--AND I'M INTERCEPTING POLICE REPORTS OF PEOPLE BEING ABDUCTED OFF THE STREETS.
UPLOAD WHAT YOU HAVE AND I'LL STAY OUT HERE AND TAKE POINT ON THAT THEN.
WHERE WAS THE LATEST ABDUCTION?
WE HAD AN UNDERSTANDING YOU'D KEEP YOUR TIME ON THE STREET LIMITED WHILE THAT BOUNTY'S IN EFFECT--
--A NEED-TO-GO BASIS ONLY.
IF INNOCENT PEOPLE ARE DISAPPEARING IT SOUNDS LIKE I NEED TO GO LOOKING FOR THEM.
I SAID I WANT YOU BACK AT--
ROBIN OUT.
...
--THANK GOD-- HELP US PLEASE--
--THEY'RE COMING--
--RIGHT BEHIND US--

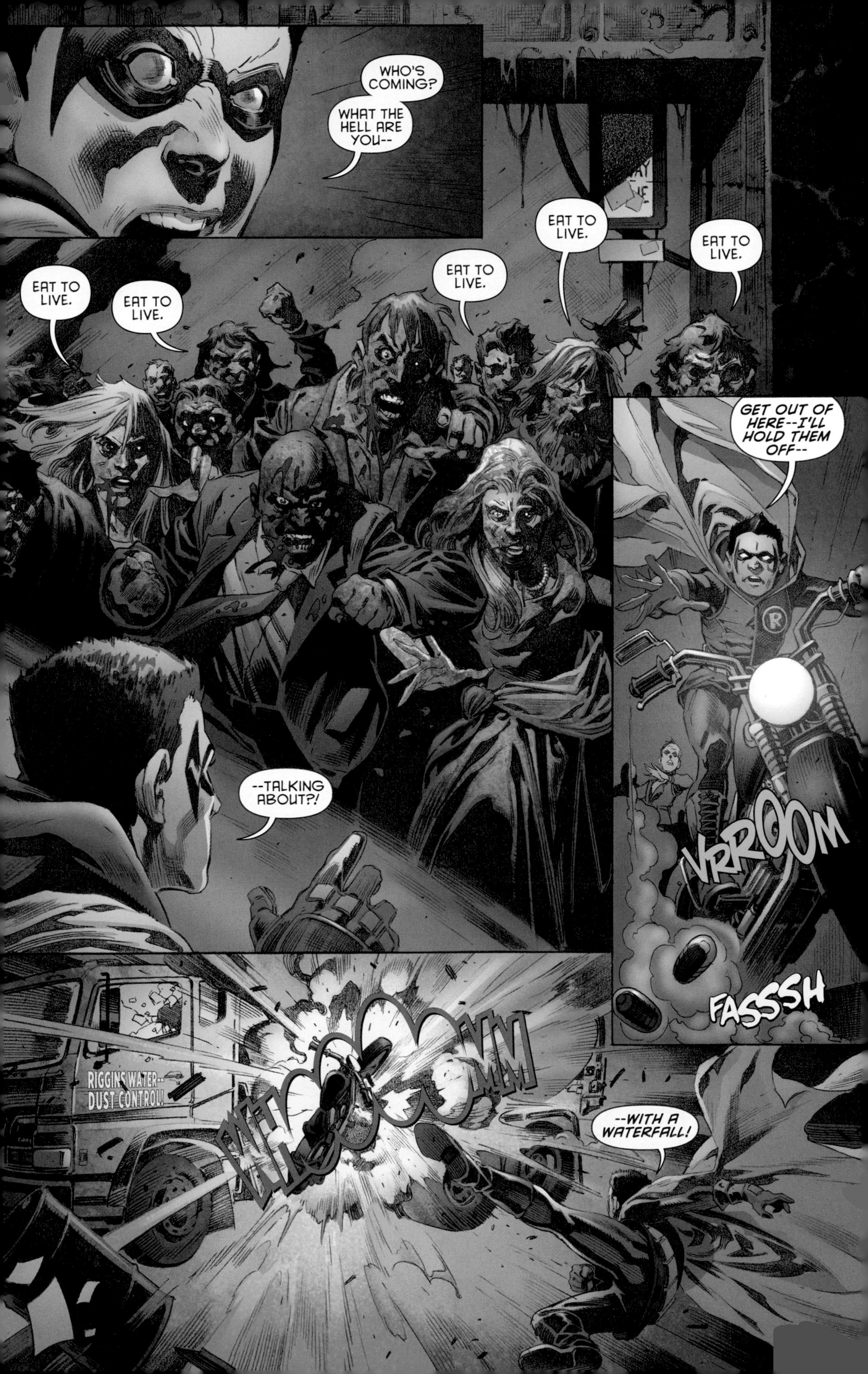
WHO'S COMING?
WHAT THE HELL ARE YOU--
EAT TO LIVE.
EAT TO LIVE.
EAT TO LIVE.
EAT TO LIVE.
EAT TO LIVE.
--TALKING ABOUT?!
GET OUT OF HERE--I'LL HOLD THEM OFF--
VRROOM
FASSSH
RIGGINS WATER-- DUST CONTROL!
--WITH A WATERFALL!

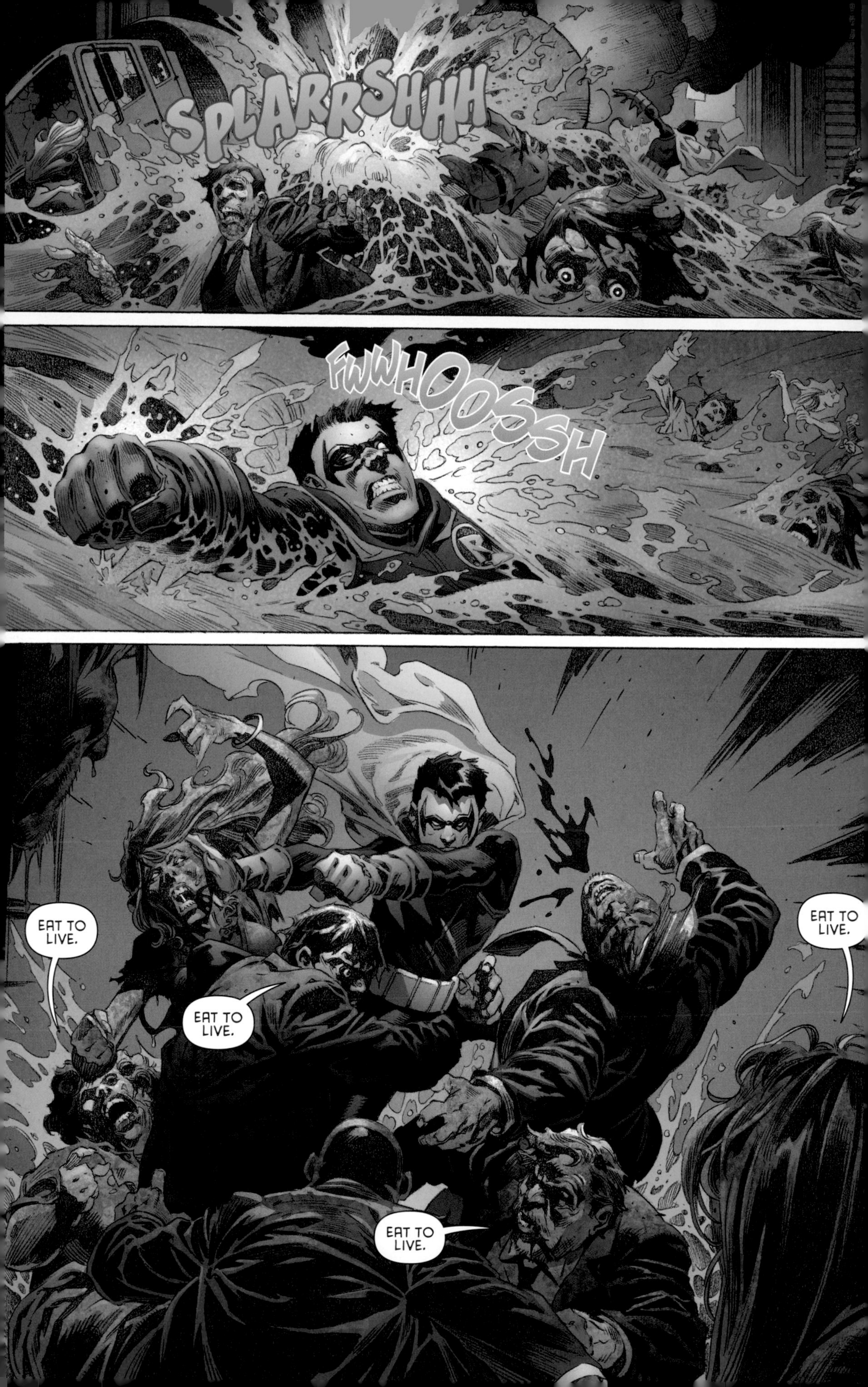
SPLARRSHHH
FWWHOOSSH
EAT TO LIVE.
EAT TO LIVE.
EAT TO LIVE.
EAT TO LIVE.

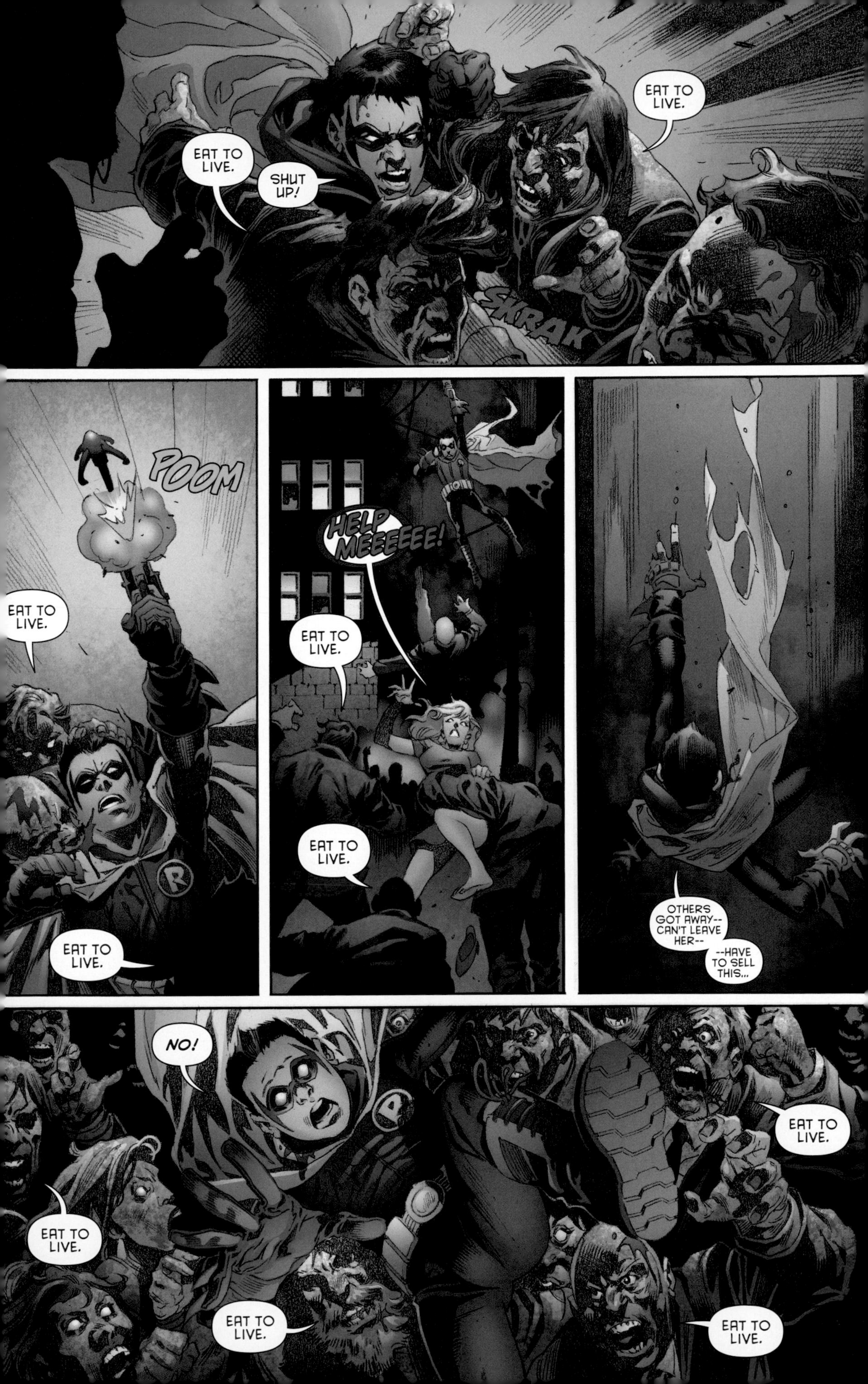
EAT TO LIVE.
SHUT UP!
EAT TO LIVE.
SKRAK
POOM
EAT TO LIVE.
EAT TO LIVE.
HELP MEEEEEE!
EAT TO LIVE.
EAT TO LIVE.
OTHERS GOT AWAY-- CAN'T LEAVE HER--
--HAVE TO SELL THIS...
NO!
EAT TO LIVE.
EAT TO LIVE.
EAT TO LIVE.
EAT TO LIVE.

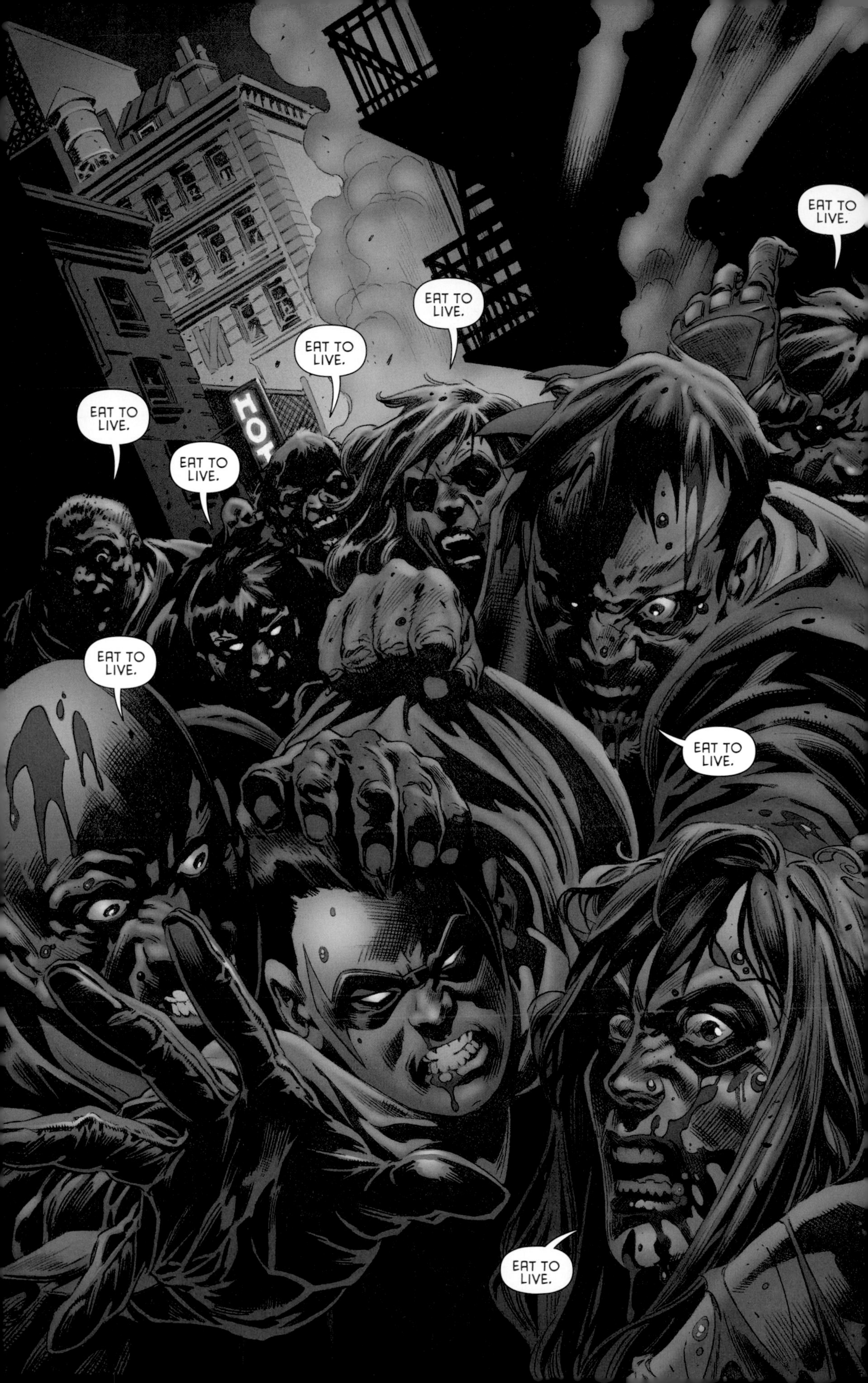
EAT TO LIVE.
EAT TO LIVE.
EAT TO LIVE.
EAT TO LIVE.
EAT TO LIVE.
EAT TO LIVE.
EAT TO LIVE.
EAT TO LIVE.

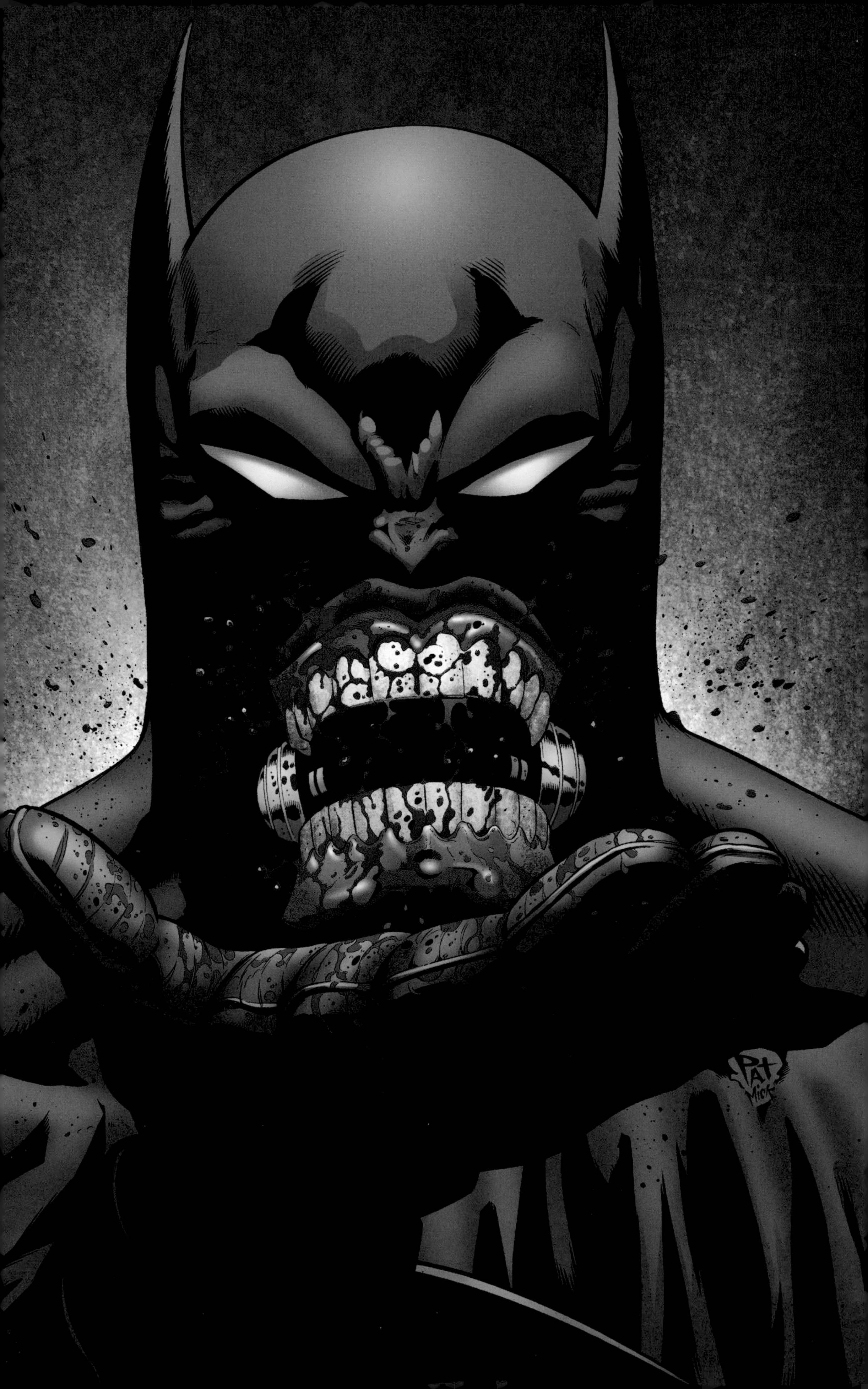
PAT
MICK

DEVOURED

PETER J. TOMASI writer **PATRICK GLEASON & TOMAS GIORELLO** pencillers **MICK GRAY** inker
cover by **GLEASON, GRAY & KALISZ**

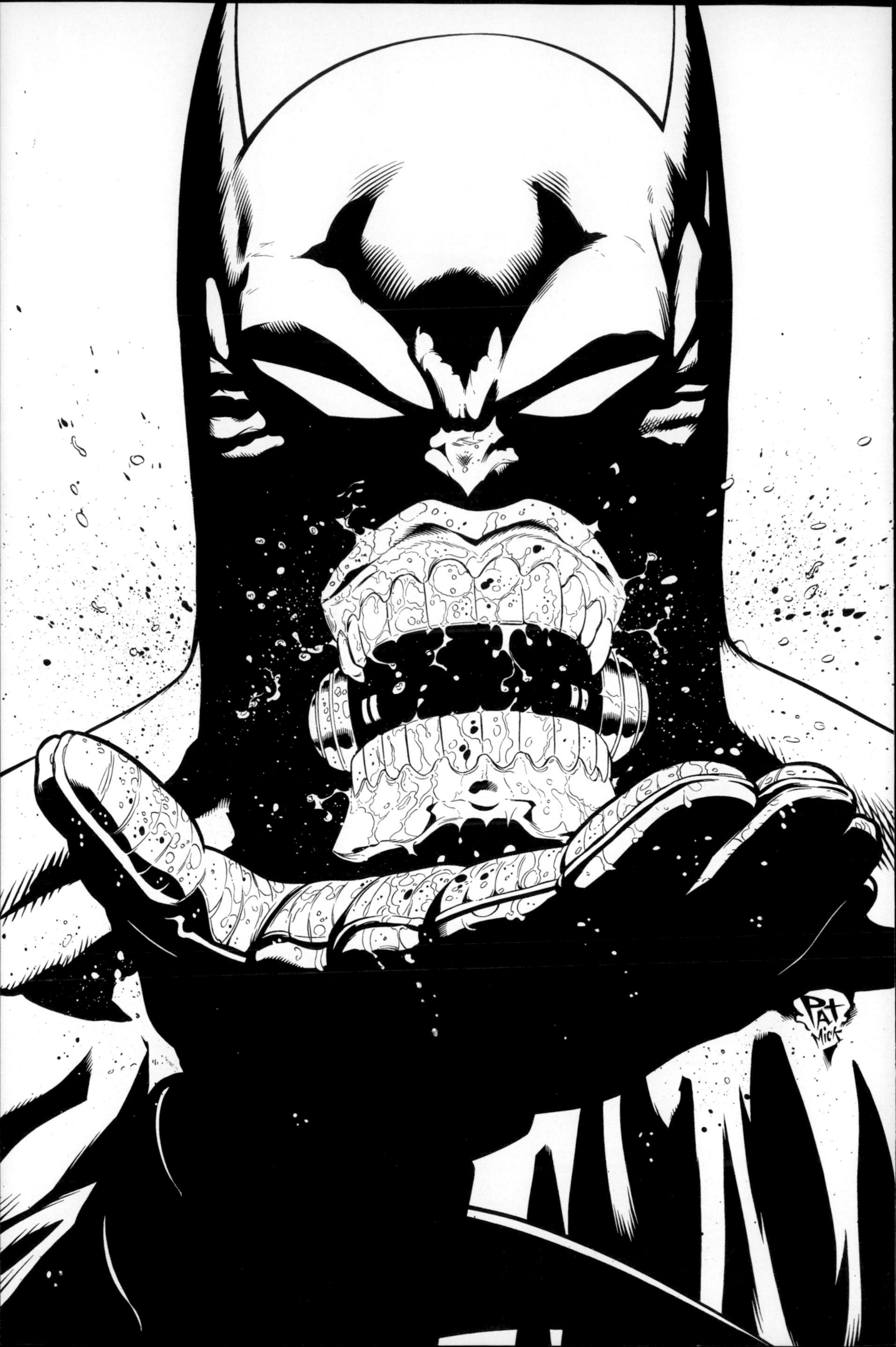
Pat
Mick

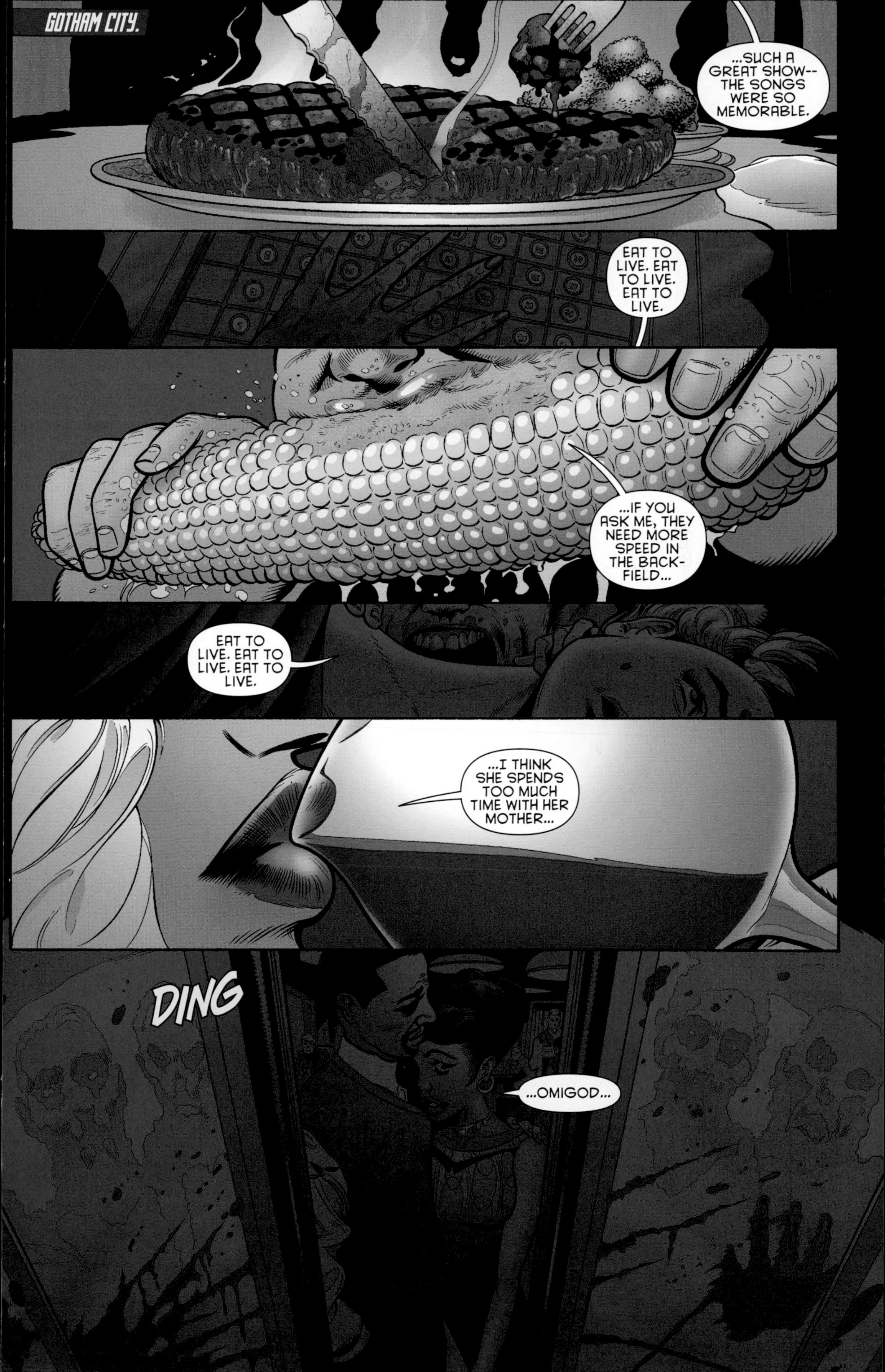
GOTHAM CITY.
...SUCH A GREAT SHOW--THE SONGS WERE SO MEMORABLE.
EAT TO LIVE. EAT TO LIVE. EAT TO LIVE.
...IF YOU ASK ME, THEY NEED MORE SPEED IN THE BACK-FIELD...
EAT TO LIVE. EAT TO LIVE. EAT TO LIVE.
...I THINK SHE SPENDS TOO MUCH TIME WITH HER MOTHER...
DING
...OMIGOD...

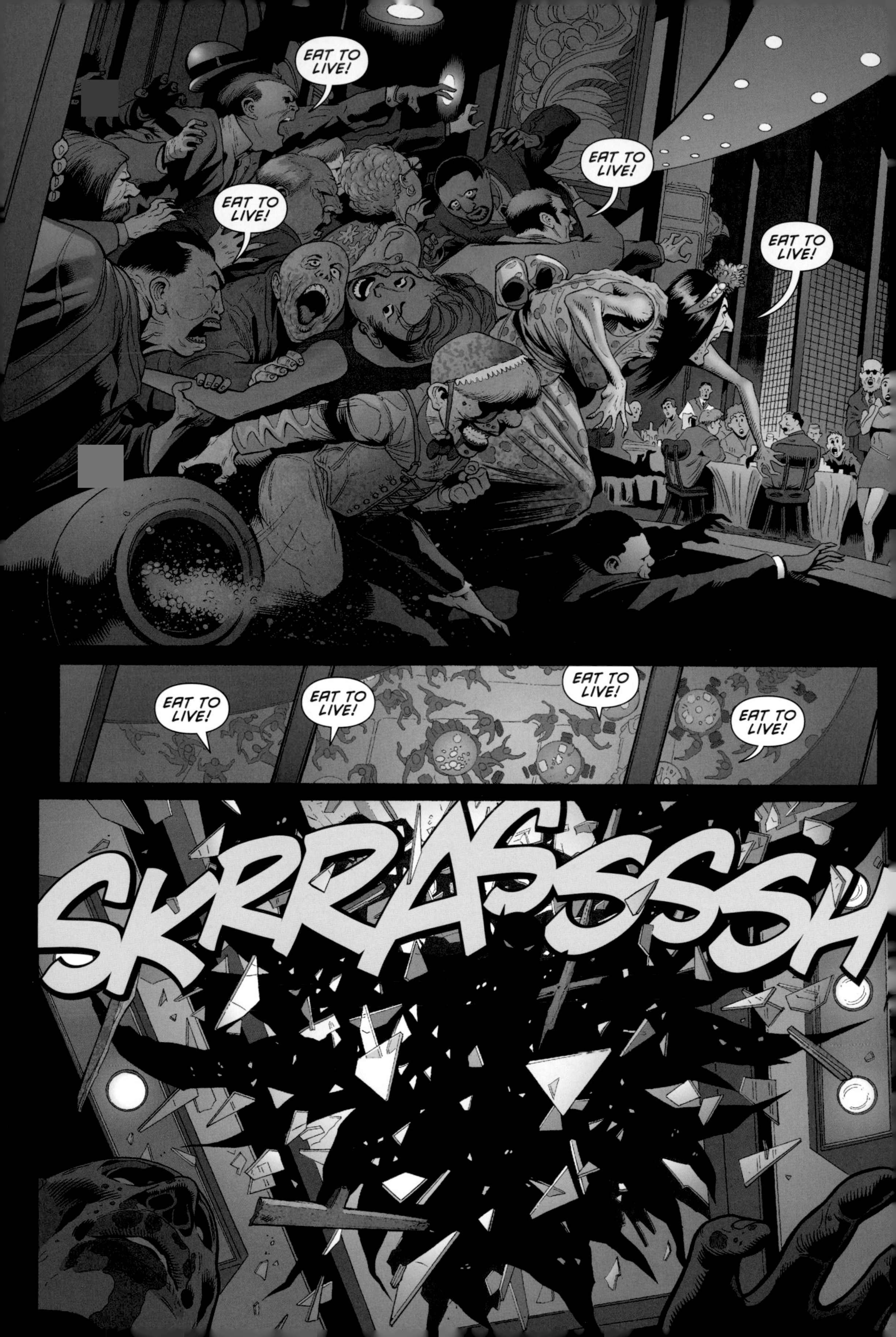
EAT TO LIVE!
EAT TO LIVE!
EAT TO LIVE!
EAT TO LIVE!
EAT TO LIVE!
EAT TO LIVE!
EAT TO LIVE!
EAT TO LIVE!
SKRRASSSH

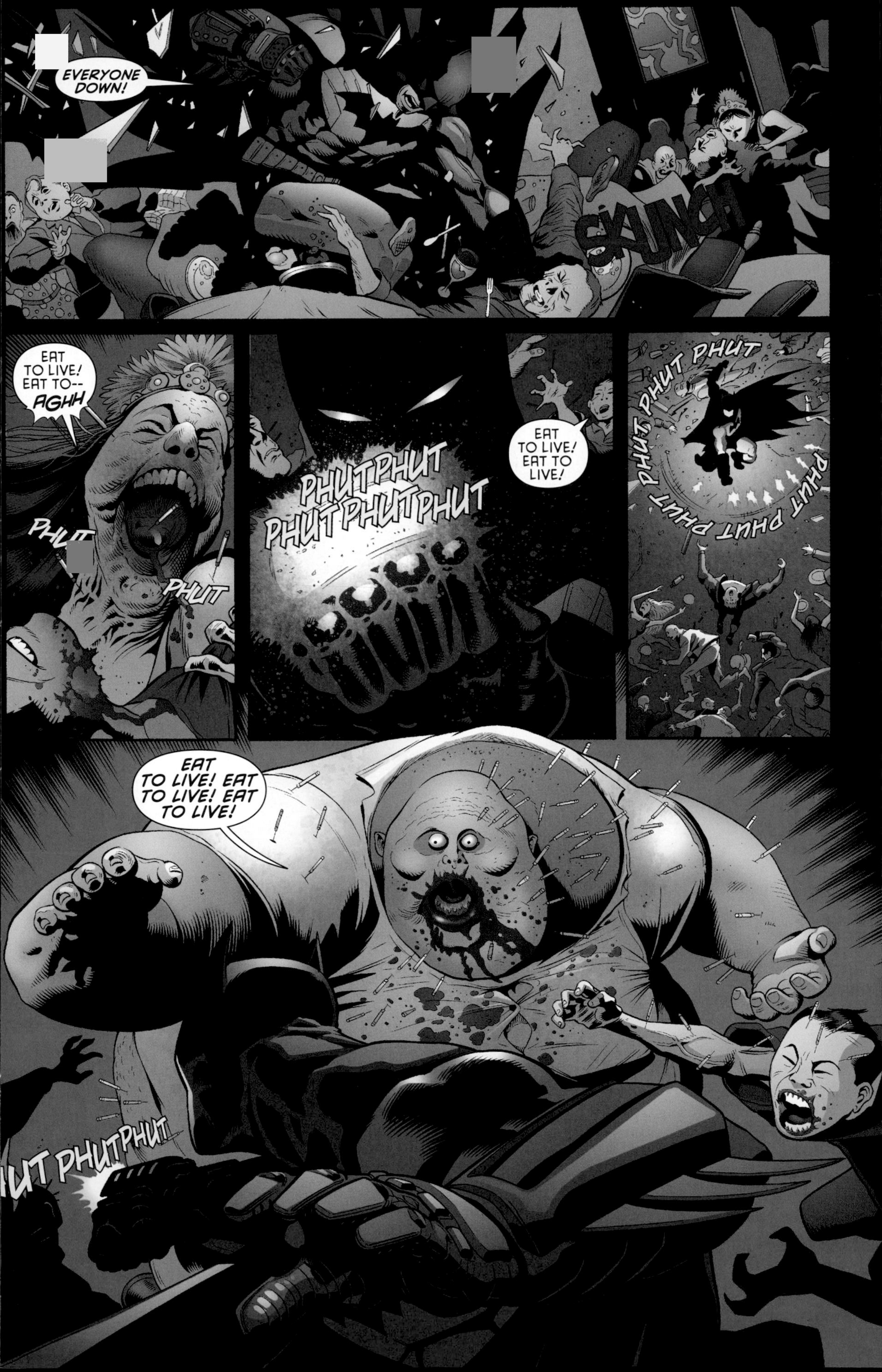
EVERYONE DOWN!
SKLUNCH
EAT TO LIVE! EAT TO-- AGHH
PHUT
PHUT
PHUTPHUT PHUTPHUTPHUT
EAT TO LIVE! EAT TO LIVE!
PHUT PHUT PHUT PHUT PHUT PHUT PHUT
EAT TO LIVE! EAT TO LIVE! EAT TO LIVE!
UT PHUTPHUT

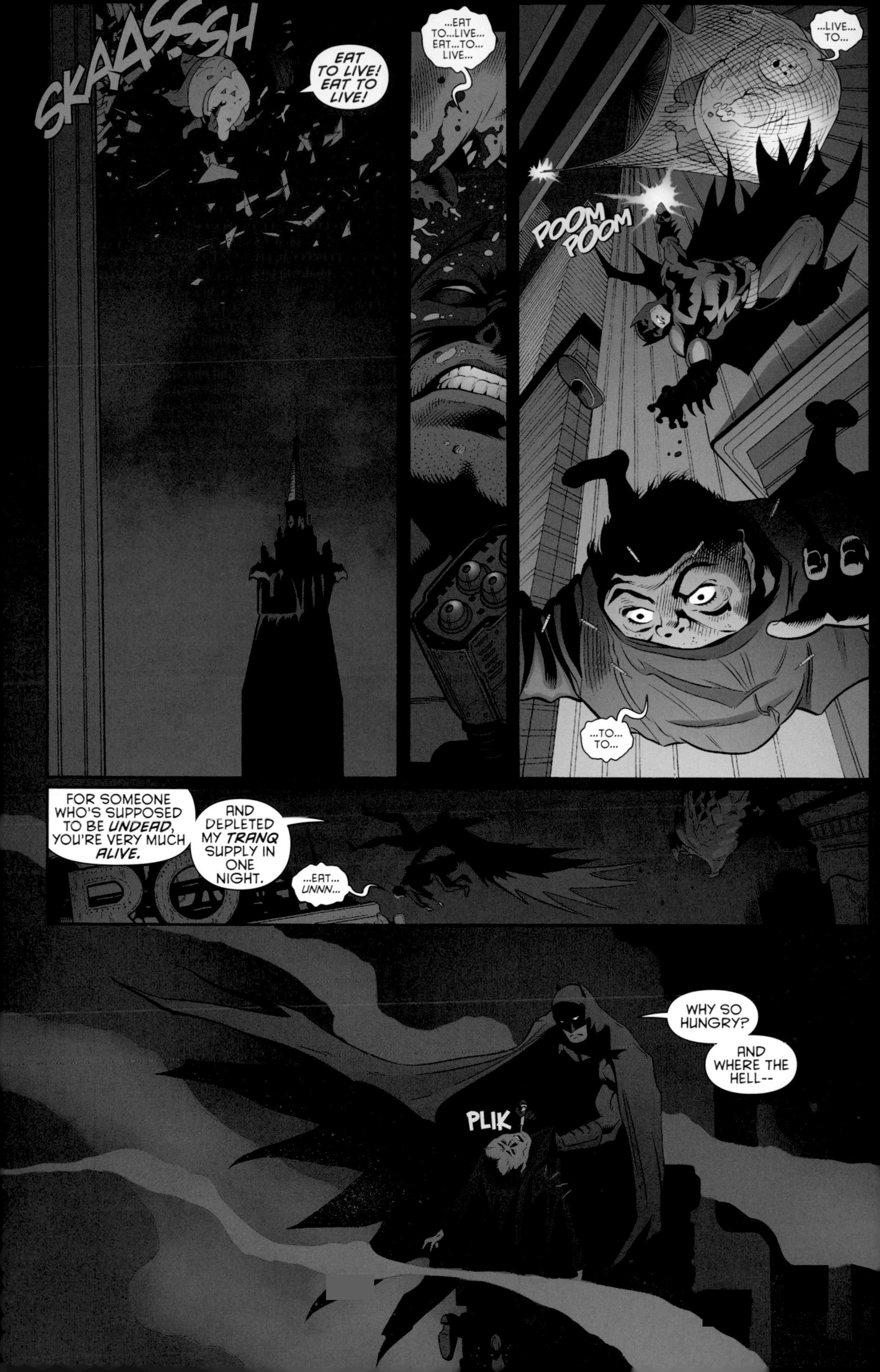
SKAASSSH
EAT TO LIVE! EAT TO LIVE!
...EAT TO...LIVE... EAT...TO... LIVE...
...LIVE... TO...
POOM POOM
...TO... TO...
FOR SOMEONE WHO'S SUPPOSED TO BE UNDEAD, YOU'RE VERY MUCH ALIVE.
AND DEPLETED MY TRANQ SUPPLY IN ONE NIGHT.
...EAT... UNNN...
WHY SO HUNGRY?
AND WHERE THE HELL--
PLIK

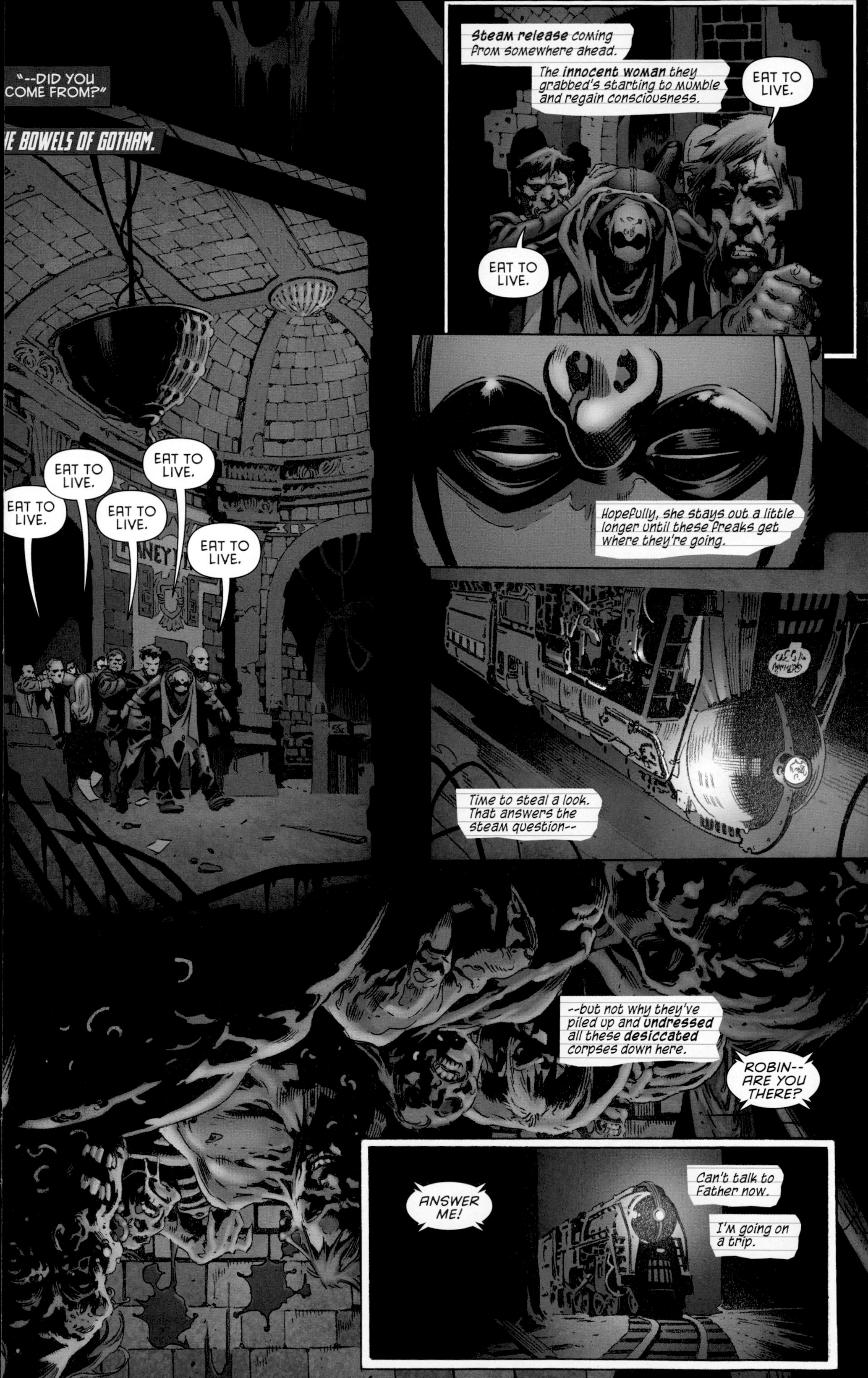
"--DID YOU COME FROM?"
...E BOWELS OF GOTHAM.
EAT TO LIVE.
EAT TO LIVE.
EAT TO LIVE.
EAT TO LIVE.
EAT TO LIVE.
Steam release coming from somewhere ahead.
The innocent woman they grabbed's starting to mumble and regain consciousness.
EAT TO LIVE.
EAT TO LIVE.
Hopefully, she stays out a little longer until these freaks get where they're going.
Time to steal a look. That answers the steam question--
--but not why they've piled up and undressed all these desiccated corpses down here.
ROBIN-- ARE YOU THERE?
ANSWER ME!
Can't talk to Father now.
I'm going on a trip.

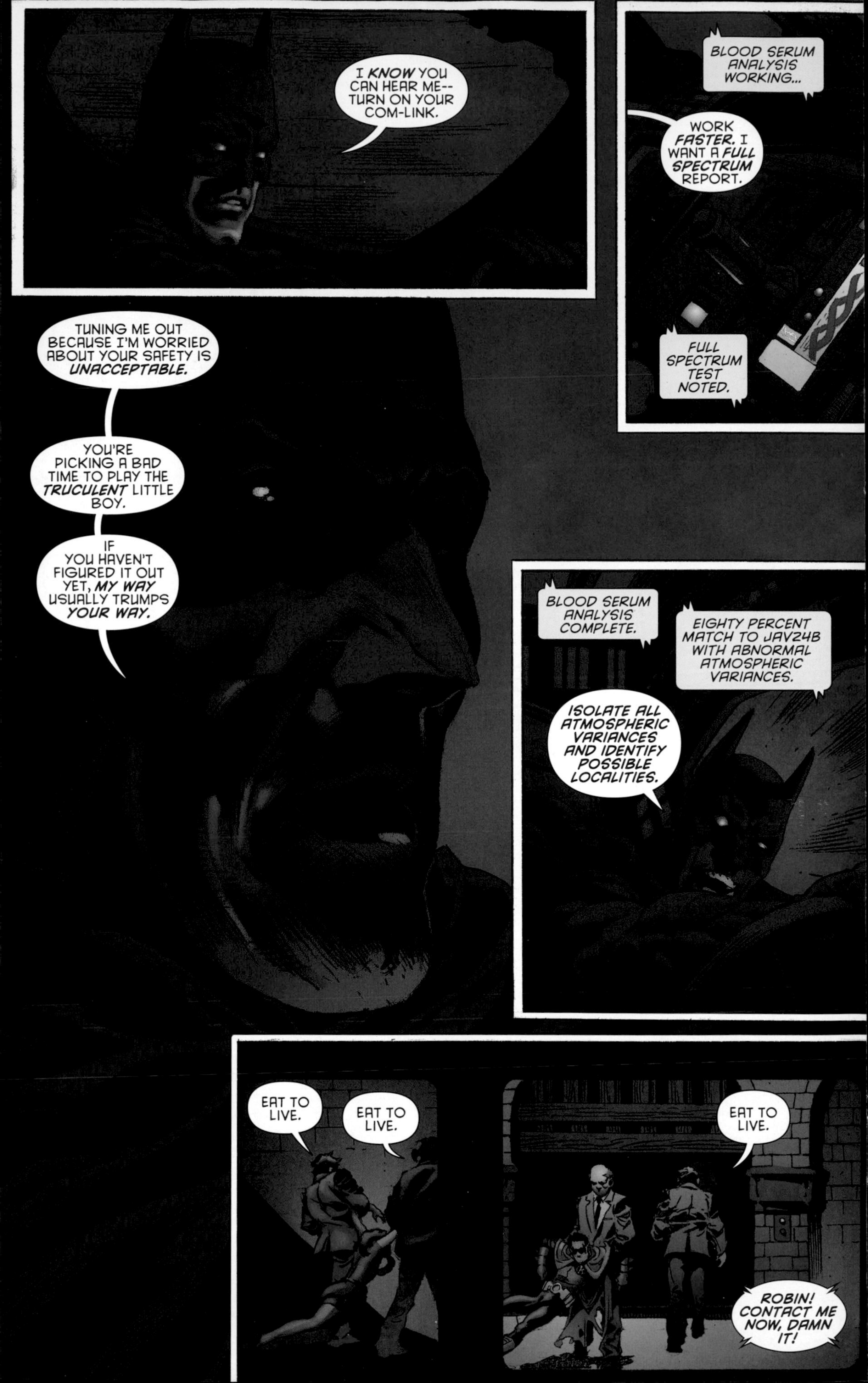
I KNOW YOU CAN HEAR ME-- TURN ON YOUR COM-LINK.
BLOOD SERUM ANALYSIS WORKING...
WORK FASTER. I WANT A FULL SPECTRUM REPORT.
FULL SPECTRUM TEST NOTED.
TUNING ME OUT BECAUSE I'M WORRIED ABOUT YOUR SAFETY IS UNACCEPTABLE.
YOU'RE PICKING A BAD TIME TO PLAY THE TRUCULENT LITTLE BOY.
IF YOU HAVEN'T FIGURED IT OUT YET, MY WAY USUALLY TRUMPS YOUR WAY.
BLOOD SERUM ANALYSIS COMPLETE.
EIGHTY PERCENT MATCH TO JAV24B WITH ABNORMAL ATMOSPHERIC VARIANCES.
ISOLATE ALL ATMOSPHERIC VARIANCES AND IDENTIFY POSSIBLE LOCALITIES.
EAT TO LIVE.
EAT TO LIVE.
EAT TO LIVE.
ROBIN! CONTACT ME NOW, DAMN IT!

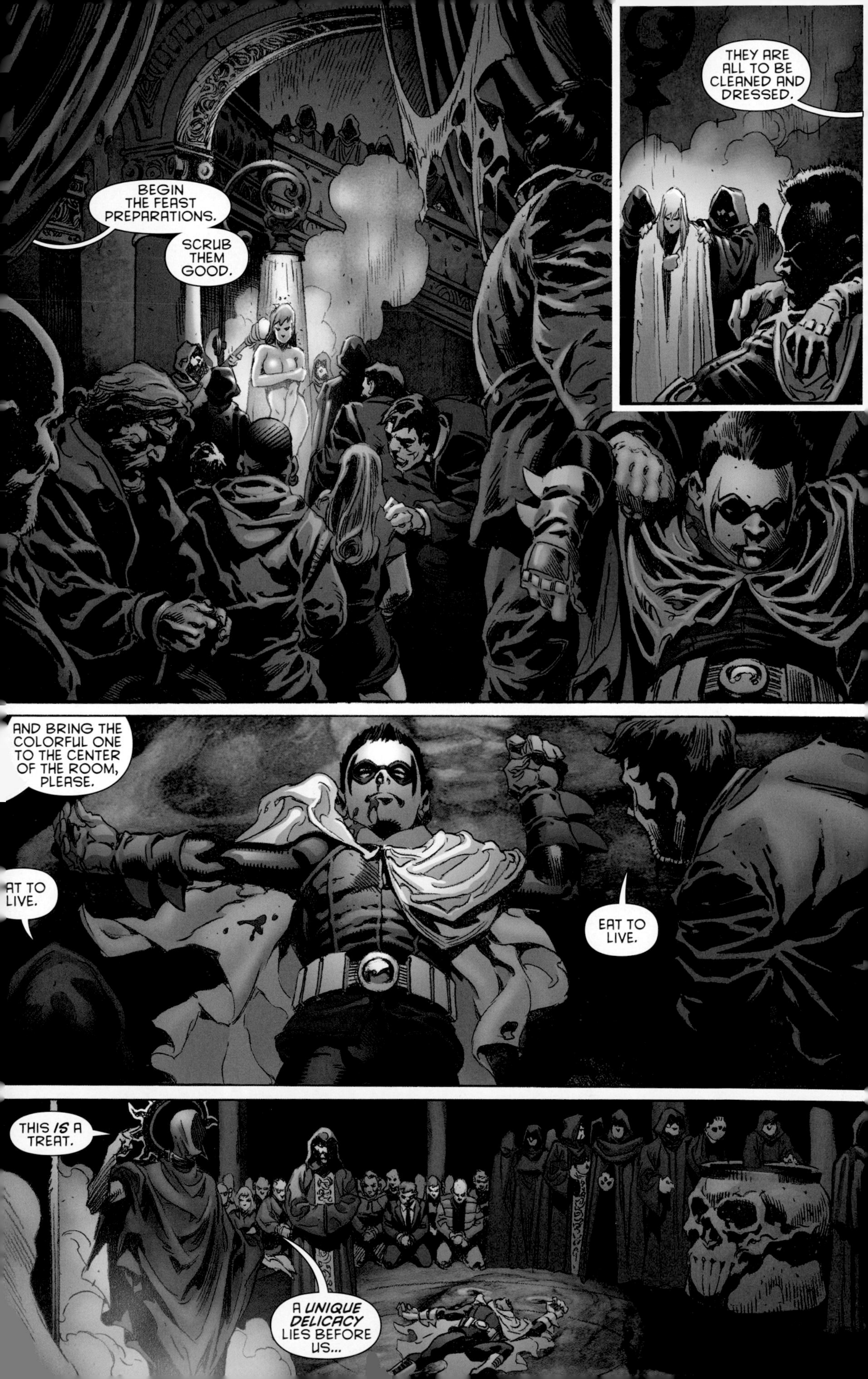
BEGIN THE FEAST PREPARATIONS.
SCRUB THEM GOOD.
THEY ARE ALL TO BE CLEANED AND DRESSED.
AND BRING THE COLORFUL ONE TO THE CENTER OF THE ROOM, PLEASE.
EAT TO LIVE.
EAT TO LIVE.
THIS *IS* A TREAT.
A *UNIQUE DELICACY* LIES BEFORE US...

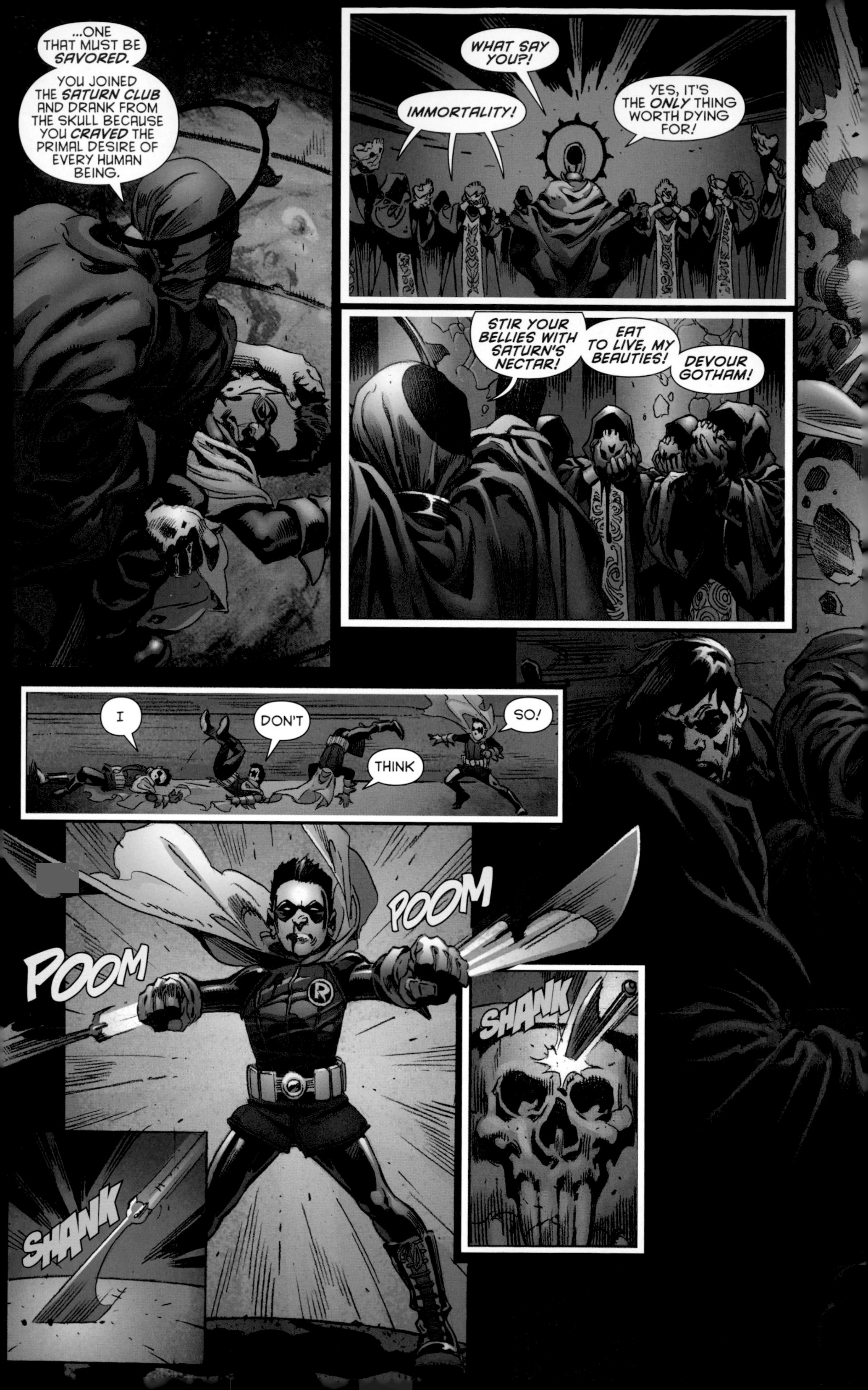

...ONE THAT MUST BE SAVORED.
YOU JOINED THE SATURN CLUB AND DRANK FROM THE SKULL BECAUSE YOU CRAVED THE PRIMAL DESIRE OF EVERY HUMAN BEING.
WHAT SAY YOU?!
IMMORTALITY!
YES, IT'S THE ONLY THING WORTH DYING FOR!
STIR YOUR BELLIES WITH SATURN'S NECTAR!
EAT TO LIVE, MY BEAUTIES!
DEVOUR GOTHAM!
I
DON'T
THINK
SO!
POOM
POOM
SHANK
SHANK

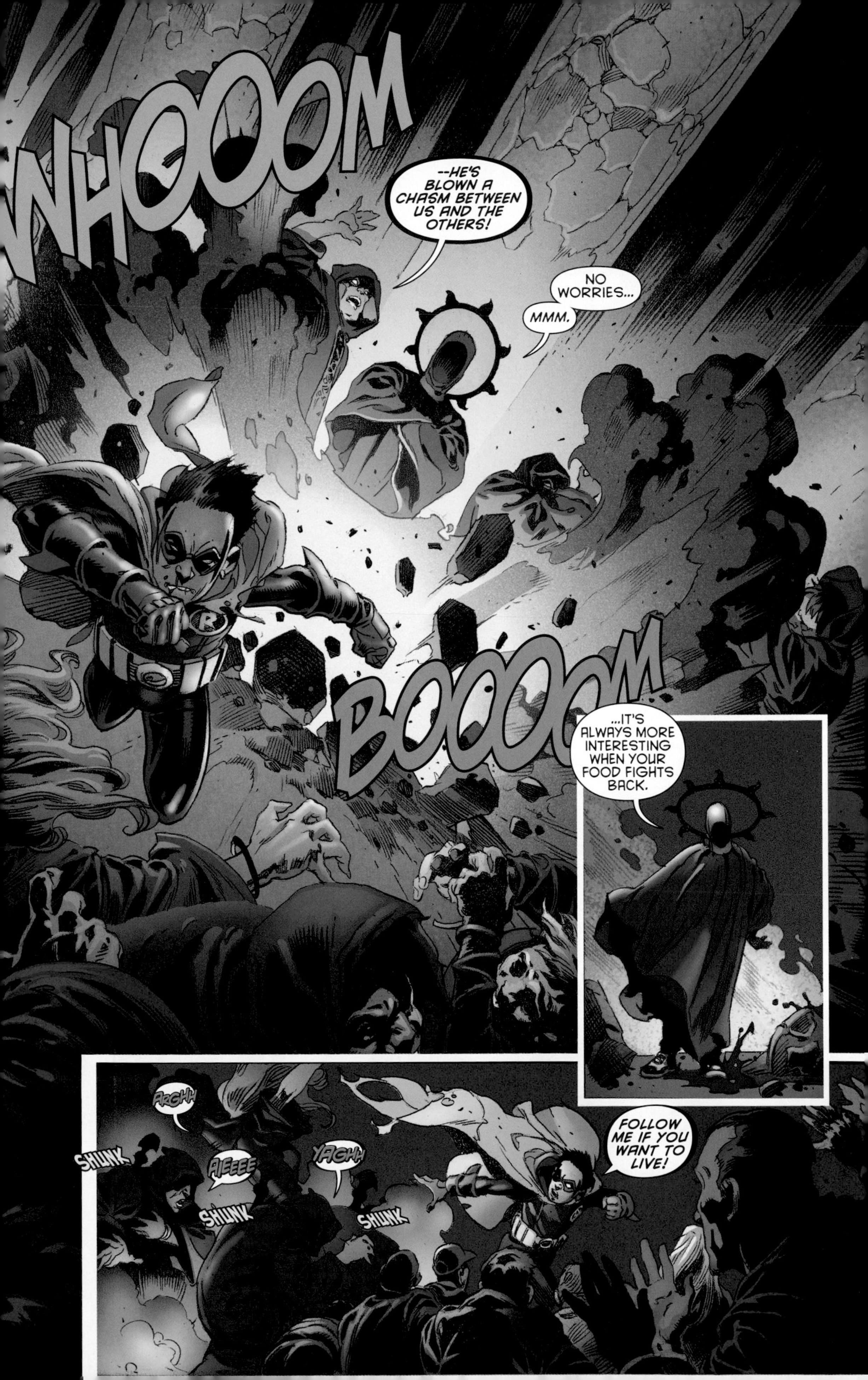
WHOOOM
--HE'S BLOWN A CHASM BETWEEN US AND THE OTHERS!
NO WORRIES...
MMM.
BOOOOM
...IT'S ALWAYS MORE INTERESTING WHEN YOUR FOOD FIGHTS BACK.
ARGHH
SHUNK
AIEEEE
YAGHH
SHUNK
SHUNK
FOLLOW ME IF YOU WANT TO LIVE!

COME ON--GET IN THIS FREIGHT ELEVATOR--HURRY!

YOUR IMMORTALITY IS ESCAPING-- WHAT ARE YOU PREPARED TO DO?

EAT TO LIVE.

EAT TO LIVE.

EAT TO LIVE.

EAT TO LIVE.

EAT T LIVE.

THAT'S THE SPIRIT!

--OMIGOD-- THANK YOU--

--SAVED US FROM THOSE MONSTERS--

IT'S MOVING TOO SLOW! WE NEED TO GET DOWN FASTER BEFORE THEY--

DON'T LET THE MEAT BEAT YOU!

EAT TO LIVE.

EAT T LIVE

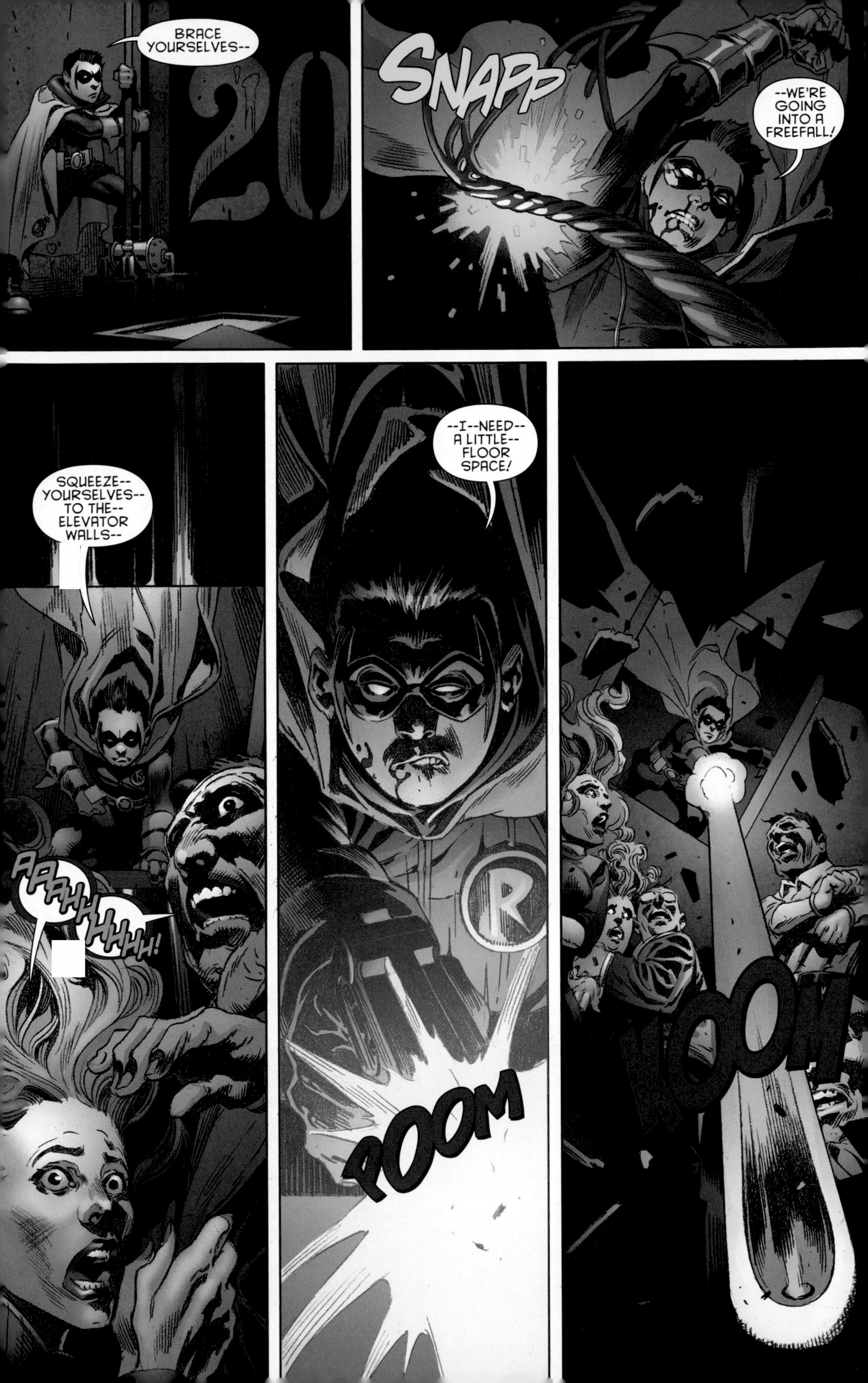
BRACE YOURSELVES--
SNAPP
--WE'RE GOING INTO A FREEFALL!
SQUEEZE-- YOURSELVES-- TO THE-- ELEVATOR WALLS--
AAAHHHHHHH!
--I--NEED-- A LITTLE-- FLOOR SPACE!
POOM
VOOOM

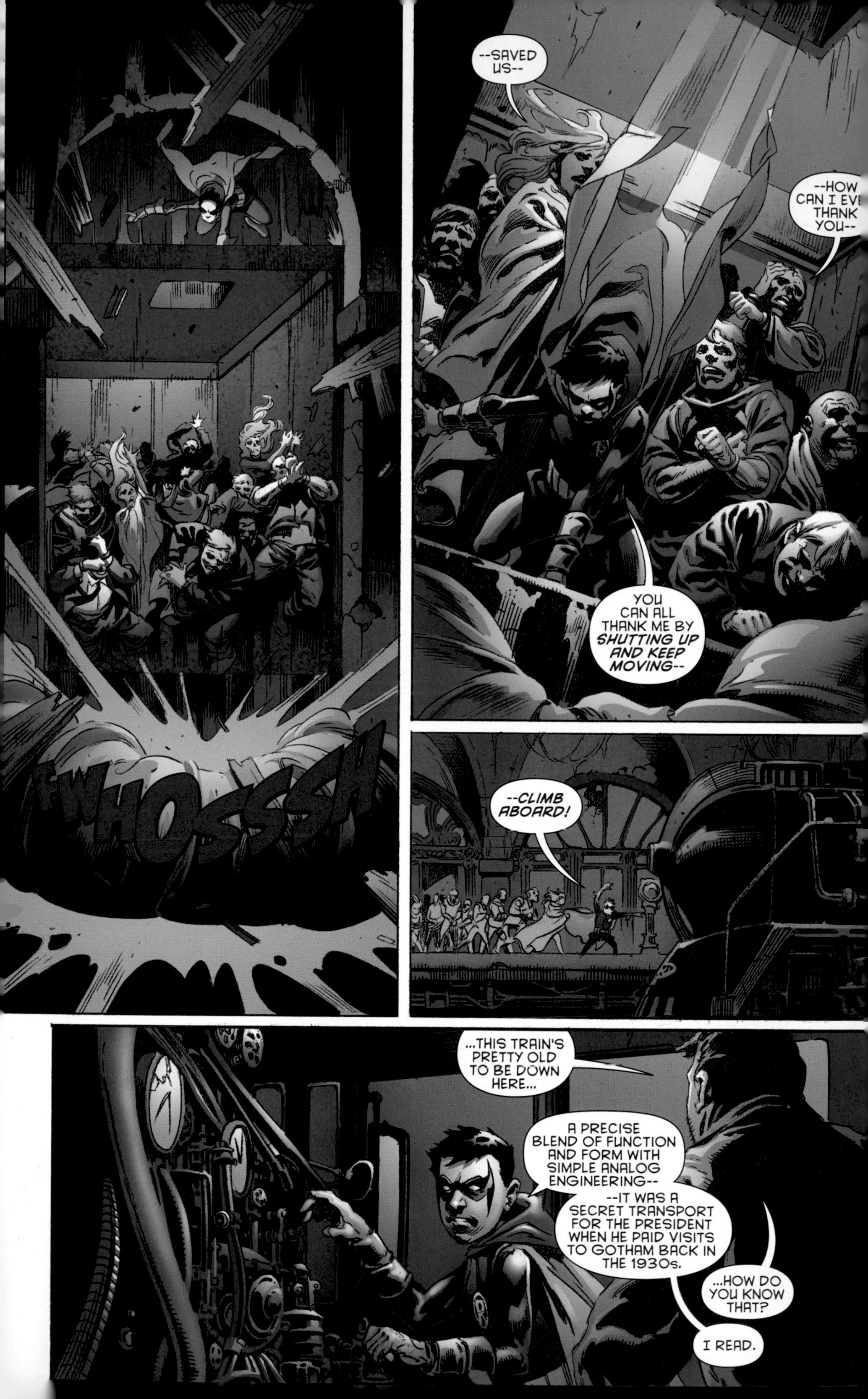

FWHOSSSH
--SAVED US--
--HOW CAN I EVE THANK YOU--
YOU CAN ALL THANK ME BY *SHUTTING UP AND KEEP MOVING--*
--CLIMB ABOARD!
...THIS TRAIN'S PRETTY OLD TO BE DOWN HERE...
A PRECISE BLEND OF FUNCTION AND FORM WITH SIMPLE ANALOG ENGINEERING--
--IT WAS A SECRET TRANSPORT FOR THE PRESIDENT WHEN HE PAID VISITS TO GOTHAM BACK IN THE 1930s.
...HOW DO YOU KNOW THAT?
I READ.

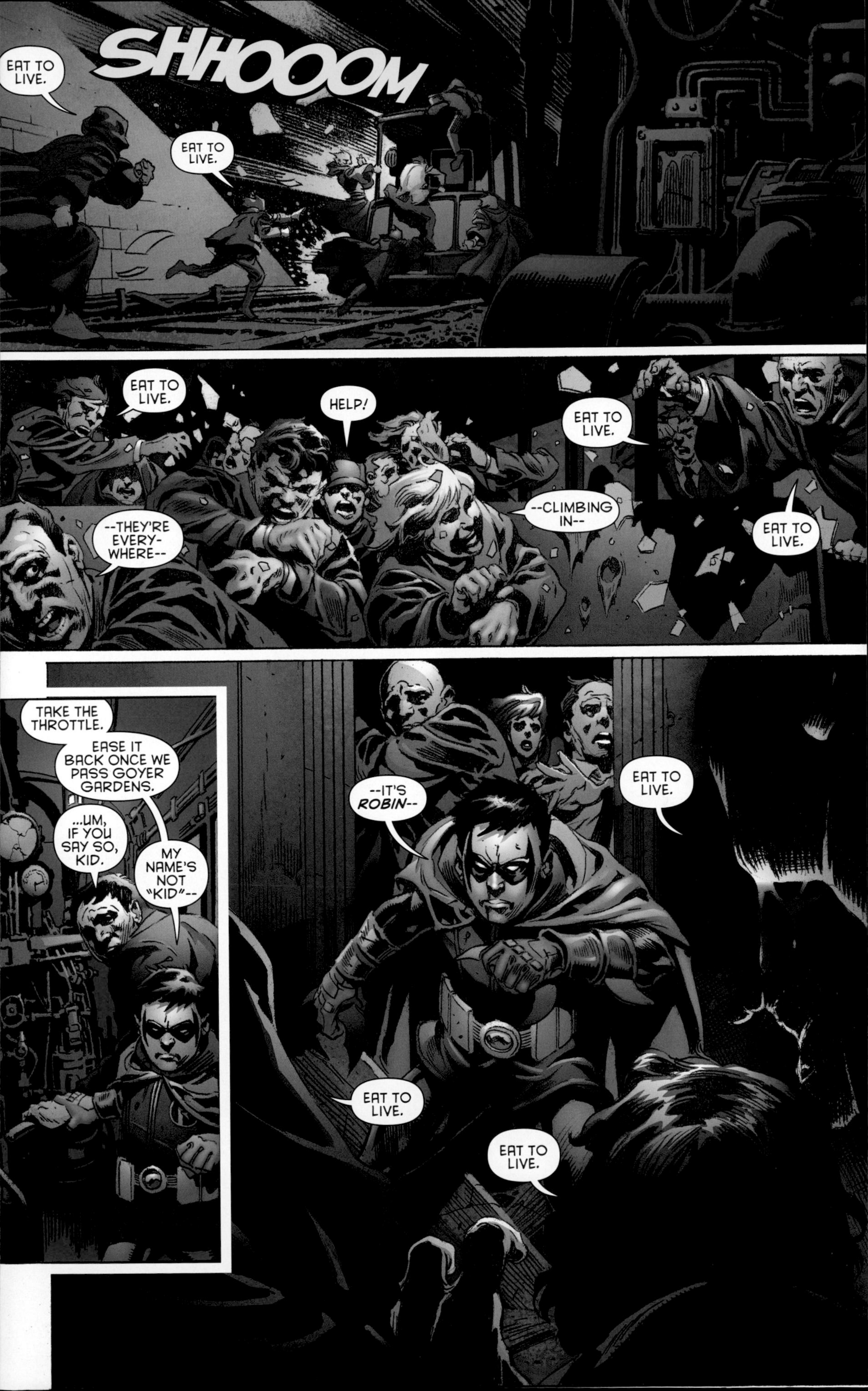
SHHOOOM
EAT TO LIVE.
EAT TO LIVE.
EAT TO LIVE.
HELP!
EAT TO LIVE.
--THEY'RE EVERY-WHERE--
--CLIMBING IN--
EAT TO LIVE.
TAKE THE THROTTLE.
EASE IT BACK ONCE WE PASS GOYER GARDENS.
...UM, IF YOU SAY SO, KID.
MY NAME'S NOT "KID"--
--IT'S *ROBIN*--
EAT TO LIVE.
EAT TO LIVE.
EAT TO LIVE.

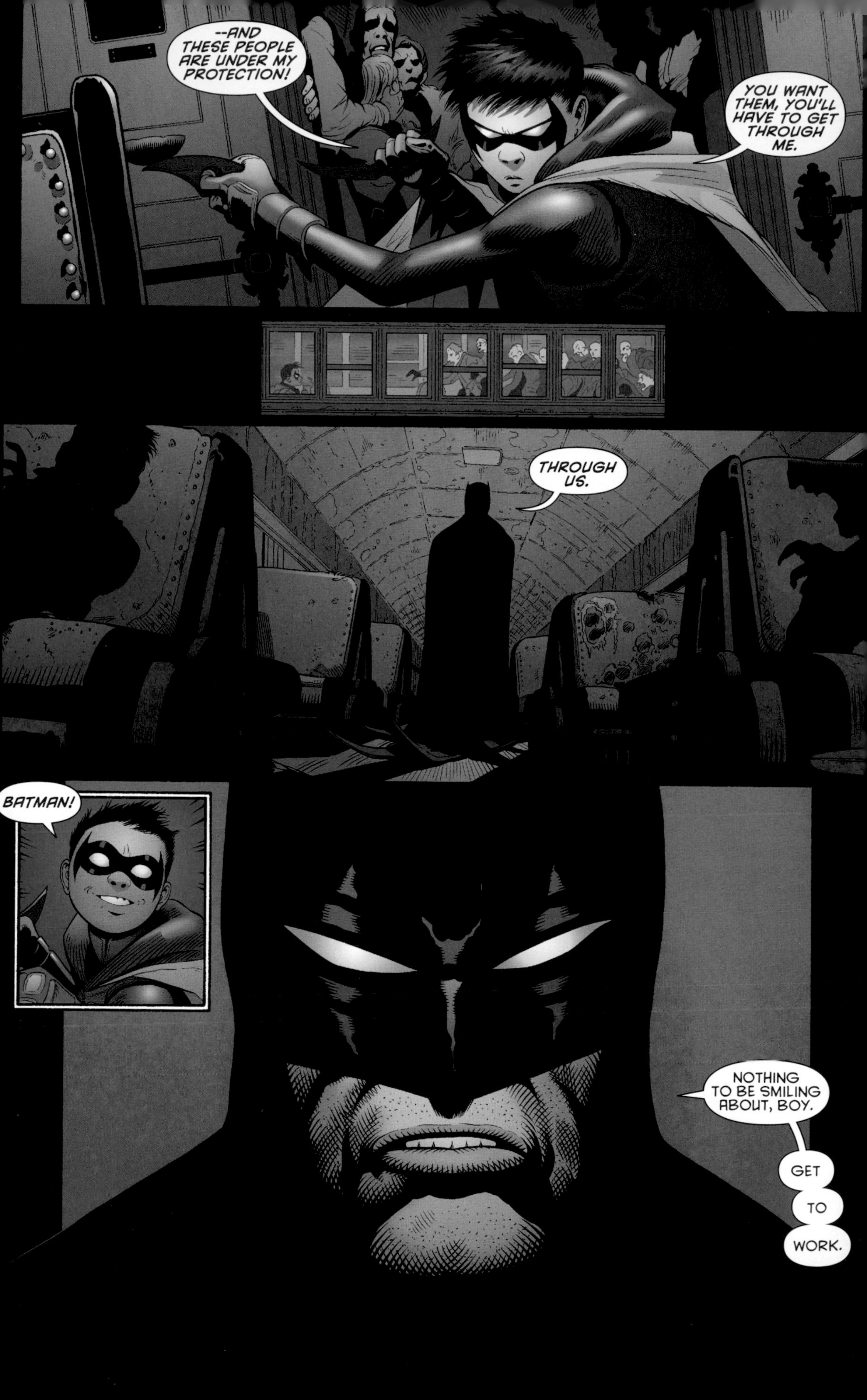
--AND THESE PEOPLE ARE UNDER MY PROTECTION!
YOU WANT THEM, YOU'LL HAVE TO GET THROUGH ME.
THROUGH US.
BATMAN!
NOTHING TO BE SMILING ABOUT, BOY.
GET
TO
WORK.

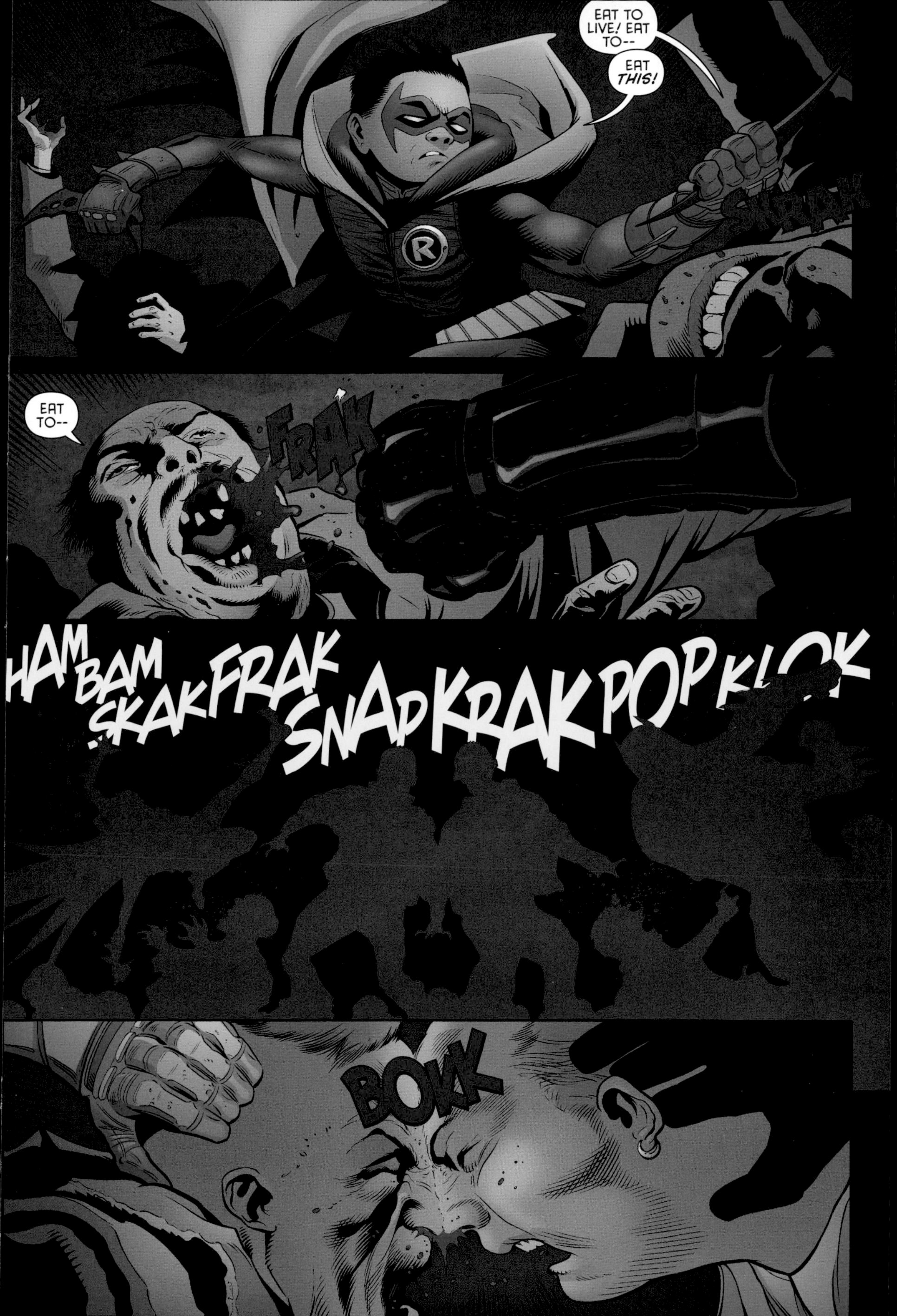

EAT TO LIVE! EAT TO--
EAT *THIS!*
EAT TO--
FRAK
HAM
BAM
SKAK
FRAK
SNAP
KRAK
POP
KLOK
BOKK

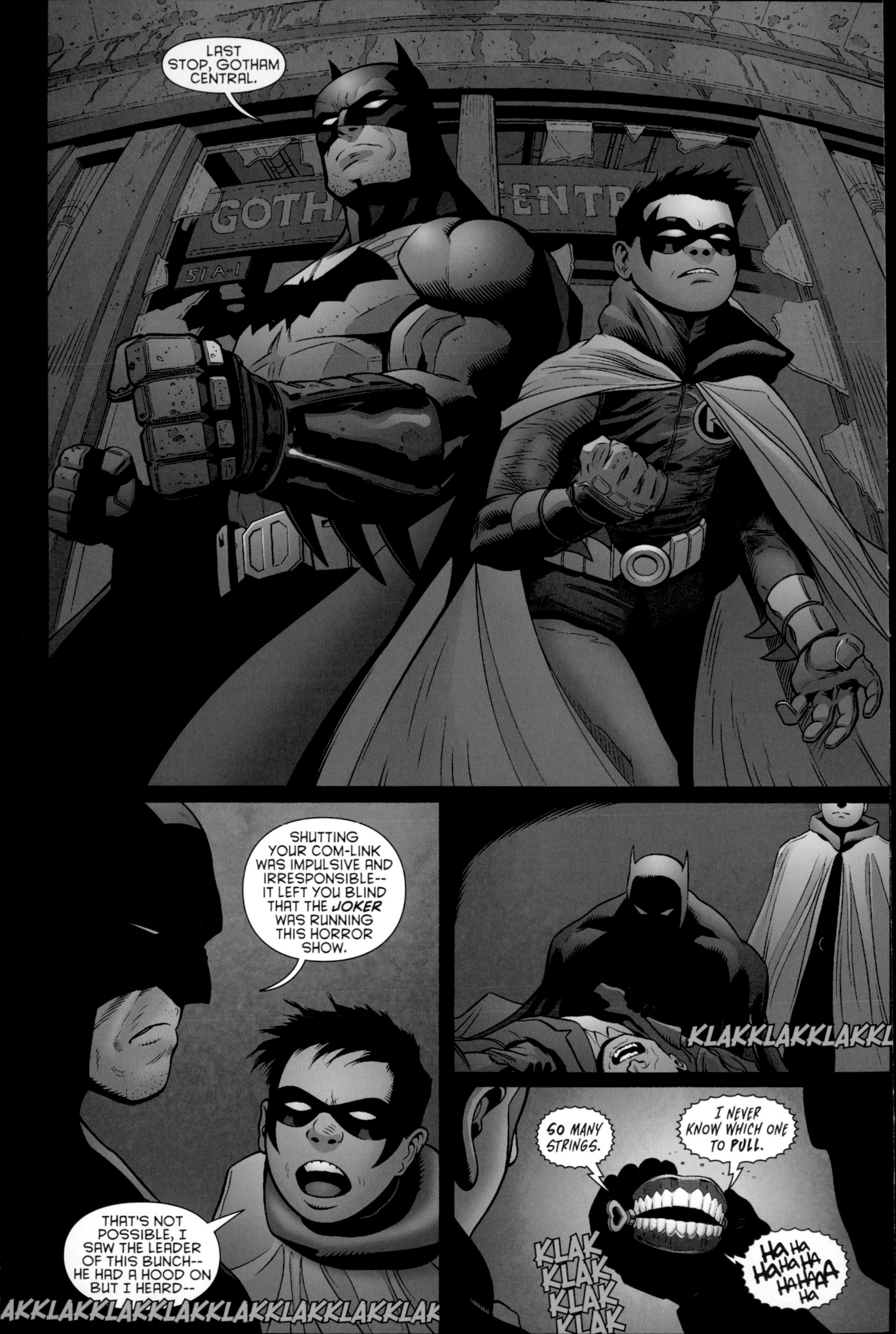
LAST STOP, GOTHAM CENTRAL.
GOTHAM CENTR
51A-1
SHUTTING YOUR COM-LINK WAS IMPULSIVE AND IRRESPONSIBLE-- IT LEFT YOU BLIND THAT THE JOKER WAS RUNNING THIS HORROR SHOW.
THAT'S NOT POSSIBLE, I SAW THE LEADER OF THIS BUNCH-- HE HAD A HOOD ON BUT I HEARD--
AKKLAKKLAKKLAKKLAKKLAKKLAKKLAK
KLAKKLAKKLAKKL
SO MANY STRINGS.
I NEVER KNOW WHICH ONE TO PULL.
KLAK KLAK KLAK KLAK
Ha Ha Ha Ha Ha Ha HaHAAA Ha

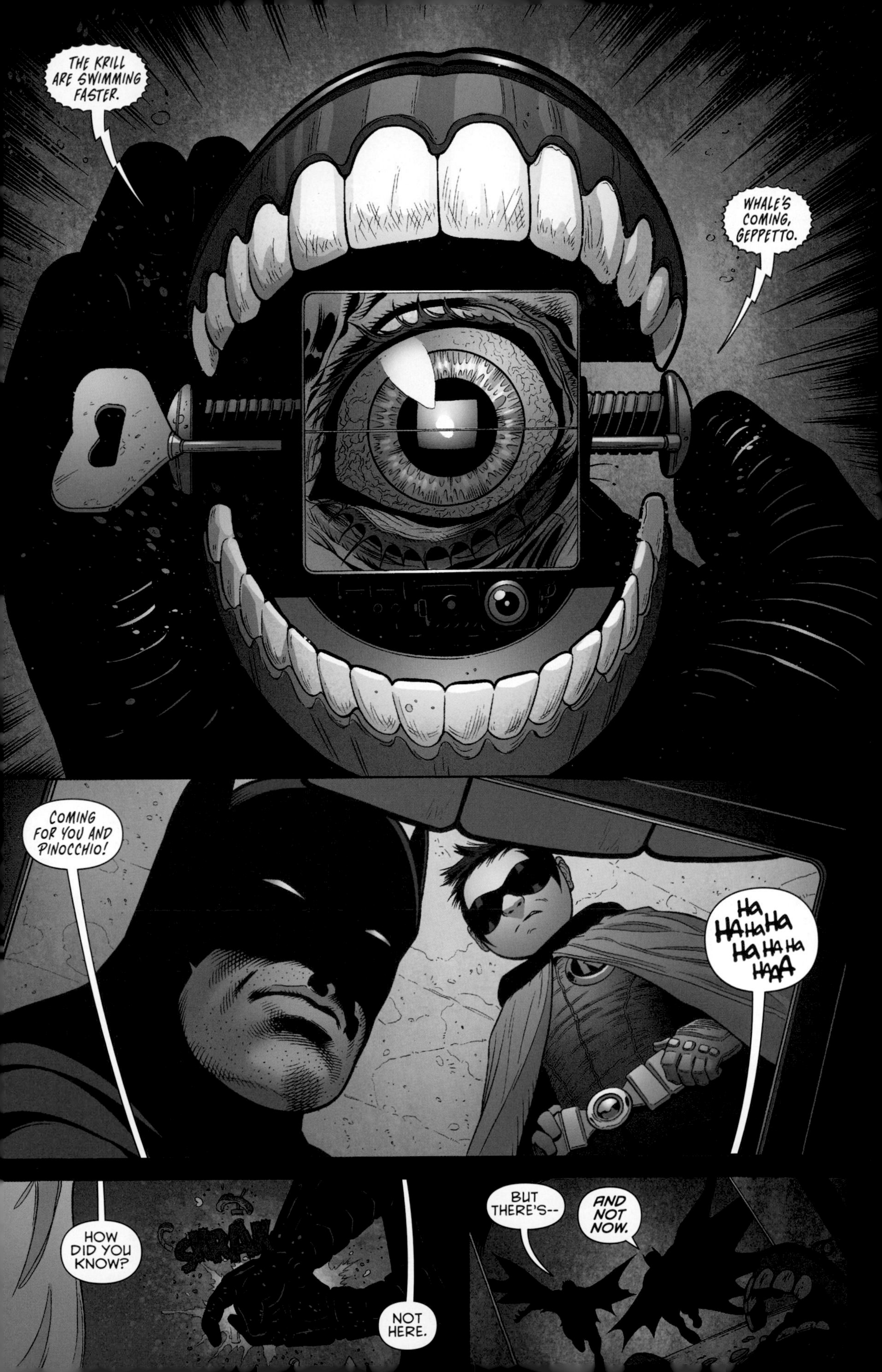
THE KRILL ARE SWIMMING FASTER.
WHALE'S COMING, GEPPETTO.
COMING FOR YOU AND PINOCCHIO!
HA HAHAHA HAHAHA HAAA
HOW DID YOU KNOW?
NOT HERE.
BUT THERE'S--
AND NOT NOW.

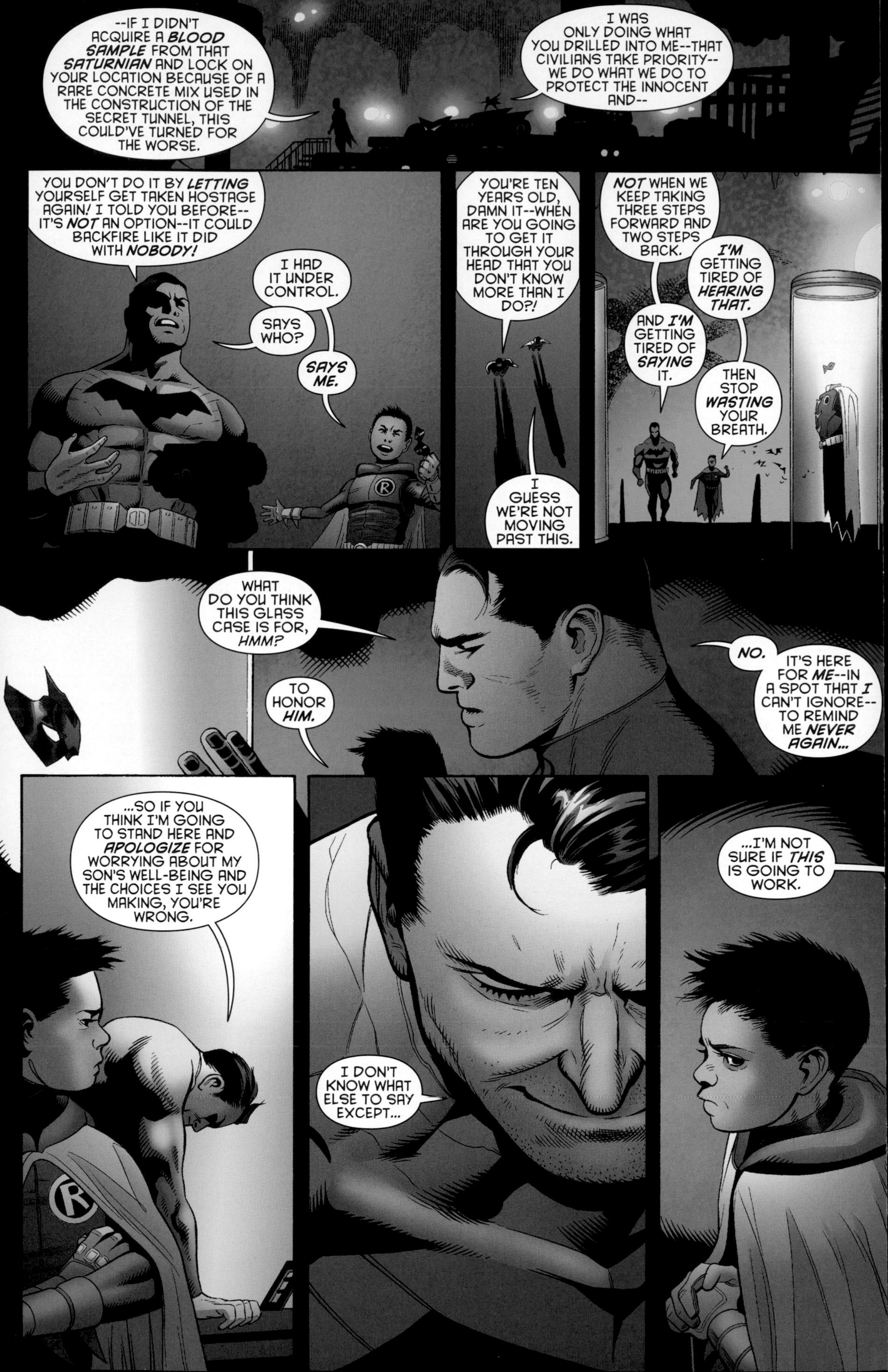
--IF I DIDN'T ACQUIRE A BLOOD SAMPLE FROM THAT SATURNIAN AND LOCK ON YOUR LOCATION BECAUSE OF A RARE CONCRETE MIX USED IN THE CONSTRUCTION OF THE SECRET TUNNEL, THIS COULD'VE TURNED FOR THE WORSE.
I WAS ONLY DOING WHAT YOU DRILLED INTO ME--THAT CIVILIANS TAKE PRIORITY--WE DO WHAT WE DO TO PROTECT THE INNOCENT AND--
YOU DON'T DO IT BY LETTING YOURSELF GET TAKEN HOSTAGE AGAIN! I TOLD YOU BEFORE--IT'S NOT AN OPTION--IT COULD BACKFIRE LIKE IT DID WITH NOBODY!
I HAD IT UNDER CONTROL.
SAYS WHO?
SAYS ME.
YOU'RE TEN YEARS OLD, DAMN IT--WHEN ARE YOU GOING TO GET IT THROUGH YOUR HEAD THAT YOU DON'T KNOW MORE THAN I DO?!
I GUESS WE'RE NOT MOVING PAST THIS.
NOT WHEN WE KEEP TAKING THREE STEPS FORWARD AND TWO STEPS BACK.
I'M GETTING TIRED OF HEARING THAT.
AND I'M GETTING TIRED OF SAYING IT.
THEN STOP WASTING YOUR BREATH.
WHAT DO YOU THINK THIS GLASS CASE IS FOR, HMM?
TO HONOR HIM.
NO.
IT'S HERE FOR ME--IN A SPOT THAT I CAN'T IGNORE--TO REMIND ME NEVER AGAIN...
...SO IF YOU THINK I'M GOING TO STAND HERE AND APOLOGIZE FOR WORRYING ABOUT MY SON'S WELL-BEING AND THE CHOICES I SEE YOU MAKING, YOU'RE WRONG.
I DON'T KNOW WHAT ELSE TO SAY EXCEPT...
...I'M NOT SURE IF THIS IS GOING TO WORK.

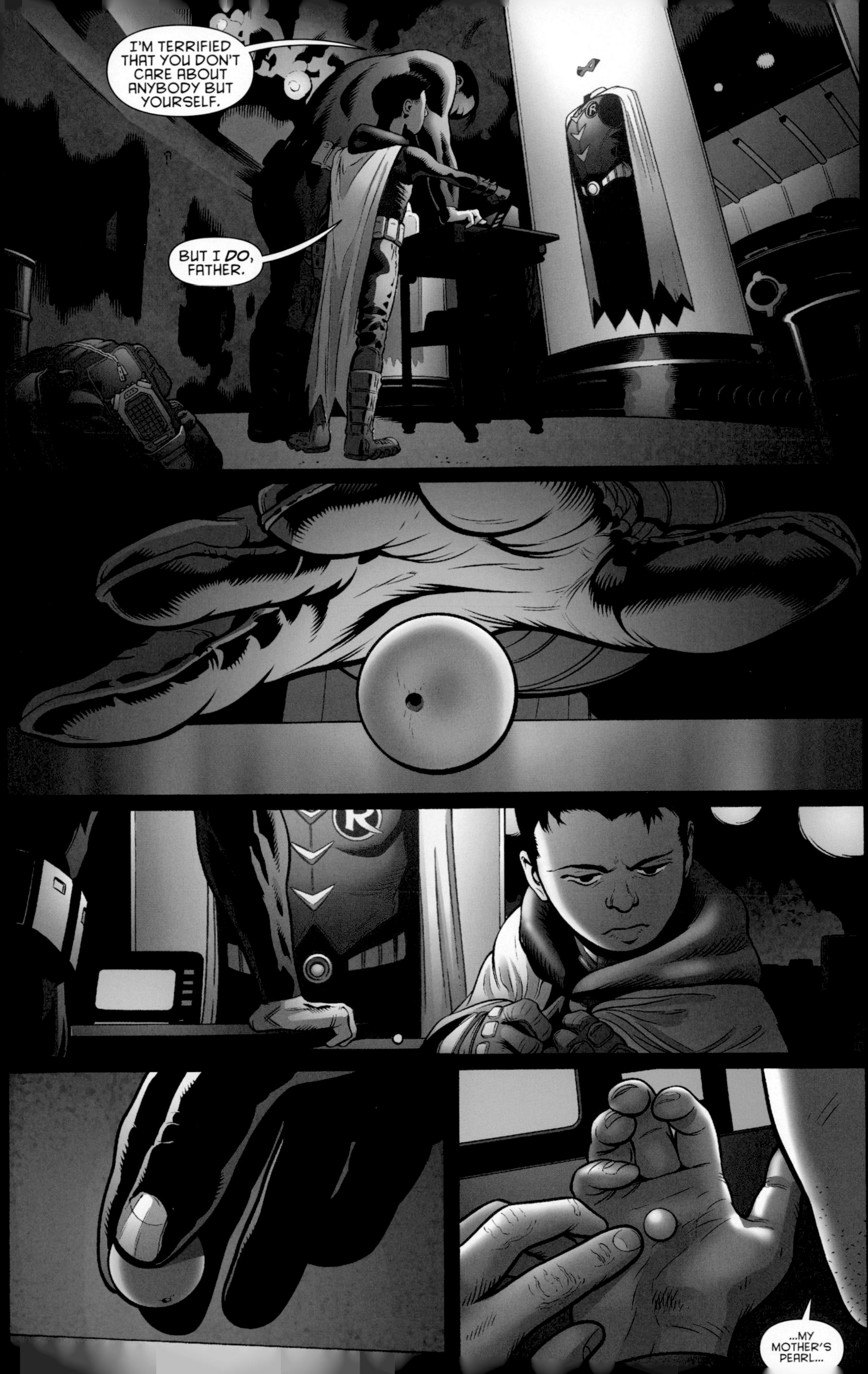
I'M TERRIFIED THAT YOU DON'T CARE ABOUT ANYBODY BUT YOURSELF.
BUT I *DO*, FATHER.
...MY MOTHER'S PEARL...

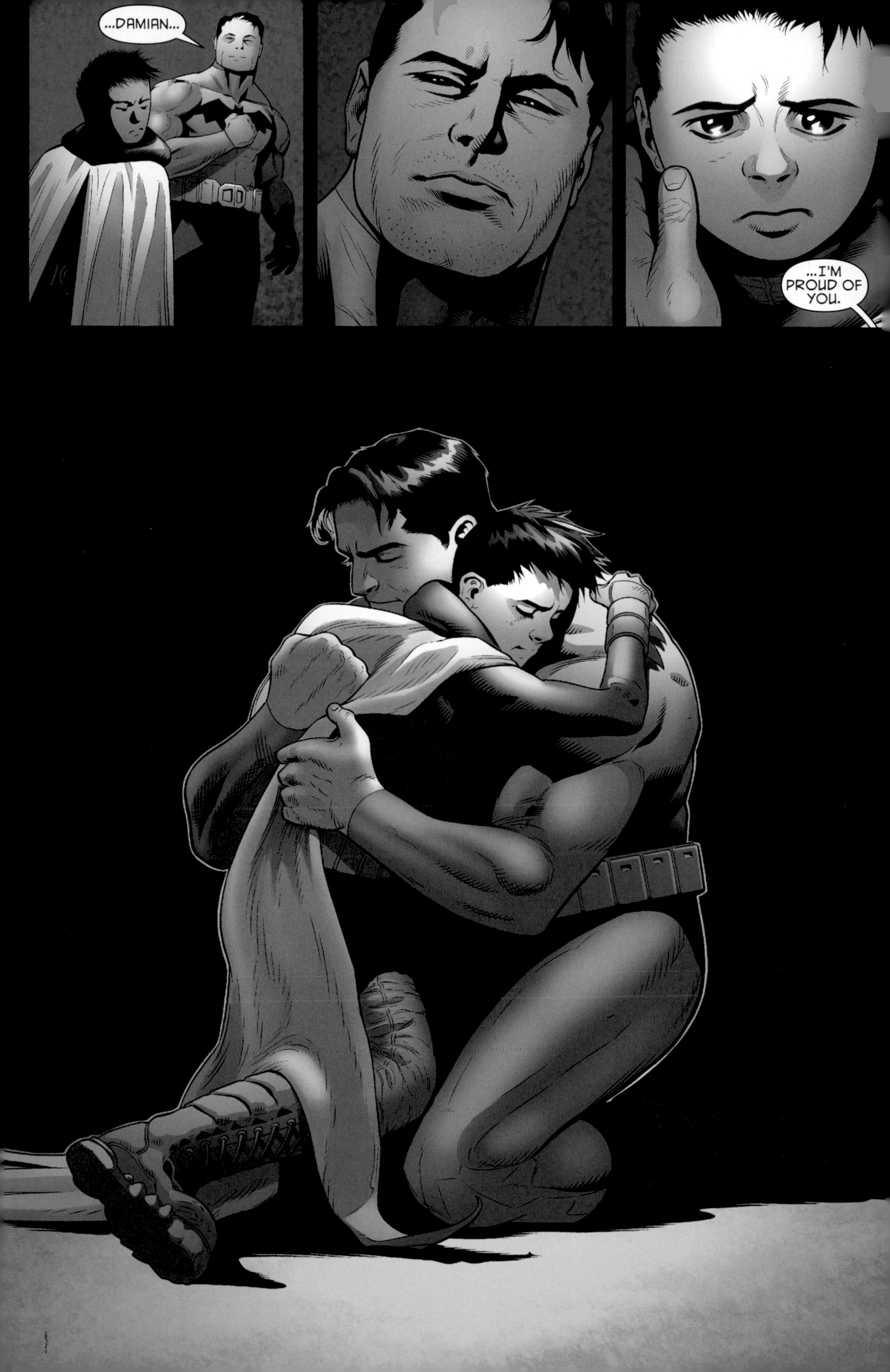
...DAMIAN...
...I'M PROUD OF YOU.

BATMAN AND ROBIN ZERO

PAGE 4
panel 1
What we're seeing is DAMIAN'S 9 MONTH OLD INFANT FACE inside the artificial womb, its special seal now open at this moment, the amniotic fluid completely drained. You know how some kids have a lot of hair when they're born, well, that's Damian, a nice mop of black hair on his itty-bitty head.

BANNER CAP: Before...

BANNER CAP: Before...

ELEC: Amniotic fluid draining...

ELEC: Incubator womb unlocked.

ELEC: Nine-month term cycle complete.

ELEC: Infant weight six pounds, ten ounces.

panel 2
Cose on TALIA from just behind Damian as she reaches her hands towards him. Beautiful and exotic, we can't tell what she's feeling just yet about her child.

TALIA: Come, my little one...

panel 3
Pull back so we see we're in the hi-tech lab on Talia's island. Check BATMAN 665 for ref, but I'd say you have a lot of latitude since it's the New 52. Make it your own. Angle on Talia, in her skintight jumpsuit, holding Damian as 2 NURSE-MAID ASSISTANTS trail her, ready to do what she needs at a moment's notice, including breast feeding. If you can add some background elements such as other small pods with other body parts being cloned in all different sizes and stages, from infant to adult. No full bodies.

TALIA: ...show me you have the strength...

panel 4
Same day, as we see Talia having walked through double doors that are still swinging, into a small pool area where she is taking the first step down into the water with Damian in her arms while her Nurse-maidens are taking positions at the edge of the pool. Also, the pool isn't for fun, there's no aesthetic sensibility to its construction. It's simple and utilitarian. Also a note, whenever you want, have League of Assassin dudes stationed around the place, standing like Buckingham Palace guards ready for anything.

TALIA: ...and willpower...

PAGE 5

panel 1
I'm seeing a riff of the famous NIRVANA ALBUM cover here, only Damian is the infant doing the swimming/floating and of course there's no money in the crystal clear water. Match the angle and positioning of the baby on the album cover, but tweak it a bit so we don't get nonsense from Legal. Also, as mentioned earlier, Damian has a bit more hair than the average infant and it's jet black too. Google Water Babies for great ref.

TALIA: ...to do what is necessary.

panel 2
Angle on Talia, still not showing any emotion yet, holding her hands out towards Damian paddling away, as one of the Nursemaids standing at the pool's edge, seems a bit worried by the baby's exertion in the water. The other Nursemaid looks nervous, giving one of those sidelong glances that say "are you crazy, keep your yap shut".

TALIA: Let me see the steel in your eyes.

MAID 1: Miss Talia, you're placing the baby at great risk with this nonsense.

panel 3
Angle on Talia as she suddenly whips a small blade from her hand without even looking at the Nursemaid. Have a speed trail right to the Nursemaid, whose head is tilted back and now holding the knife buried in her throat.

TALIA: Never tell a mother how to raise her child.

SFX: shunk

panel 4
Angle on Damian paddling away on top of the now lightly reddish water, passing the Nursemaid lying dead at the edge of the pool, her lifeless eyes wide, almost as if they're staring at him, blood from her neck running into the water. A literal 'Death's Head' already present in his first moments of life.

TALIA: Bring me another Nursemaid. He will need another breast to suckle.

panel 5
Angle on Talia as she lifts Damian under both arms from the light reddish water as it runs off his infant body. A subtle baptism of blood (well, maybe it's not that subtle, but what the hell). Also, we see for the first time the love and joy in Talia's features as she's accepted and connected to her child.

TALIA: Welcome to our world, Damian.

PAGE 6
panel 1
Another day. Angle on Damian, now a 3-year-old, and Talia, as they practice with wooden swords on the balcony. She's dressed in another of her skin tight jumpsuits while Damian has a little karate uniform on and is wielding a size-appropriate wooden sword.

DAMIAN: Mama, tell me another story about Alexander the Great.

TALIA: Of course, my son.

TALIA: Once there was a horse called Buccephalas...a wild black stallion that was given to Alexander's father, King Philip, as a gift that no one dared ride, and one day —

SFX: klak

panel 2
Angle close on Damian as he suddenly lowers his sword and stares at Talia as she taps the bottom of his sword to prompt him back into action. Remember, even at 3 years old, Damian is a precocious child.

DAMIAN: Who is my father, Mama?

TALIA: A man that lives very far away — now keep your sword up — what have I said about lowering your defenses?

DAMIAN: How come you never tell me stories about him or show me pictures?

panel 3
Angle as mother and son continue sparring.

TALIA: Because I choose not to at this time, my darling boy.

DAMIAN: Is he a king too?

TALIA: I suppose in a way he is.

panel 4
Angle close on Damian and Talia sparring. The purity of his curiosity obvious.

DAMIAN: Can I meet him?

TALIA: When you earn the right to, yes.

DAMIAN: How?

panel 1
Angle as Talia simply knocks Damian's wooden sword from his hand.

TALIA: By not losing your focus! No easy wins in life, Damian. Everything worth having is hard fought.

TALIA: Today's your birthday my love, and when you best me in a duel on your special day, that is when you will be ready to meet your father.

TALIA: Then — and only then — will I tell you his —

panel 2
A HOLO of NETZ is on a hi-tech console. Talia and Damian lower their swords.

ELEC: Miss Talia, as you requested, I have Otto Netz on a satellite link.

TALIA: Is it a secure line?

ELEC: Yes.

panel 3
Damian sees his mother talk to the HOLO of Netz. Between Damian and Talia is her bed and we can see a small ornate trunk at the foot of it.

TALIA: ...I grow weary of excuses, Netz. Make sure the Meta-Bomb program stays on schedule.

ELEC: I endeavor to make your dreams a reality.

TALIA: As well you should...

TALIA: ...but any further disruptions and you will find yourself expendable. Understood?

panel 4
Damian opens an ornate trunk at the foot of Talia's bed. He's placed his sword on her bed.

NETZ: You have my word there will be no further complications.

panel 5
Damian sees mementos of Talia's night spent with Bruce years ago: 2 champagne glasses, an empty bottle of Dom Perignon, and Batman's cowl poking out from underneath it all.

TALIA(off):   I'll have more than your word, Netz, I'll have your head.

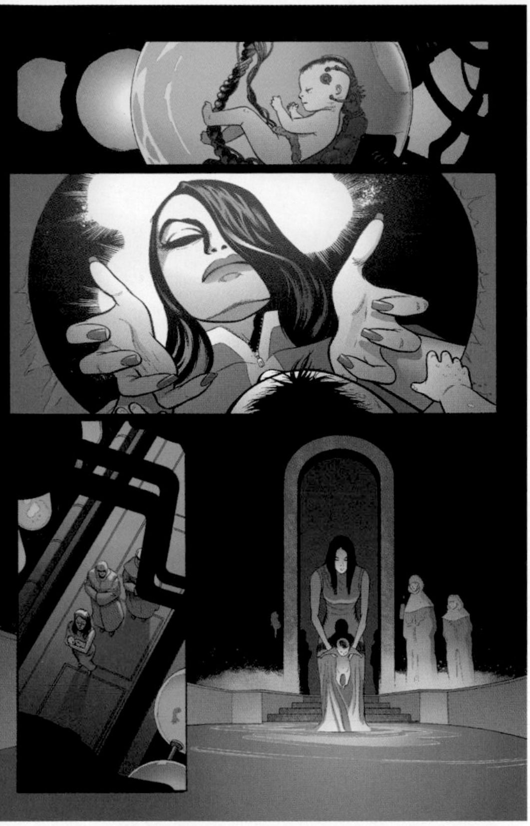
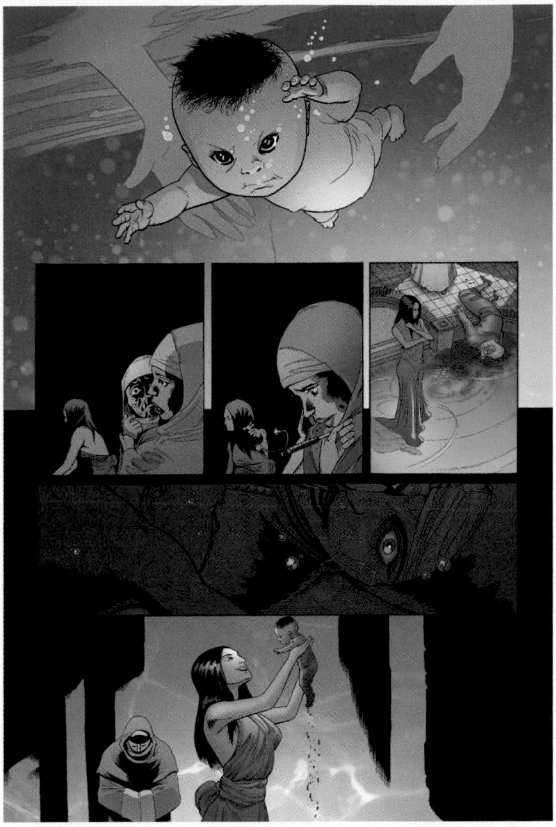
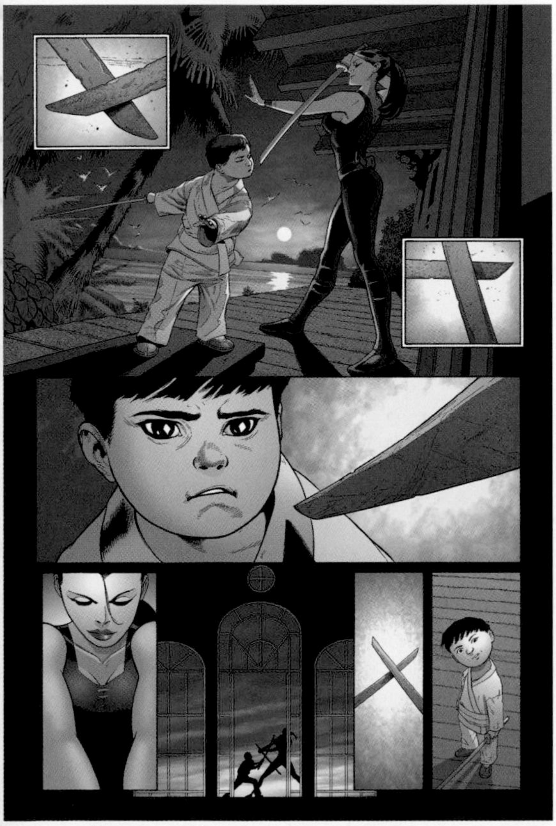
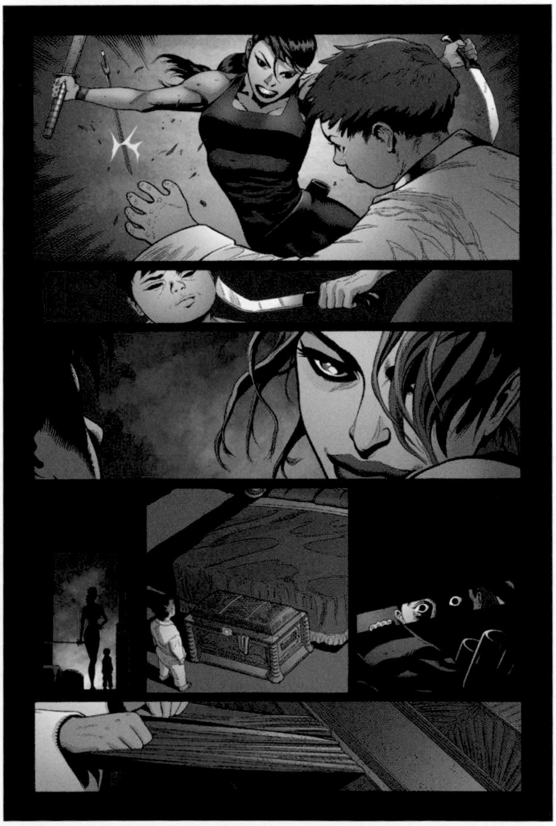

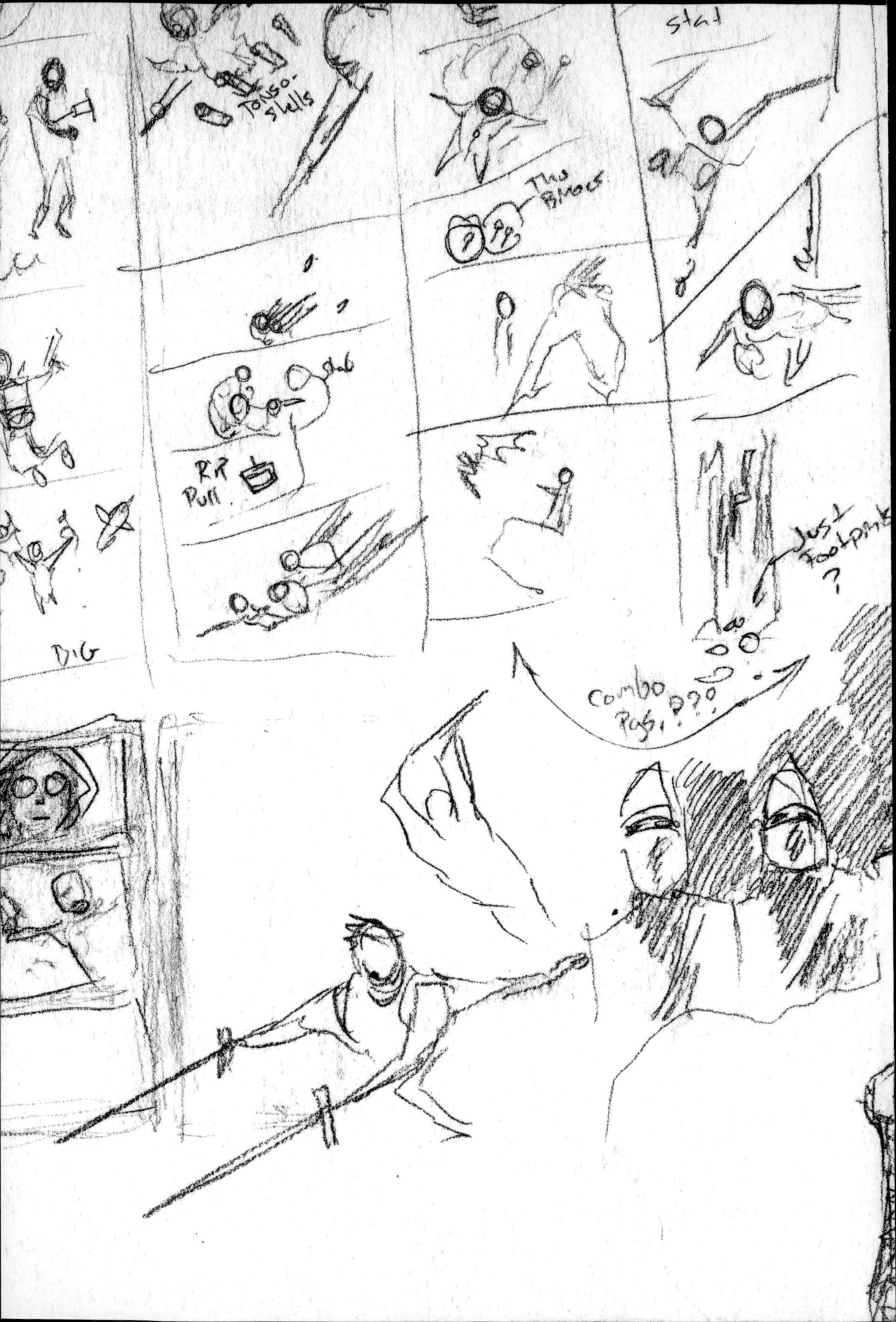
Torso-shells
Stab
Two Bmoes
Stab
Rip Pull
Just Footprint ?
DIG
Combo Pgs. ???

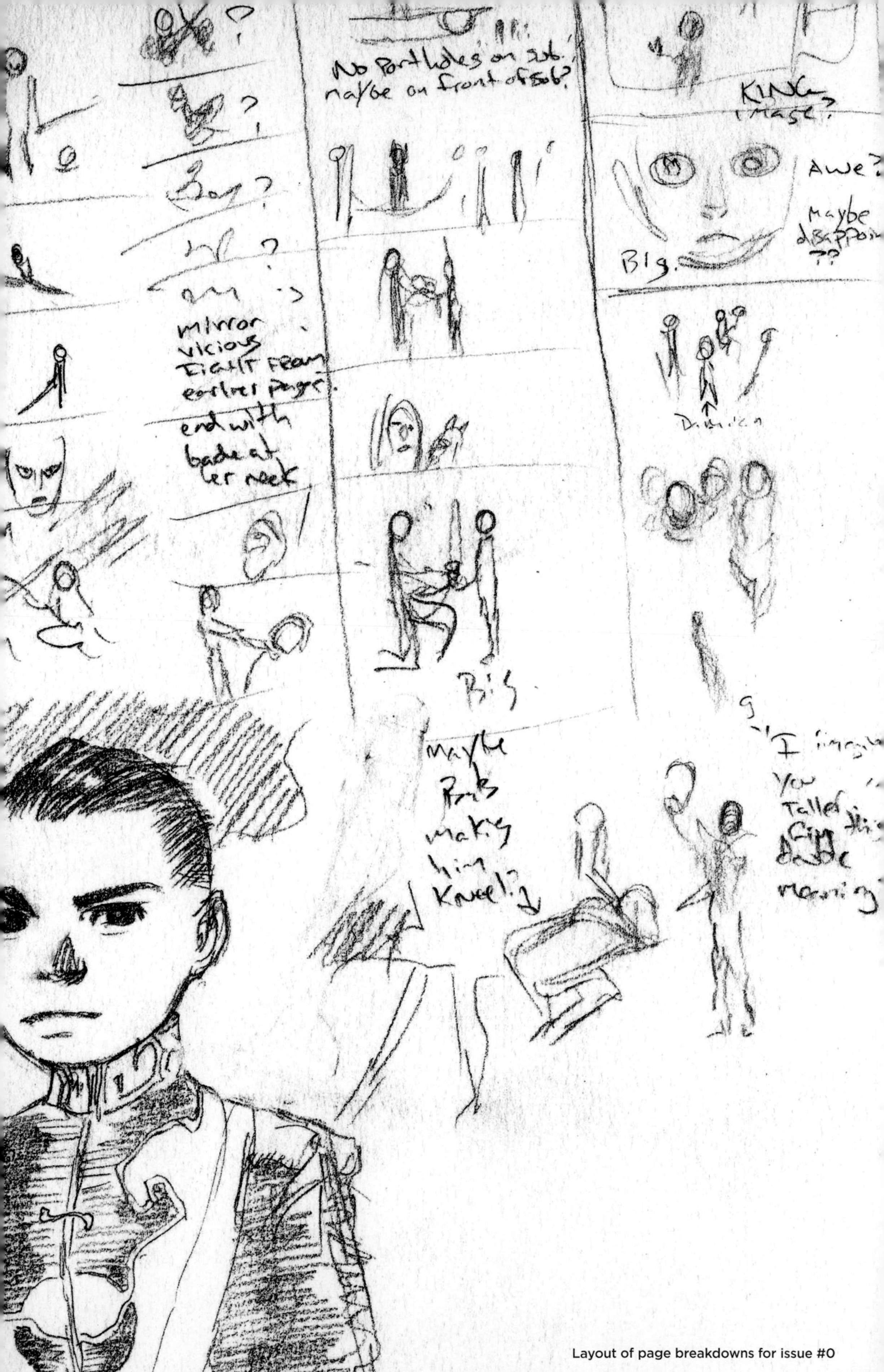
No Portholes on sub.
maybe on front of sub?
KING
Awe?
maybe
Big.
mirror
vicious
fight from
earlier page.
end with
blade at
her neck
Big

Layout of page breakdowns for issue #0

Character studies of Talia and Damian

MILITARY

DAMIAN
AGE 3-4?

NINJA

TAC-DAMIAN

KATANA ON
BACK

THROWING
STARS
ON
ARM

FIGHTING
CLAWS.

HOOKS-
CHAIN.

Bat Freak concepts

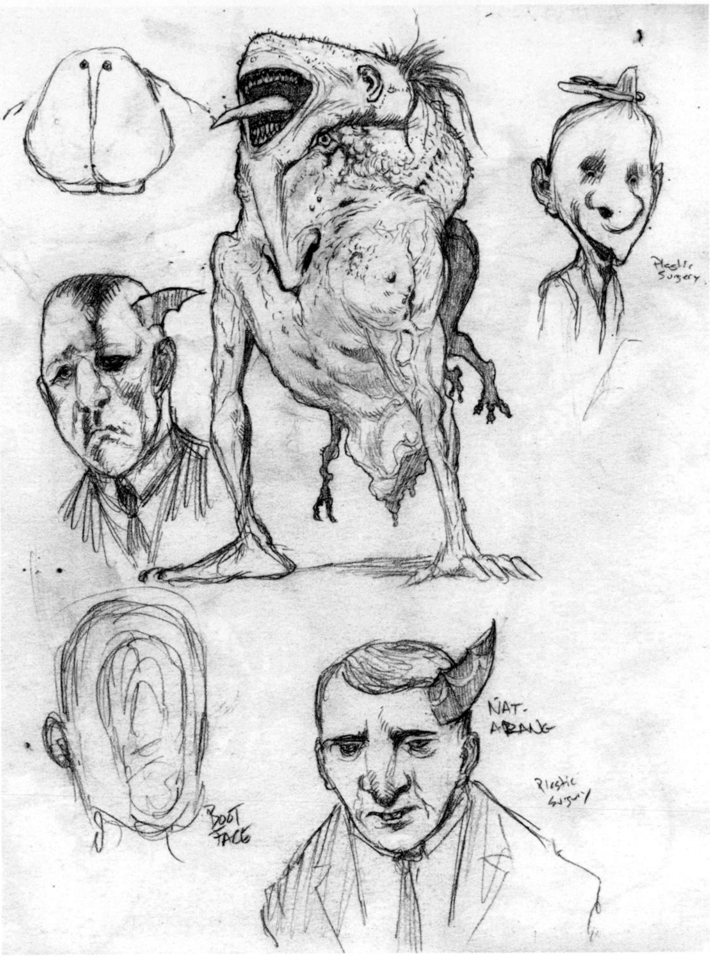
Plastic Surgery
NAT. ARANG
Plastic Surgery
BOOT FACE

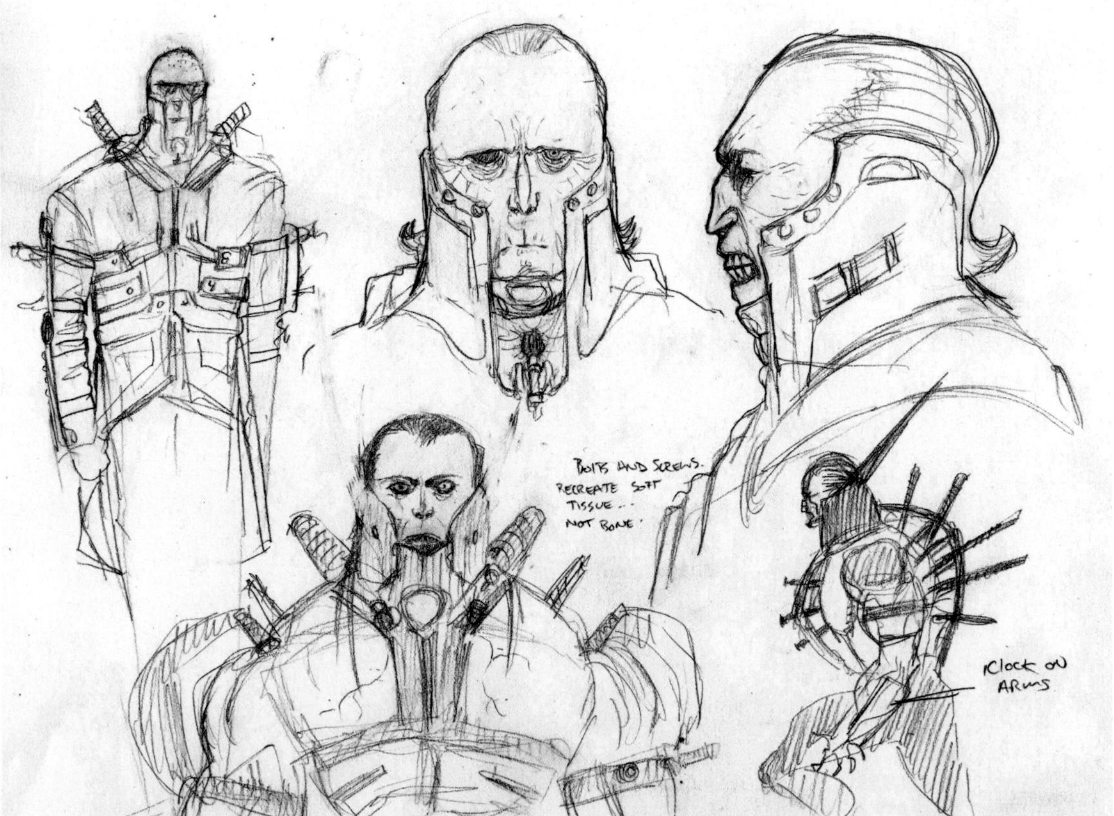
BOLTS AND SCREWS.
RECREATE SOFT TISSUE...
NOT BONE.
CLOCK ON ARMS

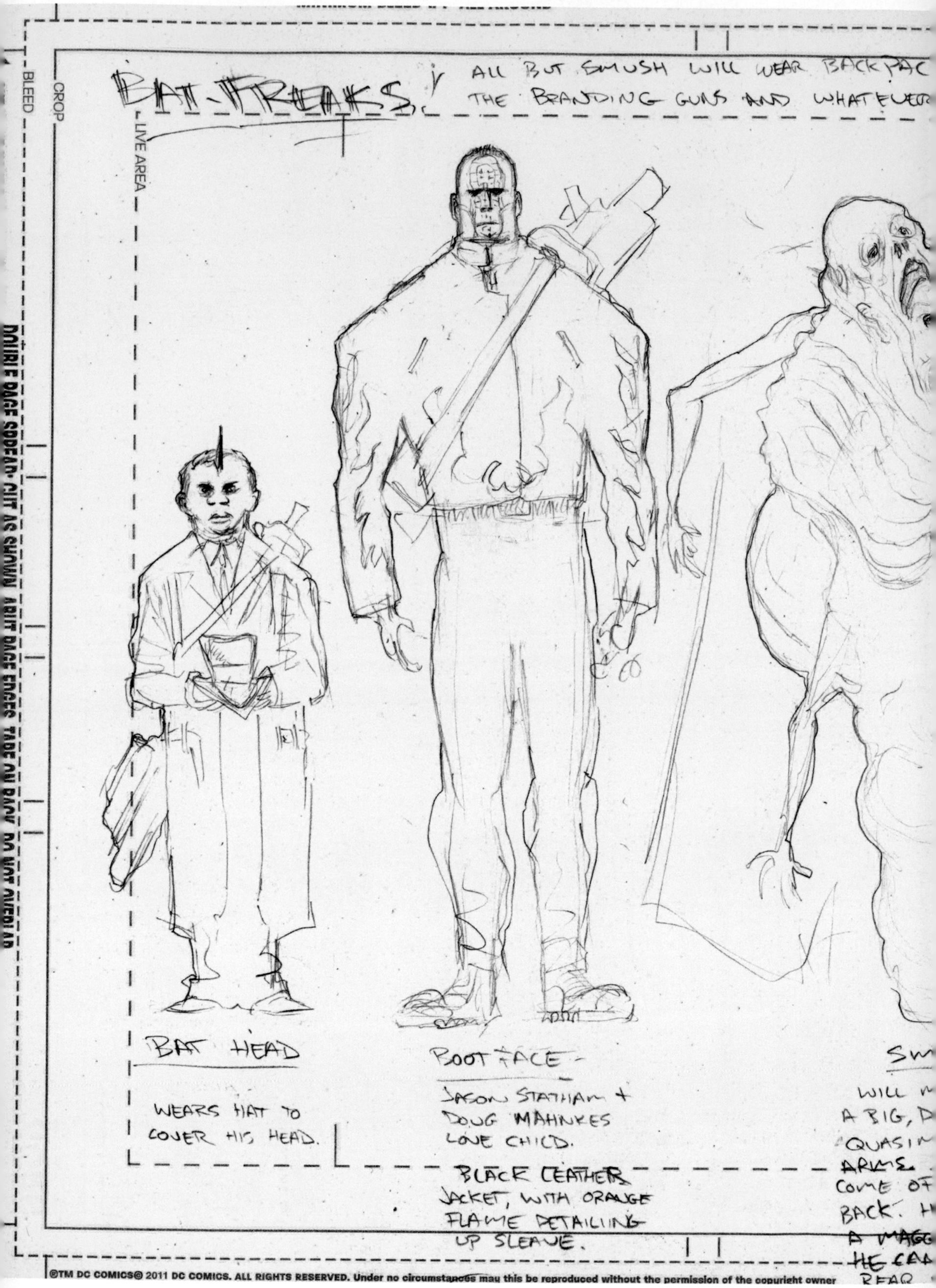
BLEED
CROP
LIVE AREA
BAT-FREAKS!
ALL BUT SMUSH WILL WEAR BACKPAC
THE BRANDING GUNS AND WHATEVER
BAT HEAD
WEARS HAT TO
COVER HIS HEAD.
BOOT FACE -
JASON STATHAM +
DOUG MAHNKES
LOVE CHILD.
BLACK LEATHER
JACKET, WITH ORANGE
FLAME DETAILING
UP SLEAVE.
WILL
A BIG,
QUASI
ARMS
COME OF
BACK.
A MAGG
HE CA
REAR

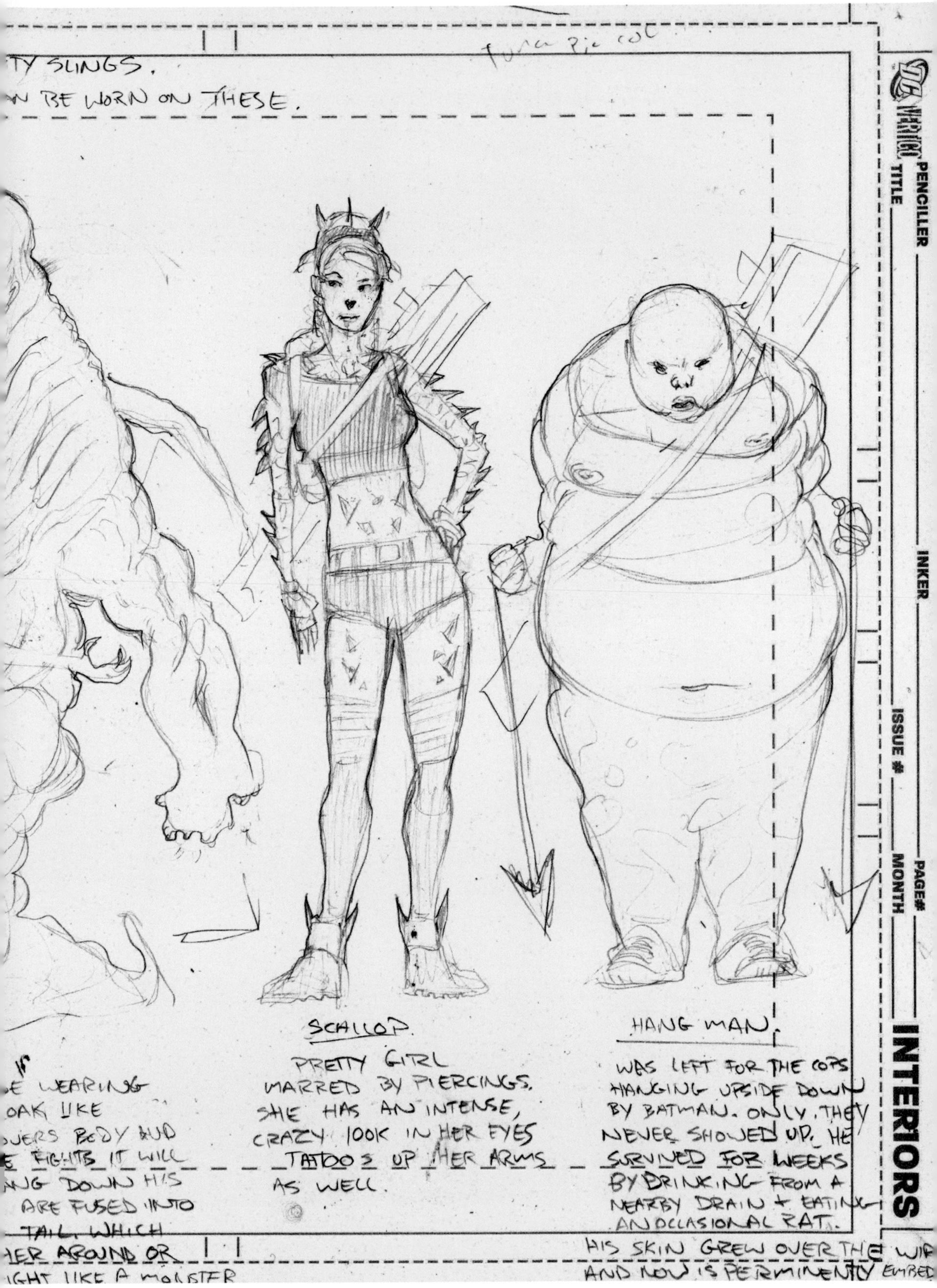
TY SLINGS.
N BE WORN ON THESE.
SCALLOP
PRETTY GIRL
MARRED BY PIERCINGS.
SHE HAS AN INTENSE,
CRAZY LOOK IN HER EYES
TATOOS UP HER ARMS
AS WELL.
HANG MAN
WAS LEFT FOR THE COPS
HANGING UPSIDE DOWN
BY BATMAN. ONLY, THEY
NEVER SHOWED UP. HE
SURVIVED FOR WEEKS
BY DRINKING FROM A
NEARBY DRAIN + EATING
AN OCCASIONAL RAT.
HIS SKIN GREW OVER THE WI
AND NOW IS PERMINENTLY EMBED
E WEARING
OAK LIKE
VERS BODY AND
E FIGHTS IT WILL
NG DOWN HIS
ARE FUSED INTO
TAIL, WHICH
HER AROUND OR
GHT LIKE A MONSTER
PENCILLER
INKER
ISSUE #
MONTH
PAGE#
TITLE
INTERIORS

Pencils from issue #0

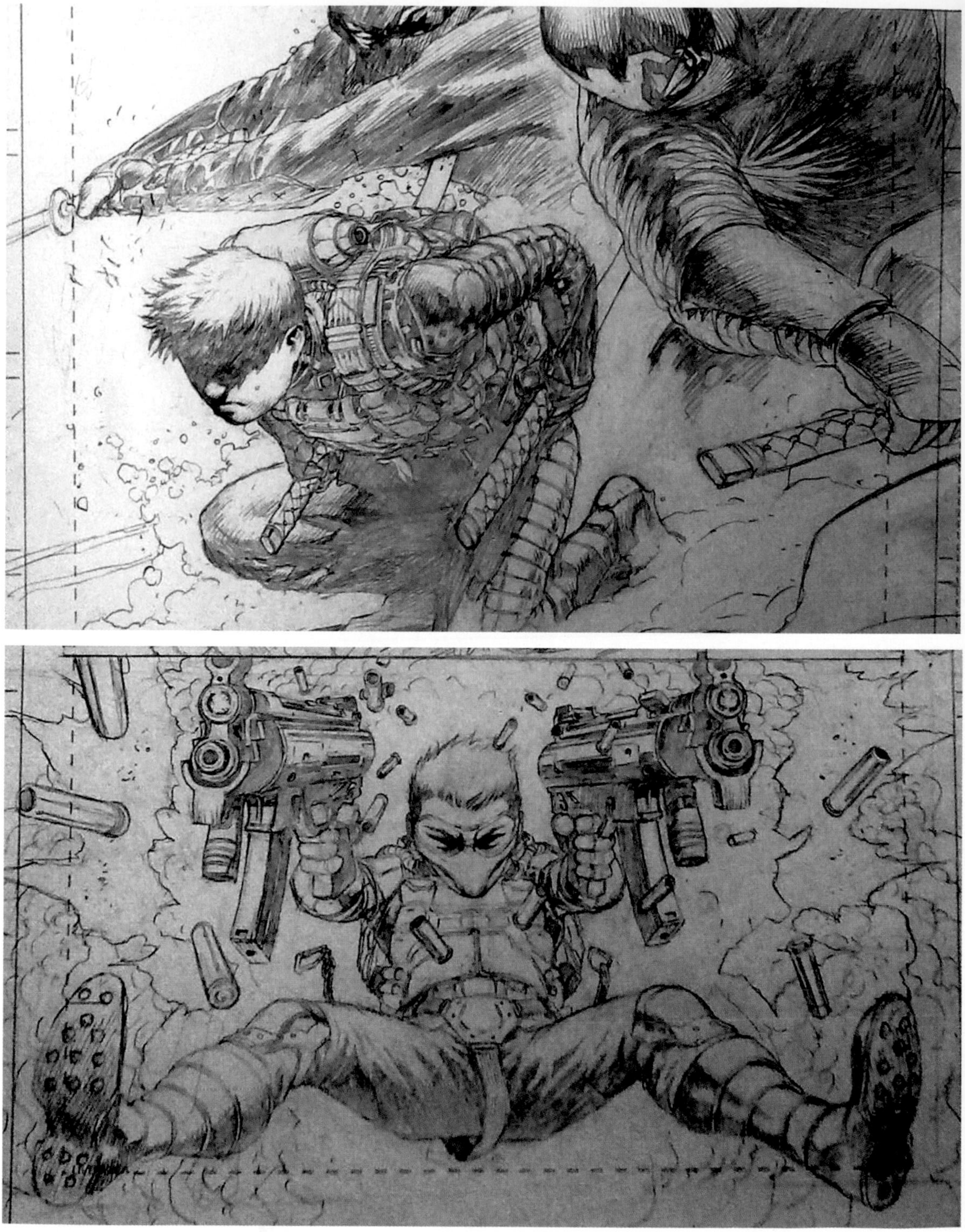

Pencils and inks from issue #12

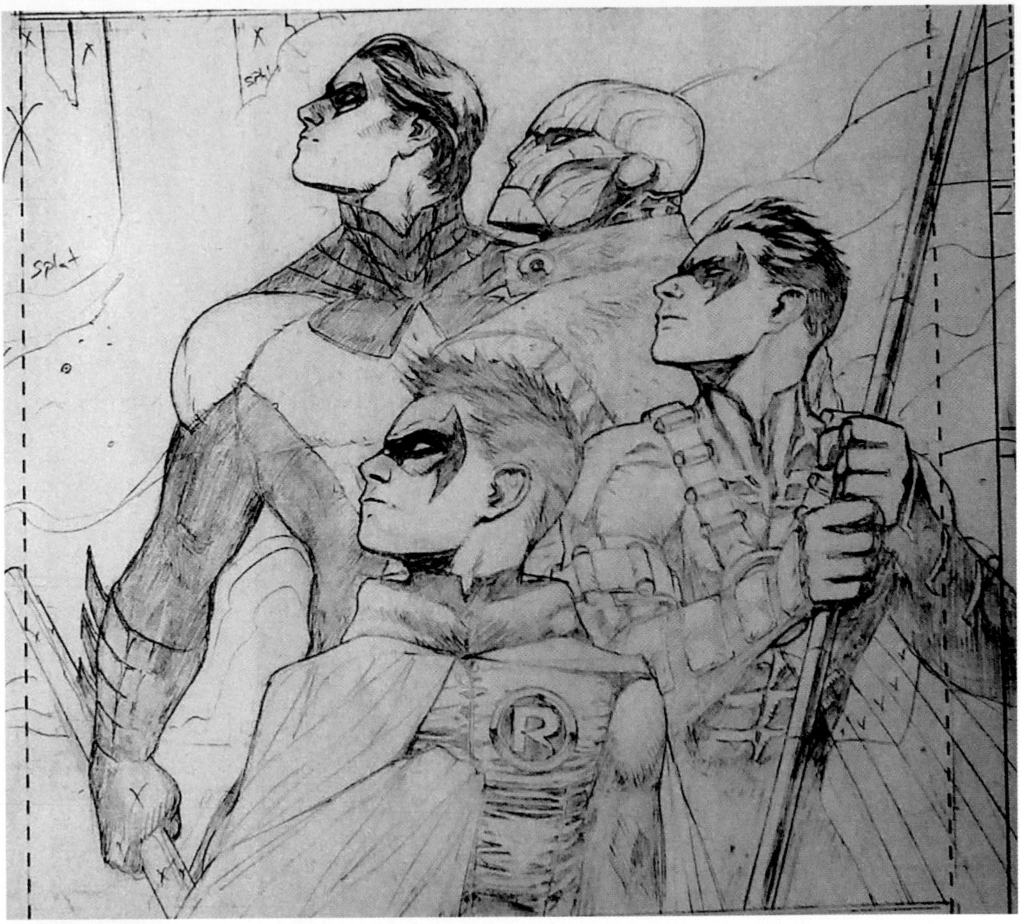
Splat

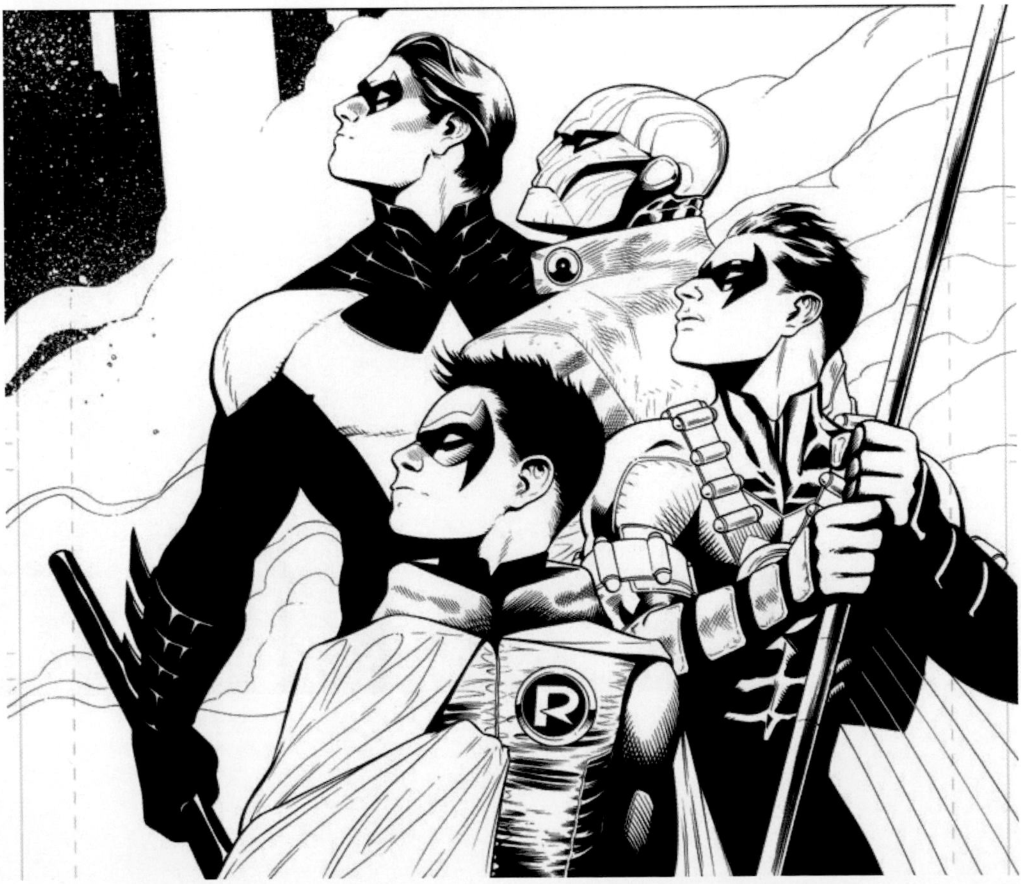

Pencils from issue #13

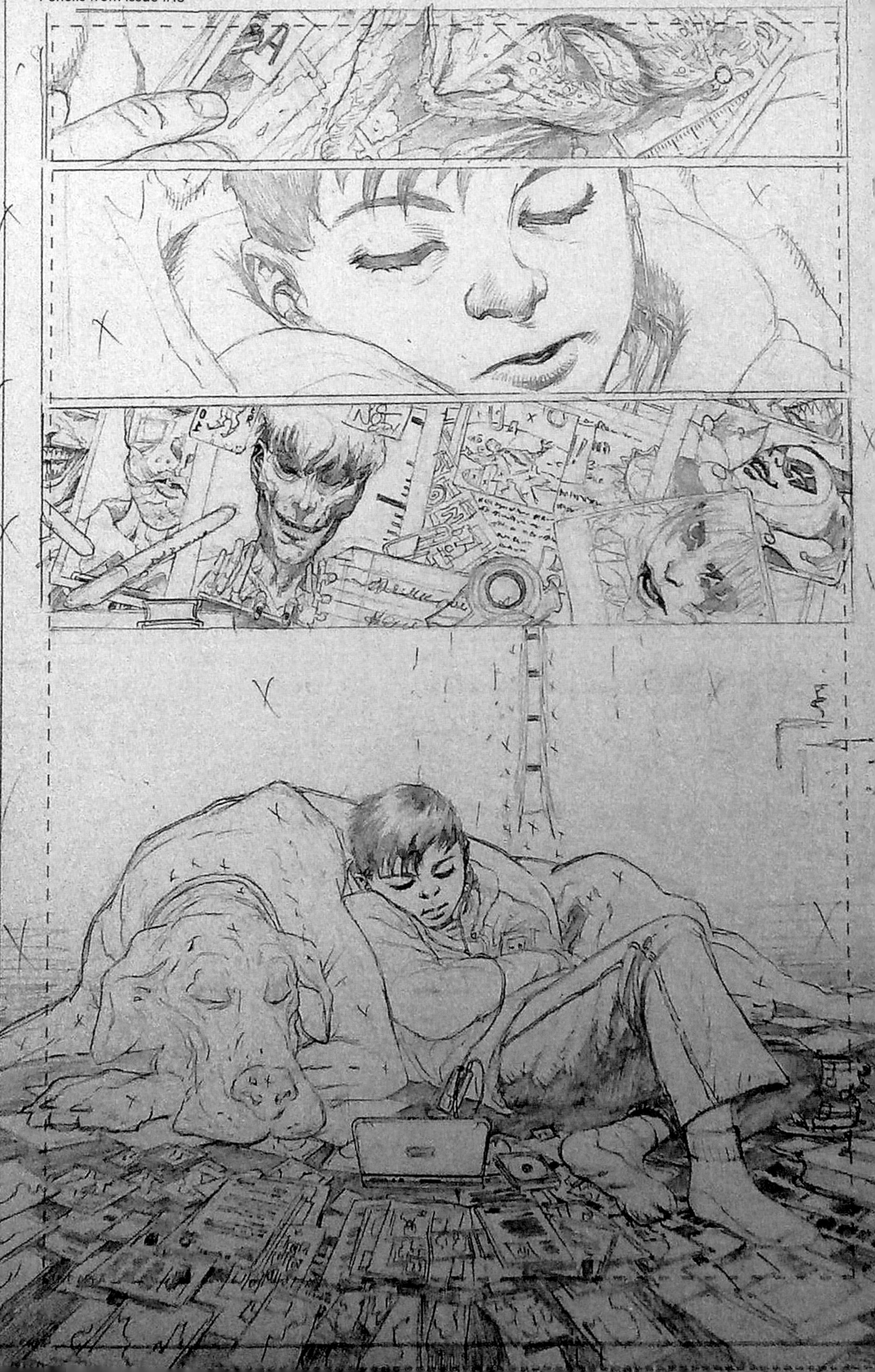

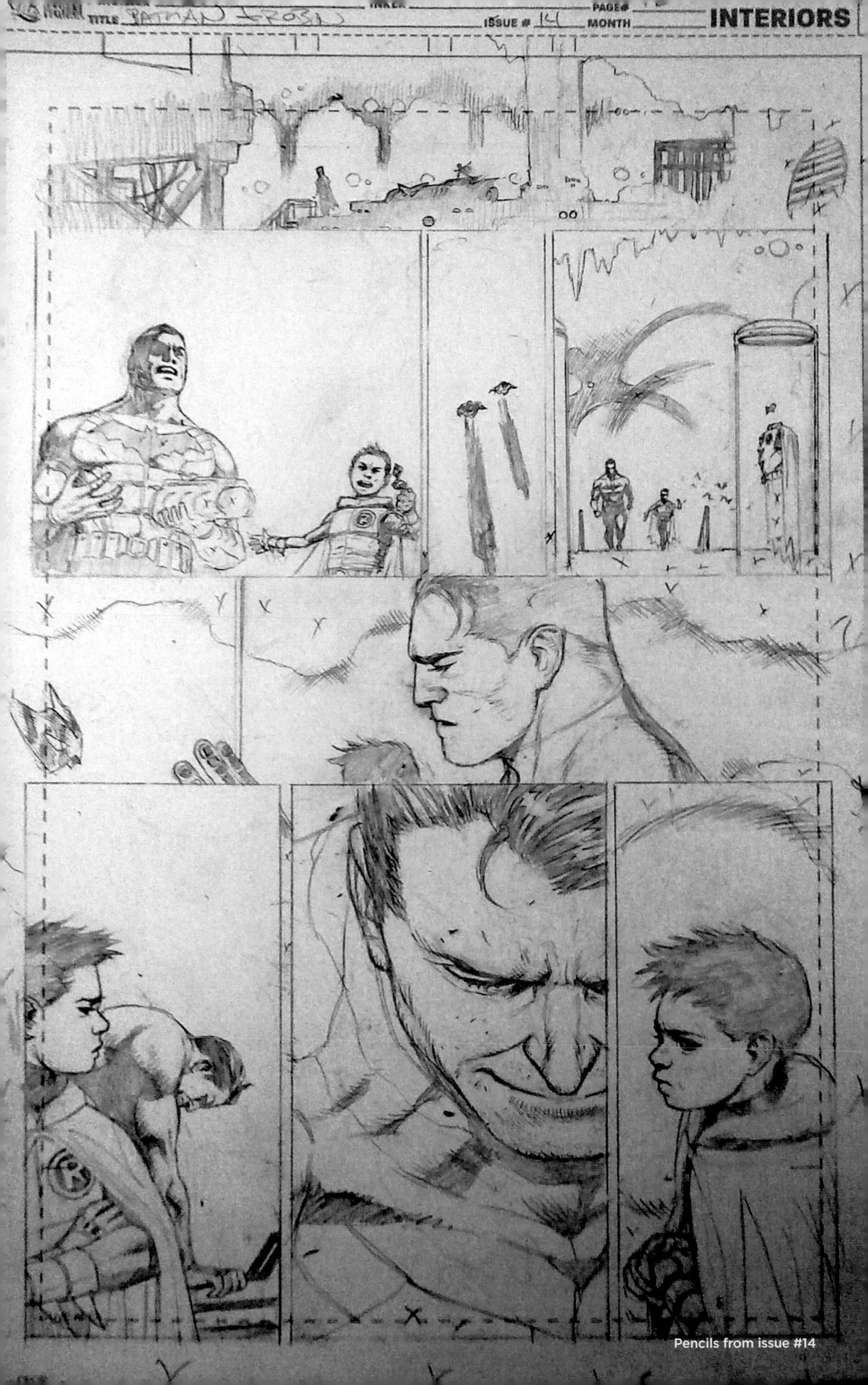
INTERIORS
ISSUE # 14
PAGE#
MONTH

Pencils from issue #14

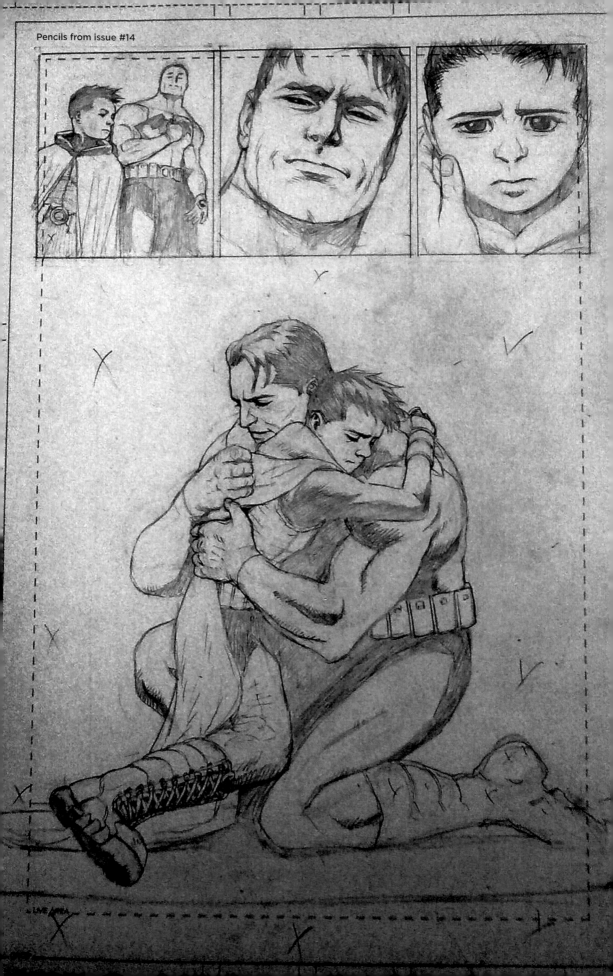

Pencils from issue #14

Pencils from issue #13

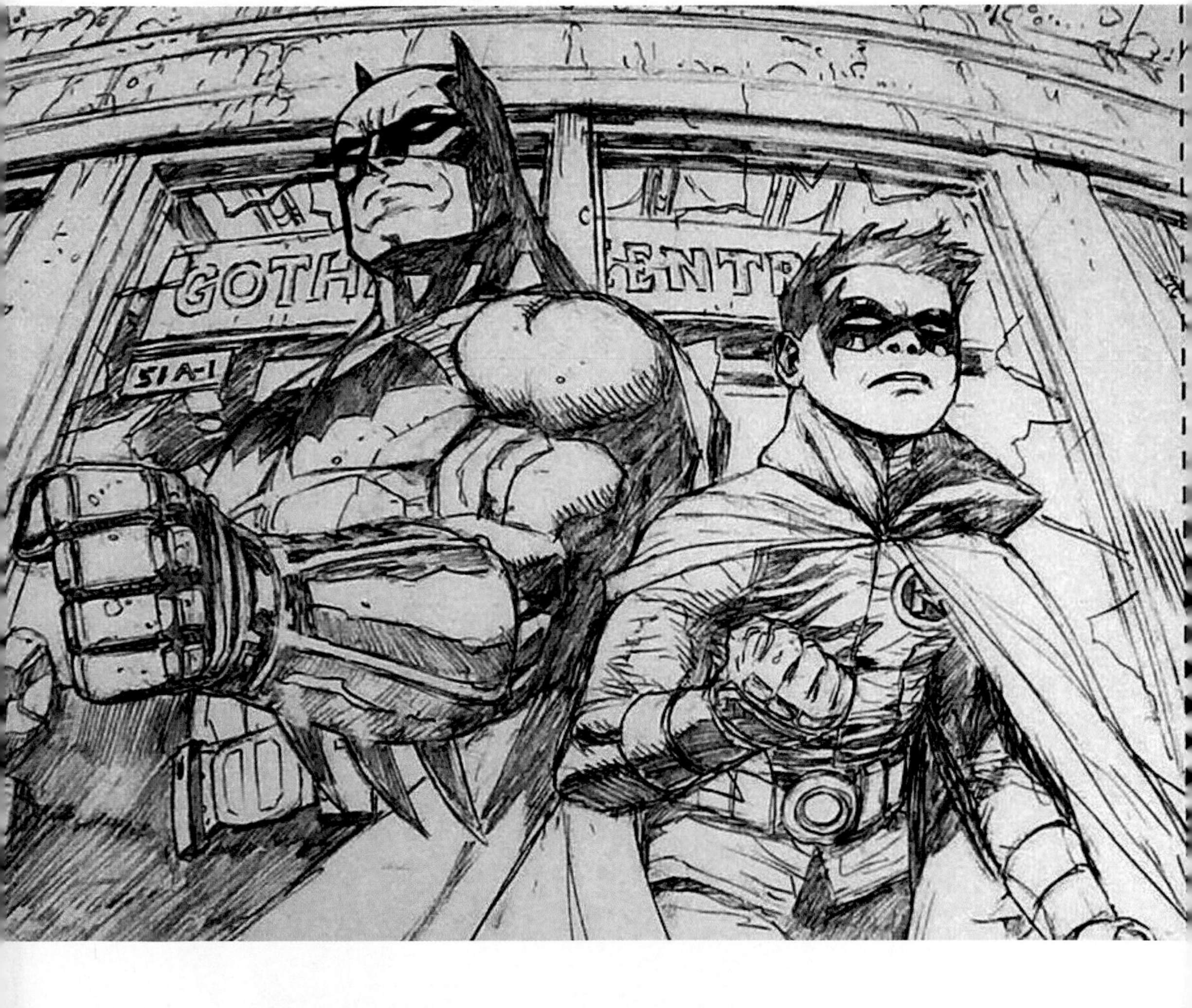
GOTH
ENTR
51A-1

DC COMICS™

"Brilliantly executed."
—IGN

"Morrison and Quitely have the magic touch
that makes any book they collaborate on stand
out from the rest." —MTV's Splash Page

"Thrilling and invigorating....Gotham City that has
never looked this good, felt this strange, or been
this deadly." —COMIC BOOK RESOURCES

GRANT MORRISON
BATMAN & ROBIN VOL. 1: BATMAN REBORN with FRANK QUITELY & PHILIP TAN

VOL. 2: BATMAN VS. ROBIN

VOL. 3: BATMAN & ROBIN MUST DIE!

DARK KNIGHT VS. WHITE KNIGHT

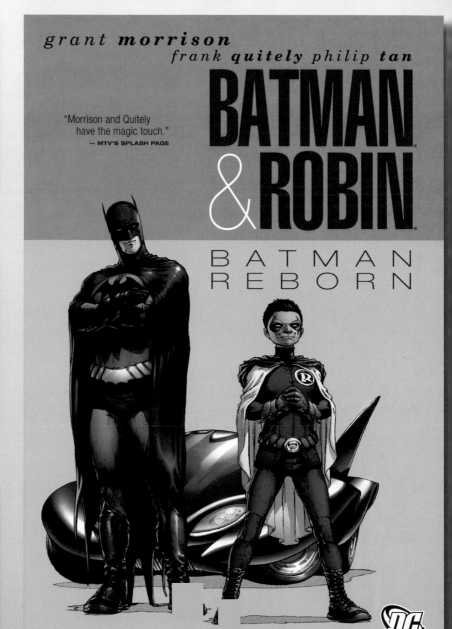